Markets, Intervention and Planning

Longman Economics Series
Series editors: Robert Millward, Michael T. Sumner and
George Zis

MARKETS, INTERVENTION AND PLANNING

B. Roper and B. Snowdon (editors),
R. Bailey, B. Craven, B. Dick,
P. Holmes, M. McNulty, N. Terry,
A. Walker, B. Wood, G. Wright,
P. Wynarczyk

Longman
London and New York

Longman Group UK Limited,
Longman House, Burnt Mill, Harlow
Essex CM20 2JE, England
and Associated Companies throughout the world.

Published in the United States of America
by Longman Inc., New York

First published 1987

British Library Cataloguing in Publication Data

Markets, intervention and planning.
 1. Economic development   2. Economic policy
 I. Roper, B.A.   II. Snowdon, B.   III. Bailey, Richard
 330.9   HD82
 ISBN 0-582-29707-9

Library of Congress Cataloging in Publication Data

Markets, intervention, and planning.

 Includes bibliographies and index.
 1. Economics – Great Britain.   2. Great Britain –
Economic policy.   I. Roper, B.A. (Brian A.)
II. Snowdon, B. (Brian)   III. Bailey, Richard.
 HB103.A2M38   1987   338.941   86-18487
 ISBN 0-582-29707-9

Set in Linotron 202 10/12pt Palatino
Produced by Longman Group (FE) Limited
Printed in Hong Kong

CONTENTS

PREFACE

This book is concerned with the role that governments could, should and do play in economic affairs. Drawing largely, but not exclusively, upon the experience of the UK economy, the book explores the theme of markets, intervention and planning from a variety of theoretical, empirical and ideological perspectives. The genesis of this book lies in our shared realisation that changes in both economics as a discipline, and in economic policy, which have occurred in the UK since the late 1970s, have rekindled discussion of these issues and have served to place them once again at the centre of attention.

The assumed reader of this book will have an introductory background in economics at 'A' level or first year undergraduate level. We assume no mathematical background beyond 'O' level.

Whilst surveying essential theoretical and empirical issues, this is not a textbook. Rather, it is designed to serve as an intermediate level reader to accompany textbooks.

The readers of this book will be studying for degrees in the Social Sciences, Business Studies or Humanities which contain economics, or will be specialising in Economics.

In inviting twelve economists to discuss this theme, one is conscious that unity will not be easily achieved. However, in drawing upon their combined teaching and research experience we are able to demonstrate a common concern over the role of government in economic affairs, an awareness that as markets can fail so too can governments, and a belief that there will remain a continuing role for government in economic activity.

All of the authors are from the School of Economics at Newcastle upon Tyne Polytechnic. In Chapter 1 the editors, Brian Roper and Brian Snowdon, present a survey of the essential theoretical issues and empirical experiences of the British economy. This augments the standard textbook presentation and serves to provide a context for subsequent chapters.

Peter Wynarczyk in Chapter 2 explores the feasibility of a pure market system in the context of the evolution of economic thought, highlighting the works of Smith, Keynes, Galbraith, Lange, Mises and Hayek. This chapter provides a clear statement of the interventionist and anti-interventionist rationale. The role of the new right is then considered as a precursor to a discussion of the minimalist state.

In Chapter 3 Brian Snowdon explains the reasons behind the demise of the Keynesian consensus and the revival of interest in monetarism. Reviewing the rich theoretical controversies by reference to the works of Keynes, Friedman and Lucas, the chapter focuses upon the key macroeconomic policy issues of inflation and unemployment.

Richard Bailey demonstrates in Chapter 4 that the international economy cannot be neatly compartmentalised but is instead an amalgam of interventionist discretion, administered rules and market structures. Within the framework of a sustainable international system he considers managed versus free trade, floating versus fixed exchange rates and integrated versus isolated capital markets.

In Chapters 5 to 10 the authors move to a micro-level discussion of their topics. Grahame Wright and Brian Roper in Chapter 5 consider the major features of post-war industrial policy in the UK and chart the emergence of the view that governments do have a role to play in industrial affairs in peace time. In reviewing the currently burgeoning literature in this field, the chapter focuses particularly upon market failure considerations and issues of organisational control and concludes by considering such current policy initiatives as franchise bidding and privatisation.

In Chapter 6 Michael McNulty establishes the magnitude and special characteristics of the labour market. Emphasis is placed on the role of training and the process of human capital formation. The structure of industrial relations, the role of trade unions and of state agencies are reviewed against the background of deteriorating employment opportunities.

In Chapter 7 Phil Holmes indicates the particular characteristics of the market for housing. Placing housing in the context of social policy in post-war Britain, the chapter explores the relationship between market and government and points to a variety of issues that need to be addressed if provision is to be improved.

Chapter 8, written by Arthur Walker, is concerned with the

economic arguments for and against government provision of
health care. Drawing upon current literature and international
experience, the chapter explores the technical and political issues
which surround this vital issue.

In Chapter 9, Barrie Craven, Brian Dick and Barry Wood discuss
the provision of education. Consideration is given to failures in
public provision, to market-based alternatives and the use of loans
and vouchers, to the idea that education is a form of investment
in human capital, and the non-economic rationale for education.

Nicholas Terry in Chapter 10 reviews the nature and structure
of the tax-benefit system in the UK. The chapter explores the trade-
off between equity and efficiency considerations and evaluates
governmental redistributive concerns and makes proposals for an
integrated tax-benefit system.

In Chapter 11 Brian Roper and Brian Snowdon conclude by
restating the key question posed in this book, what is the proper
role for government in the economy? The inescapable interweaving
of political and economic ideas, the clear (and conflicting) views
of leading economists and the possibility that economic systems
may be converging serve to remind us of the problems we face in
attempting to answer this timely and central question.

In writing this book we have tried to be comprehensive but
could not hope to be exhaustive. Frequent selective referencing has
been used to further guide the interested reader.

ACKNOWLEDGEMENTS

It is clear that this book is the product of team work. The editors are indebted to the authors and we are all, in turn, indebted to those who helped to produce the typescript. Our thanks then to Leslie Patrick, Glenda Francis and especially to Dawn Smith for her patience and forbearance. Any remaining errors are of course the responsibility of the authors.

We are grateful to the following for permission to reproduce copyright material:

Allen & Unwin Ltd for Table 10.6 based on Table B.3 *The Strategy of Equality* by J. Le Grand; The Controller of Her Majesty's Stationery Office for Tables 1.4, 9.4 *Annual Abstract of Statistics* 1984, 9.1 *Social Trends* 1984, 1.6, 6.1, 6.2 *Social Trends* 1986, 9.6 *Regional Trends* 1985, 9.3 *DES 1977 Survey of Secondary School Staffing* (Cockcroft Report 1982), 7.3 *DoE Housing and Construction Statistics* 1970–80; the Author, Prof. A. Maddison & Banca Nazionale de Lavaro for Table 1.1 *Quarterly Review* 1980; Midland Bank plc for Table 4.4 from *Midland Bank Review* 1983, Winter; National Institute of Economic & Social Research for Table 1.2 from Barker et. al. 'Macroeconomic Policy in Germany and Britain' *National Institute Economic Review* No 114, Nov. 1985; Organisation for Economic Co-Operation and Development (Paris) for Tables 1.3, 1.5 *OECD Main Economic Indicators* 1985, 4.2, 4.3 *OECD Economic Outlook* 1985; The World Bank for Table 4.1 from part Table 3.2 p 45 *World Development Report* 1986. pub. OUP.

Chapter 1

THE FALL AND RISE OF *LAISSEZ-FAIRE*

Brian Roper and Brian Snowdon

During the post-war boom, a broad consensus was established in the UK concerning the government's role in economic affairs. Both Labour and Conservative administrations accepted the idea of a mixed economy. By mixed economy we mean a capitalist market economy where government assumes and accepts an important role with regard to overall macroeconomic management as well as a more specific responsibility with regard to the provision of certain goods and services. In all the western capitalist nations, governments of various political persuasions play an important and varying part in the economic system. However, the marked deterioration in the economic performance of the major capitalist industrial nations during the 1970s and early 1980s saw a breakdown in this consensus leading to a revival of 'free market' philosophy.

In the UK the declared intention of the new Conservative administration in 1979 was clearly set out in their election manifesto. In the foreword, Mrs Thatcher declared: 'No one who has lived in this country during the last five years can fail to be aware of how the balance of our society has been increasingly tilted in favour of the State at the expense of individual freedom' (*The Conservative Manifesto*, 1979, p. 5).

The 1979 election marked a watershed in economic policy making. The consensus was rejected and the Thatcher administration embarked on a radically different course. Writing in *The Observer* in 1980, Galbraith, a notable critic of free-market philosophy and the orthodox neoclassical 'conventional wisdom' on which it is largely founded, suggested that 'Britain has in effect volunteered to be a Friedmanite guinea pig'. Friedman's championing of the cause of free markets in favour of government intervention is well known. His popular expositions of free-market ideology include *Capitalism and Freedom* (1962) and, more recently, *Free to Choose* (1980). Building on earlier work, the latter book is devoted to explaining how a complex economic system can develop and prosper without central direction, how co-ordination can be achieved without coercion. Friedman does not deny that governments may well have the best of intentions when intervening with market forces but argues that they invariably make matters worse. The adverse consequences of government policies are often the unexpected and unintended by-products of attempts to improve upon market performance. Too often governments fail to look beyond the immediate consequences of their economic policies to the adverse long-run effects. There seems to be little doubt that this Friedmanite philosophy is one which the post-1979 Conservative government would broadly endorse.

In this book we examine the debate concerning the role of government in the functioning of a predominantly capitalist economic system such as the UK. To what extent should the government interfere with market forces? Are the reasons for intervention political or economic? Does the central core of economic theory support interventionism and on what scale? Can unhindered market forces be expected to supply the goods and services in the quantity or quality desired by the population given the resources which are available? If markets do fail, can governments also fail? Is government failure on balance likely to be worse than imperfectly working market forces? Is 'planning' an answer to the economic problems which face the UK economy? In the chapters which follow, the authors address these and other questions within the context of the current debate relating to the role of government in a capitalist market economy.

In the remainder of this chapter the basis and origins of the present debate will be traced. First we must consider some broad features of recent economic performance in the UK.

Recent UK economic performance

From the end of the Second World War until the 1970s the industrial market economies enjoyed a golden age of unparalleled prosperity. Rates of growth of labour productivity and per capita incomes reached historical heights in nearly all developed capitalist economies. The mass unemployment which had tarnished the inter-war period seemed only to be of historical interest as unemployment fell to what now appears to be remarkably low levels. Economists began to ask such questions as 'Is the business cycle obsolete?'

(Bronfenbrenner 1969). But no sooner had the question been asked when the business cycle returned with a vengeance. The 1970s witnessed the emergence of 'stagflation', inflation combined with recession and unemployment. Orthodox Keynesian economic theories were thrown into disarray providing an opportunity for previously unfashionable free-market views to regain the popularity they had enjoyed in the pre-Keynesian era. By 1982 over 25 million people were unemployed in the OECD economies. Full employment, which had for so long been regarded as the norm, came to an abrupt end.

The extent of the deteriorating performance of the advanced capitalist economies can be seen in its historical context by referring to Table 1.1.

The picture which emerges from Table 1.1 is one of a marked slow-down in economic growth combined with rising inflation and unemployment in the major advanced capitalist countries, especially after 1973. By the late 1970s the growth performance was similar to that experienced in the period 1870–1950 when GDP was increasing at an average rate of 2.3 per cent. However, in contrast, inflation during 1870–1950 was only 0.1 per cent. The rise in unemployment is more dramatic if data from the 1960s is compared

Table 1.1 GDP growth, consumer prices[1] and unemployment in 16 advanced capitalist countries, 1950–79

Country	Growth of GDP %		Consumer Prices %		Unemployment %	
	1950–70	1973–79	1950–70	1973–79	1950–70	1973–78
Australia	4.7	3.1	4.2	12.0	1.9	4.4
Austria	5.4	3.2	4.3	6.4	2.9	1.5
Belgium	4.0	2.4	2.5	8.4	3.1	4.6
Canada	4.9	3.3	2.4	9.1	4.5	6.8
Denmark	4.0	1.8	4.4	10.9	3.0	4.0
Finland	5.1	2.6	5.3	12.8	1.6	3.9
France	5.0	2.9	4.9	10.7	1.9	4.0
Germany	6.3	2.3	2.3	4.7	2.9	3.2
Italy	5.6	2.3	3.5	16.3	2.9	3.2
Japan	9.8	4.0	4.9	10.0	1.7	1.8
Netherlands	4.9	2.5	3.5	4.2	2.0	5.2
Norway	4.2	4.3	4.5	8.8	2.0	1.7
Sweden	4.0	1.6	4.4	9.8	1.7	2.0
Switzerland	4.7	-0.7	2.4	4.0	0.0	0.2
UK	2.8	0.8	4.1	15.4	2.6	4.6
USA	3.5	2.3	2.4	8.2	4.5	6.6
Arithmetic mean	4.9	2.4	3.8	9.5	2.5	3.6

Source: Maddison 1980
[1] Average rates of change in consumer price level

to the 1970s since several economies, notably West Germany and
Italy, experienced relatively high unemployment during the 1950s.
The 1960s were almost universally characterised by extremely low
unemployment levels.

The decline in the growth rate of real GDP has also been
accompanied by a decline in the trend of labour productivity
growth. In the seven major OECD countries (USA, Japan, West
Germany, France, UK, Italy and Canada) average productivity was
rising by 4.0 per cent per annum in the period 1960–7. This had
fallen to 3.7 per cent in 1967–73 and 1.4 per cent in 1973–80 (*OECD
Historical Statistics* 1982). Declining productivity has led to a flower-
ing of ideas related to supply side constraints on the growth
potential of the major economies.

The overall picture for the UK during this period is one of a
rising trend in inflation and a general slow-down in the growth of
living standards (see Table 1.2).

Despite a modest recovery of output in recent years, unemployment remains unacceptably high although there has been a slow-
down in the rate of inflation compared to the 1970s. Nevertheless
during 1985 prices rose on average by 5.5 per cent in the UK, a rate
which remains higher than the UK's major competitors.

During the period 1950–70 there was a steady underlying growth
of real incomes in the UK and the business cycle was mild in
comparison to the inter-war period. It should be noted, however,

Table 1.2   Historical statistics, UK 1971–84

Year	GDP growth rate %	Industrial production growth rate %	Unemployment %	Inflation rate %	Real wage growth rate %
1971	2.7	−0.7	3.7	9.4	2.8
1972	2.3	1.8	4.0	7.1	6.2
1973	7.9	9.0	3.0	9.2	3.4
1974	−1.1	−1.9	2.9	16.0	1.0
1975	−0.7	−5.4	4.3	24.2	4.7
1976	3.8	3.3	5.7	16.5	2.8
1977	1.0	5.1	6.1	15.8	−9.6
1978	3.6	3.0	6.0	8.3	9.2
1979	2.1	3.8	5.1	13.4	1.4
1980	−2.3	−6.7	6.6	18.0	−0.7
1981	−1.4	−3.4	9.9	11.9	−1.8
1982	1.5	1.9	11.4	8.6	−1.4
1983	3.4	3.6	12.6	4.6	1.0
1984	1.8	1.2	13.0	5.0	2.5

Source: Barker *et al.* 1985

that even during the golden age, economic growth in the UK was slower than that experienced in other western European countries, the USA and Japan (see Peaker 1974). Perhaps the most worrying feature of UK economic performance emerges when making international comparisons. Although slower growth, faster inflation and rising unemployment since 1970 have been features of the international economy and not confined to the UK, it does appear that, relatively, the UK has experienced these problems in a more severe form than many of the other advanced capitalist nations. By the fourth quarter of 1983 the percentage of unemployment in the UK had risen to 13.1; this was higher than the USA (8.4), Italy (10.0), France (8.2), West Germany (7.6) and Japan (2.6). Of these nations, only Italy has had a poorer record with regard to inflation, and the UK had the weakest performance in terms of economic growth (see Pratten 1985: 18). The recent overall performance of the major seven OECD countries is summarised in Table 1.3.

It is obvious that the poor record of the UK economy must be viewed within the context of international developments which have affected all advanced capitalist market economies since 1970. However, the relatively poor performance of the UK is evident by comparing data in Tables 1.2 and 1.3 which indicate that either the inherent weakness of the UK economy has made it particularly vulnerable to adverse international developments, or domestic policies have been conducted in such a way as to make matters even worse than they otherwise would have been. Let us now briefly consider the reasons which have been suggested for the dramatic turn-around in the economic performance of major industrial nations in recent years.

Maddison (1979, 1980) has identified several special characteristics which contributed to the 'golden age' of economic performance in the period 1950–70 (see also Ch. 3 and 4). These were as follows:

1. Increased liberalisation of international transactions.
2. Active governmental promotion of buoyant domestic demand.

Table 1.3 Inflation, unemployment and growth in the seven major OECD countries 1979–84

	1979	1980	1981	1982	1983	1984
Inflation (consumer prices) (%)	9.3	12.2	10.0	7.0	4.4	4.5
Unemployment (%)	4.9	5.6	6.4	7.8	8.2	7.7
Growth of real GDP (%)	3.0	0.0	2.1	−0.7	4.2	4.7

Source: OECD Main Economic Indicators 1985

3. Favourable circumstances and policies which contributed to producing low inflation in conditions of very buoyant aggregate demand.
4. A backlog of growth possibilities following the end of the Second World War.

The break-down of the 'golden age' occurred in the early 1970s. Maddison distinguishes four major contributing factors:

1. The ultimate collapse of the Bretton Woods adjustable peg exchange rate system.
2. The emergence of strong inflationary expectations as a key determinant of prices and wages.
3. Two major supply side shocks associated with the OPEC manipulated rise in oil prices in 1973–74 and again in 1979. This had an enormous effect on inflationary expectations, the trade balances of non-oil-exporting nations and investors' confidence. A huge problem of structural adjustment emerged.
4. A weakening of governmental commitment to demand management policies along Keynesian lines combined with a resurgence of monetarist ideas and influence.

There is no doubt that all of the above factors have had an important influence on the break-down of the post-war boom. Since 1979 the government in the UK has adopted a neoclassical monetarist interpretation of recent events. This school of thought lays stress on the detrimental impact of excessive government intervention and regulation in market economies as a major cause of the deterioration in growth rates. Predictably non-monetarists attribute the severity of the recent recession in the UK to deliberate acts of government policy (Barker 1980). The causes of the recession which has so severely affected the UK economy during the early 1980s are a matter of considerable controversy. According to Worswick, this recession cannot be attributed to international factors (Worswick 1984). Unlike the 1930s, world trade has 'faltered but not collapsed', and the UK economy 'plunged into recession in the middle of 1979 well before the turn-down in any other major economy' (Worswick 1984: 223). Major international developments have checked the expansion of all economies. Critics of the strategy followed in the UK since 1979 draw attention to adverse domestic developments as an explanation. According to Coutts *et al.*:

> The cause of sudden, high unemployment in the UK is a backlash against the consensus post-war economic policies of demand management to maintain near full employment, of support for industry and of

income maintenance and the provision of social welfare services–policies which were developed in response to the experience of the inter-war years. The Thatcher Government has embraced a doctrinaire monetarist strategy for controlling inflation and a *laissez-faire* approach to the supply side of the economy without attempting to moderate the social impact of these policies (Coutts *et al.* 1981: 81).

Those economists and politicians who have faith in the market mechanism attribute much of the difficulties now facing the UK economy to the misguided interventionist strategies followed by both Labour and Conservative governments during the 1950s and 1960s. In their view, policies which had short-run appeal have produced long-term disaster. Only by turning the tide against big government can the nation's economic health be restored. Prosperity depends on fostering enterprise and effort. An enlarged role for the state by diminishing the role of the individual can only damage the long-run vitality of the economy. These views have gained ground in the past decade to the extent that they form the basis of the monetarist-inspired economic strategy of the Thatcher government. The rediscovery of *laissez-faire* philosophy and ideas combined with deteriorating economic performance allowed the critics of the post-war consensus to gain extensive influence over economic policy decisions in the period after 1979.

To what extent can free markets, unhampered by government intervention, provide the goods and services people desire? It is to this question that we must now turn. First it is necessary to understand the nature of the economic problem facing all economies and the possible ways society can organise itself in an attempt to solve this problem.

The nature of the economic problem

What is Economics about? It is perhaps ironical, given the reputation of economists for disagreement, that they would all accept that there is no single formal definition of the subject. In the west a majority adhere to the mainstream neoclassical view that economic analysis centres on the issue of the scarcity of resources in relation to a society's many and various wants as the fundamental economic problem (see Lipsey 1983; Begg *et al.* 1984; Whynes 1983). When an economy's resources are insufficient to meet all the demands placed upon them, choices must be made. As Whynes has recently noted: 'Economics exists when the resources of an individual or group are insufficient to meet the demand objectives of that individual or group. Economics is concerned with the choice that people make about how best to employ a scarce resource – if scarcity does not exist then neither does economics' (Whynes 1983: 15).

Wants do not need to be unlimited to create the essence of the economic problem. All that is necessary is for wants to exceed the existing means. However, we would not wish to deny that many wants may be 'created' via advertising (see Galbraith 1978, 1969, 1974 and Hirsch 1977).

Given the nature of the economic problem, it is crucial that society's resources are fully utilised in order to produce maximum output. The level of output will also depend on the productivity of the factor inputs and important determining variables here include the available technology, the extent and form of specialisation, and the general framework of economic control including the incentive structure, that is, the economic system.

We can define an economic system as the institutional and socioeconomic framework within which economic decisions and activity are carried out. The main difference between capitalist and socialist economic systems concern the ownership of non-human factors of production. Under socialism, capital inputs are largely collectively owned and put to use, usually by government. In capitalist economic systems most factors of production can be privately owned (see Dalton 1974; Hodgson 1984).

Given this neoclassical definition of economics it is clear that the basic economic problem is the same under capitalism and socialism. It is the same in rich and poor nations alike (for a critical appraisal of this view, see Sahlins 1972 and Malthai 1984). Political change may alter the composition of governments, or even change fundamentally the economic system, but the same core problems will remain. The differences between capitalist USA and socialist USSR, between socialist China and capitalist Brazil lies not solely in the scale of the basic economic problems they each face, but in the way they choose to solve the same problems. Inputs cannot be expected to become less scarce simply because their ownership changes. In a recent critique of Marxist economic analysis relating to the actual operation of socialist economic systems, Nove has argued that such economies must come to terms with the reality of scarcity of resources in relation to wants. To assume 'abundance' is to define away the basis of the economic problem. Only in a society with unlimited resources (or limited wants) could there be abundance in the sense that all human requirements could be met. A situation of abundance eliminates the need for choice, such that 'there are no mutually exclusive choices, no opportunity is forgone and therefore there is no opportunity cost' (see Nove 1983: 15). We might add, there is no need for Economics or economists!

Economic systems vary, the composition of governments and the nature of the economic system may change, but the same core problems will remain. In each economic system the way in which decisions are made will differ, but each society must devise some mechanism for solving three unavoidable problems:

1. All societies must solve the *allocation* problem, i.e. a decision must be taken as to which goods and services to produce and in what quantities and quality (see Ch. 7, 8, 9).
2. Having found some mechanism for deciding what to produce, it is necessary to find the most economically efficient way of producing the desired goods and services. This is the *production* problem (see Ch. 5).
3. Finally, all societies must find an acceptable method of deciding who is to receive the goods and services. This is the *distribution* problem (see Ch. 10).

No economy can avoid these *what, how* and for *whom* choices. All three questions have their origin in the basic problem of scarcity of resources. Scarcity implies choice and choice implies that opportunities must be forgone since all resources have alternative uses. But how are these fundamental choices to be made? Each society must develop some mechanism, a system to facilitate choice (Lindblom 1977). In addition, it is becoming increasingly apparent that all economies face the related choice of *where* economic activity is to be located (this issue is considered later in this chapter).

If we rule out coercion there are basically two methods available to a society for making choices. Either, economic decisions can be co-ordinated via the market mechanism, or, some form of administrative procedure must be used. Inevitably every economy will utilise some mix of both methods. Markets may be competitive or monopolistic and administrative procedures may be more or less centralised. As Lindbeck has argued, 'it may be possible to make a strong case against either markets or administrative systems, but if we are against both we are in trouble, there is hardly a third method of allocating resources and co-ordinating economic decisions' (Lindbeck 1977: 33). In poor or primitive economics a large part of economic life is often governed by ritual and tradition. In a modern economy the role of tradition will be much less important but not negligible.

The market system

Any economy is composed of numerous separate but inter-dependent units. Each day millions of decisions are being made concerning the production and consumption of goods and services. How are all these separate decisions co-ordinated so that the end result is not complete chaos and break-down of economic activity? Are Marxists right when they speak of the 'anarchy of the market'?

The interdependence of economic decisions requires a reliable co-ordinating mechanism which can ensure that the basic economic problems arising from scarcity can be effectively solved. In indus-tralised capitalist economies the market mechanism plays a crucial role in providing a solution to the what, how, for whom and where questions. In this section we will provide an account of how an ideal market system solves the basic economic problems before examining the possible sources of market failure.

Neoclassical economists view the market system as the optimal solution to the universal problem of scarcity. The core premise on which the whole edifice of neoclassical economics is erected is that markets work and that the economy will adjust to price signals which reflect changing economic conditions. The working of the market mechanism has attracted the attention and praise of econ-omists for centuries. However, it has always seemed a contra-diction to non-economists that a society consisting of a multitude of individuals, each pursuing their own self-interest, could produce any other outcome than complete chaos. Is it possible that selfish motives can produce an optimal outcome for society as a whole? In 1776 Adam Smith published his *Wealth of Nations* and provided a positive answer to this important question.

Although Adam Smith had many notable predecessors, he is regarded by most economists as the founder of their discipline. It was Smith who provided so broad and authoritative an account of the known economic doctrine that henceforth no subsequent writer could ignore his contribution (see Stigler 1983). The outstanding contribution made by Smith was his brilliant overview of the work-ings of markets. In particular, he demonstrated that the individual pursuit of self-interest, within the confines of a money-using exchange economy, can lead to social harmony, providing there is competition and governments confine their activities to a minimum. Individuals do not intend to promote the interests of the general public but nevertheless this is the outcome. In Smith's own language: 'it is not from the benevolence of the butcher, the brewer, or the baker, that we expect our dinner, but from their regard to their own interests' (Smith A. 1976).

This simple but brilliant insight has had a profound influence on contemporary advocates of the market system (see Friedman 1980). For Smith, and all subsequent writers in the mainstream classical and neoclassical traditions, individual self-interest is the dominant motivating force in a 'free' market system. But each individual who intends only his own gain is 'led by an invisible hand to promote an end which was no part of his intention'. A free market society is viewed by Smith as working like a machine, which if left to itself will tend to maximise social welfare. The 'private interests and passions of men' are led in a direction which 'is most agreeable to society as a whole'. For although each actor is self-interested, there are a host of similarly motivated individuals providing competition, and it is competition which acts as the key regulator ensuring that individual greed does not lead to exploitation.

How precisely is the competitive version of the market mechanism supposed to work? Although the terminology has changed, the analysis has become more mathematically elegant and sophisticated, and the assumptions have been more clearly exposed, the basic description of how supply and demand interact to determine an equilibrium price, and how competition forces price down towards a level that just covers production costs, has remained fundamentally the same since the *Wealth of Nations*. The modern textbook version of the 'invisible hand' explains the scenario in the following way.

1. The economy consists of numerous independent consumers and producers, none of whom is sufficiently large or powerful enough to influence market outcomes by their own individual action. Everyone is a price taker.
2. The actors are assumed to be self-interested rational beings who seek to maximise their utility or profits.
3. The utility functions of individuals are assumed to be independent rather than interdependent. Thus the individual cannot suffer feelings of relative deprivation.
4. Consumer tastes or preferences are taken as given, that is, they are exogenously rather than endogenously determined.
5. The profit-maximising behaviour of firms ensure that they will always strive to produce each level of output at least cost.

6. The market demand for a product is influenced by its price, consumers' income and preferences, the prices of alternative goods available to the consumer, the distribution of income and demographic factors such as the size of population.
7. Market supply for a particular good is influenced by its price, the costs of production, the goals of the firm, and technology.
8. In each market, providing there is no outside intervention by government, a market-clearing equilibrium price will be determined where demand equals supply.
9. There will be some vector of prices which ensures equality between demand and supply in all markets simultaneously. In such a situation the economy is said to be in a state of general equilibrium.

Economists refer to this scenario as perfect competition. The determination of price in such a market is illustrated in Fig. 1.1.

Given the demand and supply schedules D_1 and S_1 an equilibrium price P_a, and equilibrium quantity Q_a are determined. In economic analysis, equilibrium may be defined 'as a constellation of selected interrelated variables so adjusted to one another that no inherent tendency to change prevails in the model which they

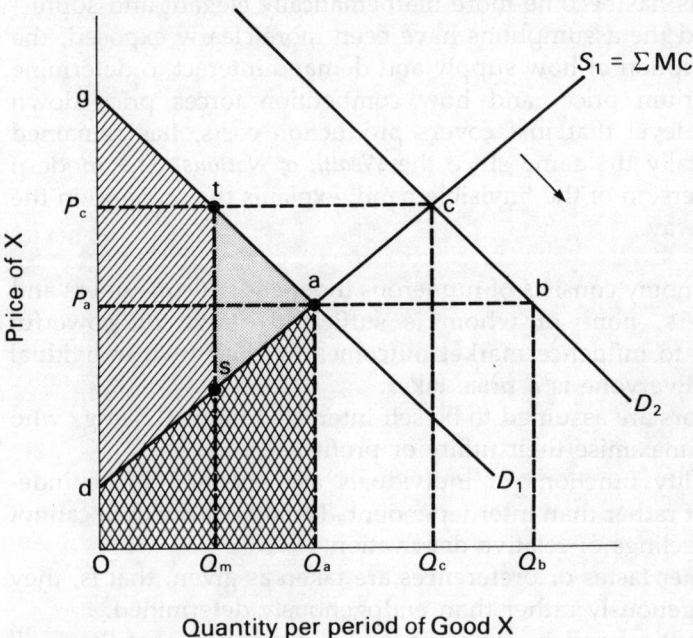

Figure 1.1 The market mechanism

constitute' (see Machlup 1958: 9). But what happens if one of the variables in the demand or supply functions changes or is disturbed? The competitive model assumes that stable adjustment will occur. The laws of supply and demand consist of statements about the consequences of shifts of the demand and supply schedules (see Lipsey 1983 or Begg *et al*. 1984). The model is put to work in the following way (see Machlup 1958: 4).

Step 1 Initial Position: 'equilibrium', that is, everything remains unchanged.
Step 2 Disequilibriating Change: 'new datum', that is something happens, for example, consumers' preferences change.
Step 3 Adjusting Changes: 'reactions', that is, things must adjust themselves.
Step 4 Final Position: 'new equilibrium', that is, the situation calls for no further adjustments.

The concept of equilibrium in neoclassical economies is a methodological device which serves as a part of a mental experiment facilitating the analysis of causal connections between events. There are four basic laws associated with the demand and supply model:

1. A decrease in supply will lead to an increase in equilibrium price and a decrease in equilibrium quantity (*ceteris paribus*).
2. An increase in supply will lead to a decrease in equilibrium price and an increase in equilibrium quantity (*ceteris paribus*).
3. A decrease in demand will lead to a fall in equilibrium price and a decrease in equilibrium quantity (*ceteris paribus*).
4. An increase in demand will lead to an increase in equilibrium price and equilibrium quantity (*ceteris paribus*).

The extent to which the adjustment is predominantly one of price or quantity depends on the elasticities of demand and supply. In Fig. 1.1 the last case of an increase in demand is illustrated. The 'initial position' is given by the schedules D_1 and S_1, with an equilibrium price of P_a and equilibrium quantity of Q_a. Let us assume that the source of the 'disequilibriating change' is an alteration of consumer preferences in favour of good X. Neoclassical economists typically do not concern themselves with the cause of such a change. Consumer preferences are taken to be exogeneously determined. Providing there are no impediments to adjustment, such as government price controls, the model predicts that the excess demand shown by the distance b–a will lead to a rise in equilibrium price to P_c. Lying behind the supply schedule are numerous perfectly competitive profit-maximising firms. If we assume that at the price of P_a each firm was making normal profits (that is P_a = Average Total Cost) the rise in price will lead to an increase in profits (price > Average Total Cost). Since the condition for profit maximisation is that firms equate marginal cost (MC) with marginal revenue (MR) and under perfect competition P = MR, then the increase in price automatically induces an increase in supply as a result of the profit-maximising behaviour of self-interested firms. The increase in supply is shown as the movement from a to c in Fig. 1.1, producing a short-run position, with an equilibrium price of P_c and equilibrium quantity of Q_c.

But each firm is now making excess profits so in Machlup's terminology this cannot be a 'final position'. Attracted by the higher profits, new firms will be encouraged to enter the industry. Since there are no barriers to entry, perfectly competitive markets are also 'perfectly contestable' (Baumol 1982). As new self-interested firms enter the industry the market supply schedule shifts to the right, lowering price and increasing the quantity bought and sold. As Smith pointed out, equilibrium price will fall until it again approximates the average cost of production. This is the 'final position' resulting from the initial disturbance caused by a change in consumer preferences.

An important feature of this model is the temporary nature of excess profits which performed a useful function in that they acted as a signal to resource users that consumers wanted more of this particular good. The outcome has indeed satisfied consumer wishes. More output of good X was forthcoming, more of society's resources were diverted to the production of good X. No planner or government regulatory body made the decision: The outcome was automatic. It was as if some invisible mechanism had guided the system towards the outcome desired by the consumer. Consumer sovereignty prevailed, no visible hand was on the rudder.

If we accept the conventional view that the basic economic problem of every society is scarcity of resources in relation to wants, then it is obviously desirable that resources be allocated in an optimal way. Can the invisible hand ensure this?

Following Pareto we can define an optimal allocation of resources as one where it is not possible to make at least one person better off without making someone else worse off (see Begg *et al.* 1984: Ch. 14 and Ch. 17; and Ch. 10). In such a situation all possible ways of increasing welfare have been exhausted given existing consumer preferences and the resource endowments and technology available to the economy. If an economy is Pareto inefficient it will be possible to make adjustments in the allocation of resources so as to increase societal welfare. Only when price equals marginal cost in the production of all goods and services will it be impossible to reallocate resources and so increase total welfare. It follows that a necessary condition for an optimal allocation of society's resources is that price is everywhere equal to marginal cost. In a perfectly competitive environment, firms, because they are self-interested, seek to maximise profits by equating costs and revenues at the margin. Under perfect competition, marginal revenue equals price, therefore profit-maximising behaviour ensures price equals marginal cost. Self-interest can therefore lead to an optimal allocation of resources, the invisible hand works!

Smith's version of the market system combined with Walras' pioneering work on general equilibrium analysis has inspired many notable contributions to the invisible hand analysis in recent years. In particular, the work of Nobel prize-winning general equilibrium theorists such as Arrow and Debreu has clarified the restrictive conditions which are necessary for Adam Smith's invisible hand to translate individual action into a socially optimal outcome. The pure theory of the invisible hand is, according to Hahn, a 'major intellectual achievement' for it 'establishes the claim that it is logically possible to describe an economy in which millions of agents, looking no further than their own interests and responding to the sparse information system of prices only, can nonetheless attain a coherent economic disposition of resources' (Hahn 1982a: 4).

But does 'logically possible' mean that actual capitalist market economies behave in the way suggested by the theory? The model outlined above is of course used as a benchmark for desirable industrial organisation. If actual economies depart significantly from this benchmark, as indeed they inevitably will, there would appear to be a strong case for deployment of the visible hand of government. Because actual markets may differ from the competitive ideal, they may fail to respond to the dictates of the consumer. Hence we arrive at the orthodox neoclassical case for government intervention, namely the presence of market failure.

Market failure and the role of government

Adam Smith and other classical economists were certainly not unaware of the limitations of the efficacy of the market mechanism. Although Smith recognised the welfare-enhancing properties of voluntary exchange within a competitive environment, he did specify a limited role for the state. In his own words:

> According to the system of natural liberty, the sovereign has only three duties to attend to; . . . first, the duty of protecting the society from the violence of invasion of other independent societies; secondly, the duty of protecting, as far as possible, every member of the society from the injustice or oppression of every other member of it, or the duty of establishing an exact administration of justice; and, thirdly, the duty of erecting and maintaining certain public works and certain public institutions, which it can never be for the interest of any individual, or small number of individuals, to erect and maintain; because the profit could never repay the expense to any individual or small number of individuals, though it may frequently do much more than repay it to a great society (Smith A. 1976).

Few modern economists would be prepared to recommend such a limited role for the state. To the extent that the conditions for perfectly competitive markets are not met, and resources prove to be less than perfectly mobile, and consumers and producers lack perfect information and knowledge, there will be inefficiencies in resource allocation. In such situations a Pareto optimum will not be forthcoming as a result of invisible market processes. As a result all real world economies are mixed in the sense that they combine the use of markets and centralised decisions for the organisation of economic activity. In the case of the UK the private sector is predominant but there is a large public sector. What does orthodox neoclassical theory have to say about government intervention?

Broadly speaking the case relates to four main issues:

1. The presence of market imperfections.
2. The presence of externalities including pure public goods.
3. The question of equity arising from dissatisfaction with the market-determined distribution of income.
4. General equilibrium problems.

A majority of economists accept a much greater role for government intervention than was envisaged by Smith since the exceptions to the universal benevolence of the invisible hand have been mounting as capitalism has developed.

Market imperfections

When economists talk of market failure they are not suggesting that markets have produced a totally unacceptable result. As Lipsey argues, 'market failure does not mean that nothing good has happened, only that the best attainable outcome has not been achieved' (Lipsey 1983: 467). Clearly in the real world there are many imperfections which prevent the attainment of the competitive ideal.

By far the most important market imperfection, judged by the attention given to it by economists, is the problem of market power. What happens to the invisible hand when market power is present? Following the refinements made to welfare economics (Pigou 1920), the analysis of imperfect competition (Robinson J. 1933 and Chamberlain 1933), and the recognition of the growing importance of increasing returns to scale as a feature of modern technology (Young 1928), it was increasingly recognised that many sectors of industrial societies would experience a break-down of competitive market structures giving rise to large enterprises with monopoly power to control prices. According to Hahn (1982a), when market power is present the 'Smithian vision of the invisible hand is lost'. Smith himself was of course well aware of the monopoly problem for it was he who wrote, 'people of the same trade seldom meet together, even for merriment and diversion, but the conversation ends in a conspiracy against the public, or in some contrivance to raise prices' (Smith A. 1976).

Economists such as Galbraith have argued that the model of perfect competition has outlived its usefulness given the nature of the modern industrial system (Galbraith 1969, 1974). The 'New Industrial State' is not dominated by atomistic price-taking firms, but by powerful firms with monopoly power (see Ch. 2). What does traditional neoclassical theory have to say about the problem of monopoly?

A monopolist is the sole supplier of an industry's product; the firm and industry are synonymous. We have already seen that profit-maximising behaviour under perfect competition produces a socially desirable outcome. But what of such behaviour under monopoly?

Following Harberger (1971) we will utilise the following social welfare function to assess the impact of monopoly. The chosen objective is the maximisation of total social benefit minus total social cost. Let W equal net welfare gain, SB represents total social benefit, and SC denotes total social cost. We can write:

$$W = SB - SC \qquad [1.1]$$

In the case of a perfectly competitive market where $P = MC$, SB is the sum total of consumers' willingness to pay, given by price times quantity (total revenue, TR) plus consumers, surplus (CS). In Fig.1.1 SB is represented by the area $OgaQ_a$. Total social cost is given by the area under the marginal cost curve, that is, area $OdaQ_a$. We can therefore write the social welfare function as:

$$W = TR + CS - TC \qquad [1.2]$$

therefore $W = OgaQ_a - OdaQ_a$
therefore $W = dga$

Now let us assume that this competitive industry is taken over by a monopolist who, in the interests of profit maximisation, equates MC to MR. Since under monopoly the firm's demand curve is also the market demand curve, MR is always less than price; therefore $P > MR = MC$, that is, price will exceed marginal cost at the most profitable level of output. In Fig. 1.1 let us assume that the most profitable output for the monopolist is given by producing an output of Q_m. Now SB is given by area $OgtQ_m$ and SC is given by area $OdsQ_m$. W is now represented by area dgts. The monopolist's restriction of output to a level of OQ_m below the competitive equilibrium output of OQ_a has resulted in a net loss of surplus. This difference in surplus, between the competitive and monopolistic outcome, is given by area sta. To see this in another way, we can ask if society would be better off by expanding output from OQ_m to OQ_a. This additional output is valued by consumers at more than the additional cost of producing the extra output, that is, area $Q_mtaQ_a > Q_msaQ_a$. Society's gain is represented by the area of net gain, sta.

In a pioneering study, Harberger (1954) made calculations of the consumer surplus losses from monopoly in the USA in the 1920s. His estimate was that the losses of consumers' surplus due to $P > MC$ for any one year was less than 0.1 per cent of USA national income. More recent studies by Cowling and Mueller (1978) and Masson and Shaanon (1984) have suggested that Harberger's study underestimated the efficiency losses from monopoly (see also Leibenstein 1966).

The traditional case against monopoly seems clear cut. Prices are higher, output is lower than the competitive outcome, and there is a resultant net loss of surplus to society. Does this mean that there is an unambiguous case against monopoly? Is theory indicating a pro-competitive anti-monopoly public policy stance? Since mergers between firms are likely to increase monopoly power, shouldn't they be prevented by government?

The real world is much more complex and the neoclassical case against monopoly is too limited. A major complicating factor is the impact of scale economies. The analysis carried out with the aid of Fig. 1.1 assumed that costs were unaffected when the perfectly competitive industry was monopolised. This is highly unlikely. If scale economies are present, and this would seem to provide a major incentive for firms to merge in the first place, we have a complex trade-off problem. In this situation, since price may be higher but cost per unit lower, society must weigh up the loss of surplus resulting from higher price and lower output against the benefits in the form of lower costs of production which will release resources for alternative uses by society. In some situations the benefits of merger may be sufficiently large as to outweigh the costs and vice versa (Williamson O. E. 1968). The trade-off approach suggests a pragmatic case-by-case approach to proposed mergers and monopoly rather than a dogmatic pro-competitive stance (Rowley 1973). If mergers produce an outcome involving large benefits in the form of scale economies such that price is lower and output higher than the competitive outcome, then from society's point of view such mergers are unambiguously good.

Leibenstein has criticised the traditional approach to monopoly and mergers on the grounds that the analysis is founded on the assumption of cost-minimising behaviour. According to Leibenstein such behaviour, although characteristic of competitive markets, is not a feature of markets where firms are not under the pressure of competition. Sheltered firms may well fail to minimise cost and this will give rise to X-inefficiency (Leibenstein 1966, 1979). X-inefficiency is the difference between actually attained and minimum attainable production costs and can therefore be distinguished from allocative inefficiency. Whereas the latter will involve the wrong level of output of a particular good, the former implies that the good in question is being produced at an unnecessarily high cost in terms of resource use, that is, X-inefficiency is pure waste. X-inefficiency theory suggests that costs will tend not to be minimised whenever competitive pressures are eased. This may be as a result of mergers, import controls, artificial barriers to entry, or the case of natural monopoly. X-inefficiency may also occur in nationalised industries and other government bodies not subject to competition.

Leibenstein's analysis points towards a more dogmatic pro-competitive public policy. If the impact of X-inefficiency outweighs the beneficial impact of scale economies, mergers should be prevented. But what if the scale economies are so significant that the market structure will tend naturally towards monopoly? Even

allowing for X-inefficiency, there will be instances where prevention of mergers and monopoly will lead to sub-optimally-sized
firms. In such a situation a number of options are open to the
government, including:

1. Nationalise the monopoly.
2. Directly regulate the monopolist's prices and profits.
3. Subject such markets to franchise bidding.
4. Simply ensure that there are no artificial barriers to entry and
   thus make such markets contestable (see Ch. 5).

The issues raised both by the orthodox neoclassical literature and
by Williamson and Leibenstein suggest a pragmatic but active
monitoring of mergers and monopoly through a variety of government policies. The basis of the traditional approach to monopoly
and merger policy is the structure–conduct–performance framework (see Ch. 5).

The competitive process school of economists regard even the
relatively weak pragmatic approach taken by the UK government
towards monopolies and mergers as being largely misconceived.
According to George, the competitive process school comes close
to saying 'that there is no need for a monopoly and merger policy
in the private sector' since given time 'all monopolies will succumb
to the forces of entry, substitution and innovation, unless they can
ward off such threats by superior efficiency' (see George
1982: 37–9). Much of the inspiration for the competitive process
school has come from the Austrian approach to monopoly (see
Shand 1984 and Ch. 2). In the Austrian view, most anti-trust
policies are misguided and harmful to economic efficiency since
monopoly profit is an incentive to entrepreneurial activity. Mergers
are an important part of the competitive process, and innovation
may be higher in monopolistic markets. Most important of all, the
Austrian school indicates that the state is the major source of
damaging monopoly power for it is here that barriers to entry may
well lead to reduced efficiency. Hence the Austrian approach has
provided inspiration to the most recent contribution relevant to
monopoly and merger policy, the theory of contestable markets
(see Baumol *et al*. 1982; and Ch. 5 below).

A perfectly contestable market is one 'into which entry is absolutely free, and exit is absolutely costless' (Baumol 1982). This
requires that all producers have access to the same technology; the
technology can exhibit returns to scale but not have sunk costs;
incumbents cannot change prices instantly; and consumers react
immediately to price differentials (see Dixit 1982).

In such a market the entrant suffers no production or price disadvantages with regard to the incumbent and can recoup any costs (less depreciation) incurred in the entry process.

The welfare implications of the contestable markets hypothesis and the consequent guidance offered to policymakers are far reaching. Since firms with extensive market power can be subject to 'hit and run' tactics, incumbents will be forced to minimise costs, refrain from cross-subsidisation, and charge prices which do not give rise to excess profits. Thus a perfectly contestable market is characterised by optimal behaviour and performance from society's point of view and yet the approach can be applied to a whole range of market structures including oligopoly and monopoly. A perfectly contestable market does not need to be perfectly competitive although the latter by definition will always be perfectly contestable. Baumol argues that perfect contestability is not meant to represent reality any more than the perfectly competitive model, but it does provide a much broader benchmark for desirable industrial organisation than is offered by the latter.

Baumol (1982) lists three major welfare propositions which follow from the hypothesis of perfectly contestable markets. First, a contestable market never offers more than normal profits even if the structure is non-competitive since excess profits provide potential entrants with earnings opportunities and invite hit and run tactics. Second, production inefficiencies (including X-inefficiency) will be absent from such markets since unnecessary costs invite entry. Finally, in equilibrium, prices will equal marginal cost as is required for Pareto optimality.

These welfare implications of the contestable markets hypothesis 'extend enormously the domain in which the invisible hand holds sway. In a perfectly contestable world it would seem to rule everywhere' (Baumol 1982). The performance and conduct of firms in such markets does not depend on market structure and hence the model directs policymakers' attention away from such issues as industrial concentration towards the key issue of barriers to entry and their removal. Baumol's theory, combined with Austrian views on the market process, suggest that in the past governments have tended to over-regulate industry. Where entry and exit are completely free, firms with substantial market power can only prevent hit and run entry by acting virtuously, that is by offering consumers an outcome normally associated with a highly competitive structure. An industry with a high concentration index and a history of absence of entry should not necessarily be interpreted as a signal for governmental regulatory action. Providing the market is contestable, these features will represent evidence of virtuous behaviour (see Shepherd 1984).

According to Bailey (1981), the contestable markets theory is extraordinarily helpful in the design of public policy for even if the cost-minimising market structure calls for a single seller (natural monopoly), provided such a market can be readily contested it will perform in a competitive fashion. In general the contestable markets theory suggests a change in the direction of government policy as well as its extent. Austrian writers appear to advocate complete disengagement by the state with regard to the regulation of private enterprise monopolies and proposed mergers.

These issues are also of relevance to the recent debates concerning privatisation. The contestable markets hypothesis does not necessarily provide a case for the privatisation of nationalised industries since the theory indicates that the source of the monopoly problem is not one of ownership but rather the artificial prevention of potential competition. Providing nationalised industries are subject to the threat of competition there may be no strong case for privatisation (see Button 1985; Shackleton 1984; and Ch. 5 below).

Externalities and public goods

We have already noted that in a world of perfectly competitive markets a Pareto-optimal allocation of resources will result. However, this assumes that there is no divergence between private and social costs and benefits. Where private costs and benefits diverge from social costs and benefits, the market outcome will involve too much or too little of a particular good, that is, resources will have been misallocated. Begg *et al.* define an externality as arising 'wherever an individual's production or consumption decision directly affects the production or consumption of others, other than through market prices' (Begg *et al.* 1984: 334). Obviously in the real world there are numerous situations where one person or group may carry out activities which have significant effects on the welfare of other persons or groups. Indeed, as the economic system becomes increasingly urbanised and interdependent, the presence of externalities will invariably increase.

Where an individual's action results in beneficial effects on others, for which they do not pay, an external economy has occurred, and social benefits have diverged from private benefits. On the other hand, when one person's action leads to costs falling on other individuals or groups, without compensation, an external diseconomy has been generated. In this case social costs have diverged from private cost.

We have seen that optimal resource allocation requires as a necessary condition that $P = MC$. However, self-interest leads firms to consider only their marginal private costs (MPC). If an externality is present in the production process (e.g. pollution) marginal social costs (MSC) will exceed MPC such that $P = MPC < MSC$. Efficient resource allocation requires $P = MSC$. Hence this particular good has been overproduced from society's point of view and resources have been misallocated. This is illustrated in Fig. 1.2.

In Fig. 1.2 we illustrate the case of a production externality in the form of pollution causing a divergence between MPC and MSC. The free-market outcome will lead to an output of OQ_1 ($P = MPC$). However, from society's point of view the optimal level of output is OQ_2 where $P = MSC$. The extra output of $OQ_1 - OQ_2$ adds Q_2baQ_1 worth of extra benefit to society but

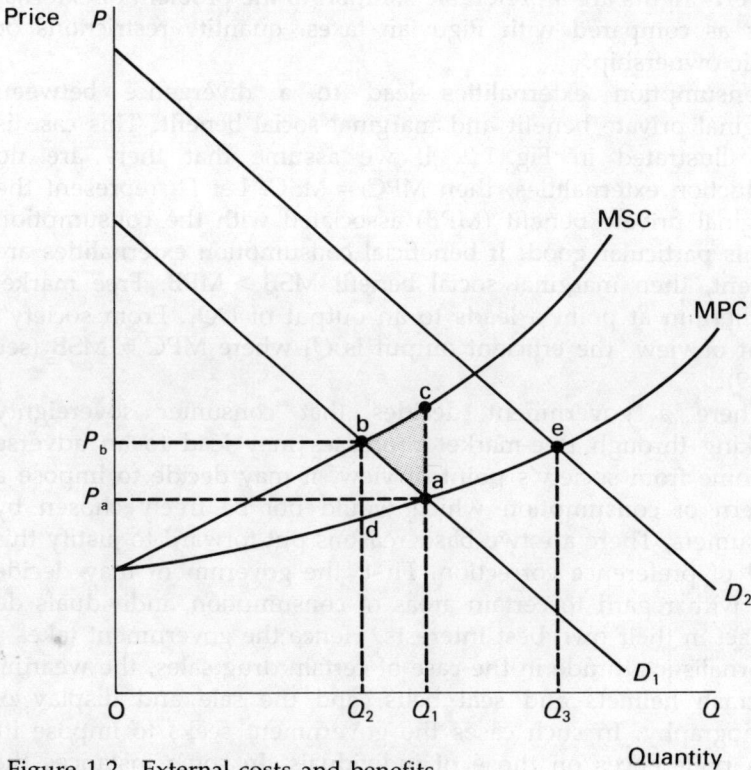

Figure 1.2 External costs and benefits

Q_2bcQ_1 worth of additional cost. The triangle abc indicates the excess of social cost over social benefit involved in producing OQ_1 rather than OQ_2.

The presence of externalities implies that the pursuit of self interest will not necessarily lead to an outcome which is socially optimal. This provides a case for government intervention, providing the costs of such do not outweigh the benefits. In the example discussed above, a Pigovian tax of bd per unit would lead to the desired outcome as it converts MPC into MSC. Alternatively, the government could specify that output shall not exceed OQ_2. Both the tax and quantity restriction solutions involve problems of measurement and information.

Some economists stress the importance of property rights and bargaining in discussions of externalities and argue that the most efficient solution is for externalities to be internalised through the use of litigation. In this case those responsible for the external costs would be required by law to provide compensation to the victims (Coase 1960). According to this view, sufficiently well defined property rights are a preferable solution to the problem of external costs as compared with Pigovian taxes, quantity restrictions or public ownership.

Consumption externalities lead to a divergence between marginal private benefit and marginal social benefit. This case is also illustrated in Fig. 1.2. If we assume that there are no production externalities, then MPC = MSC. Let D_1 represent the marginal private benefit (MPB) associated with the consumption of this particular good. If beneficial consumption externalities are present, then marginal social benefit MSB > MPB. Free market equilibrium at point a leads to an output of OQ_1. From society's point of view, the efficient output is Q_3 where MPC = MSB (see Ch. 9).

Where a government decides that consumer sovereignty working through free-market processes may lead to an adverse outcome from society's point of view, it may decide to impose a pattern of consumption which would not be freely chosen by consumers. There are two basic reasons put forward to justify this kind of preference correction. First, the government may decide that with regard to certain areas of consumption, individuals do not act in their own best interests. Hence the government takes a paternalistic attitude in the case of certain drug sales, the wearing of crash helmets and seat belts, and the sale and display of pornography. In such cases the government seeks to impose its own preferences on those of individuals. In some instances the problem may be more to do with the government's access to better information rather than a difference in preferences, for example the sale of dangerous toys or electrical equipment. The second reason involves the externality argument. If the MSB of an individual's consumption of education or health care exceeds the MPB, then too little education and health care will be demanded. In this case governments may choose to encourage the production and consumption of 'merit goods' such as education, health care and housing, although this encouragement may take a variety of forms (see Ch. 7, 8 and 9). Proponents of free markets remain unconvinced that the merit good argument provides a legitimate case for government interference in the provision of such goods.

In addition to merit wants, there are also certain goods which have the characteristic that once they are available to one person it is impossible to exclude other members of society from receiving the benefits. The principle of non-excludability (except at a prohibitive cost) is one of the key characteristics of a 'pure' public good. The second feature of this kind of good is non-rivalry in consumption. This means that one person's consumption of the good in no way reduces the amount available to others. In the UK, as elsewhere, national defence is regarded as a pure public good. In providing an anti-missile defence system for any one individual, all other members of society automatically enjoy the same benefits. Pure public goods can be thought of as exhibiting very strong externalities.

Because of their characteristics, pure public goods will be especially vulnerable to 'free rider' problems. Individuals pursuing their own self-interest are unlikely to pay for the benefits they would receive from the provision of a pure public good if others will receive the same benefits without paying. If, on the other hand, each individual can be assured that everyone else will contribute to the cost of providing such goods, they too will be willing to pay.

Private markets will not produce a socially efficient output of pure public goods and here there is a clear case for government intervention, on efficiency grounds, to provide goods and services with such characteristics. Even *laissez-faire* enthusiasts such as Adam Smith and Milton Friedman have accepted this (see Friedman 1980). Additional problems arise in association with the incomplete development of forward and contingent markets due to problems of moral hazard, adverse selection and informational gaps (see Begg *et al.* 1984: Ch. 14; and see Ch. 8 below).

One severe limitation of applying piecemeal adjustments in

order to correct various market distortions is that unless all the conditions of Pareto optimality are simultaneously satisfied throughout the whole economy it may not be desirable to aim to satisfy Pareto conditions in any particular market: for example, the desirability of marginal cost pricing rules in nationalised industries does not follow if $P \neq MC$ everywhere else. Partial Paretianism is refuted by the theory of second best (see Webb 1976).

Equity and income distribution

The orthodox assessment of the welfare implications of the market mechanism adopts the neoclassical Paretian framework. The Pareto criterion is concerned with ensuring that resources are efficiently allocated amongst competing ends. However, there are several Pareto optima, each corresponding to a different distribution of income. This raises an obvious problem for, as Sen points out, 'if the utility of the deprived cannot be raised without cutting into the utility of the rich, the situation can be Pareto optimal but truly awful' (Sen 1985: 10).

Indeed, if society regards greater equality as a desirable objective, a non-Paretian position with a reasonably equitable distribution of income may well be preferable to a Pareto optimum which is also highly inegalitarian. The suggestion that a perfectly competitive equilibrium is a 'good thing' is certainly not value neutral. The optimality of the equilibrium position rests on the acceptability of the distribution of income. To argue that the market mechanism is a 'good thing' not only rests on the value-laden assumption that only individual preferences are to count, but also on the additional value judgement that egalitarian concerns are either irrelevant or of no importance. But to argue that inequality is of no concern becomes very hard to defend 'when inequalities are so great that some people live in extreme misery, or indeed die of starvation or hunger' (Sen 1985: 14). Where individuals are deprived of entitlement to food through no fault of their own, free-market solutions would invite disastrous consequences, and public fall-back mechanisms of redistribution are both desirable and inevitable (see Snowdon 1985). Indeed, following Sen, we can view the social security systems associated with the development of welfare state capitalism as a basic means of guaranteeing a minimum standard of entitlement to the population (Sen 1981; Rawls 1972).

The alteration of the free-market outcome with regard to income distribution is a major reason for government intervention in the economy (see Ch. 10). However, such interference is highly controversial. Some writers doubt the wisdom of such intervention in any form (Nozick 1974). The justification for such a position rests on the grounds that such inequalities that do exist are 'largely the result of people's varied capabilities and motivations' (Bauer 1981: 19). This personal production view becomes difficult to sustain where inequalities are extremely wide, where opportunities are limited by sex, class, race or religion, where production is a highly interdependent process involving team production, and where the starting positions of individuals are unequal and determined by luck or inheritance.

Dissatisfaction with the market-determined distribution of income has led the governments of all advanced capitalist market economies to institute redistributive policies. This trend was reinforced as the franchise was extended to the poorer members of society. Several issues are of immediate concern to economists. Will policies designed to achieve equity have a detrimental impact on efficiency? What form should the tax-benefit system take? Should redistribution to the poor be in the form of cash or kind? Has the evolution of the welfare state reduced inequality compared to what it would have been in the absence of such a development (see Le Grand 1982)? Does inequality provide a sound reason for government intervention in the production and consumption of education, housing and health care (see Ch. 10)?

In modern economies the redistribution of incomes is achieved through the use of income, wealth and sales taxation as well as through the subsidised provision and sale of government-produced goods and services. These policies affect both efficiency and equity in a complex way and form the basis of much of the discussion in several of the chapters to follow (see Phelps 1973).

General equilibrium problems

General equilibrium analysis examines the interrelationships among the many markets which comprise any economy and represents the dominant price-theoretic research programme of the post-war period. The modern developments of this approach, by Arrow, Hahn and Debreu, develop mathematically Smith's insight that a system of social co-operation can be facilitated by a network of interrelated markets (see Arrow and Hahn 1971; Weintraub E. R. 1974). The central purpose is to extend the neoclassical analysis of market forces and their equilibrating tendencies to the economy as a whole by demonstrating that all prices and quantities produced can adjust to mutually consistent levels. The originator of this approach to economic analysis was Leon Walras who in 1874 published his *Elements of Pure Economics* (see Blaug 1978).

The essential feature of any economic system is the interdependence of its constituent parts. Since the markets for all productive factors and for all goods are interrelated, prices in all markets will be determined simultaneously. The Walrasian approach raises several important questions, the major one of which is the problem of whether the independent, self-interested behaviour of individual economic agents is consistent with an end result where each agent attains equilibrium. Thus general equilibrium theory deals with the problem of whether 'the independent action by each decision-maker leads to a position in which equilibrium is reached by all' and a 'general equilibrium is defined as a state in which all markets and all decision making units are in simultaneous equilibrium' (Koutsoyiannis 1979: 486).

In addition to the 'existence problem' (does a general equilibrium solution exist?), there are two further difficulties. Even if there is a set of prices which established a competitive market-clearing equilibrium, there is the question of whether the equilibrium is unique. The 'uniqueness problem' raises the possibility that there may be multiple equilibria. Finally, there is the 'stability problem'. If an equilibrium solution exists, is it stable, and if the equilibrium is disturbed will market forces set up automatic pressures which will restore the system back to its general equilibrium?

In the macroeconomic sphere the most interesting question is, does the general equilibrium solution also generate 'full employment', defined as the absence of 'involuntary unemployment'? The issue of involuntary unemployment was most eloquently raised by John Maynard Keynes in his *General Theory of Employment, Interest and Money*, published in 1936. Prior to this work (apart from a few heretical exceptions) unemployment was explained as being due to lack of labour mobility, wage inflexibility, the abuse of monopoly power by labour unions, or simply as reflecting a preference for leisure by certain members of the labour force (see Ch. 6). Such explanations appeared to be implausible in the face of the great depression and it was Keynes who attempted to provide a new structure of analysis in order to explain the existence of mass underutilisation of 'scarce' resources in a market system.

Keynes' contribution to economic theory remains, fifty years after the publication of his *General Theory*, a matter of considerable debate. However, by the mid-1960s, Patinkin and others had developed a consensus view, known as the 'neoclassical synthesis', where Keynes' model was represented as a special type of aggregate general equilibrium system consisting of four markets: goods, money, bonds and labour. Increasingly, Keynes' contribution was discussed within the confines of a simultaneous equation model. The synthesis view is that Keynes failed to provide a more General Theory than the classics. Keynes' claim that it is possible to have equilibrium with excessive unemployment is denied since this implies long-term labour market disequilibrium. In Patinkin's general equilibrium model, involuntary unemployment cannot persist since the assumption of wage and price flexibility ensures the simultaneous achievement of equilibrium in all four markets. Thus Keynesian underemployment equilibrium is viewed as a special case of the general neoclassical equilibrium system: it results from assuming that wages are inflexible. As Friedman has noted: 'all sorts of frictions and rigidities may interfere with the attainment of a hypothetical long run equilibrium position at full employment . . . but there is no fundamental flaw in the price system that makes unemployment the natural outcome of a fully operative market mechanism' (Friedman 1970).

During the late 1960s attempts were made to restore Keynes' claim to have produced a more General Theory. According to Clower (1965) and Leijonhufvud (1968) it was Keynes' intention to demonstrate that even in the absence of price rigidities the market system would not automatically gravitate towards a general equilibrium solution without involuntary unemployment. This amounts to saying that equilibrium prices will not be attained even if prices are completely flexible (see Levacic and Rebmann 1982: Ch. 16).

According to Leijonhufvud, the efficient working of the price mechanism requires that it fulfils two essential functions simultaneously. First, prices need to disseminate the information necessary to co-ordinate economic activity and, second, prices should provide the incentives for agents to adjust their activities in such a way that they have an aggregate consistency. Hines has summed it up as follows: 'if the market clearing vector of relative prices is known by all transactors, and if each transactor adjusts to these parameters, the system simultaneously generates an optimal allocation of resources and ensures that they are fully employed' (Hines 1971). Keynes accepted the second proposition but, according to the reinterpretation by Leijonhufvud, he denied that the appropriate information was conveyed with sufficient speed and efficiency in order to ensure a full employment outcome.

In the Walrasian general equilibrium system the information is disseminated via a fictional auctioneer, who helps the tatonnement process, by which the market gropes its way towards equilibrium. The auctioneer calls out prices and only allows trade to finally take place when the vector of intertemporal relative prices which would simultaneously clear all markets is known. In the real world there is no auctioneer, and trade will more than likely take place at disequilibrium prices ('false trading'). Hence in a world where uncertainty exists, information is imperfect and false trading is the norm, involuntary unemployment as a result of deficient effective demand can emerge, even where prices are perfectly flexible (see Morgan 1978). In this view the neoclassical monetary general equilibrium theory is a special case where uncertainty is ignored and agents have access to perfect information (see Shackleton 1982).

During recent years the UK economy has once more been plagued by a growing level of unemployment. We have seen earlier in this chapter that various forms of market failure can give rise to inefficient resource allocation. Many economists would argue that by far the most significant failing of a market economy is its inability to reach an equilibrium where all resources are fully employed. However, monetarist models, particularly those of the new classical breed, explicitly adopt a Walrasian general equilibrium framework as their basis (see Hoover 1984; Hahn 1980). In such models unemployment, which emerges as an equilibrium phenomenon, is a 'natural' and hence voluntary condition. In such models activist demand management is either ineffective or positively harmful if unexpected. The cure for unemployment is seen to lie in reducing the natural rate via microeconomic policies (see Ch. 3). But since it was Keynes who first effectively challenged the old view concerning the self-righting properties of the market system, let us review his vision of the capitalist system.

Keynes and the management of capitalism

Since 1945 we have become accustomed in Britain to the government taking an active role in economic affairs. However, this runs counter to much of the classical and neoclassical tradition in economics. The main message to emerge from Adam Smith's *Wealth of Nations* was that selfish individualism under competitive conditions would translate the activities of millions into a social optimum via the invisible hand of market forces. Following Smith, political economy had an underlying bias towards *laissez-faire*. The dominant view of the classical economists was that the state should confine its activities to ensuring a peaceful competitive environment within which citizens would pursue their individual objectives as fully as possible. Order and harmony rather than chaos would be the result. Only the evils of monopoly power or too much state involvement in economic affairs could prevent the market mechanism from yielding maximum national output given the constraint of scarce resources.

In contrast to the prevailing neoclassical orthodoxy, the most revolutionary aspect of Keynes' work from the mid-1920s onwards was his clear and unambiguous message that with regard to the general level of employment and output there was no invisible hand channelling self-interest into some social optimum. Here we find Keynes the iconoclast, challenging the existing conventional wisdom. An examination of his work in the 1920s and 1930s reveals that he was one of the first writers to form a distinctive vision of the kind of economic system which has evolved in post-war Britain. Managed welfare state capitalism, with a commitment to full employment, was the kind of system that he had in mind when in the concluding section of his famous essay *The end of Laissez-faire* he argued that:

> For my part, I think that capitalism, wisely managed, can probably be made more efficient for attaining economic ends than any alternative yet in sight, but that in itself it is in many ways objectionable. Our problem is to work out a social organisation which shall be as efficient as possible without offending our notions of a satisfactory way of life (Keynes 1972: 294).

The most objectionable feature of capitalism for Keynes was the intolerable level of unemployment which emerged during the 1920s and 1930s. This unemployment was inevitably associated with capitalistic individualism. On occasions Keynes' frustration with the economic system as it existed in the inter-war period resulted in almost revolutionary outpourings. At the bottom of the slump in the 1930s he wrote:

> The decadent international but individualistic capitalism in the hands of which we found ourselves after the [first world] war is not a success. It is not intelligent, it is not beautiful, it is not just, it is not virtuous

– and it does not deliver the goods. In short, we dislike it, and we are beginning to despise it (Keynes 1933: 760–1).

The inability of the capitalist system to provide for full employment was the main blemish on an economic system which he otherwise held in high regard. It was in determining the level of output rather than its direction that the existing system had broken down.

Keynes challenged the existing neoclassical orthodoxy which assumed that full employment was the normal state of affairs. The reality of the 1920s and 1930s was very different:' . . . it is an outstanding characteristic of the economic system in which we live that it seems capable of remaining in a chronic condition of subnormal activity for a considerable period of time without any marked tendency towards recovery or towards complete collapse' (Keynes 1973a: 249).

As early as 1929, Keynes was arguing forcefully for government programmes to expand aggregate demand via deficit financing in full support of Lloyd George's pledge to the nation. The Liberal policy was 'one of plain common sense' while the Conservative view, which Keynes regarded as being 'crazily improbable', seemed to suggest that it is 'financially sound to maintain a tenth of the population in idleness for an indefinite period'. No man who had not had his head 'fuddled with nonsense for years and years' could accept this view (Keynes 1972: 90–1). But to confront this existing orthodoxy Keynes needed to challenge the underlying theory on which policies were based. The objections to the Liberal programme were based on abstract economic theories whose assumptions were contrary to the facts. We therefore find Keynes from 1930 onwards groping towards his *General Theory*, a book which unlike many of his earlier writings was addressed to his fellow economists.

But could the experience of the capitalist economies from 1929 onwards not have been interpreted as the fulfilment of Marx's prediction that capitalism would ultimately collapse as a result of its own internal contradictions? Keynes was notoriously blind to the work of Karl Marx and his exchange with George Bernard Shaw is of interest here. During 1934 and 1935 Shaw had suggested to Keynes that he take a fresh look at the writings of Marx and Engels because in his view their work made sense of the Great Depression. On 1 January 1935 Keynes replied to Shaw that he could find nothing but 'out of date contraversialising' in the work of Marx, but perhaps more importantly:

To understand my state of mind, you have to know that I believe myself to be writing a book on economic theory, which will largely revolutionise . . . the way the world thinks about economic problems. When my new theory has been duly assimilated and mixed with politics and feelings of passions, I can't predict what the final upshot will be in its effects on action and affairs. But there will be a great change . . . I can't expect you or anyone else to believe this at the present stage. But for myself I don't merely hope, in my own mind I'm quite sure (Keynes 1982: 42).

Once published, the *General Theory* caused an immense stir. In replying to his critics, Keynes summarised his contribution as 'a theory of why output and employment are so liable to fluctuation' (Keynes 1973b: 1212). The main driving force behind these fluctuations was the behaviour of investment. The dependency of output and employment on investment would not be so important if investment expenditure were stable from year to year. Unfortunately the investment decision is a difficult one because machinery and buildings are bought now to produce goods that will be sold in the future. Expectations about future levels of demand are involved in the calculations, allowing hopes and fears as well as hard facts to influence investment behaviour. Thus, unavoidably, employment was dependent on an unstable factor. Keynes succinctly summed up this aspect of his theory in 1937 in the following way:

. . . given the psychology of the public, the level of output and employment as a whole depends on the amount of investment . . . not because that is the only factor on which aggregate output depends, but because it is usual in a complex system to regard as the causa causans that factor which is most prone to sudden and wide fluctuations . . . it is those factors which determine the rate of investment which are most unreliable, since it is they which are influenced by our views of the future about which we know so little (Keynes 1973b: 121).

For the above reasons, Keynes regarded the 'social control' of investment as central to his scheme for increased employment and economic stability. In other words, investment was not something to be left solely to private decisions. The way to improve economic performance was to raise the average level of investment. Since the instability of investment is a direct result of the instability of business expectations, Keynes laid special emphasis in the *General Theory* on the problems of risk and uncertainty (Lawson 1985). It is a theme which has been constantly stressed by those of his disciples referred to as 'chapter 12 Keynesians' (Coddington 1983).

Since ignorance can be reduced by the provision of better and more accurate information, Keynes was convinced that risk and uncertainty could be reduced by better social organisation. The establishment of more calculable markets by appropriate government policies could reduce the severity of economic fluctuations which were largely the result of the instability of investment (Meltzer 1981).

From this brief discussion we can see that Keynes wanted to reform capitalism. He had no sympathy with the individualistic *laissez-faire* capitalism which many diehard conservatives wished to preserve. What is also equally clear from his works and correspondence is his rejection of planning as a solution to economic problems. Keynes believed in the management of capitalism rather than planning (Cairncross 1971).

Keynes was a propagandist and most of his writings from the mid-1920s onwards indicate that in his view the successful preservation of capitalism would require an increase in government intervention. He did not consider that the economic system was sufficiently self-correcting in a way which would allow the government to sit back and watch. In a radio talk given by Keynes in 1934 entitled 'Poverty in Plenty: is the economic system self adjusting?', he distinguished between two groups of economists.

> On the one side are those who believe that the existing economic system is, in the long run, a self adjusting system, though with creaks and groans and jerks, and interrupted by time lags, outside interference and mistakes . . . On the other side of the gulf are those who reject the idea that the existing economic system is, in any significant sense, self adjusting . . . The strength of the self adjusting school is that it has behind it almost the whole body of organised economic thinking and doctrine of the last hundred years . . . Thus, if the heretics on the other side of the gulf are to demolish the forces of nineteenth century orthodoxy . . . they must attack them in their citadel . . . Now I range myself with the heretics! (Keynes 1973c: 485–92).

The idea that the economy is not self-adjusting, particularly at the macroeconomic level, that unemployment will not automatically be cured by market forces, is the major trademark of those who adhere to the Keynesian tradition. In this sense Keynes and his followers are challenging the Smithian vision of the smooth working of the invisible hand. The Keynesian approach to economic analysis puts considerably less faith in the corrective powers of the market mechanism to achieve full employment. The pursuit of self-interest via the market need not necessarily coincide with a socially harmonious outcome. As Keynes observed, 'the world is not so governed from above that private and social interest always coincide . . . Is it not a correct deduction from the principles of economics that enlightened self-interest always operates in the public interest' (Keynes 1972: 287–8).

Keynes was determined to provide the 'right analysis' of the problems of capitalism so that the disease could be cured whilst maintaining freedom and efficiency. But what would happen if the cure worked and full employment capitalism became a reality (Bleaney 1985; Worswick and Trevithick 1983)?

Although Keynes did not consider in any systematic way the likely behaviour of money wages under conditions of full employment, he did make several references to their likely behaviour in such conditions.

> If money wages rise faster than efficiency, this aggravates the difficulty of maintaining full employment . . . and it is one of the main obstacles which a full employment policy has to overcome . . . The more aware we were of the risk, the more likely we should be to find a way round other than totalitarianism. But I recognise the reality of the risk (quoted by Kahn 1978).

On occasions Keynes was extremely pessimistic with regard to the future of full-employment capitalism because of the likely wage inflation problem:

> . . . a capitalist country is doomed to failure because it will be found impossible in conditions of full employment to prevent a progressive increase in wages. According to this view severe slumps and recurrent periods of unemployment have been hitherto the only effective means of holding efficiency wages within a reasonably stable range. Whether this is so or not remains to be seen. The more conscious we are of this problem, the likelier we are to surmount it (Keynes 1943).

Just one year before his death, Keynes was writing:

> One is also, simply because one knows no solution, inclined to turn a blind eye to the wages problem in a full employment country (quoted by Kahn 1974).

We cannot be sure of course what form of anti-inflationary policy Keynes would have supported had he lived to witness full-employment capitalism. But in Kahn's view an examination of Keynes' works and correspondence indicates that he would have been in favour of some measure of incomes control (see Ch. 6). For Kahn the reference by Keynes to the upward movement of money wages under conditions of high employment being a 'political rather than an economic problem' is indicative of the stance which he would have adopted in the post-war period (Kahn 1978). Trevithick's view is that 'certainly Keynes would recommend a policy of prices and incomes restraint as a necessary adjunct to a restrictive demand policy' and his research on Keynes' work during the Second World War has persuaded him that Keynes' eventual conversion to a policy of incomes control took place in this period (see Trevithick 1975; 1980). This view is clearly at odds with those who claim that Keynes was a monetarist at heart (see Levacic 1985).

What can we conclude from all of this? An examination of Keynes' works and correspondence seems to indicate a measure of support for the following conclusions:

1. Keynes was well aware of the dangers of inflation and that this was likely to be the main problem to confront full-employment capitalism.
2. He regarded the upward pressure on the money wage as essentially a political problem and would have opposed policies which relied on deflation alone as a means of reducing wage inflation. He would have supported some form of policy towards incomes as a necessary adjunct to demand management policies.
3. Keynes recognised that the management of capitalism under conditions of full employment would be an extremely complicated task (see Kalecki 1943).

The relevance of equilibrium theorising

We have seen that the orthodox case for government intervention in the economy is based on the notion of market failure, including failure at the macroeconomic level. But some economists would go much further in their critical evaluation of the equilibrating properties of unregulated market forces. In Kaldor's view, market forces cannot be relied upon to counteract adverse developments in an economy and various forms of government intervention are desirable in order to prevent a vicious circle of economic decline (Kaldor 1972). The Kaldorian approach to government intervention is based on Myrdal's theory of cumulative causation which we will now develop in relation to the debate concerning the emergence of regional disparities and the appropriate policy response of government. This analysis has also been applied to the issue of de-

industrialisation and the explanation of this in terms of a balance
of payments constraint (see Thirlwall 1974; 1979; 1981; 1982).

The regional problem

The essential feature of the regional economic problem is long-term
disequilibrium in the labour market arising out of a severe imbalance between the growth of labour supply and the growth of job
opportunities in particular regions. The symptoms of this imbalance manifest themselves mainly in the form of divergencies in
regional incomes, unemployment rates, activity rates and net
outward migration. Table 1.4 indicates the extent of the problem
in the UK in its most obvious form, unemployment rates above the
national average.

It is evident from Table 1.4 that severe regional disparities exist
in the UK and have done so for a considerable period of time.
Traditional neoclassical theory suggests that such severe imbalance
should not persist due to the self-correcting nature of market
forces. In a neoclassical world, factor prices are flexible and this
induces labour to move from low-wage regions to the more prosperous high-wage regions. Capital, on the other hand, is attracted
to the low-wage regions where higher profits can be achieved.
Thus the movement of labour and capital brings about factor price
convergence, in effect the regional problem cures itself (see
Armstrong and Taylor 1985).

The fact that regional disparities persist suggests that either the
market mechanism has been prevented from operating or that it
is working inadequately, perhaps even perversely. The models
developed by Myrdal and Kaldor offer an explanation for the
persistence of the regional problem (see Dixon R and Thirlwall
1975).

Does the unhampered operation of market forces give rise to
regional disequilibrium? The view expressed by Myrdal (1957) is
in sharp contrast to the main features of the neoclassical model
outlined above. In a neoclassical world, market forces are equilibrating. Regional rates of return and growth rates are unlikely to
diverge for any significant length of time providing market forces
are allowed to work. But Myrdal's argument is that:

> . . . in the normal case there is no such tendency towards an automatic
> self-stabilisation in the social system. The system is by itself not moving
> towards any sort of balance between forces, but is constantly on the
> move away from such a situation. In the normal case a change does not

Table 1.4   Regional unemployment rates, UK

Rates of unemployment
Analysis by standard regions

Percentages

Annual averages	1974	1975	1976	1977	1978	1979	1980	1981	1982	1983	1984
United Kingdom	2.6	4.0	5.5	5.8	5.7	5.3	6.8	10.4	12.1	12.9	13.1
Great Britain	2.5	3.9	5.4	5.7	5.6	5.2	6.7	10.2	11.9	12.7	12.9
North	4.6	5.8	7.2	8.0	8.6	8.3	10.4	14.7	16.6	17.9	18.3
Yorkshire and Humberside	2.5	3.8	5.3	5.5	5.7	5.4	7.3	11.4	13.2	14.1	14.4
East Midlands	2.2	3.5	4.5	4.8	4.7	4.4	6.1	9.6	11.0	11.8	12.2
East Anglia	1.9	3.3	4.7	5.1	4.9	4.2	5.3	8.3	9.7	10.3	10.1
South East	1.5	2.6	4.0	4.3	3.9	3.4	4.2	7.0	8.5	9.3	9.5
South West	2.6	4.6	6.2	6.5	6.2	5.4	6.4	9.2	10.6	11.2	11.4
West Midlands	2.1	3.9	5.5	5.5	5.3	5.2	7.3	12.5	14.7	15.7	15.3
North West	3.4	5.2	6.7	7.0	6.9	6.5	8.5	12.7	14.7	15.8	15.9
Wales	3.7	5.5	7.1	7.6	7.7	7.3	9.4	13.5	15.4	16.0	16.3
Scotland	3.8	5.0	6.7	7.7	7.7	7.4	9.1	12.4	14.0	14.9	15.1
Northern Ireland	5.4	7.4	9.5	10.5	11.0	10.7	12.8	16.8	18.7	20.2	20.9

Source: Annual Abstract of Statistics. HMSO 1986 edn

call forth countervailing changes, but instead, supporting changes, which move the system in the same direction as the first change but much further. Because of such circular causation a social process tends to become cumulative and often to gather speed at an accelerating rate (Myrdal 1957: 13).

Myrdal admits that this process may be stopped by new exogenous changes or policy interferences, but this of course is very different from the neoclassical view that equilibrating forces are endogenous to the economic system. Myrdal's conclusion is that market forces work towards inequality, and the cumulative movement may be in either a favourable or unfavourable direction: 'the main idea I want to convey is that the play of the forces in the market normally tends to increase, rather than decrease the inequalities between regions' (Myrdal 1957: 26).

Economic activity will tend to cluster in certain favoured localities. These may have natural geographical advantages or it may simply be the outcome of historical accident. Whatever the reason, the initial competitive advantage combined with the ever-increasing internal and external economies sustain the continued expansion of the favoured locality at the expense of other less fortunate localities and regions.

Myrdal contends that expansion in one locality has unfavourable ('backwash') effects in other localities. In contrast to the neoclassical model, 'the movements of labour, capital, goods and services do not by themselves counteract the natural tendency to regional inequality' (Myrdal 1957: 27). Indeed, in cumulative causation models, factor movements have a disequilibrating influence.

Economic activities which yield above-average returns tend to cluster in certain localities at the expense of others. The advantages of the prospering regions far outweigh any limited advantages of the depressed regions such as cheap labour. The movements of capital are predominantly towards the prosperous expanding region. As a result, factor flows are disequilibrating favouring the rich region at the expense of the poor.

There are of course favourable ('spread') effects which pass from the prosperous to the less prosperous region. However, the combined impact of backwash and spread effects is to produce disequilibrating regional growth patterns. Again in Myrdal's words:

> If things were left to market forces unhampered by any policy interferences, industrial production, commerce, banking, insurance, shipping and, indeed, almost all those economic activities which in a developing economy tend to give a bigger than average return and, in

addition, science, art, literature, education and higher culture generally – would cluster in certain localities and regions, leaving the rest of the country more or less in a backwater (Myrdal 1957: 26).

As far as factor flows are concerned, Myrdal has this to say:

By themselves, migration, capital movements and trade are rather the media through which the cumulative process evolves – upwards in the lucky regions and downwards in the unlucky ones. In general, if they have positive results in the former, their effects on the latter are negative. (Myrdal 1957: 27).

The main problem with Myrdal's analysis is that it is very generalised and consequently difficult to model. In order to rectify this, Kaldor (1970) put forward a variant of the cumulative causation hypothesis which yields testable hypotheses in the form of the following propositions:

1. The rate of growth of an autonomous demand factor will govern the rate of growth of the economy as a whole.
2. From the point of view of any particular region, the autonomous component of demand is the growth rate of exports.
3. The rate of growth of exports depends on an exogenous factor, the rate of growth of world demand for the products of a region, and an endogenous factor, the movement of efficiency wages in the region relative to other regions.
4. The movement of efficiency wages is determined by the relative movement of money wages and productivity.
5. The rate of growth of money wages will tend to be the same across regions.
6. The rates of growth of productivity will be higher, the higher the rates of growth of output (the Verdoorn Law).
7. Efficiency wages will tend to fall in those regions with above-average productivity growth.

It is through this mechanism that the process of cumulative causation works with comparative success or comparative failure, having self-reinforcing effects on industrial development.

Unquestionably, Kaldor's thinking has been very much influenced by the pioneering work of Young in the 1920s (Young 1928). It was Young who noted that the forces making for continuous change are engendered from within the economic system. With increasing returns, change becomes progressive and propagates itself in a cumulative way.

The policy implications of the theory of cumulative causation are far reaching. Market forces cannot correct disequilibrating tendencies since they themselves are the source of the problem. Hence Kaldor concludes that active government regional policy is required in order to narrow regional disparities. Advocates of regional policies argue that market forces either work, but far too slowly, or work in a perverse way as suggested by the Myrdal–Kaldor model.

Regional policies can involve a variety of instruments designed to achieve a more even spatial balance of economic activity. In the UK these have included the use of policies designed to alter factor prices, to influence industrial location and improve regional infra-structure. The effectiveness of these policies has been questioned. Although regional imbalance persists, it is possible that the existing situation would have been much worse in the absence of inter-vention (see Moore and Rhodes 1973).

De-industrialisation and the balance of payments constraint

Several writers, including Kaldor, have used the cumulative caus-ation framework to explain the poor economic performance of the UK economy as a whole. For example, Robinson and Wilkinson argue that:

> . . . market forces generated disequilibrium. Differences in competitive power, whatever their origin, set up a spiral of divergence. A country such as West Germany, with growing exports, could maintain a high rate of investment and therefore growing productivity, which enhanced its competitive power, and allowed real wages to rise so that workers were less demanding. In the United Kingdom, any increase in employ-ment causes an increase in the deficit in the balance of payments so that every hopeful go had to be brought to an end with a despairing stop. Thus strong competitors grow stronger the weak, weaker (Robinson and Wilkinson 1977: 10).

Further support for this position is given by Singh, who argues that Britain is suffering from a process of cumulative decline which cannot be corrected by a *laissez-faire* policy stance:

> Once the economy is in long-run disequilibrium, for whatever reason, continued participation in international economic relations on the same terms as before may produce a vicious circle of causation. As a consequence, a country in a weak competitive position may have balance of payments difficulties, which lead the government to have a lower level of demand, which leads to lower investment and hence

lower growth of productivity and continuing balance of payments difficulties. There may be no automatic market mechanism to correct the disequilibrium (Singh 1977: 133).

In general, post-Keynesian writers stress the influence of differences in the pressure of demand between countries as an explanation of variations in growth rates. The problem is not that Keynesian employment theory has become defunct, rather it is because a weak balance of payments (BOP) has imposed a constraint on demand preventing the implementation of Keynesian policies (see Cornwall 1977).

In recent years there has been much discussion of the relative decline of the UK manufacturing sector in a process referred to as de-industrialisation. Economists who adhere to the cumulative causation model reject the 'crowding out' hypothesis of Bacon and Eltis (1976) which attributes this de-industrialisation to the rapid growth of the non-market sector of the UK economy. Instead, the relative decline is attributed to an interlocking cumulative process whereby a weak BOP leads to slow growth which in turn leads to a further deterioration in our competitive position (see Moore and Rhodes 1976; Eatwell 1982). The main argument is that the growth of industrial productivity in the UK has consistently failed to match that of our major industrial competitors. This is both a cause and a consequence of our failure to compete in world markets. The stop–go cycle of the 1950s and 1960s adversely affected business expectations and hence the willingness of manufacturing firms to invest in new plant and machinery. These low levels of investment imply a relatively slow rate of adaption by industry to technical progress, changing demand patterns, innovation in new product ranges, and the need to modernise the whole production and marketing process. Thus we have a vicious circle of cause and effect.

Of particular concern to the policymaker is the number of studies which indicate that the UK income elasticity of demand for foreign manufactured goods is much higher than the world income elasticity of demand for UK manufactured exports (Thirlwall 1974; 1982). Thirlwall has consistently argued that currency depreciation, which improves (at least in the short term) the price characteristics of UK goods, 'may aggravate a structural problem by ossifying the industrial structure which is the source of the problem' (Thirlwall 1974: 25). Many writers now support the view that the basic trade problem lies in the 'character' of the goods produced (Singh 1977; Kaldor 1982). In Kaldor's view, a 'supply side problem' does indeed exist. But it is not a lack of capacity to produce (the neoclassical supply side view); rather it is due to 'an inferiority in the quality of British products which cannot be attributed to excessive costs and prices' (Kaldor 1982: 66). According to Thirlwall, the UK income elasticity of demand for imports is not particularly high. It is the world income elasticity of demand for UK goods which is much lower compared to our industrial competitors.

With regard to intervention, the Myrdal–Kaldor hypothesis of cumulative causation has been very influential with respect to the development of the Cambridge Economic Policy Group's (CEPG) thinking, concerning their arguments supporting import controls. Kaldor has recently argued that the 'reactivation of idle resources may be possible only if some form of import controls are introduced' (Kaldor 1982: 66). Cripps and Godley of the CEPG have summarised their position as follows: 'fiscal expansion accompanied by direct control of imports is the only practical means by which the UK and probably several other industrial countries can sustain expansion of national output sufficient to restore full employment in the next decade' (Cripps and Godley 1978). However, there are many objections to import controls which are well known (Bailey and Snowdon 1982; Lall 1981).

Clearly the important issue is how can a policy be constructed which will increase the rate of innovation, investment and transformation in UK manufacturing. Cumulative causation theory suggests that demand side policies need to be supplemented by measures on the supply side which help relieve the BOP constraint. A neoclassical 'supply side' industrial policy relies on returning to the market. Deregulation, privatisation and incentives are the cornerstone. Keynesian supply side policies are more interventionist, that is, Keynesians advocate supply side policies whilst rejecting neoclassical supply side economics.

What is clear from the foregoing analysis is that any industrial strategy must be based on a more detailed understanding of why UK manufacturing industry has performed badly in world markets (see Smith K. 1984; Lawson and Kirkpatrick 1980).

The growth of government

Big government is a fact of life in nearly all western industrial market economies and this is essentially a development which has taken place in the last one hundred years. The most general observation that can be made concerning government activities is that they have grown both relatively and absolutely. In the middle of the last century, classical political economy gave support to the philosophy of *laissez-faire* and government activities were very limited; maintaining law and order and providing defence of the realm were the primary concerns (see Ch. 2).

Why has the government sector grown so much over the past century to the extent that government activities have developed far beyond the minimalist conception of the nightwatchman state (Larkey *et al.* 1981)? Several factors have been important and include the demographic pressures associated with an ageing population and the implied old-age security and health require-ments, the costs of extending national defence as high-technology weapon systems have become increasingly expensive, and the various problems and expenses associated with urbanisation such as crime prevention, transportation, housing and improved sani-tation. In recent years the recession has also induced large increases in public expenditure associated with the provision of benefits to an increasing number of unemployed workers.

The tendency for government expenditure, as a proportion of the GDP, to rise over time has long been noted by economists. In 1883 Wagner attempted to establish certain empirical observations about the growth of government expenditure. On the basis of his findings, Wagner put forward his 'law' of expanding state activity which suggests that government expenditure would inevitably increase at a faster rate than national output in any 'progressive' state (see Bird 1971). With regard to the UK, Peacock and Wiseman's seminal study of government expenditure growth in the period 1890–1955 showed that total government expenditure had risen relative to GNP over the period. The government sector was taking an increasing proportion of economic resources for its own activities and there was a clear upward 'displacement effect' associated with the two world wars (Peacock and Wiseman 1967).

Table 1.5 shows government expenditure as a percentage of GDP for the major OECD countries and Table 1.6 shows its composition in the UK. Overall the trend everywhere has been for an increase in this ratio (see Alt and Chrystal 1983: Ch. 8 and 9).

As Heald (1984: 32) has noted, 'if increases in the public expend-iture/GDP ratio count as evidence of sin there are many sinners'. Although controversy surrounds the correct way to measure public expenditure, it is clear that there have been massive increases during the present century and 'very different countries demon-strate remarkably consistent experiences' (Alt and Chrystal 1983: 219). Various forms of market failure and the impact of the Keynesian revolution gave the stimulus and facilitated this trend.

Table 1.5   Government expenditure as a percentage of GDP

Country	1965	1970	1975	1980	1981	1982	1983	Increase in % points 1965–83
United States	27.9	32.4	35.6	35.0	37.7	37.7	38.1	+10.2
Japan	—	19.3	27.3	32.4	34.5	34.4	34.8	+15.5
Germany	36.6	38.6	48.9	48.4	49.2	49.4	48.6	+12.0
France	38.4	38.9	43.5	46.4	49.1	50.8	51.5	+13.1
UK	36.1	39.0	46.4	45.1	47.8	47.3	47.2	+11.1
Italy	34.3	34.2	43.2	46.1	51.4	54.9	57.4	+23.1
Canada	29.1	35.7	40.8	40.9	41.8	46.0	46.8	+17.1
Total above countries	30.8	32.8	38.2	39.3	40.0	41.5	41.6	+10.8
Total OECD	30.6	32.7	38.4	40.1	40.9	42.3	41.7	+11.1

Source: OECD Main Economic Indicators 1985

Percentages for country groups are calculated from the total GDP and total outlays of governments for the group. The increase in percentage points for Japan is taken over the period 1970–83.

The climate for public expenditure growth following 1945 could not have been more favourable. We have already noted that Keynes himself sought to inspire a 'conservative' revolution in order to preserve capitalism. But at the same time his ideas appealed to social democrats who appreciated that a general acceptance of this new stabilisation role for the state would also provide a more relaxed attitude towards the size of the public sector. Maddison (1984) lists four main reasons why this growth has taken place.

1. Welfare state expenditures, such as income transfers, and the provision of services like education, housing and health care, have grown substantially, averaging almost 30 per cent of GDP in the advanced capitalist countries.
2. The government, at least until very recently, has increasingly become involved in using fiscal policy to steer the economy as advocated by Keynes. Activist macroeconomic management became a post-war feature of all capitalist economies.
3. The state has become a significant employer and producer in its own right.
4. Various forms of microeconomic intervention in resource-allocation processes are now commonplace with the government employing legal prescriptions, regulation, taxes and subsidies to achieve particular economic and social objectives.

Table 1.6 Public expenditure in real terms*: by programme

| | United Kingdom £ million (base year 1983–84 prices) | | | | | | | |
Programme	1979–80	1980–81	1981–82	1982–83	1983–84	1984–85	1985–86	Percentage of total 1985–86
Social security	29 061	29 591	32 796	34 923	36 301	37 369	37 801	31
Health and personal social services	16 067	17 255	17 619	17 942	18 341	18 762	18 757	15.5
Education and science, art and libraries	16 522	16 939	16 813	16 964	17 080	16 747	15 836	13
Housing	8 242	6 971	4 687	3 932	4 277	4 071	3 079	2.5
Environmental services	4 883	4 747	4 410	4 640	4 703	4 554	4 077	3.4
Transport	5 753	5 844	5 731	5 530	5 324	5 493	5 046	4.2
Employment services†	1 684	2 256	2 398	2 350	2 734	2 789	2 772	2.3
Law, order and protective services	4 474	4 660	4 963	5 169	5 457	5 704	5 642	4.7
Defence, overseas aid and other overseas services	16 353	15 592	15 829	17 264	18 089	18 856	18 902	15.7
Other expenditure on programmes‡	8 772	9 656	11 318	9 722	7 992	7 956	8 756	7.3
Total public expenditure on programmes	111 809	113 513	116 566	118 437	120 298	122 301	120 672	
Of which, expenditure by local authorities§	31 399	30 745	29 724	30 547	33 165	32 738	30 383	

* Real terms figures are the cash outturn or plans adjusted to 1983–84 price levels by excluding the effect of general inflation as measured by the GDP deflator.
† Great Britain only.
‡ Includes employment services in Northern Ireland, local authority current expenditure not allocated to specific programmes, the Reserve, special sales of assets and general allowance for shortfall.
§ Includes local authorities' current expenditure not allocated to specific programmes.

Source: Social Trends 1986

The climate of opinion has now changed and over the past decade all forms of government intervention and expenditure have been put under scrutiny. For many the role of the state has been extended too far. For example, as early as 1968 we find Margaret Thatcher arguing that:

> I believe that the great mistake of the last few years has been for the government to provide or to legislate for everything. Part of this policy has its roots in the plans for reconstruction in the post-war period when government assumed all kinds of new obligations. The policies may have been warranted at the time but they have gone far further than was intended or is advisable (quoted by Coates and Hillard 1986: 64).

The emphasis upon the more detrimental impact of various forms of government intervention have been a feature particularly of government statements since 1979. The combined impact of government expenditure and revenue programmes are seen as blunting incentives and distorting the allocation of resources. In general there has been a loss of confidence in the ability and desirability of government intervention in the economy. Parallel with this has been a restoration of faith in the dynamic properties of market forces freed from the visible hand of government. A large and continuously expanding public sector has come to be seen as 'an inferior substitute for a dynamic private sector rather than as an essential complement to it' (Saunders 1985).

For some economists the growth of government has had an extremely detrimental impact on economic performance. In the mid-1970s the Bacon and Eltis thesis that poor economic performance in the UK was the result of too rapid a growth of the non-market (largely public) sector caused considerable controversy (see Hadjimatheo and Skouras 1979). However, international cross-sectional evidence appears to provide little support for the hypothesis that government size and growth have necessarily had an adverse impact on economic efficiency and economic performance (Saunders 1985; Parker 1985).

Nevertheless almost every OECD country has employed a variety of methods to control public spending in recent years, including the use of privatisation. However, more targets have been set than met due to political and administrative resistance and the paradoxical impact on government revenue and expenditure resulting from austerity programmes in economies with significant built-in stabilisers (see Tarschys 1985).

Government failure

We have seen that the orthodox case for government interference in a capitalist economic system is based on various forms of market failure. In this sense, Keynes was orthodox in that he saw the principle of market failure as the basis upon which macroeconomic interventionist policies could be founded (Beenstock 1980). In addition, cumulative causation theorists would argue that the problem is more fundamental than neoclassical economists are prepared to admit.

But in recent years there has been a resurgence of faith in the welfare-generating properties of the market mechanism and growing disillusionment with the ability of government to improve on market outcomes, even where markets are working imperfectly. Imperfect markets may well produce more desirable results than imperfect government. Sources of government failure now attract the attention that economists for so long directed towards imperfections in market processes. Several factors have been important in stimulating this counter-revolution:

1. As noted above there has been widespread disappointment with recent economic performance in the capitalist economies where government intervention in the post-war period had become generally accepted as desirable.
2. The apparent failure of Keynesianism to explain and solve the emerging problem of stagflation combined with the monetarist and new classical revivals inspired by Friedman and Lucas (see Ch. 3).
3. The influence of the comparative institutional approach to public policy issues inspired by economists such as Demsetz.
4. The analysis associated with the public choice theorists represented by economists such as Buchanan and Niskanen.
5. Widespread disillusionment with the results of planning, especially central planning, in many eastern bloc economies.

Market failure is a necessary but by no means sufficient condition for state intervention since there is no guarantee that governments have the capacity or desire to successfully correct such failures. Much of the early literature on market failure inspired by the Paretian framework tended to ignore problems which were likely to emerge when government attempted to interfere with imperfect markets. Demsetz has referred to this as the 'nirvana' approach to public policy where the relevant choice is

presented as being one between an ideal norm (perfect government) and an existing imperfect institutional arrangement (imperfect markets). Demsetz argues for the adoption of a comparative
institutional approach in which the relevant choice is between
alternative real institutional arrangements, that is imperfect
markets and imperfect government.

This approach attempts to assess 'which alternative real institutional arrangement seems best able to cope with the economic
problem' (Demsetz 1969). It is therefore essential to compare the
outcomes associated with imperfect government with imperfectly
working markets if public policy is to achieve improvements in
social welfare. In general, economists who place great faith in the
market mechanism do not accept that governments can improve
upon the market outcome (see Friedman 1980).

There is, however, an emerging view in certain political circles
that governments have a role to play in helping markets work.
Thus Sherman has noted that:

> . . . there is no necessary correlation between intellectual acceptance of
> the market as a self-operating system and rejection of government econ-
> omic intervention. It is possible to appreciate the historic role of the
> market process and therefore to hold that government involvement is
> needed both to safeguard its operation against endogenously generated
> aberrations, and to realise its full potential (Sherman A. *The Guardian*,
> 7 April 1986).

Buchanan's critique of Paretian welfare economics focuses on
the treatment of government as an exogenous element. Public
choice theorists treat government action as endogenous and politicians as utility maximisers whose utility functions contain re-
election prospects as well as a concern for social welfare. Of further
concern is the role of the bureaucrat since many public sector
goods and services are delivered through bureaucratic organisations. Typically bureaucracies are regarded as being large,
hierarchical, inefficient and inflexible. The bureaucrat is not
accountable, as is the politician, to an electorate, and the bureaucrat's specialist knowledge gives them considerable power and
influence. What do bureaucrats seek to maximise? According to
Niskanen (1973), the bureaucrat's utility function will contain variables such as salary, reputation, power, promotion prospects etc.
Politicians supply funds to the bureau with the expectation that a
desired level of output (e.g. education, health care etc.) will be
forthcoming. Niskanen assumes that bureaucrats aim to maximise
the relative size of their bureaux and that the end result will be

excessive output from individual bureaux. Allocative inefficiency shows up as budgets that are too large.

Several writers have drawn attention to the possibility that where governments are subject to a re-election constraint they may be tempted to manipulate the economy for political profit (Buchanan *et al.* 1978). One of the consequences of the Keynesian revolution has been that governments are held responsible by the electorate for the state of the economy. A government's ability to stay in power will depend on the prevailing economic conditions at the time of the election. Political trade-cycle models therefore predict that incumbent politicians will engineer a favourable pre-election boom (Nordhaus 1975). The construction of politico-economic models (politometrics) in which the government is an endogenous part of the circular flow calls into question the whole idea of the government steering the economy in a way which maximises social welfare (Frey 1978; Mosley 1984).

Pro-marketeers have argued that one of the most important lessons of recent economic history has been that planning cannot replace the market. It was noted earlier that an economic system consists of a network of institutions and arrangements designed and directed towards solving basic economic problems. The discussion so far has concentrated on the extent of government involvement in capitalist market systems. An alternative method of solving the basic economic problem is for decisions to be centralised with some central body or planning agency. The task for the planning agency is to collect and use information so that the production and distribution of goods and services can be organised. If the what, how, for whom and where decisions are centralised in this way, the economic system operates through a process of command.

One immediate problem stands out. How can the planners obtain accurate up-to-date information concerning the productive possibilities of government-run enterprises and the preferences of households with respect to consumption and work so that the goods people desire are actually produced in the correct quantities and quality? Advocates of the price mechanism, such as Hayek and Friedman, stress the advantages of a decentralised market system in terms of its subtle ability to co-ordinate decisions without any central authority requiring masses of information.

If the planners had perfect knowledge, then the calculation of efficient plans would be relatively easy. However, the central authorities will always lack adequate information on which to base their decisions. According to Ellman, planners will inevitably suffer partial ignorance for two reasons. First, the planning process actually creates ignorance because inaccurate information is deliberately created, some information is destroyed in the process of transmission, and the addressees of information may never receive it. Second, some ignorance is unavoidable since the real world is characterised by a sequence of unforeseen changes (Ellman 1978). According to orthodox Marxist–Leninist theory, a national economic plan is the means by which a socialist economy can avoid the anarchy of production which is regarded as inevitable under capitalism. The major weakness of this view is that: 'it fails to take any account of ignorance . . . It also fails to take account of stochastic, as opposed to deterministic processes. It assumes a perfect knowledge, deterministic world, in which unique perfect plans can be drawn up for the present and the future' (Ellman 1978).

Austrian economists, such as Mises and Hayek, view the market economy as a spontaneous institution which efficiently coordinates economic activity in a complex and continuously changing world. In their view, real socialist economies are certain to produce economic chaos (see Ch. 2).

The initial advocacy of planning, which favoured centralism, controls, directives and targets, has fallen into disrepute given the experiences in many eastern bloc countries (see Nove 1983). Many socialists have recognised the inefficiencies and problems associated with bureaucratic red tape, corruption and delays. Of course, the planning attempted in capitalist market systems has not been of this highly centralised nature but of an indicative variety. Indicative planning is a procedure 'by which government works out, after consultation with private industry, a set of more or less disaggregated output targets, for the various commodity groups within the national product . . . these targets, do not correspond to binding obligations imposed on individual firms' (Richardson 1971). Indicative planning avoids the dangers of bureaucratic intervention and its role is essentially one of avoiding mistakes which can arise through lack of co-ordination. Interest in the role of this kind of planning resulted from disappointment with the relative growth performance of the UK economy during the 1950s and the apparent success of such planning in France. The failure of the indicative planning experiment in the mid-1960s added fuel to the critics of dirigiste philosophy (see Ch. 5). Indeed, planning of all types has been the subject of severe criticism both in developed and underdeveloped countries (see McFarlane 1984; Lall 1983; Killick 1976; Budd 1978).

One of the main sources for the dissemination of these pro-market influences has been the Institute of Economic Affairs which was formed in 1957 as a research and educational trust specialising in the study of markets and pricing systems as technical devices for registering preferences and apportioning resources. The main policy conclusions to emerge from the numerous pro-market publications of the IEA over nearly thirty years include the following (see Heald 1984: 90):

1. Generally the extent of state involvement in the economy should be dramatically curtailed.
2. Services such as health care and education should not be provided free at the point of consumption. There is a strong case for the private provision of such services (see Ch. 8 and 9).
3. Choice ought to be restored to the consumer in such areas as education by the use of vouchers (see Ch. 9).
4. Income redistribution should be carried out via cash transfers rather than in the form of benefits in kind (see Ch. 10).
5. Keynesianism in general should be abandoned. Governments should be prevented from running deficits by constitutional rules (see Ch. 3).
6. All forms of centralised planning and attempts by governments to control market forces will inevitably produce economic chaos.
7. Rent controls damage the operational efficiency of the housing market (see Ch. 7).
8. In the international sphere, floating exchange rates are the most desirable exchange rate regime (see Ch. 4).

Since 1979 the welfare state has been 'the object of a sustained intellectual attack' (Le Grand and Robinson 1984a; Gough 1979). Most of the above arguments would be endorsed in large measure by the present government. But what are the ultimate aims of economic policy?

The objectives of economic policy

Governments implement economic policies in order to achieve some specific goal or goals. In the UK during the post-war period, successive governments, at least until 1979, have been held responsible for achieving multiple, often conflicting, objectives which include full employment, the maintenance of a high (and rising) living standard, price stability, equilibrium in the balance of payments, a more even regional balance of economic activity, and reduced inequality of incomes and wealth. These objectives can be regarded as contributing to the welfare of society since individual welfares are linked to their achievement. Now although it may be agreed by everyone that the ultimate aim of all economic policies ought to be the promotion of social welfare, this leaves open the complex issue of what precisely is social welfare?

At the core of policymaking is to be found a usually implicit and ill-specified statement of societal objectives, what neoclassical economists have come to term the social welfare function, what policymakers (and voters) more usually refer to as the public interest.

It is appealed to in times of crisis (domestic and international), and used (and abused) by politicians of all persuasions. Strange indeed would be the politician who publicly advocated a policy that was 'not in the public interest'. Yet the frequency of its invocation has not facilitated its clarification.

The vacuity which usually surrounds this issue is well attested to in the work of Bailey. Thus: 'there is perhaps no better example in all language of the utility of myth than the phrase "the public interest". It is balm for the official conscience. It is oil on the troubled waters of public discontent. It is one of society's most effective analgesics . . . Happily for policy makers, the public is often quite easily satisfied' (Bailey S. K. 1967: 97).

On the (relatively) rare occasions when neoclassical economists explicitly consider the public interest, a certain wariness is evident. Steiner has commented that:

> My dominant reaction to rereading the discussion among economists about the 'public interest' is surprise at its defensive tone, as if we are somehow disloyal when we find a role for extramarket forces in the economy. Perhaps because economists have felt defensive, much of the economic discussion has revolved not around the issue of how to define the public interest but how to demonstrate that there is a *de minimis* role of government activity that clearly benefits everybody. Much of welfare economics consists of such a possibility theorem (Steiner 1977: 40–1).

The definition, articulation and representation of the public interest is the domain of the state. What then can we say of the state? Notice first that 'the state' is not synonymous with 'the government'. Thus Ballard (1936) argues that government is the mechanism through which the state acts. Williams sees the government as '. . . the legitimate power holding *group*: the State is the structure by which the group's activity is defined and regulated' (Williams R. M. 1951: 202). It is our view that economists, in their continued preoccupation with the notion that governments are 'the' or 'the only' source of economic policy, and that governments are dispassionate as regards the competing interest groups in the economy, invite an accusation of naivety and over-simplification. A number of influential and determining forces are at work. Thus:

> Alongside this capitalist class, there are the people who occupy the top positions in the institutions of the state – leading politicians, top civil servants, the managers of state enterprises, judges, high-ranking military and police chiefs . . . lawyers, accountants, church leaders, and other specialists in communications. Together these people control the means of production, the means of persuasion, and the means of coercion. They constitute the 'dominant class' in Britain, the 'ruling class', the 'power elite', the Establishment. It is they who are in charge of the main institutions through which power, responsibility, and influence are mainly exercised . . . (Miliband 1982: 6–7).

The aggregation procedures embedded in modern welfare economics are far removed from the antagonisms and conflicts which permeate actual political processes. Consider the following contribution:

> The claim that Britain, in terms of how life is experienced, is 'one nation', or has been moving towards being 'one nation', is wishful thinking or wilful-mystification. There is one nation of large claims on resources, . . . and another nation of wage labour. The main function of the political system is to maintain and protect these arrangements, and to contain the pressure against them (Miliband 1982: 11).

There would appear to be little hope of reconciliation here.

Of course, this is not to say that governments are not important in economic policy formulation and they are clearly essential in policy implementation. But what of the other actors who, together with the government of the day, make up the state? There has developed over the past twenty years a considerable literature surrounding this complex issue, some of which has latterly been contributed by economists.

Much of the early literature (Lindblom 1965; Wildavsky 1966) characterises the policy process as being essentially pluralistic with the achievement of workable compromises between conflicting interest groups, e.g. trades unions, corporations, professional bodies, consumer protection groups etc., operating both within and without the government. Within this environment progress is made by trial and error, no specification of overall goals and the routes by which they are to be achieved, being made. This process avoids direct conflict between competing interests but tends to produce rather vacuous policy statements which are frequently incapable of evaluation.

This rather even-handed and benign view of the policy process has, of course, been challenged.

Indeed, in later work Lindblom acknowledges that the process of mutual adjustment might be rather more uneven than earlier suggested, in that those interest groups which are capable of affording special pleading to the executive tend to prevail (Lindblom 1977). Another source of bias emanates from the failure, *ex ante*, to specify the criteria by which policies are to be evaluated (Schultze 1968).

Further, it has been argued that there is a need to evaluate policy from a wider perspective than that of the immediate concerns of government so as to enable them to get beyond 'muddling through' (Nelson 1977).

The formation of interest groups has attracted attention, as has their continuation in the presence of the 'free-rider' problem, under which others enjoy the benefits of their activity without paying for it (Olson 1965; Stigler 1974). It is scarcely surprising that another, increasingly influential, group of researchers should be attracted to interest group explanations of the policy process, these being Marxists.

This vast literature is increasingly being acknowledged as insightful even by those working outside of the Marxian framework. Thus Atkinson and Stiglitz have stated 'we have emphasised the self-interest approach . . . but we do not suppose that it provides the full picture. Just as the act of voting may be based on considerations other than rational calculation of expected net benefit, so too group activity may arise from a wider social context' (Atkinson and Stiglitz 1980: 319).

There are of course many variants of Marxism but they have as a common core a concern with conflict between capital and labour, the exploitation of the latter by the former and the determination of class by reference to one's role in the productive process, that is, one's ownership of capital. A person's interests are defined by their class; collective decision-making problems do not arise since members of the same class have common interests. On the issue of the relationship between the dominant class (capitalists) and the state, there is a range of view.

Whilst noting the impact of increasing concentration and the evolution of giant firms and the divorce of ownership from control upon the capitalist mode of production, Miliband argues that it remains legitimate to refer to a capitalist class.

It has been argued that the state is formed by the conflict between workers and capital over the appropriation of surplus value (Foley 1978). By contrast, an instrumentalist analysis would have it that the state simply reflects the power of the dominant class and that decisions are made so as to further its interests, notably the accumulation of capital, in the face of recurrent crises (O'Connor 1973). The illuminatory value of such analysis is however tempered by the difficulty of generating and testing the hypotheses which it implies. Interest group analyses (Marxist and non-Marxist) are but one type of theory of the state. To them must be added bureaucratic models and voting theories.

In contemporary democracies considerable responsibility for the administration of legislation resides with bureaux. Some politicians have suggested that bureaux have even greater significance as makers of policy (Crossman 1975; 1976). Following upon the early work of organisational theorists and sociologists, economists were initially, and perhaps unsurprisingly, content to see public bureaux as polar opposites of the neoclassical private firm. The difficulty of specifying the objectives of public bureaux as against the stark simplicity of the maximisation of expected profits for the private firm and the nature of worker incentives in the polar cases furthered the dichotomisation of these organisational types. Recent developments in our understanding of both types has led to a blurring of this sharp distinction and the increased application of concepts such as the internal economics of organisations and the divorce of ownership from control (initially developed in the theory of the private firm) to public agencies.

We must however be cautious in over-stretching the analogy. Public agencies still frequently enjoy a monopoly position aided by entry barriers. Often the consumers of their services can only use 'voice' (i.e. complain) they cannot 'exit'; in the market both are possible (Hirschman 1970).

The relative decentralisation of the functions of the state permits of a degree of autonomy for state agencies and for the bureaucrats. This raises the possibility that there may be allocative inefficiency in the bureaux (Niskanen 1971). Whilst welcoming the fertility of this approach, some commentators (Atkinson and Stiglitz 1980) consider it to be rather too stark in ascribing 'overwhelmingly dominant monopoly power' (Niskanen 1971: 30) to the bureau.

Voting models are concerned with the relationship between preferences and decisions, the development of a voting equilibrium and its implications for representative democracy. In a world where everyone had perfect knowledge of policy trade-offs, and identical preferences and endowments, the role of the state would collapse to that of enacting agreed decisions as efficiently as possible. In a direct democracy, where decisions are made by voters directly rather than through their elected representatives, if everyone had the same preferences, endowments and policy trade-offs then there would be no disagreement. Where preferences differ we have no problem with private goods, each chooses their desired quantity. In the case of public goods we need a mechanism to reconcile conflicting preferences. We could permit one person (despot) to make the decision by imposing his preferences upon the rest. It would generally be considered that such a solution, although determinate, is not acceptable. In a one-man, one-vote system we could proceed by pure majority voting. With an odd number of voters who do not misrepresent their preferences for some ulterior motive there will be a majority voting equilibrium which corresponds to the preferences of the median voter. As policy changes so too will the identity of the median voter. The predictive power of this approach is considerable but is bought (as usual) at the expense of strong assumptions, not the least of which are informational in nature. The model requires that voters be in receipt of information about policies and their impact and this is costly to acquire. This, of course, is a precondition for the development of mediating agencies and spurs the transition from direct to representative democracies with voters' informational demands being increasingly met by pressure and lobby groups and political parties. Median voter models have been econometrically tested but a number of problems arise such as the identification of the median voter, voters' misconceptions of policy issues (e.g. under or over-statement of the cost of public services) and factor price variations in cross-sectional data. Their state of development is such that even where they have achieved a reasonable explanatory level they are not yet clearly superior to other approaches.

In the absence of a majority voting equilibrium the familiar voting paradox may arise. Thus, incomplete transitivity may result in there being no overall majority decision. Having been noted two centuries ago, it is to the seminal work of Arrow that one must turn for systematic analysis of this issue (Arrow 1951).

Modelling with relatively weak conditions, Arrow demonstrated that only dictatorial methods are capable of guaranteeing the existence of equilibrium with every possible configuration of individual preferences.

The second wave of (analytical) attack has, as frequently occurs in neoclassical economic theory, concentrated on the relaxation of

Arrow's specified conditions, e.g. by limiting voters' choices to small regions around the existing position and by restricting the range and distribution of preferences.

In the absence of a majority voting equilibrium, more recent work has focused upon voting other than in accordance with one's true preferences (strategic voting) and preventing this; exploring the sensitivity of the outcome to the order in which votes are taken; supporting another voter on one issue in return for his support on a different issue (log-rolling) via a process of vote trading (see Mueller 1979).

With the exception of infrequent referenda, most policy decisions are, in practice, taken by our elected representatives and their appointed bureaucrats.

In a two-party political system in which the winning of elections is paramount (rather than policy prescriptions *per se*), Downs (1957) has argued that the preferred location on the right–left spectrum for each party would be the median point. This approach does, however, clearly understate the ideological anchorage of many political parties and underplays thc variation of opinion within parties (degrees of 'right-ness' and 'left- ness'). Further, it is at least arguable that voters are more influenced by their perceptions of individuals (party leaders and rebellious backbenchers) than they are by issues and policies. Getting beneath this imagery so as to form a rational preference of course involves the voter in costs. These may be partly borne by the political parties (but presumably with the expectation of a return). Even fully informed, the voter may choose not to vote in the knowledge that his vote is extremely unlikely to be decisive and the acquisition of information is not cost-less. That voters participate to the extent that they do may, in the light of the above, be better explained by reference to social norms, expectations and pressures than by the pursuit of self-interest.

On a broader level, research has concentrated on modelling the relationship between economic policy and policy instruments and electoral fortunes, that is, the political business cycle (Frey 1978; and MacRae 1977). In view of the specification and estimation problems involved and in the light of the rather patchy history of developments elsewhere in macroeconometrics, this work may best be described as embryonic.

Whether the state ought to behave in any of the ways suggested above is of course a rather different question. Recent writing on political philosophy reveals a spectrum of opinion from those who regard it as axiomatic that economic activity should be under some form of collective control through those who see the state as undertaking only those activities which command unanimous approval through to those who see a role only for the minimalist state with functions limited to law enforcement and protective services (see Ch. 2). These perspectives have widely differing informational requirements and make very different assumptions about the interpersonal comparisons of utility which are required to aggregate to a social welfare function.

Our interest in these matters is however not merely technical since these issues are central to the formulation of policy objectives and have fundamental implications both for the way in which the economy operates and also for the analytical and empirical agenda which we have surveyed above.

Conclusion

In this chapter we have explored the analytical foundations of the debate over markets, intervention and planning. We have established that the essential and inescapable imperative is to address the central economic problem of choice in the presence of scarcity. In exercising these choices we have seen that society has available to it a range of possible solutions and have noted that in the western democracies some form of 'mixed economy' has evolved in response. We have grounded our empirical commentary upon the recent economic history of the UK and have noted the comparative performance of the economy, the decline of manufacturing industry and problems of spatial imbalance.

This discussion serves to remind us that we need also to address fundamental issues about the nature of economic policy and the underlying objectives upon which it is predicated. We must, however, be careful not to overstate public concern with economic affairs.

In a salutary comment, Sherman reminds us that:

> For government in a mature democracy to achieve great changes for better or worse, its members and supporters must be moved by disproportionately great passions. History shows no cases where economic ideas alone have fuelled such passions . . . Embodiments of logic or hedonism, like the market economy, Gross National Product or free enterprise, have yet to inspire martyrdom (Sherman A. *The Guardian*, 7 April 1986).

We have raised a series of crucial questions to which we return in subsequent chapters. In doing so we are well aware of the danger of raising an expectation of determinate solutions. Even in areas of theory, economists are necessarily prone to disagree. In matters of policy the differences, as we have seen, can be so profound as to threaten the continued unity of the discipline.

Complex, controversial and intractable though they may be, these questions cannot be avoided since they lie at the centre of both the discipline and of the policy debate. There is thus an obligation upon economics and economists to provide some guidance to policymakers, advisers and voters upon these pivotal issues.

Chapter 2

IS A PURE MARKET SYSTEM FEASIBLE?

Peter Wynarczyk

Introduction

Economists and politicians are currently engaged in the process of rediscovering the potency of markets. We are witnessing the re-emergence of the belief that a market economy is capable of self-generating and self-sustaining an acceptably high and growing level of output and employment if freed from the de-stabilising influence of government interference of its micro and macro foundations. Market systems are now being presented in a much more positive way than they have in the past.

The established modern, liberal, conventional wisdom which argues that free-market economies face inherent limitations and need deliberate correction through the machinery of the state has come increasingly under attack. One of the most disputed questions in economic theory and policy today relates to the proper limits of the functions and agency of governments. There is a need to determine afresh the role or agenda of government from its non-agenda.

In considering whether a pure market system is feasible, i.e. whether pure market forms can exist in the real world without the necessity of legitimate state action, we must concern ourselves with the practically realisable rather than the merely theoretically conceivable. Our interest is with the possible rather than the purely imaginable.

We must also concern ourselves with the fundamental question of whether markets are preferable (superior) to non-market systems. Such an endeavour requires that we make a comparative appraisal of the relative efficiencies of the market and the state in getting things done.

Traditionally, economists have been over-hasty in suggesting that government should intervene to solve a problem which the market did not appear to solve efficiently (Stigler 1975: ix–x). The belief that governments should step in to correct market failure has come under increasing attack. Experience of government intervention and its political failings demonstrates that apparent market break-down should not be seen as giving an automatic green light to government interference. There is no reason to believe that governments reach perfect solutions either (why should governments be able to refresh those parts that the market does not reach?). What is required is a comparison to be made between the likely errors of the market and of government in the real world and to use the least inefficient. As Tullock has argued: 'there is a legend of a Roman emperor who, being asked to judge a contest between two singers, heard only the first and gave the prize to the second, assuming he could not be worse. This is not an optimal selection procedure' (Tullock 1976: 10).

From classical to modern liberalism

Adam Smith is generally accredited with having established the first systematic prototype of the classical liberal position. His advocacy of such was firmly entrenched within a system of natural liberty and was clearly a reflection of influences drawn from the Anglo-Scottish enlightenment (most notably Hutcheson, Hume, Ferguson and Mandeville).

In the *Wealth of Nations* we get the argument supporting a restricted role for government – the recognition that state interference is necessary but must be limited. It was by freeing industry and trade rather than by directing it that economic progress would occur. One must fully comprehend the tremendous innovative force of Smith's support for greater individual liberty and more restricted government at a time when common practice and interested thought favoured large-scale government control and regulation of the economy and the individual. We get the demonstration within the *Wealth of Nations* that unfettered private markets generally promote consequences which are beneficial not only to the individual but also to society at large; whilst government distortions of the workings of the market place tend to lead to consequences which are injurious to individuals and the public good. The visible foot of mercantilism had to be replaced by the invisible hand of the market. To govern better, one had to govern less.

Smith appeared to argue for a rather austere economic role for the state. He believed that the state (or sovereign) had three essential duties to perform: first, the state needed to protect society from without – from external aggression; secondly, the state needed to protect society from within – from internal rights violation; thirdly, the state needed to provide and maintain certain public institutions and public works which facilitate the commerce of society.

It may be contested that this latter function of government opened up a wide caveat through which much later government interference could easily be endorsed. Smith himself was of the opinion that the aforementioned duties of the state were related to the particular stage of development that society had reached and he was pragmatic and eclectic enough to realise that he was not attempting to establish principles applicable for all societies at all times. Certainly the duties that Smith assigned to the state at the particular time that he was writing must be viewed as an endeavour to limit the agenda of government interference so that it would support, instead of hinder, the enlarging sphere of market activity.

Smith displayed a strong preference for private economic activity because of his belief in the efficiency of the system of natural liberty and the disinterestedness of the invisible hand as compared with the inefficiencies of the state and the interests of the politicians. The invisible hand allowed for the free and open play of all interests, as Stigler has argued 'the price system lays the cards face up on the table' (Stigler 1975: 36). It was the result of the unintended consequences of human action.

Mandeville had argued even earlier than Smith that 'the worst of all the multitude did something for the common good' (de Mandeville as quoted in Hayek 1978a: 251), and Ferguson had correctly perceived the important social point that 'every step and every movement of the multitude, even in what are termed enlightened ages, are made with equal blindness to the future; and nations stumble upon establishments, which are indeed the result of human action but not the execution of human design' (quoted by Kristol 1983: 151).

This can be contrasted with the vested interests and the political market of state legislation. Not only did Smith find the competence of the state wanting, he was deeply suspicious and distrustful of the motives of the state. Smith saw the state as being directed not by the common good but rather by 'the clamorous importunity of partial interests' (quoted by Stigler 1975: 41). He had forcefully argued in *The Wealth of Nations* that 'to hurt in any degree the interest of any one order of citizens, for no purpose but to promote that of some other, is evidently contrary to that justice and equality of treatment which the sovereign owes to all the different orders of his subjects' (Smith A. 1976: 654).

Smith, then, advocated a limited role for government in the economy – the state should provide the necessary framework and stable environment within which the market can be allowed to work unhindered, as Smith claimed:

> Commerce and manufactures can seldom flourish long in any state which does not enjoy a regular administration of justice, in which the people do not feel themselves secure in the possession of their property, in which the faith of contracts is not supported by law, and in which the authority of the state is not supposed to be regularly employed in enforcing the payment of debts from all those who are able to pay (Smith A. 1976: 910).

Whilst Smith was well aware of the superiority of market processes in general to political processes, he did not deny that efficient markets had to be competitive and pointed to the existence of monopoly as an important source of market break-down. He also realised that some government involvement in the economy may prove to be beneficial. The state should be actively engaging itself in supplying those goods and services which the system of natural liberty and the market are unable to provide because the provision of such is not in the interests of any individual (or small group of individuals) to supply even though the availability of such goods and services would be to the advantage of society as a whole.

Smith believed that the revenue required to cover the costs of such limited government involvement should be raised by means of a 'general contribution of the whole society, all the different members contributing, as nearly as possible, in proportion to their respective abilities' where such expenditure was for the benefit of the whole society and by means of a local or particular contribution where such expenditure was for the benefit of a particular area or body of individuals. It is interesting to point out at this juncture that Adam Smith's maxims of taxation take no real account of the willingness or desire of individuals to pay the contributions which are requested of them. They are expected to pay such taxes so long as they are levied according to the following four maxims, namely: first, contribution in proportion to the ability to pay; secondly, certainty of the amount of tax to be paid; thirdly, convenience of time and mode of payment; finally, the tax to be as gentle and sufficient as required for the limited provision of the agenda of the state (see also Ch. 10).

The Smithian commitment to a rather undogmatic and conditional form of *laissez-faire* and limited government as well as a pragmatic attitude towards necessary government interference was shared by most of the classical economists. Smith was writing at the dawn of the British Industrial Revolution and between the publication of his *The Wealth of Nations* (1776) and Mill's *Principles of Political Economy* (1848), the economy had radically transformed itself into the workshop of the world. The profound changes occasioned by the twin processes of industralisation and urbanisation called for a reassessment of the agenda of legitimate government interference.

Although Mill declared that '*laissez-faire*, in short, should be the general practice: every departure from it, unless required by some great good, is a certain evil' (Mill 1895: 609), he did recognise that there were good grounds for government interference. He believed that there was no universal solution to the question of the proper duties of government and advanced a characteristically pragmatic position in arguing that

> . . . the admitted functions of government embrace a much wider field than can easily be included within the ring-fence of any restricted definition, and that it is hardly possible to find any ground of justification common to them all, except the comprehensive one of general expediency; nor to limit the interference of government by any universal rule, save the simple and vague one that it should never be admitted but when the case of expediency is strong (Mill 1895: 514).

Of the necessary duties of government entertained by Mill, we have the standard one of the protection of person and property from force and fraud. He also believed that the *laissez-faire* principle of non-interference does not apply to such areas as colonisation and relief of the indigent as well as the case of where 'important public services are to be performed, while yet there is no individual specially interested in performing them, nor would any adequate remuneration naturally or spontaneously attend their performance' (Mill 1895: 626). There was a need for government to provide a greater amount of education because the provision of such should not depend on the 'mere demand of the market' (see Mill's *Autobiography*) but should be viewed as a merit good civilising and improving economic actors. Although Mill did recognise that the government must not claim a monopoly for education as he did not deny that it may be better done by others. He also believed that the government should be actively engaged in providing advice and promulgating information where required and that it had a responsibility to protect those who were unable to look after their own interests. The government needed to act as the great economic stabiliser and the great social civiliser as the stationary state of constrained capitalism was approached.

Mill not only recognised that the lot of the working classes could be improved through education but also effectively demonstrated that not only the existing institutions but also the laws governing the distribution of income in society were 'merely provisional' and unlike the laws of production were not immutable but socially determined.

Whilst Mill endorsed the provisional nature of the *laissez-faire* doctrine and was willing to support interventionist legislation, this did not prevent him from being deeply suspicious of government. He feared the authoritative interference of government, believing that any increase in government power could jeopardise individual rights and lead to their violation. Mill argued that 'there is a circle around every individual human being, which no government, be it that of one, or of a few, or of the many, ought to be permitted to overstep' (Mill 1895: 604) and he seriously questioned the legitimacy of authoritarian governments which crossed such boundaries. He was well aware that 'every increase of the functions devolving on the government is an increase of its power, both in the form of authority, and still more, in the indirect form of influence' (Mill 1895: 605) and he was apprehensive of the ability of all governments, including democracies, to 'encroach unduly on the liberty of private life'. Of course, the larger the active agenda of government the greater the need for revenue to finance the burgeoning leviathan and, although Mill does not address the issue with a thorough discussion of all of its possible ramifications, he did recognise that an important means of such revenue was compulsory taxation (Mill 1895: 604–5) which is viewed by many present-day libertarians as organised coercion and legalised rights violation.

Mill was especially fearful of centralised government and was deeply influenced by the work of Tocqueville supporting decentralisation and the need for much of the collective business of society to be performed by the people themselves. He argues that 'in all the more advanced communities, the great majority of things are worse done by the intervention of government, than the individuals most interested in the matter would do them, or cause them to be done, if left to themselves' (Mill 1895: 606–7).

One must keep such reservations on government's effectiveness and its threat to liberty clearly in mind if one is to fully understand Mill's position. Where private initiative is found wanting and government action is felt to be necessary and expedient, then a suitable rationale for interference may present itself. As Mill argued, 'in the particular circumstances of a given age or nation, there is scarcely anything, really important to the general interest, which it may not be desirable, or even necessary, that the government should take upon itself, not because private individuals cannot effectually perform it, but because they will not' (Mill 1895: 627).

The pragmatic and conditional advocacy of *laissez-faire* by the classical economists was continued into the era of neoclassical economics by Alfred Marshall. He was well aware of the need not to 'assign any universality to economic dogmas', believing that economics should rather be 'an engine for the discovery of concrete truth' (see Pigou 1925: 159). His magnum opus *The Principles of Economics* (1890), which set the tone of British economics for a generation, was a clear reflection of this philosophy, being representative of a Cambridge tradition which advocated a bold pluralistic, eclectic and pragmatic methodological approach.

Marshall presented economics as the 'study of mankind in the ordinary business of life' (Marshall 1920: 1) and he believed that we should never lose sight of the ultimate objective or end of economic study – to contribute to the solution of urgent and concrete social problems. Economics should be concerned with problem-solving and the provision of 'guidance in the practical conduct of life' particularly 'social life' (Marshall 1920: 42). Certainly the age of Marshall was the age of grave social problems – particularly that which Winch has termed the 'social question', namely the problems of urban poverty in the midst of plenty (see Winch 1972: 33–42), and Marshall himself recognised this in arguing that 'never was there an age so full of great social problems as ours' (Pigou 1925: 172). He desired to promote the social amelioration of the people and aimed to despatch into the world disciples 'willing to give some at least of their best powers to grappling with the social suffering around them' (Pigou 1925: 174).

Whilst Marshall recognised and conceded some extension of the potential agenda of the state in his day – to deal with such matters as the blatant inequalities of capitalism and the control of the growth of non-perfectly competitive firms – he maintained his faith in the workings of the private enterprise system because he believed that the alternative of bureaucratic management by the state would be burdensome, inefficient and representative of vested interest groups. Marshall was convinced that '. . . so soon as collectivist control had spread so far as to narrow considerably the field left for free enterprise, the pressure of bureaucratic methods would impair not only the springs of material wealth, but also many of those higher qualities of human nature the strengthening of which should be the chief aim of social endeavour' (Pigou 1925: 334).

He put little faith in the feasibility of socialism, seeing it as a utopian pipe-dream. Marshall was committed to the belief that increasing state encroachment in areas of production which demanded initiative and 'ceaseless creation' should be seen as being dangerous and downright anti-social because such intervention would retard 'the growth of that knowledge and those ideas which are incomparably the most important form of collective wealth' (Pigou 1925: 339).

Marshall's successor at Cambridge, Pigou, identified and provided the first sytematic account of what he believed to be an important area of market break-down which may need the corrective remedial action of the state – externalities – in *Wealth and Welfare* (1912) and more fully in his *The Economics of Welfare* (1920).

A great impetus to further government intervention in the economy was provided by Keynes' revolutionary work *The General Theory of Employment, Interest and Money* (1936) which supplied not only a refutation of part of the classical orthodoxy of his day (namely that part endorsing Say's Law of Markets) but also an economic rationale for state interference on the grounds that macro market systems were unable to guarantee stable full employment equilibria unassisted but, rather, were prone to aggregate demand failures culminating in high levels of involuntary unemployment (see Ch. 1 and 3).

Keynes believed that a modified form of capitalism would ensure the full employment of all resources but would require an extension of the agenda of the state. The government needed to act as a prime bulwark of the system – through its orchestrating of the macroeconomy by means of not only fiscal and monetary policy but also direct public investment expenditure (when required) – in order to maintain aggregate demand at the level required. Capitalism is viewed by Keynes to be a generally efficient economic system which is able to safeguard individual freedom and unleash private initiative. Wisely managed, it is preferable to any alternative. But, as Keynes argued in *The End of Laissez-Faire* (1926), if the government is to be effective it should not concern itself with 'those activities which private individuals are already fulfilling, but to those functions which fall outside the sphere of the individual, to those decisions which are made by *no one* if the State does not make them' (Keynes 1972: 291).

Whilst capitalism passed the test so far as economic efficiency and individual liberty went, it failed when it came to the criteria of full-employment provision and the need for social justice. Keynes could find no justification for the large and significant disparities of wealth and incomes that existed in his own day. Indeed, the theoretical schema presented in his path-breaking work suggested that such inequalities were more likely to impede rather than generate economic progress. One important message coming out of *The General Theory* was the demonstration that the reduction of such large relative inequalities in wealth and incomes would aid the future management of the economy because it would be likely to increase society's willingness to spend on consumption whilst at the same time decrease the need to exploit and exhaust all foreseeable investment opportunities in the endeavour to maintain aggregate demand at a sufficiently high level to guarantee full employment.

Whilst there was a need to strengthen the position of the weak and disadvantaged (as well as ignorant) in society, Keynes recognised that there were limits to the degree of redistribution which could take place. He believed that significant inequalities should continue to persist because the capitalist system would not be able to function effectively without the existence of a system of incentives and rewards and any attempt to impose egalitarianism would threaten individual liberty and stifle private initiative.

The economics of Galbraith provides us with our final destination in the intellectual itinerary taking us from Adam Smith's classical liberal position endorsing limited government to the modern liberal statement supporting wider government intervention.

The notion of power in economic life has a crucial role to play in, and remains central to, all of Galbraith's work. Indeed, the state is needed to redress some of the basic power imbalances that exist in society and lead to unequal development within economies. Galbraith believes that we can divide the economy up into two quite distinct parts: a relatively weak market system dominated by a large number of small firms functioning within a competitive framework; and a relatively strong planning system composed of the largest corporations functioning within an atmosphere of collusion and accepted symbiosis (see his *The New Industrial State* (1969) and *Economics and the Public Purpose* (1974)). One of the most significant features of the planning system is that there is a divorce of ownership from control. It is the technostructure, with its specialised knowledge and skill, which makes the decisions and not the owners of capital. So long as the technostructure acts in a profit-satisficing manner and achieves an appropriate and acceptable rate of return, it may follow a more autonomous course and pursue other more highly regarded objectives such as growth and sales maximisation.

Size is crucial to the business/organisational unit within the planning system. It provides for, among other things, financial strength, product diversification, and the ability to influence price determination – all factors providing the large corporation with greater security. Further stability is provided by: first, the government's manipulation and underwriting of aggregate demand to ensure that the economy has the wherewithal (or ability) to purchase the output of the planning and market networks; secondly, the executive branch of government's support for, and stake in, the continuance of an industrial/military/government complex allied with the demonstrated ineffectiveness of traditional type legislative action against monopoly behaviour; thirdly, the large corporations' manipulation of consumer preferences bringing with it a created desire to purchase and the decline of consumer sovereignty so that we have Galbraith's 'revised sequence' or dependence effect occurring with the planning system dog wagging the consumer tail rather than the consumer dog of conventional economics wagging the planning tail.

The problem posed by consumer manipulation extends into the choice between public goods and private goods. Galbraith refers to the social imbalance that can take place when the individual is manipulated into accepting a much larger ratio of private to public goods than is socially required. As a corollary to this, Galbraith argues that certain types of public goods which are beneficial to the planning system, in particular defence, have a tendency to be oversupplied relative to such areas as health, welfare and education. In his *The Affluent Society* (1958) he criticises orthodox economics on the grounds that it has displayed an over-concern with economic growth and the quantity of life rather than with much needed redistribution and an improvement in the quality of life. Galbraith believes that society is characterised by its deep-rooted tendency to underestimate the degree of private vices and public virtues.

Galbraith recognises that the planning system stands in need of reform. He advocates the enhancing of the power of the market system at the expense of the planned. The government is seen to have an active role to play here. Not only should there be the public operation of weak parts of the market system but the government should intervene to assist the growth of firms belonging to the market network. There is also the need to implement more effective control of the planning system. As a means to that end, the legislative branch of government should have an upgrading of its power relative to the executive so that the emancipation of the state away from the planning system can take place. An alliance between the government and the market system should make an effective countervailing force against the power of the planning system.

The interventionist rationale

Given the historical narrative presented in the preceding section, it would appear that economists became increasingly aware of certain negative aspects of the market system which were believed to be inherent and systematic failings:

1. At the macro level, it was argued that *laissez-faire* economies would face effective demand failures.
2. It was felt that there was a distribution problem under unfettered capitalism which went against any notion of social justice and that the state should provide the disadvantaged with a safety net below which they would not fall.
3. It was believed that markets were unable to provide public goods which were necessary to the effective functioning of any complex economy.
4. Markets were unable to internalise externalities.
5. Under market economies there was the problem posed by the growth of non-perfect competition which needed to be controlled.

Such underlying faults of market economies were seen as forms of market failure which required correction by the state. The invisible hand had demonstrated that it failed in certain specific areas and that the visible foot of government should and would be able to remedy these allegedly inherent market failings. The market system had been found wanting and the state could do no worse in its provision (indeed, it was necessary to ensure it). The failures of a market system in the real world were to be corrected by some ideal conception of the government working in the 'public interest'. The economic rationale for the interventionist strategy was based upon the two goals of efficiency and equity and the pragmatic principle of expediency. No serious doubts were entertained about the ability of the state to perform its delegated tasks nor was any earnest effort made to provide a comparative judgement of the effectiveness of the market and government – both considered, warts and all. The danger is that 'we may tell the society to jump out of the market frying pan, but we have no basis for predicting whether it will land in the fire or a luxurious bed' (Stigler 1975: 113).

New views on an old debate: economic calculation under socialism revisited

The interventionist rationale of the preceding section was widely accepted by the majority of economists who recognised that a pure market system was unworkable and that there was the need for a mixed economy with the government playing an integral role. Given that some state involvement in the economy was generally endorsed, the question naturally arises as to the degree of such interference. If markets demonstrably failed and governments presumably succeeded, then why not introduce a totally state-directed and controlled economic system consciously designed to guarantee more efficient and equitable results? Were there not limits to state encroachment and costs borne by market displacement?

In endeavouring to answer these rather pertinent questions we shall look at the episode known as the economic calculation under socialism debate. With the recent revival of the philosophy of the market place has come the re-opening of old wounds once considered healed. With revival has come reappraisal and reinterpretation and this is especially true of this debate where the orthodox version of the episode has recently been challenged and found wanting (see Rothbard 1976; Vaughn 1980, 1981; Murrell 1983).

Between 1920 and 1940 there took place a debate upon whether it was possible for a real economy to operate efficiently without free markets and the private ownership of capital and land. The orthodox telling of the story has gone somewhat as follows:

1. Mises asserted that rational economic calculation under socialism was impossible because the information necessary for

such calculation was missing. The problem lay with the allocation of capital goods – there was no way to evaluate the relative resource scarcities effectively because the absence of market prices for the factors of production meant that any computation of profit or loss would be impossible to make. This had led Mises to conclude that 'we have the spectacle of a socialist economic order floundering in the ocean of possible and conceivable economic combinations without the compass of economic calculation' and thus 'there is only groping in the dark. Socialism is the abolition of rational economy' (see Mises 1920, as reprinted in Nove and Nuti 1972: 80).

2. The demonstration (following the work of Barone and others) that economic calculation under socialism was *theoretically* possible. Barone had argued that a collectivist theoretical equilibrium solution existed and that it would be based upon the same system of equations as that of free (or perfect) competition so that what he took to be the two fundamental conditions of perfect competition (i.e. the production of output at minimum cost and the equalisation of price with marginal cost) could be achieved (see Ch. 1).

3. Hayek's alleged acceptance of the theoretical solution and his so-called retreat to a second line of defence which challenged only the *practical* possibility of implementing economic calculation under socialism.

4. The Lange *et al.* demonstration of the *practical* solution by advancing the concept of 'market (or competitive) socialism' and its trial and error market clearing. The state was to imitate the workings of the Walrasian auctioneer in finding the equilibrium prices. Lange allegedly provided the satisfactory resolution of the debate when he asserted that:

> Our study of the determination of equilibrium prices in a socialist economy has shown that the process of price determination is quite analogous to that in a competitive market. The Central Planning Board performs the functions of the market. It establishes the rules for combining factors of production and choosing the scale of output of a plant, for determining the output of an industry, for the allocation of resources, and for the parametric use of prices in accounting. Finally, it fixes the prices so as to balance the quantity supplied and demanded of each commodity. It follows that a substitution of planning for the functions of the market is quite possible and workable (see Lange and Taylor 1938, as reprinted in Nove and Nuti 1972: 99).

It was argued that Mises and Hayek had been refuted. The debate was seen by many as one of capitalism versus socialism –

and it was believed that it had been shown that economic calculation under socialism was a possibility (not I hasten to add an inevitability) but not necessarily superior to capitalism.

As stated earlier, this traditional interpretation of the debate has been questioned. The new way of viewing the old debate has been to see it as a clash between two theoretical models – both of which belong to neoclassical economics. The economic theory of socialist calculation was based upon neoclassical static general equilibrium analysis (with all its inherent restrictive conditions) whilst the Mises–Hayek position was characteristically Austrian with its dynamic rather than static perception, its stress on uncertainty and the partial distribution of knowledge and information. The new view supports the Mises–Hayek position and argues that they were not refuted but, on the contrary, they rather than the competitive socialists had effectively demonstrated the superiority and feasibility of *real world* capitalism functioning with universal individual property rights and free markets and the impossibility of *real world* socialism functioning with restricted individual property rights and without free markets. Socialist planning on the basis of equilibrium models would not work in a world characterised by uncertainty, lack of information and the possession of partial knowledge.

The competitive socialists' adoption of the Walrasian conceptual framework of static general equilibrium models and the use of such models for planning purposes had simply assumed away the significant problems for economic calculation in the real world. Mises believed that the static nature of equilibrium theorising presumed by the competitive socialists corresponded to no real state of affairs because 'this state of equilibrium is a purely imaginary construction. In a changing world it can never be realised. It differs from today's state as well as from any other realisable state of affairs' (Mises 1949: 707). He argued that the problem of economic calculation only arises as a consequence of change so that where change does not occur one can dispense with it entirely.

In the conceptual world of static equilibrium, the entrepreneurial function is redundant; it needs no reward because it serves no purpose. In the real world of ceaseless change and flux, the entrepreneurial function is essential to the process of continual re-adjustment. Mises presented the capitalist system as being primarily an entrepreneurial system which depended upon private property rights in the means of production. This could be contrasted with the socialist system which was primarily a managerial system which depended upon public property rights in the means of production. Socialist managers could never be substitutes for market entrepreneurs. Mises believed that 'one cannot play speculation and investment' (Mises 1949: 705) so that socialist managers lacked the will and the means to play at entrepreneurs. It must also be stated that socialist managers could not play at being perfect competitors because they lacked the power and the information to follow the procedural rules of producing at minimum cost and setting price equal to marginal cost.

It is interesting to note that 'when Lange was asked to help in the actual establishment of a control system for the Polish economy, he never recommended that his model of the thirties be implemented. He himself must have thought it impossible that any economy could be controlled exclusively by means of equilibrium prices' (Kornai 1971: 350–1).

Mises not only challenged the feasibility of the economic order of socialism but he also argued that any attempts to intervene with market processes were also doomed to failure. He was fearful of government intervention because he believed that 'government interference always means either violent action or the threat of such action' (Mises 1949: 715) and so is established by means of coercion and compulsion. Mises rejects interventionism as a viable alternative to unhampered market capitalism because it fails to 'attain those ends which those advocating and resorting to it are trying to attain' (Mises 1949: 729, also see 854). Interventionism is unworkable because it is frustrated by the responses of spontaneous market forces so that such isolated acts of interference must be given up or applied more intensively and extensively until further expansion is no longer possible and all of the spontaneous market forces have been extinguishcd so that socialism has ensued.

Hayek (1973a) points to two contrasting forms of rationalism: *constructivist* rationalism with its belief in the power of human wisdom, its perfectability and infallibility, and its product designed blueprints such that 'if you want good laws, burn those you have and make yourselves new ones' (Voltaire, as quoted in Hayek 1978a: 5) because the constructivist believes that 'since man has himself created the institutions of society and civilisation, he must be able to alter them at will so as to satisfy his desires or wishes' (Hayek 1978a: 3); *critical* rationalism with its recognition of the imperfectability and fallibility of man and the limits of human reason. Hayek argues that collectivist/socialist views have grown out of this constructivist rationalism and that their belief in the efficacy of planning must be seen as an error of such constructivism. Whilst the Austrian perspective follows the tradition of the

Anglo-Scottish enlightenment in endorsing critical rationalism and arguing for the need to distinguish between unmade orders spontaneously formed and made orders deliberately created. Many of the most effective institutions of society such as the market, money, and the law came about not as a result of conscious design but rather evolved organically as the unintended consequences of human action. Such spontaneous organisms have an important role to play in an economy dominated by uncertainty with regard to the future and ignorance with regard to the present and function most effectively when left freely alone.

The Austrian vision presents the market as the great communications system in complex societies. It is the price system which allows not only a division of labour but also a co-ordinated utilisation of resources to be possible in a world where each individual possesses only a fragment of all possible knowledge: 'we are only beginning to understand on how subtle a communications system the functioning of an advanced industrial society is based. This communications system which we call the market, turns out to be a more efficient mechanism for digesting information than any that man has deliberately designed' (Hayek 1975: 42).

Different people know different things and it is up to the price system to co-ordinate people's actions. The pricing system allows each individual to possess less knowledge than would usually be required to make correct decisions: 'the most significant fact about this system is the economy of knowledge with which it operates, or how little the individual participants need to know in order to be able to take the right action' (Hayek 1945: 526–7).

Hayek argues that the price system can only fulfil its role of communicating information so long as prices are free to move. If they become more inflexible or even rigid, then they will not work as well as they should. The essential ingredient for a successful price mechanism is the existence of competition. Competitive markets provide and co-ordinate information which allows complex societies to develop and function effectively in a world characterised by change, uncertainty and the division/decentralisation of knowledge.

The key to the working of the competitive market process is the entrepreneur. Kirzner (1973) has presented the entrepreneur as an economic actor who is alert to new opportunities for profit whether by means of arbitrage, speculation or innovation. The market process is viewed as a process of the systematic discovery and correction of true error. Whenever error occurs there is scope for entrepreneurship. Entrepreneurial activity ensures a tendency towards co-ordination so that it is the entrepreneurial function which acts as a deviation counteracting device.

Hayek and his fellow Austrian economists believe that the economic problems of society will not be solved by a movement towards centralisation. He states that the economic problems of society will not be solved by 'first communicating all this knowledge [in the possession of a large number of individuals] to a central board which, after integrating *all* knowledge, issues its orders' (Hayek 1945: 524). The economic problems of society will only be solved if we allow each individual to make decisions with the help of the unique information that each possesses. Only in this way will the beneficial use of his knowledge be to the advantage of society as a whole. Governments lack the knowledge and information to allocate efficiently. In their endeavour to co-ordinate resources without markets, they turn towards the use of authority and rules rather than incentives. Entrepreneurial activity is replaced by state inactivity and the economic system is reliant upon the stick rather than the carrot. Experience has demonstrated that the centralised state is a poor auctioneer. A totally planned economy without the utilisation of any markets whatsoever is unable to function effectively in the real world and many of the command economies are presently engaged in carrying out much needed reforms such as the re-introduction of a price-incentive system.

Recent work from within rather than without the socialist fold by Nove (1983) and Hodgson (1984) convincingly questions the possibility of any form of completely centralised planning (and raises severe doubts about the existence of pure types of economic orders whether capitalist or socialist). Both authors recognise that there is an essential need for markets to help cope with the enormous complexity and variety of contemporary industrial society.

The New Right and the revival of the philosophy of the market place

The thinkers who may be subsumed under the common label of the New Right do not constitute a monolithic homogeneous school. The united, politically simplified front that is presented against state interference and planning (indicating agreement on where they would *not* like to end up rather than where they would) conceals important philosophical differences (see Barry 1983) and diverse intellectual origins and development (see Bosanquet 1983).

Certainly if we take the view that the 'New Right is mainly based in economics and on ideas about individualism and markets' (Bosanquet 1983: 1) then the diverse nature of the New Right becomes clearly apparent: its foundations are built upon three main schools of economic thinking which are not fully compatible with each other – the Chicago School (of Friedman and Stigler), the Austrian School (of Mises and Hayek) and the Virginia School (of Buchanan and Tullock). Outside of the strictly economic sphere but still included under the New Right umbrella are the right theorists such as Rand, Nozick and Rothbard.

The New Right itself appears to display strong traces of two seemingly contradictory influences: classical liberalism (with its faith in free markets, limited government and the rule of law) and conservative traditionalism (with its emphasis upon the need to maintain and return to 'the old values').

Apart from its success at the ballot box, the most notable achievement of the New Right appears to have taken place within economics itself. There has certainly taken place a revolution in thinking and policy. The belief in the power of an unhindered market economy and in the de-stabilising influence of governments has become, once again, the conventional wisdom. The new slogan has become 'markets work, governments do not'.

Belief in the efficacy of markets as allocators and employers has reached new heights. Markets, we are told, will work provided that the right environment is created so that they will be allowed to work. The existence of large-scale unemployment demonstrates the need for allowing markets to work rather than indicating possible market break-down or malfunctioning. The recipe for the creation of the right environment is to get competition in and government out. Even Keynes' refutation of Say's Law and with it his demonstration that a capitalist economy is unlikely to provide full employment has been overturned. Say's Law has been rehabilitated and Keynes' explanation of the Great Depression has been challenged. We are presently in the process, it would appear, of relearning the lessons of the inter-war period.

The anti-interventionist rationale

It has become increasingly apparent that government too can fail and that the state faces severe inherent limitations. Government failure was recognised to be in-built and the belief in a 'benevolent despot' seen as naive. Government bodies were seen as self-interested and highly fallible. It was claimed that the arguments with regard to market failure were not inherent to, or the fault of, markets per se. It was not that markets were tried and found wanting, but rather that they had not been tried at all. Many of the contributory causes of market failure resided in government interference. The state had been provided with the overriding function of creating the correct legal/political framework to allow market systems to function effectively and this it had failed to do. There had taken place political failure. Such profound criticisms of the machinery of government, matched with a growing disenchantment with state interference, and allied to the increasing realisation of the potency of markets, led to the development of an anti-interventionist rationale in direct contrast and as a counter-response to the above section:

1. Effective demand failures were seen to be distortions of the market mechanism which had been government induced.
2. In attempting to solve the distribution problem, the state had taken away choice and used collectivised coercion to infringe upon individual rights.
3. The recognition, especially among the anarcho-capitalists, that the market could and should provide public goods.
4. The demonstration that externalities could be solved through the market mechanism by means of the extension of clearly defined and defended property rights.
5. One could not solve the problems posed by the growth of non-perfect competition by utilising the standard neoclassical argument that we should try to make all firms conform to the ideal of perfect competition or that we should believe that the replacement of private monopolistic elements by state-owned institutions will solve the problem. To safeguard and maintain the competitive framework, one should ensure that there is freedom of entry (and as a means to that end patent laws should be removed) so that only short-run profits can be gained.

In defence of the minimal to zero state

Whilst it would be considered unwise to over-homogenise the intellectual elements that compose the New Right, it would be permissible to argue that the Chicago, Austrian and Virginia School economists generally endorse the minimal state of classical liberalism where one has the protective and productive state playing a minor but necessarily sufficient role. Government interference is looked upon with apprehension and there is a recognised need to control and contain such activity. It is the libertarian rights theorists, however, who put forward the most aggressive case against the state.

Libertarian rights theorists generally begin by arguing that all individuals have certain universal rights which function as protective boundary lines around individuals and that these rights should not be violated by others. Their concern with rights is paramount and tends to precede any concern with efficiency. They are fearful of the state because it has demonstrated its capacity, in the past, to invade the rights of individuals in pursuance of the collective interest which is deemed to be unjustifiable.

We may split the libertarian rights theorists up into two main groups: *the minimal staters* who argue that we need the night-watchman state of classical liberalism to protect rights by means of it having control of, and a monopoly in, coercive power. It is recognised that the state is necessary in practice (although one is unclear of its standing in principle) and that any funding of state activities should be voluntary and not coercive; *the anarcho capitalists* who argue for the complete dissolution of the state as the best safeguard of rights because it has not only historically been the principal violator of rights but its continued existence depends upon the levying of compulsory and, therefore, coercive payments.

The work of Rand and Nozick is representative of the minimal staters' position. Ayn Rand in *Capitalism: the Unknown Ideal* (1967) claims that capitalism, in its undiluted form, is the only system that allows the essential nature of man to rise to the surface whilst socialism and collectivism stifle innate egoism and entail parasitism. Robert Nozick in *Anarchy, State and Utopia* (1974) believes that past rights violation is permissible if compensation is paid to the victims (so that there is a need to establish legitimate entitlement to ownership gained by means of acquisition or transfer).

Rothbard in his *Man, Economy and State* (1962) and *For a New Liberty* (1978) succinctly presents an anarcho capitalist position by synthesising Austrian economics and the rights doctrine. He advocates an ethics of ownership which argues that an individual has a right to self-ownership as well as a right to homestead, i.e. to acquire property rights in things. It is maintained that a pure market system completely rid of government is the most efficient and ordered economic system known to man and the best guarantee of safeguarding rights – 'not only does the free market directly benefit all parties and leave them free and uncoerced; it also creates a mighty and efficient instrument of social *order*' (Rothbard 1970: 880). This may be contrasted with government intervention which is viewed as being coercive, inefficient and chaotic. Rothbard believes that 'intervention is the intrusion of aggressive physical force into society; it means the substitution of coercion for voluntary actions' (Rothbard 1970: 766). Complete *laissez-faire* is seen to be not only desirable but also highly feasible. We need to introduce the zero state society and have a society based upon the contractual and voluntary mutual benefit of the market rather than the command and obedience of the state. Government is dangerous because 'empirically, the vast bulk of interventions are performed by States, since the State is the only organisation in society legally equipped to use violence and since it is the only agency that legally derives its revenue from a compulsory levy' (Rothbard 1970: 766).

Rothbard provides us with a typology of intervention which is significantly different from that proposed in the above section. He argues that there are three main types of interference: first, there is *autistic intervention* where the intervener *restricts* the subject's use of his own property, e.g. prohibition of speech; secondly, there is *binary intervention* when the intervener *compels* some exchange between an individual subject and himself or attempts to force a gift from the subject, e.g. taxation, conscription to jury service, slavery; finally, there is *triangular intervention* when the intervener either *compels* or *forbids* an exchange between two subjects, e.g. price control, licensing (see Rothbard 1970: 767). The dissolution of the state will lead to the ending of such intervention based upon hegemonic power relationships and its replacement with a market order based upon voluntary and free exchange.

Concluding remarks

Whilst the arguments of the anarcho capitalists (such as Rothbard) are extremely consistent and persuasive, and stand in direct contrast to the rather inconsistent and suspect position of the minimal staters, one must be aware of the needs to have sane historical perspective. We are living at t_{1986} and not t_0 so that total abolition of the state may not be feasible at present (given the national and international power structures) although it could gradually occur in time. Government displacement takes place slowly and needs to be done carefully. We must be wary of remorseless, presently utopian, logicians who argue that all government is inexpedient at all times and who may direct us to some real future bedlam.

There are certainly lessons to be learned from the philosophy of the market place. Probably the most important lessons to be learned are that capitalism is a more robust species than we expected and that markets are sophisticated mechanisms in a world characterised by uncertainty and ignorance. One must be very wary of arguments that try to force us into making a choice between either a completely centralised planning system or a completely *laissez-faire* market system. The evidence appears to indicate that such pure types have never existed nor possibly could exist. There is no reason why the fallibility of man should drive us to believe in the infallibility of markets. Certainly if we accept that man is fallible (and I see no evidence to the contrary) then we should be extremely cautious in endorsing blueprints and utopian plans.

In a world characterised by limited and dispersed knowledge, uncertainty and doubt, we must be pragmatic, eclectic and pluralistic. If we are, then we can be aware of the mistakes of the past, conscious of the constraints on the present, and more prepared for the problems of the future.

Chapter 3

THE CLASSICAL REVIVAL IN MACROECONOMICS

Brian Snowdon

Introduction

This chapter is concerned with the intellectual influences which have shaped the conduct of macroeconomic policy in the fifty years following the publication of Keynes' *General Theory*. The main policy message to emerge from Keynes' theory was that active government intervention designed to regulate aggregate demand was necessary, indeed unavoidable, if a satisfactory level of total output and employment were to be maintained. As Keynes himself summed it up: 'it is in determining the volume, not the direction of actual employment that the existing system has broken down' (Keynes 1973a: 379).

In the post-war world, demand management policies, with the explicit aim of stabilising output and employment, became synonymous with Keynesianism. In 1944 Beveridge published his *Full Employment in a Free Society* and the government committed itself to a high and stable level of employment in a White Paper on employment policy. The age of Keynes had begun.

The justification for activist stabilisation policies in the initial post-war period was based on the argument that market processes work slowly and imperfectly, perhaps even perversely, in correcting macroeconomic disturbances. This essentially Keynesian view has in the past twenty years been vigorously challenged by a group of economists inspired by the ideas of Milton Friedman. The monetarist research programme represents a counter-revolution in economic thought. According to Johnson (1971), by far the most helpful circumstance for the rapid propagation of a new orthodoxy is the existence of an established doctrine which is clearly inconsistent with the 'most salient facts of reality'. The monetarist revival based its comeback on the alleged failure of

Keynesian theory to solve the predominant post-war economic problem, inflation. This appeared to be the Achilles heel of Keynesian theory.

During the past decade discussions and controversies in the macroeconomic literature have been dominated by the influential work associated with Lucas who launched a new wave of monetarist ideas. This body of analysis has been labelled 'New Classical' because of the similarity between the old and new schools with regard to their policy conclusions and the faith of its adherents in the ability of the market mechanism to demonstrate self-righting properties.

As a result of the renaissance of classical macroeconomics the Keynesian bandwagon, which dominated the post-war consensus, has suffered a serious intellectual setback. In addition, the ideas of the new classical school have undoubtedly influenced policy-making in the UK under Mrs Thatcher's administration. The Thatcher experiment is not an incoherent expression of a deranged system of thought but has solid intellectual foundations which can be traced back over 250 years to the work of David Hume (1752) and Adam Smith (1776).

The remainder of this chapter will examine these controversies, beginning with the arguments presented by Keynes in his *General Theory* which challenged the old classical theory.

The *General Theory* – revolution or reform?

Historians of economic thought are divided between those who adhere to an 'absolutist' position and others who adopt a 'relativist' position concerning changes in economic theory. According to Blaug, 'the relativist regards every single theory put forward in the past as a more or less faithful reflection of contemporary conditions each theory being in principle equally justified in its own context; the absolutist has eyes only for the strictly intellectual development of the subject, regarded as a steady progression from error to truth' (Blaug 1978: 2). While the marginalist revolution in the 1870s is a good example for the absolutists, the *General Theory of Employment, Interest and Money* was undoubtedly a product of the Great Depression and is perhaps the best example of the development of a theory in response to contemporary conditions.

In the 1930s the existence of an established theory which appeared to be inconsistent with events was the most helpful circumstance for the rapid propagation of a new 'revolutionary' theory. Indeed, it is difficult to imagine that the *General Theory* would ever have been written but for the events which characterised the industralised economies during the inter-war period.

Remarkably, economists are still deeply divided over the significance of the *General Theory* and controversy still rages over the basic ideas contained in the book some fifty years after it was published. Opponents are either convinced that Keynes was entirely wrong or, alternatively, that he was saying nothing new. Hayek has recently reaffirmed his view that Keynes 'was wholly wrong in the scientific work for which he is chiefly known' and Friedman regards Keynes' theory as having been contradicted by the evidence (Hayek 1983; Friedman 1983). Keynesians are themselves divided between those who regard the policy implications of the *General Theory* as moderately conservative and others who see Keynes' work as representing a revolutionary break from mainstream classical doctrines (Coddington 1983). However, economists of all persuasions would probably agree that the *General Theory* has had more influence on policymaking, for good or ill, than any other book on economics this century.

Part of the problem involved with interpreting the *General Theory* is that it is a highly complex book which enables economists of different persuasions to find statements which support their own vision of Keynes' contribution. Numerous attempts have been made to summarise and interpret Keynes' contribution and this has resulted in the development of a huge and complicated literature (see Meltzer 1981). At present there is no definitive interpretation of Keynes which commands universal support, and the turbulence he has caused in economics shows no sign of abatement. The major reason for this is that the very issue with which Keynes was concerned, namely the effectiveness of market forces in generating a stable full-employment equilibrium without active government intervention, is still at the centre of macroeconomic debate.

Keynes was essentially an applied economist always concerned with practical problems, impatient and anxious to set the world right. The main characteristic of the inter-war period in the UK was the high degree of resource underutilisation. Inevitably Keynes' attention became focused on the problem of unemployment which was high throughout the 1920s in the UK and was then increased by the world-wide slump which began in 1929. Unemployment data for the 1920s and 1930s are contained in Table 3.1 (Aldcroft 1984; Tomlinson 1983).

Table 3.1   Unemployment in the 1930s

	UK			USA	
	%	Numbers (millions)		%	Numbers (millions)
1929	7.3	1.5		3.2	1.5
1930	11.2	2.4		8.7	4.3
1931	15.1	3.3		15.9	8.0
1932	15.6	3.4		23.6	12.0
1933	14.1	3.1		24.9	12.8
1934	11.9	2.4		21.7	11.3
1935	11.0	2.4		20.1	10.6
1936	9.4	2.1		16.9	9.0
1937	7.8	1.8		14.3	7.7
1938	9.3	2.2		19.0	10.4
1939	5.8	1.3		17.2	9.5

Source: UK data, Feinstein 1972: Table 12b; USA data, Historical Statistics of the United States. US Department of Commerce, Bureau of the Census 1960

In Keynes' view the classical model was bankrupt, for in the face of mass unemployment in the 1930s it suggested that little corrective action could or should be carried out by government. In time full-employment equilibrium would be automatically restored via market forces. Neither central planning along Soviet lines nor lesser forms of intervention were necessary. Keynes decisively rejected this view; instead, he sought to find a workable solution to the predominant economic problem of his day.

The General Theory was addressed to Keynes' fellow economists, it was they he needed to convince if a lasting solution was to be found. He was helped in this task by the inability of the classical model to satisfactorily account for the collapse of output and employment in the 1930s. This failure, more than anything else, paved the way for an alternative explanation. The General Theory evolved into a study of the forces which determine changes in the scale of output and employment as a whole. In providing an explanation which focused attention on aggregate demand, Keynes was to generate a research programme highly critical of the prevailing non-interventionist policy stance taken by governments towards the general level of economic activity.

Pre-Keynesian conventional wisdom was dominated by 'Say's Law' which maintained that a general excess supply of output could never emerge for any significant length of time. Thus capitalist market economies will normally have output limited by supply rather than demand constraints. With the exception of a few heretics (notably Marx and Malthus) the majority of classical and neoclassical writers argued that a general deficiency of demand was an impossibility (see O'Brien D. 1984). Aggregate output was determined by real forces on the supply side, namely, the labour supply, capital stock and the state of technology. Fluctuations of nominal aggregate demand would have a neutral effect on real variables, only influencing nominal variables such as the general level of prices. The real level of output and employment are independent of the level of prices in the classical model.

Although the classical view is a great deal more complex than the conventional textbook account, it is convenient here to regard their general position as being one of regarding the aggregate supply curve as perfectly inelastic at the full employment level of output. This result follows on naturally from the classical economists' analysis of the labour market. With a given capital stock and technology, the marginal product of labour declines as employment expands because of the law of diminishing returns. Assuming firms seek to maximise profits, they will hire labour until the marginal product of labour is equated with the real wage. Hence the demand for labour is a negative function of the real wage (W/P) with employers deciding on how much labour to employ by comparing the money wage rate to the value of additional output produced when another worker is employed.

The supply of labour is a positive function of the real wage and this reflects the assumed utility-maximising behaviour of workers. A higher real wage is necessary to induce workers to give up leisure and supply more labour. Labour market equilibrium requires that the demand and supply of labour are equal. This equilibrium will therefore be associated with a particular market clearing real wage $(W)/P)^*$ and level of employment $(L)^*$. These relationship are shown in Fig. 3.1.

The schedule LF indicates the total size of the labour force which responds positively to the real wage. Thus OL^* workers are employed and unemployment is equal to ab. Such unemployment is voluntary (and 'natural') and consists of people changing jobs and others engaged in job search activity.

Why is aggregate output insensitive to nominal demand fluctuations in this model? Figure 3.2 illustrates the classical case in terms of the familiar aggregate demand (AD) and aggregate supply (AS) model.

As indicated in Fig. 3.2 an increase in aggregate demand from AD_1 to AD_2 has no real effects, output remains unchanged at Y^*. The only effect is on the general level of prices, with the price level rising from P_1 to P_2. This result follows given the assumption of price and wage flexibility which lies at the heart of the classical

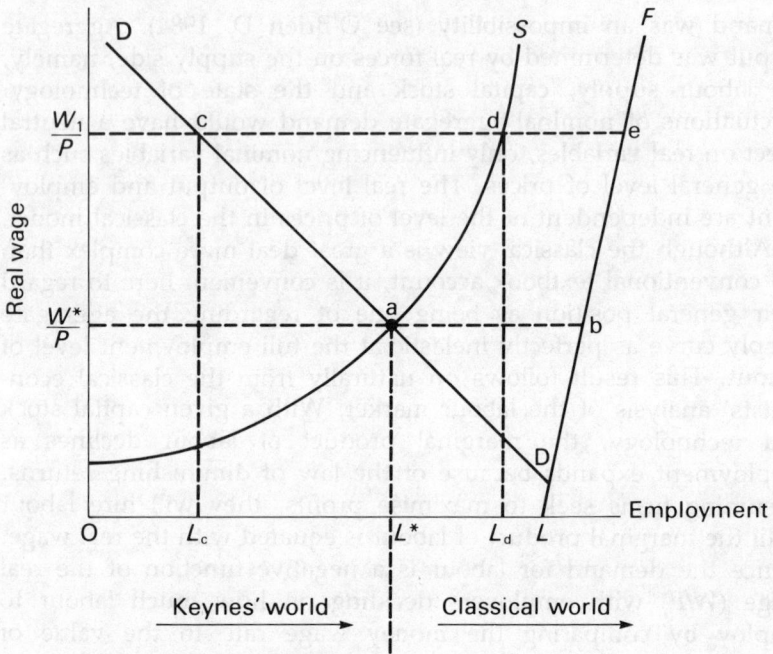

Figure 3.1   The labour market

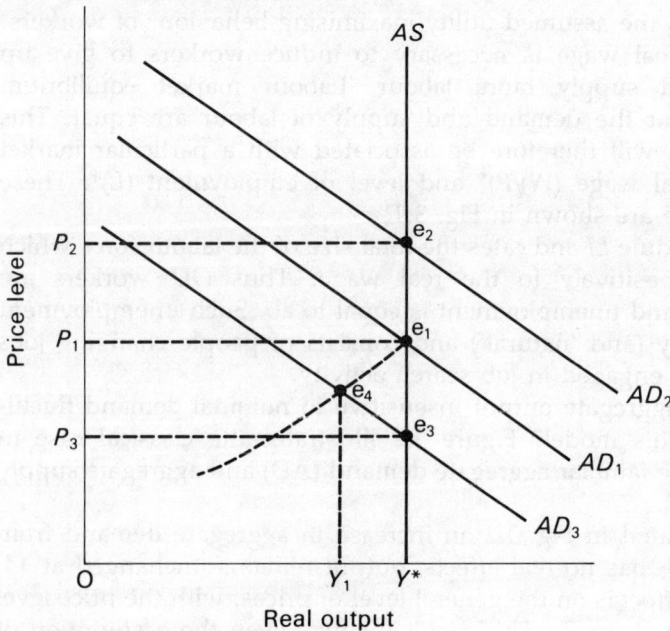

Figure 3.2   The classical model

model. Workers and employers consider only real wages when selling and hiring labour. Initially an increase in aggregate demand will raise the price level and depress the real wage below its market clearing level $(W/P)^*$. This creates an excess demand for labour and nominal wages rise to re-establish the market clearing real wage. Thus there are no permanent effects on either the real wage or on employment. Aggregate output is independent of the price level and the impact of a change in aggregate demand has been neutral. Classical economists regarded any government-induced expansion of demand as a totally ineffective way of stimulating employment and output. This is also the familiar prediction of the classical quantity theory which is really a concomitant of Say's Law. The quantity theory relationship is given by the following equation.

$$M\bar{V} = P\bar{Y} \qquad\qquad [3.1]$$

where M is the stock of money, V is the income velocity of circulation of money, P is the general level of prices and Y is real income. Both Y and V are assumed to be constant so that any change in M will affect P, leaving Y unchanged. This result is illustrated in Fig. 3.2. The left-hand side of the equation is the total money value of transactions over a given period and is simply another way of expressing aggregate nominal demand. The right-hand side measures the total money value of the flow of output in the economy, in effect GDP at current prices. The two sides are equal by definition since what is bought must be the same as the money value of goods sold. The classical analysis of the labour market leads to the conclusion that Y is predetermined at its equilibrium full-employment level Y^*. Thus any variation of aggregate demand (MV) will lead by definition to an adjustment of P with Y unchanged. As Keynes himself put it: 'the view that any increase in the quantity of money is inflationary is bound up with the underlying assumption of the classical theory that we are always in a condition where a reduction in the real rewards of the factors of production will lead to a curtailment of their supply' (Keynes 1973a: 304).

In other words, the labour market is assumed to be permanently in equilibrium as indicated by point a in Fig. 3.1.

Why is full employment guaranteed in the classical model? Let us assume that there is an autonomous decline in aggregate demand to AD_3 in Fig. 3.2. The excess supply created in the goods market leads to a fall in prices which in turn raises the real wage to $(W/P)^1$ in Fig. 3.1. The rise in real wages causes an excess supply of labour equal to cd. In a competitive labour market, money wages will be bid down leading to a fall in real wages and a return to full employment, but at a lower general price level of P_3 and a lower level of nominal wages. Thus the assumption of full wage and price flexibility is critical to the classical argument.

In sharp contrast to the classical argument. Keynes did not accept that a flexible wage policy is capable of maintaining a state of continuous full employment. A competitive market economy 'cannot be made self-adjusting along these lines' (Keynes 1973a: 267). To begin with, money wages tend to be sticky downwards. Workers' resistance to cuts in money wages reflect their concern over relativities, one group of workers being unlikely to accept a money wage cut unless all other workers do so. General wage cuts are therefore only likely to be possible 'in a highly authoritarian society where sudden, substantial, all-round changes could function with success' (Keynes 1973a: 269).

With money wages slow to adjust, involuntary unemployment becomes a distinct possibility. Keynes defines involuntary unemployment as follows: 'men are involuntarily unemployed if, in the event of an overall rise in the price of wage goods relatively to the money wage, both the aggregate supply of labour willing to work for the current money wage and the aggregate demand for it at that wage would be greater than the existing volume of employment' (Keynes 1973a: 15).

We can interpret this definition by referring back to Fig. 3.1. If a decline in aggregate demand has reduced the price level and raised the real wage to $(W/P)^1$ then the amount of labour demanded is L_c and the amount of labour supplied is L_d. Total unemployment is equal to ce with cd representing involuntary unemployment and the remainder, de, being voluntary and frictional unemployment.

At the real wage $(W/P)^1$ only L_c workers have employment and although they are receiving a real wage of $(W/P)^1$ they would continue to supply their labour even if the real wage were less than $(W/P)^*$. Note that the labour supply curve indicates that all members of the labour force between L_c and L^* are prepared to work for a real wage less than $(W/P)^1$. Hence Keynes' point that the aggregate supply of labour willing to work for the current money wage will increase even if the real wage falls from $(W/P)^1$ to $(W/P)^*$. The apparent paradox in Keynes' definition of involuntary unemployment, that both the demand and supply of labour will increase with a fall in real wage, is solved once it is realised that the labour supply schedule indicates the maximum amount of labour willingly supplied at each wage rate. Keynes argued that it was perfectly reasonable to assume that workers would accept a reduction in real wages brought about by a rise in the general price level since it affects all workers alike. Therefore, rather than relying on the downward spiral of wages and prices to restore full employment via their indirect and unreliable influence on aggregate demand, it was preferable for the monetary authorities to stimulate aggregate demand directly, which by putting upward pressure on the general price level would lower the real wage and stimulate output and employment (see Thirlwall 1981). As Keynes put it, 'Having regard to human nature and our institutions, it can only be a foolish person who would prefer a flexible wage policy to a flexible money policy . . . to suppose that a flexible wage policy is a right and proper adjunct of a system which on the whole is one of *laissez-faire*, is the opposite of the truth' (Keynes 1973a: 268–9). In addition, Keynes also argued that falling money wages may well induce further falls in the price level, so much so that the desired reduction in real wages could never be achieved. An atmosphere of price instability could also make business calculations futile and create further uncertainty. In such circumstances, falling wages and prices could induce further perverse shifts of the aggregate demand schedule to the left, deepening rather than correcting the recession.

Keynes' aggregate supply schedule is positively sloped and is indicated by the dashed line in Fig. 3.2. A fall in aggregate demand in the classical model shifts the economy from e_1 to e_3 with no real effects. However, in Keynes' model, wage stickiness causes output to fall as employment falls to L_c in Fig. 3.1. Output is reduced to Y_1 in Fig. 3.2. The solution is in principle relatively simple: engineer a shift of the aggregate demand schedule from AD_3 to AD_1. This will raise the price level, reduce the real wage, stimulating employment and output.

Classical economists explained unemployment by reference to the real wage. Unemployment was seen to be a supply side problem which could easily be corrected if workers would accept cuts in their money wage as a method of reducing the real wage. To increase government spending was futile since the system was supply rather than demand constrained. A public works programme would simply 'crowd out' an equivalent amount of private expenditure. If such a programme was financed by printing new money rather than by borrowing, the result would be inflation as the quantity theory predicts.

As far as Keynes was concerned, the classical theory was a 'special case' applicable to periods of full employment only. Since in Keynes' view the outstanding characteristic of the industrial market economies was their tendency to remain 'in a chronic condition of sub-normal activity for a considerable period without any marked tendency either towards recovery or towards complete collapse', the classical model is 'misleading and disastrous if we attempt to apply it to the facts of experience' (Keynes 1973a: 249 and 3). In the *General Theory*, Keynes agreed with the classical economists that a cut in real wages was necessary to stimulate employment (Trevithick 1980). However, he did not accept that cuts in nominal wages were feasible in a democracy and in any case, even if they were, such cuts could not guarantee a reduction in the general level of real wages. In this sense the problem of unemployment could not be blamed on the trade unions since the 'general level of real wages depends on other forces in the economic system' (Keynes 1973a: 14). Thus unemployment was largely an 'involuntary' phenomena and it was the responsibility of the government to do something about it. Market forces themselves were too slow and unreliable in reaching full employment. Macroeconomic rather than microeconomic forms of intervention were required.

Keynesians have traditionally regarded fiscal policy as being the major macroeconomic instrument of intervention to stabilise the economy. According to Keynes' theory, the output of an economy is constrained not by supply considerations except in conditions of the classical 'special case'. In Keynes' general case it is demand constraints which are important, and the major source of unemployment was traced to a deficiency of effective demand. The aggregate of planned expenditures of consumers and investors is insufficient to produce a level of output sufficiently large to provide employment for the whole of the labour force. Effective demand could be stimulated by either cuts in taxation in order to stimulate consumer spending or direct increases in government spending to augment private investment. Monetary policy should be supportive of fiscal policy since by itself the influence of monetary policy on effective demand was weak and indirect. In terms of equation [3.1], Keynes had shown that an increase in MV could affect Y because of the existence of involuntary unemployment.

The main policy conclusions of Keynesian economics have significant political implications since it concludes that the performance of capitalist market economies can be significantly improved by government intervention in the form of demand management. This is to be achieved mainly by the use of fiscal policy rather than detailed forms of microeconomic intervention at the level of individual markets. Capitalism can remain intact, there is no need for massive programmes of socialisation of the means of production along Marxist lines with the consequent loss of 'individual freedom'. Keynes had inspired a conservative revolution by suggesting ways in which the system could be saved from itself. Keynes summed this up as follows:

> Whilst, therefore, the enlargement of the functions of government, involved in the task of adjusting to one another the propensity to consume and the induceent to invest, would seem to the nineteenth century publicist or to a contemporary American financier to be a terrific encroachment on individualism, I defend it, on the contrary, both as the only practicable means of avoiding the destruction of existing economic forms in their entirety and as the condition of the successful functioning of individual initiative (Keynes 1973a: 380).

Following the end of the Second World War, governments of both left and right appeared to accept the central message of the *General Theory* that macroeconomic intervention was required if the system was to achieve a stable equilibrium with full employment. Until the 1960s the initial optimism associated with Keynesian economics seemed well founded. This whole period was characterised by a social democratic consensus, a consensus inspired very much by Keynes' research programme.

At the theoretical level, the interpretation of the *General Theory* provided by Hicks (1937) was combined with the existing neoclassical general equilibrium framework to produce the 'Keynesian neoclassical synthesis'. This approach dominated most of the teaching in macroeconomics until recently. The more radical Keynesians have pointed out that the only way that neoclassical general equilibrium theory could absorb Keynes was to first of all remove the least digestible parts of the *General Theory*, in particular the discussion of uncertainty and money wage determination (see Robinson J. 1971). Nevertheless the synthesis succeeded in providing a common framework of analysis within which debates concerning the relative effectiveness of monetary and fiscal policy could take place (Morgan 1978). The conventional interpretation of the outcome of these theoretical debates which took place in the first twenty-five post-war years was as follows:

1. Keynes had not provided a more 'general theory' superior to the classical model because his conclusion concerning underemployment equilibrium depended on introducing rigidities into the analysis, for example downwardly sticky money wages. Once these impediments to the working of the market mech-

anism are removed it could be demonstrated in theory that price flexibility was sufficient to restore full employment. It seemed that the neoclassical belief in the self-equilibrating properties of a capitalist market economy had not been overthrown by the Keynesian revolution after all. An unregulated price mechanism could deliver full employment.
2. However, as this process would be slow and cumbersome there was a case for government intervention to speed up the process via direct forms of demand stimulation, i.e. budget deficits.
3. Keynes 'special case' therefore was the relevant one for short-run policy.
4. A consensus view emerged and it was generally agreed that 'the classics won the intellectual battle; Keynes won the policy war' (Hines 1971).

Thus demand management was justified even to those who accepted the general framework of neoclassical economics. A central feature of the macroeconomics associated with the synthesis was that demand management was at least possible even if such policies were difficult to implement with a high degree of accuracy.

This consensus view has now been completely shattered by two simultaneous events, the deteriorating performance of the indus-trial economies during the 1970s combined with theoretical devel-opments in macroeconomics.

The demise of orthodox Keynesianism

Although Keynes laid the theoretical foundations for further research into market failure at the macro level and supported the need for government-induced demand stimulations in periods of substantial spare capacity, nowhere did he argue that managing capitalism along a path of full employment would be an easy task. Unfortunately in the first few decades after 1945 a bastardised form of Keynesianism emerged which, in attempting to capture the essence of Keynes' great and subtle work, presented his model in a simplistic and mechanistic form. Weintraub (1961) has referred to this hydraulic interpretation of the *General Theory* as 'Classical Keynesianism', and Keynes' model has been typically represented in basic textbooks by the Hicksian *IS–LM* model. Under the influ-ence of Classical Keynesianism, Keynes' contribution became diluted and somewhat distorted, in particular his ideas tended to become synonymous with fiscalism.

The major Keynesian development in the post-war period was the incorporation of the Phillips curve into the prevailing macro-economic models (Phillips 1958; Lipsey R. G. 1978). In Phillips' seminal contribution he drew attention to the existence of a non-linear negative relationship between the rate of increase of money wage rates and the rate of unemployment. Phillips concluded from his empirical research into the UK economy for the period 1861–1957 that the 'Phillips curve' was stable. It was Lipsey (1960) who first provided a theoretical framework to explain the existence of such a relationship and Samuelson and Solow (1960) who popularised the concept in a modified form indicating a stable trade-off between price inflation and unemployment (see Snowdon 1981).

Following Samuelson and Solow's paper, the Phillips curve was increasingly interpreted as offering an explanation of the post-war policy dilemma resulting from the incompatibility between high levels of employment and price stability. Policymakers in asking the question 'how can one have price stability and high employment?' were informed by the Phillips relationship that such a combination was impossible given the existing structural relationships in the economy. Policymakers would have at best a choice between various combinations of inflation ($\dot{P}$) and unemployment (U). Figure 3.3 shows the Samuelson–Solow modified version of the Phillips curve which is labelled PS_1. All governments would like to achieve targets of low unemployment and low inflation such as the combination $\dot{P}_x + U_z$, or anywhere in the shaded area to the left of U_z. However, the existence of the Phillips curve acts as a constraint: governments can only achieve combinations indicated by the relationship PS_1 or anywhere above and to the right of PS_1. If the government wished to achieve price stability, then it seemed from Phillips' fitted relationship that 'the associated level of unemployment would be a little under 2.5 per cent' (Phillips 1958: 339). Should the government desire a lower level of unemployment, then this could be achieved via expansionary policies. But in deciding on targeting for lower levels of unemployment such as U_x, U_y or U_z, the government must accept that this will involve a cost in terms of higher, but stable rates of inflation as indicated in Fig. 3.3 by $\dot{P}_x$, $\dot{P}_y$ and $\dot{P}_z$. Policymakers were faced with a menu of choice, *but at least they did have a choice* according to this brand of Keynesianism. As we shall see, the essential message of the revised version of classical macroeconomics is that no such

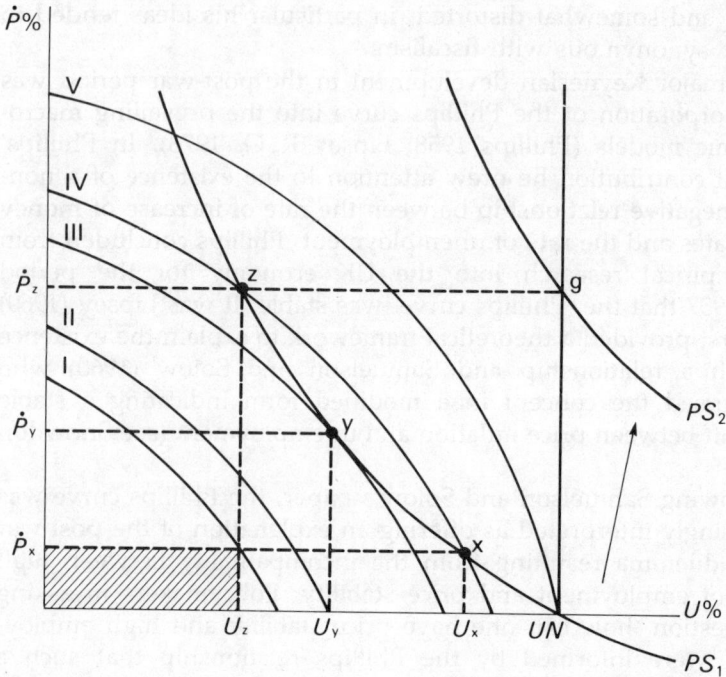

Figure 3.3   The Phillips curve

choice exists in the long run, and probably not even in the short run. In extreme monetarist models the government is powerless to influence the level of unemployment via systematic macroeconomic intervention.

In Fig. 3.3 combinations of inflation and unemployment can be ranked according to their distance from the origin, and the indifference contours I, II, III and IV indicate successively lower levels of societal welfare. The indifference contours are concave to the origin since there are 'bads' on the axes rather than goods. According to this analysis the best that any government can achieve via macroeconomic intervention is to push the economy towards point y on the PS curve. Given a stable Phillips curve, this position is optimal from society's viewpoint assuming the government has an accurate knowledge of societal preferences.

A consensus of economists accepted that a reasonably stable inverse relationship between $\dot{P}$ and U existed in the UK until the late 1960s (see Santomero and Seater 1978). The emergence of stagflation, accelerating inflation combined with higher and higher levels of unemployment, ended that consensus and paved the way

Table 3.2   Prices, money wages and unemployment 1966–1984 (year to year % changes)

Year	Retail price Index	Index of basic weekly wage rates	Unemployment %	% change in money wage rates predicted by Phillips equation*
1966	3.9	4.6	1.4	5.1
1967	2.4	3.9	2.2	2.3
1968	4.8	6.6	2.3	2.1
1969	5.4	5.3	2.3	2.1
1970	6.3	9.9	2.5	1.8
1971	9.4	12.9	3.7	0.7
1972	7.1	13.8	4.0	0.5
1973	9.2	13.7	3.0	1.2
1974	16.0	19.8	2.9	1.3
1975	24.2	29.5	4.3	0.4
1976	16.5	19.3	5.7	0.0
1977	15.8	6.6	6.1	−0.1
1978	8.3	14.1	6.0	−0.1
1979	13.4	15.0	5.1	0.0
1980	18.0	18.8	6.6	−0.2
1981	11.9	10.2	9.9	−0.5
1982	8.6	6.9	11.4	−0.6
1983	4.6	5.6	12.6	−0.6
1984	5.0	6.8	13.0	−0.6
1985	5.5	—	13.5	−0.6

Source: National Institute Economic Review, Nov. 1985, Economic Trends Annual Supplement 1985, and Department of Employment Gazette, Dec. 1985
* Phillips equation was: $\dot{W} = -0.9 + 9.638(U)^{-1.394}$

for a monetarist-inspired classical revival in macroeconomics. Table 3.2 indicates the extent to which the Phillips curve relationship disintegrated after 1966 (see also Tables 1.1, 1.2 and 1.3 in Ch. 1).

From the above data it is clearly evident that the Phillips curve ceased to provide a reliable guide to wage and price increases after 1966. The higher levels of unemployment which characterised this period ought to have been associated with lower rates of inflation, but the opposite was the case. These experiences of the late 1960s and 1970s dealt a severe blow to the temporary revitalisation of 'classical Keynesianism' which had been provided by the Phillips curve.

There were four basic explanations which were seriously put forward to explain these experiences of the late 1960s and early 1970s.

1. The first explanation is that suggested by Phillips himself when in conluding his 1958 article he noted that:

   The statistical evidence seems in general to support the hypothesis that the rate of change of money wage rates can be explained by the level of unemployment and the rate of change of unemployment, except in or immediately after those years in which there is suffi- ciently rapid rise in import prices to offset the tendency for increasing productivity to reduce the cost of living (Phillips 1958: 299).

With the devaluation of sterling in November 1967 combined with the general accleration of world inflation, import prices did indeed move substantially upwards in this period. So even Phil- lips himself would have been surprised if there had been a good fit after 1967.

2. Other economists preferred to argue that there had been an upward shift in the underlying level of unemployment. Some economists saw this as a supply side phenomenon, while others viewed the increase in unemployment as being caused by a 'shake out' of hoarded labour, i.e. a demand side explanation (see Gujarati 1972; Taylor 1972). Both explanations implied that wage inflation would now be higher for every level of unem- ployment than had previously been the case, i.e. that a right- ward shift of the Phillips curve had occurred.

3. At the time, by far the most popular view put forward for the acceleration of wage inflation in the late 1960s and early 1970s in the UK was the cost-push explanation. Cost-push theorists are a heterogeneous group but they share a common belief that inflation originates on the supply side of the economy and in particular they view money wages as being exogenously rather than endogenously determined. The members of this school of thought were not surprised by the breakdown of the Phillips curve as they had never accepted the foundations on which it had been built (see Kaldor 1959).

4. The fourth and final explanation for the breakdown of the Phil- lips curve was the monetarist view. This fourth explanation will be developed more fully in the next section as it has had the most influence on recent macroeconomic policymaking in the UK and elsewhere.

The monetarist counter-revolution

It is now obvious that macroeconomic policies based on the hydraulic variety of Keynesianism, with an almost total emphasis on aggregate demand and neglect of aggregate supply, were naive in the extreme. Inevitably these models generated an unrealistic degree of confidence in the precision with which demand management policies could achieve their often conflicting objectives. As time moved on, the Keynesian medicine appeared to be working less and less effectively, interventionist policies became easy targets for an intellectually well-armed opposition.

To trace the origins of the monetarist counter-revolution and the classical revival in macroeconomics, it is necessary to examine the influential work of Milton Friedman and his followers. Since the late 1960s he has been exerting an increasing influence on his fellow economists and from the mid-1970s onwards his ideas have entered the realms of the policymakers. Friedman's doctrines are, as he would be the first to admit, a more sophisticated version of pre-Keynesian orthodoxy. His ideas on the desirability of unregulated markets reach back to Adam Smith's *Wealth of Nations*, and the central plank of monetarism, the quantity theory of money, stretches back to David Hume's classic essay *Of Money*. Indeed, according to Mayer (1980), most of the fundamental propositions which characterise monetarism date back to Hume's essay published in 1752.

James Tobin, a leading neo-Keynesian, has distinguished between two brands of monetarism which he has labelled 'monetarism mark I' and 'monetarism mark II' (Tobin 1981). The first variety is the orthodox monetarist research programme inspired by Friedman himself. Monetarism mark II has come to be better known as the 'New Classical Macroeconomics' and the foundations of this research programme were provided by Professor Robert Lucas Jnr building on the earlier work of Friedman (Cross 1982a).

Monetarism like Keynesianism is not a homogeneous monolith. Is it therefore possible to talk of monetarism as a coherent body of thought? Several authors have attempted to provide a list of generally accepted theorems which embody the essence of monetarism (Stein 1976; Laidler 1981). According to Burton, monetarism can be regarded as a coherent body of thought 'because there are certain basic ingredients that are common to all brands of monetarism' (Burton 1982: 15). The following four propositions seem to capture the essence of all neoclassical monetarist models.

1. A belief in the inherent stability of the private sector in the absence of government interference.
2. Acceptance of the long-run neutrality of money.
3. Rejection of the possibility of a stable long-run Phillips curve relationship.
4. A preference for non-activist economic policy.

Where orthodox monetarism would modify propositions (2) and

(3) as far as the short run is concerned, new classical theorists believe that money is neutral in the short run also, with the implication that there is no short-run Phillips curve relationship to be exploited by systematic interventionist macroeconomic policies.

How have these four propositions come to dominate monetarist thinking? It is convenient to trace the monetarist counter-revolution in four distinctive stages.

Stage 1 (1948–56)

In the first stage of the monetarist revival, Friedman began to attack the ideas of hydraulic Keynesianism that governments could stabilise output and employment relatively easily by manipulating the budget deficit in an appropriate counter-cyclical manner. As early as 1948, Friedman was challenging naive Keynesian models. Chicago University has become the recognised bastion of the proponents of *laissez-faire* market capitalism, and it is appropriate that 1948 was the year Friedman joined its department of economics (Butler 1985).

Friedman's 1948 paper suggested that activist stabilisation policies would more than likely be destabilising in their effects. The reason put forward in support of this view was the presence of time lags in the policy process, both in its implementation and in its effects. The stimulation of aggregate demand via budget deficits requires that the government can forecast the future path of aggregate demand and supply. Because it takes time to implement policies and see their effects, problems need to be anticipated in advance. But the lags in the system 'could conceivably be so long and variable that the stimulating effects of the deficit would often be operative only after other factors had already brought a recovery rather than when the initial decline was in progress' (Friedman 1948: 254). Forecasting could only avoid this problem if such forecasts were accurate. The combined effects of recognition, decision and effect lags, together with forecasting errors, led Friedman to argue that the monetary authorities would invariably take action 'too late' and to make matters worse they would then attempt to do 'too much'.

Throughout the 1950s Friedman continued to challenge the macroeconomic foundations upon which full-employment policies were based. It was by no means clear to him that full employment could be guaranteed by the management of demand. Friedman's early suspicion that fiscal policy could be destabilising has more recently been given support by Peacock and Shaw (1978: 108) who conclude that 'it is now generally admitted, by even the staunchest advocates of fiscal interventionism that the earlier Keynesian models to which fiscal variables were related, were extremely simplistic and generated an unrealistic degree of confidence in the precision of the fiscal world'. In a much publicised study of the UK economy, Dow echoed Friedman's 1948 fear when concluding from his research that 'as far as internal conditions are concerned then demand management policy failed to be stabilising and must on the contrary be regarded as having been positively de-destabilising' (Dow 1964). Hansen's seven-country study reached similar conclusions (Hansen 1969).

During this early period Friedman was also developing a clear preference for market systems rather than government intervention. It is evident from his early work at Chicago that he adhered to and advocated the first proposition of monetarism, that the private sector is inherently stable. Acceptance of this proposition together with the potential for destabilising activist programmes provided early opposition to the Keynesian consensus. But such criticisms only scratched the surface of orthodox Keynesianism: more powerful weapons were needed.

Stage 2 (1956–68)

Stage 2 in the development of monetarism lasted from the mid-1950s until 1968. During this period Friedman's work was mainly concerned with re-establishing the discredited quantity theory of money. His article 'The quantity theory of money – a restatement' (1956) has become the classic redefinition of the quantity theory. The key insight of this contribution was the recognition that the quantity theory stands or falls according to the stability of the demand for money. If it was highly stable, then the quantity theory view that monetary expansions would lead to fluctuations in nominal income was justified. Given the stability of the private sector, the long-run implications of monetary expansion would be inflation.

Friedman's theoretical and empirical work during this stage challenged the naive Keynesian view that money did not matter. This work culminated in his famous study co-authored with Anna Schwartz, *A Monetary History of the United States*, published in 1963. This empirical work demonstrated the importance of the supply of money and its relationship to prices and incomes over a long historical period. Friedman and Schwartz concluded from their work that the events of the Great Depression were in fact 'a tragic testament to the effectiveness of monetary policy, not demonstration of its impotence' since the government in the USA had failed to prevent a fall in the quantity of money by one-third in the period 1929–33.

At the end of stage 2, a fierce debate was taking place between Keynesians and monetarists concerning the direction of causation in money–income correlations. In providing theoretical and empirical support for the monetarist view that the causation was predominantly one of money to income rather than vice versa, Friedman had undermined the confidence Keynesian economists had placed in the power of fiscal policy. He had demonstrated how exogenous changes in the stock of money interacted with a stable money demand function to 'cause' the observed movements in nominal income.

The policy implications of these early orthodox monetarist contributions were profoundly anti-Keynesian. Activist demand management policies would lead not to stability but would promote fluctuations of economic activity. Given the inherent stability of the private sector and the self-righting properties of market forces, governments should concern themselves with establishing a stable monetary environment. This requires government adherence to a monetary rule rather than fiscal activism.

Stage 3 (1968–73)

As already noted, during the decade 1958–68 the famous Phillips curve was incorporated into the prevailing macroeconomic models. At about the same time as the Phillips curve relationship began to disintegrate, Professors Friedman and Phelps in the USA were developing theories which predicted that the Phillips curve could only be a short-run phenomenon (Friedman 1968; Phelps 1967). Friedman's 1968 paper 'The role of monetary policy' has had a profound affect on macroeconomic policymaking and has been labelled as 'the most influential article written in macroeconomics in the past two decades' (Gordon 1981). In retrospect it can be viewed as part of a long continuing research programme specifically aimed at subsuming Keynesian economics within a resuscitated quantity theory of money, a process that had begun with Friedman's 1956 'Restatement'.

The most important hypothesis to emerge from Friedman's 1968 paper concerns the idea that market economies gravitate towards a 'natural' rate of unemployed defined as follows:

> At any moment of time, there is some level of unemployment which has the property that it is consistent with equilibrium in the structure of real wage rates . . . The 'natural rate of unemployment', in other words, is the level that would be ground out by the Walrasian system of general equilibrium equations, provided there is imbedded in them the actual structural characteristics of the labor and commodity markets, including market imperfections, stochastic variability in demands and supplies, the cost of gathering information about job vacancies and labor availabilities, the costs of mobility and so on (Friedman 1968: 8).

The natural rate of unemployment is therefore that level which remains when the labour market is in equilibrium and is equivalent to the distance ab in Fig. 3.1. The main thrust of Friedman's argument is that a government cannot increase employment (reduce unemployment) permanently beyond L^* in Fig. 3.1 by the use of expansionary policies along Keynesian lines. To understand this argument we must take a closer look at the concept of the natural rate of unemployment.

The natural rate of unemployment is determined by real forces in the economy. These real forces lie behind the labour demand and supply functions in Fig. 3.1. On the demand side the productivity of labour is determined by the size and composition of the capital stock as well as the technology embodied within it. On the supply side of the labour market the important determining variables include the behaviour and strength of trade unions, the disutility associated with work, and the net income available to workers should they be unemployed. But there is a puzzle which monetarists need to solve. How can a nominal variable such as aggregate monetary demand affect real variables such as employment and output? The empirical evidence conclusively shows a positive correlation between aggregate demand and employment and yet such a relationship flies in the face of the neutrality proposition. In terms of equation [3.1], shifts of MV do cause movements of Y. Friedman's 1968 paper provides an ingenious explanation of these observed positive correlations between real output and nominal aggregate demand in terms of a model which has been highly influential in reshaping policymakers' attitudes to Keynesian demand management policies.

Friedman criticises the analysis of Phillips and Lipsey on the basis that it ignores the important role of inflationary expectations. Equation [3.2] represents Friedman's 'expectations augmented' version of the modified Phillips relationship.

$$\dot{P} = f(U) + \alpha \dot{P}^e \qquad [3.2]$$

where $\dot{P}^e$ stands for the expected rate of inflation and α is a coefficient with a value lying between zero and one. In effect it is a measure of the extent to which wages and prices adjust to expected inflation; if $\alpha = 1$ then this implies full adjustment. However, if $\alpha < 1$ money wages rise less than inflation. But if workers do not make full allowance for the effect of expected inflation on the real value of their money wages, they are in effect behaving irrationally. Since the majority of monetarists adhere to the neoclassical paradigm which has at its heart the principle of rational maximising behaviour, they take a value of $\alpha = 1$ in their models. If $\alpha = 1$ and we subtract $\dot{P}^e$ from both sides of equation [3.2] we have equation [3.3]

$$\dot{P} - \dot{P}^e = f(U) \qquad [3.3]$$

Now in the long run $\dot{P}^e$ will converge towards the actual rate of inflation such that $\dot{P} = \dot{P}^e$. Therefore in Friedman's model there can be no long-run trade-off. With $\dot{P} = \dot{P}^e$ we have equation [3.4]

$$\dot{P} - \dot{P} = f(U) = 0 \qquad [3.4]$$

Equation [3.4] tells us that there is no trade-off once the labour market is in equilibrium and the natural rate of unemployment is established. In terms of Fig. 3.3, the long-run Phillips curve is a vertical line at the natural rate of unemployment. How precisely does this process of expectational adjustment take place? In the next section we will follow Friedman's own argument presented in his 1968 paper.

Suppose the government decides that a level of unemployment of 2.5 per cent is too high and has as its target a level equal to U_z in Fig. 3.3. If we assume that the natural rate of unemployment is 2.5 per cent (UN in Fig. 3.3) then the monetary authorities will be attempting to reduce natural unemployment, a real phenomenon, with a nominal instrument. The original interpretation of the Phillips curve suggested that it was possible to buy a lower level of unemployment such as U_z at the cost of a higher stable rate of inflation equal to $\dot{P}_z$. According to Friedman, such policies were misguided and doomed to failure in the long run. The reason for this was that workers and firms would gradually come to expect higher rates of inflation. Inflationary expectations would affect price and wage-setting behaviour so as to shift the Phillips curve in a north-easterly direction. Instead of one Phillips curve, there were several, each associated with a particular rate of expected inflation. But why is there any expansion of output and employment at all in response to the increase in aggregate demand? We can understand Friedman's argument by referring back to Fig. 3.1.

It is clear from Fig. 3.1 that an expansion of employment beyond L^* can only occur if firms know that the real wage has fallen and workers *believe* that their real wage has risen. This can happen because 'selling prices of products typically respond to an *unanticipated* rise in nominal demand faster than prices of factors of production', thus 'real wages received have gone down – though real wages anticipated by employees went up, since employees implicitly evaluated the wages offered at the earlier price level' (Friedman 1968). In effect, workers have been deceived into accepting jobs because they have not yet adjusted to the new unanticipated higher rate of inflation. Unemployment falls below the natural rate as job search declines and in terms of Fig. 3.1 employment expands to a point such as L_d. But unemployment can only be held below the natural rate as long as workers miscalculate the real value of their nominal wage. Sooner or later workers will adjust their expectations in line with the new higher rate of inflation, and employment will contract as the real wage returns to the market clearing level in response to rising money wages. In Fig. 3.3 the Phillips curve has shifted to PS_2. Instead of price stability being associated with UN we now have the economy located at point g on the vertical long-run Phillips curve. An inflation rate of $\dot{P}_z$ is now anticipated and is equal to the actual rate. The fall in unemployment to U_z was a temporary phenomenon and could only be maintained so long as workers' expectations of inflation were out of line with the actual rate. Stable inflation rates are achievable at the natural rate of unemployment, and the vertical long-run Phillips curve indicates that there are numerous stable inflation rates consistent with labour market equilibrium. Thus the quantity theory holds in the long run, inflation is a monetary phenomenon, and unemployment is determined by real forces. The short-run deviations of output and employment which are actually observed can be explained using Friedman's expectations-augmented Phillips curve incorporating the concept of the natural rate of unemployment (we shall refer to this as the natural rate hypothesis NRH).

The preceding argument can also be presented in terms of an aggregate demand and supply framework and this will enable us to understand more easily the monetarist critique of interventionist demand management policies. Figure 3.4 indicates the Friedmanite version of the aggregate supply curve. Imagine the economy is initially located at the natural rate of unemployment (UN in Fig. 3.3, and L^* in Fig. 3.1). The output consistent with labour market equilibrium given the existing real forces in the economy is Y^* in Fig. 3.4. The classical quantity theory predicts that an increase in aggregate demand (MV) from AD_1 to AD_2 will raise the price level from P_1 to P_3 leaving real output unchanged at Y^*. Friedman's model allows for a temporary increase in real output to occur as employment expands (to L_d in Fig. 3.1) and unemployment falls (to U_z in Fig. 3.3). The increase in real output shown in Fig. 3.4 lasts only so long as expectations of inflation are out of line with the actual rate. But as expectations adjust, the short-run aggregate supply curve shifts to AS_2. Thus the economy has displayed a short-run expansion along the path indicated by abc in Fig. 3.4. In the long run, when expectations have fully adjusted, the economy has moved from a to c. Hence in Friedman's model a positively sloped short-run aggregate supply schedule co-exists with a vertical long-run aggregate supply schedule ($LRAS^*$), just as a short-run negatively sloped Phillips curve co-exists with a vertical long-run relationship.

Friedman's persuasive theoretical argument, combined with

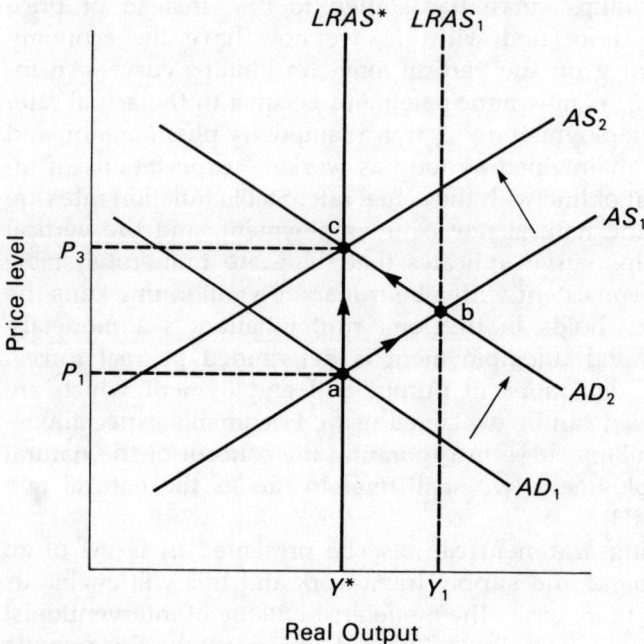

Figure 3.4 Short- and long-run aggregate supply

predictions, which appears to be verified by events in the late 1960s and 1970s, led to the NRH being quickly absorbed into the macroeconomics literature. Orthodox monetarism gained many adherents during this period as it displayed all the characteristics of a progressive research programme (see Cross 1982b).

The NRH, if accepted, has profound implications for the whole framework of stabilisation policy. It established the 'hard core' monetarist proposition that unemployment is independent of aggregate demand in the long run. Instead of having room to manoeuvre, which was the implication of the stable Phillips curve, the NRH implies that the government is powerless to influence the level of unemployment in the long run via the use of macroeconomic demand management policies. This does not mean that the natural rate of unemployment is immutable. It can be influenced by policy but, as Laidler has pointed out, 'monetarist analysis suggests that it is the tools of high employment policy rather than its goals which must be changed' (Laidler 1975: 47). Such tools will be microeconomic rather than macroeconomic in nature. In recent years monetarists have concentrated on policies to lower barriers to labour mobility as a means of reducing the natural rate. Such policies would include reform of trade unions as well as giving attention to the level of unemployment benefits (see Minford *et al.* 1983). Unemployment can only be permanently reduced if either the labour demand and/or supply schedules of Fig. 3.1 shift to the right (assuming the size of the labour force remains unchanged). Microeconomic policies which succeed in reducing the natural rate of unemployment will shift the long-run aggregate supply schedule in Fig. 3.4 to the right (see $LRAS_1$). Thus unemployment can be reduced and output increased in the long run by interventionist policies, but not of the kind advocated by Keynesians.

Friedman's arguments in 1968 provided additional weight to his call for the monetary authorities to adopt a monetary growth rate rule. Only if the money supply was increased at a rate consistent with long-term productivity growth could there be price stability. Such an environment would allow market forces to work more effectively. In contrast to Keynes, Friedman's analysis suggests that the greatest threat to economic stability comes not from the private sector, but from well-intentioned but misguided governments weaned on Keynesian analysis.

Initially monetarists appeared to suggest that the natural rate of unemployment in the UK was around 2.5 per cent (Laidler 1975). This raised a problem. Why had inflation not accelerated during the 1950s and early 1960s when unemployment in the UK had consistently been below 2.5 per cent? The answer to this puzzle was provided by the 'international monetarist' analysis associated with the monetary approach to the balance of payments and exchange rates (see Johnson 1973a).

Johnson's analysis suggests that under the Bretton Woods fixed exchange rate system, monetary expansions lead to a deteriorating balance of payments position for the economy concerned as excess demand spills out of it. The rate of inflation in a small open economy operating with a fixed exchange rate is governed by the rate of inflation prevailing in the rest of the world rather than domestic monetary expansion. Since the world rate of inflation was low until the late 1960s, the UK rate was also low – hence a stable Phillips curve with low levels of unemployment was to be expected. However, once a floating exchange rate regime is adopted, the rate of domestic inflation is governed by the rate of domestic monetary expansion. Thus after the break-down of the Bretton Woods system in the early 1970s and the move towards floating exchanges, rates of inflation in the advanced countries would be expected to diverge as the rate of monetary expansion in each country differed. Monetarists point to the divergence of inflation rates after 1973 as evidence in support of their theory. For Keynesians, this divergence after 1973 has more to do with the varying ability of different market economies to deal with the impact of the huge increases in oil prices which occurred at this time. Those economies, such as the UK, where real wage resistance was strong, experienced dramatic increases in their rates of inflation (see Hicks 1974).

Stage 4 (1973–   )

Friedman's analysis in 1968 had been founded on the assumption that price expectations would be formed by extrapolating previous experience of inflation via an error-learning mechanism. This adaptive expectations hypothesis (AEH), first used by Cagan in 1956, postulates that agents revise current expectations on the basis of past forecasting errors. Individual agents raise or lower their expectations of inflation only after higher inflation has been experienced. This expectations formation mechanism is backward rather than forward looking.

To those wedded to the neoclassical paradigm, the AEH is clearly unsatisfactory as it implies irrational non-maximising behaviour, long lags of adjustment and the persistence of systematic errors. Since the early 1970s a new school of monetarist theorists have developed models which are more clearly rooted in neoclassical microeconomic foundations. The seminal contribution to the 'New Classical' school of macroeconomics was provided by Lucas in 1972 with the publication of his influential paper 'Expectations and the neutrality of money'. In this paper Lucas derives a Phillips curve relationship, a systematic relation between the rate of change of nominal prices and the level of real output, within a framework 'from which all forms of money illusion are rigorously excluded: all prices are market clearing, all agents behave optimally in light of their objectives and expectations, and expectations are formed optimally' (Lucas 1972: 103).

As we have already noted, neoclassical microeconomics is based on the notion that economic agents, to the limits of the information available to them, are consistent and successful optimisers, i.e. they are continuously in equilibrium (Hoover 1984). This in turn implies that:

1. agents' real economic decisions are based only on real not nominal factors, and
2. agents make no systematic errors in assessing the economic environment in which they live, i.e. they hold rational expectations.

Lucas had set out to develop a theory of the business cycle in strict adherence to the above neoclassical principles. In a world of free competition and wealth-maximising behaviour, market-clearing prices and quantities will be generated implying that all perceived profitable opportunities have been fully exploited. This in turn implies that the business cycle must be viewed as an equilibrium phenomenon when adopting competitive neoclassical microfoundations (see Zarnowitz 1985; Mullineux 1984).

At the heart of the new classical doctrine is an acceptance of the rational expectations hypothesis (REH). Although the REH is necessary to generate new classical results, by itself it is not sufficient. It must be combined with the assumption of continuous market clearing before the startling predictions of the new classical models can be derived. Let us examine these two assumptions in turn.

The refinement of the idea of rational as opposed to adaptive expectations was the natural outcome of the assertion that economic agents will not *systematically* make mistakes. The AEH was seen to be an *ad hoc* approach to the modelling of expectations because such a hypothesis allows individuals 'to make systematic forecasting errors period after period, without requiring any amendment to the basis of the forecasting rule itself' (Begg 1982). Although the REH was introduced into the economic literature by John Muth in 1961, it was Lucas (1972) who provided the earliest application of the idea to macroeconomic modelling. The REH postulates that in forming expectations, economic agents will use all publicly available information which is relevant to the factors determining the variables about which expectations are being formed and that no systematic errors will be made. Errors in expectations are therefore random and hence completely unpredictable (Sheffrin 1983). Muth's hypothesis was presented as follows: 'I should like to suggest that expectations since they are informed predictions of future events, are essentially the same as predictions of the relevant economic theory' (Muth 1961: 316).

In other words, if agents work with a model of the economy where the rate of inflation is determined by the rate of growth of the money supply, then rational agents will forecast a rate of inflation based on the current and expected growth of the money supply.

Now the second assumption of continuous market clearing in a competitive (non-monopolistic) environment implies that the economy will gravitate towards the natural rate of unemployment. But both Friedman and Lucas accept the possibility of a short-run positively sloped aggregate supply function which a shift of aggregate demand can take the economy along. Whilst Friedman's 1968 model relies on an asymmetry in the availability of information to workers and employers to produce this result, Lucas' model is based on the assumption that firms and workers cannot always distinguish temporary from permanent price and wage changes because of information gaps. A business cycle (short-run Phillips curve) can result where expectations are formed rationally, providing there is incomplete information.

The problem for any seller is that they must decide how much of a given change in the current price of their product is a relative price change and how much is the result of a general (or 'global') price change. If a general (inflationary) price movement is misinterpreted as a relative price change, then maximising agents will supply more output and labour. A business cycle will be observed as the economy moves up a short-run aggregate supply schedule. Such a movement will obviously be temporary: sooner or later rational agents will realise that they made their supply decisions on the basis of faulty information. The economy will quickly return to the natural level of employment and output, but at a higher rate of inflation.

Clearly, systematic aggregate demand variations producing global price movements will be incorporated into the agent's information set. Building on the work of Friedman and Lucas, Sargent and Wallace (1976) put forward what may be referred to as the Lucas–Sargent–Wallace policy ineffectiveness proposition. This proposition suggests that any systematic policy will be totally ineffective since the consequences will be forecast by rational agents. Suppose the government announces that it wishes to reduce unemployment to U_z in Fig. 3.3 by increasing aggregate nominal demand. If the forecasts of economic agents are based on a monetarist model, then a higher rate of inflation equal to the new expected growth of the money supply will be expected. Thus there will be no possibility of the government engineering a deviation of the actual rate of inflation from its expected rate. Since with rational expectations $\dot{P} = \dot{P}^e$ for any announced expansion of the money supply, agents will not have mistaken global price movements for relative price movements. Labour supply will not increase and output and unemployment will remain at their natural rates. In terms of Fig. 3.3 the economy will move immediately to point g on the vertical long-run Phillips curve. In Fig. 3.4 the economy moves immediately from point a to point c on the long-run aggregate supply schedule ($LRAS^*$).

The implications of this analysis for Keynesian stabilisation policy appear to be devastating. Only *unanticipated* random demand and supply shocks to the economic system can cause actual output and unemployment to diverge from their natural levels. In a Lucas–Sargent–Wallace world, the economy (in the absence of random shocks) is always located on a vertical aggregate supply schedule or long-run Phillips curve.

We can now summarise the main conclusions of the new monetarist macroeconomics.

1. In an economy with complete wage and price flexibility and where agents are utility maximisers, output and unemployment will tend towards their equilibrium or natural levels.
2. Friedman's analysis using the NRH combined with AEH implies that money is neutral only in the long run. The new classical theorists go much further, anticipated money is neutral in the short run also.
3. Full employment should not be regarded as an absolute technical limit but the equilibrium outcome of optimising choices made by economic agents.
4. There is no short-run Phillips curve or positively sloped aggre-

gate supply schedule to be exploited by systematic expansions of aggregate demand.

5. Output and employment can only deviate from their natural (full employment) levels if $\dot{P} \neq \dot{P}^e$. Since price expectations will be formed by utility maximising agents, deviations of $\dot{P}^e$ from P can only be the result of random changes in the government's monetary growth in relation to the rate of growth of output.
6. A random monetary policy can increase the variability of output; it cannot alter its natural level.
7. The new classical school support Friedman's recommendation that monetary policy should be conducted on the basis of rules rather than discretion. It is the determinateness or non-randomness of Friedman's rule that new classicals support on the basis that this will eliminate fluctuations induced by governments.
8. The rate of inflation is entirely determined by the rate of monetary growth in relation to the rate of growth of output.

In certain aspects of their analysis, the new classical theorists have presented a challenge to Friedman's brand of orthodox monetarism (see Laidler 1981). The original monetarist critique of fine tuning was based on the argument derived from the NRH that such policy was ineffective in the long run and also because of the long and unpredictable lags experienced in the implementation of and effects from demand management policy. The implication of the new classical analysis is somewhat different. Here announced policy is totally ineffective because of the short lag between its implementation and effects. When policies are repeated time and again, people catch on. Rather than causing damage, systematic policy does nothing!

If the best advice that Keynesian macroeconomists can give the politicians is 'don't just sit there – do something' – the message from the new school of monetarists is 'don't just do something – sit there' (Davies G. 1985).

Monetarism and the policymakers

As we have already noted, between the end of the Second World War and the mid-1970s the UK government's macroeconomic policies were largely influenced by what we have called 'Keynesianism'. Although the high water mark of Keynesian influence was probably during the 1960s, it was Prime Minister James

Callaghan who formally announced the end of the Keynesian era when speaking at the Labour Party conference in 1976. He gave the following Friedmanite view of the world. 'We used to think that you could just spend your way out of recession and increase employment by cutting taxes and boosting government spending. I tell you in all candour that that option no longer exists, and that insofar as it did exist, it worked by injecting inflation into the economy.' This view has more recently been echoed by Nigel Lawson who declared at the Conservative Party conference in October 1984, 'let us be quite clear, you will not reduce unemployment by increasing what governments spend or borrow'. Obviously these statements reflect the increasing influence of monetarist as opposed to Keynesian thinking on policymakers. Although the Labour government adopted certain macroeconomic policies which had a monetarist flavour, it is the Conservative administration under Mrs Thatcher's leadership which has been 'unashamedly monetarist in its approach' (Davies G. 1985: 11). According to Davies, Chancellor Lawson's approach to macroeconomic management has a distinctly 'new classical tinge'. In his Mais Lecture delivered in June 1984, the Chancellor denied that macroeconomic policy could reduce the level of unemployment; he asserted that inflation was 'above all a monetary phenomenon'; he supported the REH when declaring that 'the private sector is bound to take into account its expectations of the behaviour of the government when deciding its own behaviour'; and finally the Chancellor indicated that the curse of unemployment could only be eliminated if market forces were 'progressively liberated from rigidities and distortions'. There can be no doubt that the legitimacy of the Thatcherite macroeconomic strategy rests heavily on the validity of monetarist theories (see Tomlinson 1986).

In the USA the monetarist experiment lasted precisely three years from October 1979 until October 1982 (Brimmer 1983). During this short period, inflation was checked but at the cost of a sharp rise in unemployment. Since the end of 1982 output and employment in the USA have recovered sharply, but there is considerable controversy concerning the cause of this recovery. Was it induced by President Reagan's 'supply side' policies, or was the recovery due to an old-fashioned Keynesian reflation? What is clear is that since 1982 the monetarist strategy was abandoned in the USA but not in the UK (see Peterson and Estenson 1985).

Since 1979 the Conservative government's primary objective has been the control of inflation via 'proper monetary discipline' which requires 'public stated targets for the rate of growth of the money supply' (*Conservative Manifesto* 1979). With the control of inflation given a high priority, full employment as an objective was dropped. Thus Britain was truly made the subject of a monetarist experiment (Keegan 1984). It is now evident that many influential Conservative politicians and financial journalists were converted to the monetarist creed as a result of the failure of the reflation of the economy carried out by the 1970–74 Conservative administration led by Prime Minister Heath. Following this episode, Sir Keith Joseph became a leading monetarist evangelist while Peter Jay writing in *The Times*, and Samuel Brittan writing in *The Financial Times*, were particularly influential in propagating the new monetarist wisdom (see Grant and Nath 1984).

Control of the money supply is the centre piece of any monetarist economic strategy. Thus the conduct of policy since 1979 has been marked by the following features. First, monetary policy has become far more important than fiscal policy. Second, the focus of monetary policy has shifted from the Radcliffian concern with interest rates to the Friedmanite emphasis on the quantity of money and its rate of growth (Kaldor 1982). Third, inflation and its control have become the overriding objective of government policy. Finally, the government has claimed that its concern is with the long-run consequences of policy rather than the short-run (Llewellyn 1984). Thus since 1979 economic policy has been conducted within the framework of a 'medium term financial strategy' and the setting of monetary targets.

There is one sense in which the Thatcher brand of monetarism is different from that of Friedman and Lucas. Orthodox Keynesianism accepted that inflation and unemployment were alternatives; Friedman's 1968 analysis suggested that higher inflation would reduce unemployment in the short run but not in the long run; Lucas and his associates have argued that unemployment and inflation are independent of each other in both the long and the short run; Mrs Thatcher's economics, in contrast to the above approaches, indicate that inflation causes unemployment. In terms of Fig. 3.4, this latter view can be interpreted in one of two ways. Either the shift of aggregate demand from AD_1 to AD_2 must induce a leftward shift of the short-run AS schedule beyond point c so that real output falls below its initial level of Y^*. Or, the effects of inflation on the co-ordinating mechanisms in the economy produce adverse supply side effects so as to shift the long-run AS schedule to the left. Again real output finishes below its initial level of Y^* (Gowland 1985). These adverse effects of inflation on the real economy seem to have more in common with Hayek's brand of monetarism than the new classical approach. After all, if money is super neutral and has no real effects should we really worry about mild forms of inflation at all?

Has monetarism failed?

The solution to any economic problem invariably depends on identifying what causes it and upon taking appropriate action. At the present time the UK is confronted with many serious economic problems. But the Conservative government since 1979 have declared inflation to be public enemy number one. It would therefore seem reasonable to answer the above question in the following way.

1. Has the strategy adopted succeeded in reducing inflation?
2. What have been the costs of the strategy?
3. If the costs have been excessive, is this due to faulty analysis underlying the strategy or has it been due to poor implementation of the policies?

With regard to the first question, the answer must be yes. Inflation has been reduced as Table 3.2 indicates. We can therefore move quickly to a consideration of the second question. Presumably inflation is worth reducing because it has real effects on the economy. In particular, variable rates of inflation are seen as destabilising by both Friedman and Lucas (Friedman 1975). In Hayek's view (1973) any positive rate of inflation is damaging to the real economy. For monetarists of all persuasions, monetary stability is a pre- condition for economic growth. However, many economists have questioned the extent of the real costs of inflation (Bootle 1981; Higham and Tomlinson 1982; Hahn 1982b). Even more at dispute are the unemployment costs of deflationary strategies. This controversy revolves around the nature of the trade-off between unemployment and inflation.

In Friedman's model, reducing the rate of growth of the money supply will produce a temporary rise in unemployment above the natural rate. This will last as long as it takes inflationary expectations to adjust to the new monetary environment. The new classical theorists are much more optimistic. Reductions of inflation require nothing more than an announced reduction of monetary growth. Since agents have rational expectations, inflation will fall almost immediately with little or no effects on output and employment. In effect, the economy tumbles down a long-run Phillips curve. Assuming the real costs of inflation are significant, these temporary losses of output, if any, would appear to be worth paying.

For Keynesians the costs of monetary deflation have been excessive and these costs are the inevitable price being paid for implementing an economic strategy which is based on faulty analysis (Kaldor 1983; Barker T. 1980; Coutts *et al.* 1981).

At the theoretical level, critics have cast doubt on the validity of models incorporating the strong version of the REH (Gomes 1982; Struthers 1984). This version states that rational expectations are the same as the predictions of the relevant economic theory. Economic agents, to make such predictions, would need to know the true structure of the economy and yet economists cannot agree on what is the 'correct model'. In a new classical world everyone is conveniently a monetarist, they accept the basic propositions of the quantity theory, they accept the Lucas–Friedman surprise aggregate supply function, the NRH, price and wage flexibility etc. Not surprisingly, most Keynesians reject economic policies which are based on models which have as a key element this strong version of the REH.

Other critics are prepared to accept the REH but reject the other components of the new classical doctrine, in particular the assumption of continuous market clearing. The empirical evidence suggests that prices and wages are not sufficiently flexible to ensure continuous market clearing. With sticky prices and wages, involuntary unemployment becomes a possibility and we are back in a Keynesian world where employment can be stimulated by an increase in effective demand. The equilibrium price auction model of the new classical theorists which treats the labour market in the same way as any other flexiprice market is seen to be fatally flawed. Wages and prices are likely to be sticky for rational reasons, not least of which is the need to maintain the morale of the workforce and customer goodwill (Thurow 1983; Okun 1983; see also Ch. 6 below).

Keynesians are prepared to agree that the UK government's monetarist strategy has resulted in a fall in inflation. However, they would not agree that the mechanism has been via a process of expectational adjustment along monetarist lines. Instead they would argue that deflation is used as a method of creating 'enough unemployment to bring the trade unions to heel, and thereby bring the level of pay settlements sufficiently below the current rate of inflation' (Kaldor 1982; 55). In effect, Keynesian policies are deliberately being put into reverse to break the power that workers acquire during a long continuous period of full employment (see Kalecki 1943).

Unlike monetarists, Keynesians accept that inflation can be generated on the supply side of the economy. In an oligopolistic economy with powerful trade unions, a conflict over real wages and profit mark-ups between firms and workers will result in a wage–price spiral. Such cost inflations cannot be broken by monetary restraint alone without a substantial cost in terms of lost output and employment. The majority of Keynesians support the use of incomes policy as a necessary adjunct to demand management policies in order to minimise the damage monetary restraint alone will have on output (Snowdon 1983; Trevithick 1980). For monetary deflation to affect only prices and wages rather than output and employment requires a particular response from wage bargainers. This requirement is that negotiated aggregate wage increases are no higher than the new lower money supply growth rate. Given the fragmented nature of wage bargaining in the UK and the concern over relativities, it does not make sense to assume that the macroeconomic outcome of unco-ordinated wage bargains taking place during a period of deflation will not involve significant costs in terms of unemployment. Thus Keynesians do not deny that deflation will eventually lower inflation; rather they claim that it will be a long and costly process and point to recent UK experience as evidence of this fact.

Since most Keynesian economists are also wedded to the advantages of free markets in performing allocative functions better than governments, the use of incomes policies is not a 'cheery outlook' but an unfortunate necessity. However, they regard the costs in terms of resource misallocation to be 'trivial' compared to the losses of output associated with monetarist deflationary policies unaided by incomes policy (Tobin 1977; Lipsey R. G. 1984).

More radical Keynesians who view the ultimate source of inflation as being due to a conflict over the distribution of the national product see the need for incomes policy on a *permanent* rather than *temporary* basis. Fear of unemployment as a method of restraining the inflationary bias in the system is unlikely to work in the long run. In contrast to the monetarist position more, not less, government intervention is required in order to help capitalist economies function properly. The sustained period of full employment in the 1950s and 1960s fostered an inflationary bias in market economies requiring new forms of intervention to deal with it. The attraction of the monetarist solution was always dependent on the assumption that the unemployment cost of monetary deflation would be small. Unfortunately, large-scale unemployment appears to be a more credible signal to the workforce than announced monetary targets. To avoid such an approach, radical Keynesians argue that 'there is no alternative to a permanent incomes policy for achieving wage and price stability at full employment' (Cornwall 1984: 175; see also Fine and Murfin 1984).

It is recognised by radical Keynesians that a permanent incomes policy needs to be preceded at the political level by some minimal societal agreement as to how the gains from economic growth are to be distributed (see also Hirsch 1977). In this sense, inflation is always and everywhere a political phenomenon. Keynes hinted at this problem in 1943 when he noted that: 'the task of keeping efficiency wages reasonably stable is a political rather than an economic problem' (see Kahn 1978).

To Keynesians of all persuasions the major lesson of the past fifty years appears to be that with the existing labour market institutions of advanced capitalist economies' low unemployment induces excessive wage inflations and that non-inflationary levels of demand give rise to serious unemployment and slow growth (Brown A. J. 1985).

This is all very depressing, but it has long been evident that the simultaneous achievement of full-employment price, stability and free collective bargaining are incompatible objectives. It seems we can have any two but never all three simultaneously. In attempting to resolve this problem, Keynesians would prefer to reform the institutional framework within which collective bargaining takes place. But incomes policies are no soft option and the problems of implementation are well known. The Conservative administration's approach is to give way on full employment or simply to redefine what it means. However, the universal increase in unemployment in recent years would seem to be inconsistent with the voluntary unemployment thesis and yet present government policy seems to be based on this approach.

Unemployment: voluntary or involuntary

Nowhere in the *General Theory* does Keynes recommend the use of expansionary demand management policies to reduce unemployment once the economy has attained the classical equilibrium position of full employment. Such a policy would be pointless and inevitably end in producing 'true inflation'. *Keynes and Keynesians were and are concerned with explaining how a capitalist market economy can be pushed towards its natural rate of unemployment, not beyond it* (see Fig. 3.1). As Hahn notes, 'If the economy is there already, we can all go home' (see Hahn 1982b: 75). It is not surprising that many Keynesians are somewhat puzzled to find out that the essence of the monetarist argument is that expansions of demand will not reduce the full-employment level of unemployment. Whoever claimed otherwise?

The essential issue raised in the *General Theory* is that capitalist market economies will not normally or automatically find themselves in a state of full-employment equilibrium, this was to be regarded only as a 'special case'. In the special case, all unemployment is voluntary and frictional and equivalent to Friedman's natural rate. If classical theory is only applicable to the special case of full employment, obviously it is 'fallacious to apply it to the problems of involuntary unemployment' (Keynes 1973a: 16).

Keynes' criticism of the classical economists is equally applicable to monetarist theories. The starting point of monetarist analysis of either the Friedman or Lucas variety is a state of full-employment equilibrium, i.e. the economy is located at L^* in Fig. 3.1 and Y^* in Fig. 3.4. Monetarists then proceed to demonstrate that expansions of demand cannot permanently reduce unemployment. But Keynes in the *General Theory* was not concerned with this issue. Indeed, as early as page 7, Keynes was explaining how microeconomic policies are necessary to increase employment to a position to the right of L^* in Fig. 3.1. Friedman and Lucas, by adopting the classical position, deny that employment can be expanded by reducing the real wage via demand expansions. Keynes agreed: 'there will only be one level of employment consistent with equilibrium . . . this level cannot be greater than full employment, i.e. the real wage cannot be less than the marginal disutility of labour' (Keynes 1973a: 28). If aggregate demand was increased when the economy was already located at L^* what precisely did Keynes argue would happen? His statement in the *General Theory* is unambiguous and strictly in keeping with classical economics.

> The conditions of strict equilibrium require therefore, that wages and prices, and consequently profits also, should all rise in the same proportion as expenditure, the 'real' position including the volume of output and employment, being left unchanged in all respects. We have reached a situation in which the crude quantity theory of money is fully

satisfied; for output does not alter and prices rise in exact proportion to MV (Keynes 1973a: 289).

Keynes argued that macroeconomic effective demand expansions by government could work when employment was less than L^* in Fig. 3.1 but such policies had no role to play once the economy reached L^*. Beyond L^* we are in the world of the classical special case. In such a situation involuntary unemployment does not exist, and we have no need for Keynes.

The crucial question at the present time would seem to be: 'Is the UK economy fully employed in the sense of labour market equilibrium?' The Conservative administration's approach to unemployment only seems to make sense if the answer to this question is yes. In their view, unemployment has increased in the UK due to supply side deficiencies, not a lack of demand. These include a lack of incentives to work, in particular too high a level of taxation and over-generous unemployment benefit; a lack of flexibility in the labour market; too high real wages due to trade union monopoly power, minimum wage legislation etc., and a lack of adequate training facilities (Minford 1983). Government policies are aimed at removing these impediments to the supply side of the labour market so as to create a more flexible economy which can generate growth without inflation. Thus it is not a lack of aggregate demand that has generated the dramatic rise of unemployment particularly since 1979, but the growth of artificial impediments to the proper working of a market system. Removal of these impediments will enable the market system to automatically generate full employment.

Keynesian economists remain unconvinced that the major part of recent rises in unemployment can be explained by artificial impediments. By resorting to claims that the path of unemployment can be explained by shifts of its natural rate, the monetarist research programme would seem to be showing signs of degeneracy (Cross 1982b). According to Dornbusch (1985), demand factors account for 70 per cent of the change in unemployment in the period 1979–85, macroeconomic factors have totally outweighed all the microeconomic determinants of unemployment. Keynesians regard the monetarist case against using demand management to fight the present UK recession unproven. Indeed, some economists have argued that a 'hands off' policy which allows unemployment to lie above the natural rate for considerable periods can lead to a rise in the natural rate due to a deterioration of human capital which long periods of unemployment inevitably produce (Cross

1982a; Davies G. 1985). In sum, Keynesians support a much more active macroeconomic approach to the problem of unemployment than the present monetarist-inspired Conservative administration are prepared to accept. To non-monetarists, what looks like involuntary unemployment is involuntary unemployment. (Solow 1980).

How dead is Keynes?

If the new classical theorists are right, the whole Keynesian episode was one very long fruitless diversion from the wisdom of the classical/neoclassical framework. In Rowley's view (1983), the Keynesians have been vanquished and should 'leave the field of battle'. This view is not supported here. The Keynesian research programme has been enriched by the appearance of the new classical models. Just as economists did not fully understand the classical economic system until Keynes produced his *General Theory*, forcing the supporters of this school to re-examine the very foundations of their analysis, the revival of classical macroeconomics has, and will continue to force Keynesians to refine their analysis (Snowdon and Wynarczyk 1984).

New classical monetarism is firmly embedded in the tradition established by Walras – the general equilibrium framework. This framework attempts to analyse the economy by analysing all markets simultaneously, allowing for feedback and interdependencies. Since Walrasian theory represents the world in terms of a series of simultaneous equations, the interesting question for economists is: will there be a vector of prices which will yield the equality of demand and supply, in all markets simultaneously? Monetarist models with their assumptions of continuous market clearing and rational expectations yield an equilibrium outcome to market interaction. The invisible hand works. Incomplete information and unforeseen shocks can throw the economy temporarily off its natural rate path but market forces will quickly restore it back to equilibrium.

The essence of the Keynesian approach is to adopt a non-Walrasian framework. In particular, markets do not always clear, uncertainty prevents the formation of rational expectations, and sticky prices and wages are a stabilising rather than destabilising influence on the economic system. Capitalism certainly cannot survive with price rigidity, but neither could it survive the perfect price flexibility of the new classical models, unless all price adjustments took place at a single point of time. This would require the existence of a Walrasian auctioneer. No such auctioneer exists in reality.

Modern monetarists criticise Keynesians for assuming that the government has sufficient knowledge of the structure of the economy to manipulate it. In the next breath we are introduced to workers and firms who know the true model of the economy! In this author's view the Keynesian research programme still has much to offer. There is no instant theoretical kill in economics. Indeed, it is better that the economics profession admits to the differences which exist between economists. It is quite incorrect to suggest as Friedman did in his famous 'Theoretical framework' paper in 1970 that the differences are empirical. Clearly, they are also theoretical.

Keynesian economics has in the past suffered from having weak, inconsistent or undisclosed micro foundations. This 'no bridge' problem has been exposed by Lucas. A macro theory should certainly be consistent with its micro foundations. The perfectly competitive neoclassical world is not an appropriate foundation for meaningful Keynesian economics. Hopefully the future development of Keynesian economics will incorporate fruitful ideas from Kalecki, Robinson, Tobin, Okun and others to challenge the new classical view that all unemployment is the result of an intertemporal choice between having leisure now or later. It is certainly true to say that the new classicals have forced Keynesians to restate and remake their case for stabilisation policies. This has been useful and necessary given the unhealthy state of orthodox Keynesianism is the 1960s which had become a degenerating research programme. Orthodox Keynesianism undoubtedly gave insufficient attention to the supply side of the economy. The new classical analysis as a polar extreme gives insufficient attention to the demand side. Macroeconomics should be concerned with aggregate demand and supply, the determination of output depends on the interaction of both, not one or the other. The effects of an expansion of aggregate demand depends crucially on the aggregate supply schedule. Is it L-shaped, vertical or positively sloped? The introductory textbooks are only just coming to terms with these questions (Lipsey R. G. 1983; Begg *et al.* 1984).

How dead is Keynes? Tobin (1977) in answering this question drew attention to four central propositions of the *General Theory*.

1. Prices and wages are 'sticky' in their response to excess demand and supply.

2. Modern industrial capitalist economies are subject to periodic bouts of involuntary unemployment.
3. Capital formation is dependent on long-run expectations of profit and risks.
4. Flexible prices and wages will not stabilise an economy subject to supply and demand shocks.

These propositions seem as relevant in the 1980s as they were in the 1930s. The new classical models, in presenting a case against macro interventionalist policies, must come to terms in particular with (2) above and in Buiter's view: 'there is no presumption at all that a government that sits on its hands and determines the behaviour of its instruments by the simplest possible fixed rules is guaranteed to bring about the best of all possible worlds' (Buiter 1980: 48).

In a situation where recessions persist for considerable periods of time, Keynes is alive and well. The new classical models have failed to satisfactorily explain the length of the recent recession and that experienced during the 1930s. Explanations which rely on outbreaks of contagious laziness amongst workers remain unconvincing (Modigliani 1977).

Conclusion

Can demand management affect output and employment? This question raises two others. First, can government shift the aggregate demand curve to the right? A consensus of economists accept that this is within any government's capability. Second, given that aggregate demand increases can be engineered by governments, what is the shape of the aggregate supply curve? In the classical world it is vertical, and in the new classical world there is only a short-run positive slope if agents suffer expectational errors. In both cases the long-run impact on output and employment is neutral. For Keynesians, where there exists substantial spare capacity and involuntary unemployment, the aggregate supply curve has a positive slope which can be exploited by demand management to produce a lasting increase in output and employment. Thus the shape of the aggregate supply curve is crucial in modern macroeconomic debates. It is hardly surprising that the supply side of the macroeconomy is now receiving the attention it deserves from economic theorists.

In this chapter we have sought to explain the reasons for the revival of classical macroeconomics. This revival has been particularly influential on policymakers in the UK since 1979. Modern monetarist analysis supports the case for less active government interference in the economy in the macroeconomic sphere. At the microeconomic level, policies which unleash free market forces from artificial impediments are advocated.

Keynesians, especially radical Keynesians, see these developments as a step backwards. To those who see the inherent inflationary bias in capitalist market systems as providing the greatest challenge to the future health of such economies, more enlightened forms of intervention in the labour market are required. Certainly the idea that all that is required for a healthy macroeconomy is some strict adherence to a monetary growth rate rule plus microeconomic policies to restore incentives is rejected by non-monetarists.

The debates of the 1980s bear an uncanny resemblance to those between Keynes and his critics in the 1930s. This is because the central issue then and now is the ability of an unhindered market mechanism to generate a fully-employed growing economy without inflationary consequences. Monetarists possess faith in the power of market forces to achieve this desirable goal. Keynesians remain pessimistic and look towards improving government performance in correcting macroeconomic market failures.

Chapter 4

MANAGING A DISINTEGRATING WORLD ECONOMY

Richard Bailey

Introduction

In this chapter the theme of planning and markets is addressed somewhat obliquely and it is, therefore, necessary to make some initial comments on the approach adopted.

The central issue concerns the operation and maintenance of structures which facilitate processes of economic transactions on an international scale. It is argued below that in the context of the inter-state system which has emerged in the last 300 years, the economists' distinction between free market relations (no central intervention) and structured, administered or managed transactions is not practically or politically meaningful. Given a world consisting of nation-states, any sustainable framework of economic relationships will be a messy combination of market structures, administered rules and interventionist discretion. The issue of a sustainable system resolves into questions of achieving a balance between transactor integration through market processes and the economic autonomy of the nation-state. Within this broad framework of analysis, the specific issues of managed versus free trade, floating versus fixed exchange rates, and integrated versus isolated capital markets will be considered as contributing towards solutions to the general problem of sustaining a network of international transactions.

World economy: some preliminary ideas

The terms 'world economy' and 'international economy' are

frequently used interchangeably, but rarely are attempts made to define them. Here, the focus will be on the concept of an 'international market economy' (IME), broadly conceived of as a structure wherein the the principal intermediator between transactors of differing nationalities is the market. Historically, the emergence of an IME has been placed variously at the beginning of the seventeenth century and the second quarter of the nineteenth century. Writers in the Marxist-inspired world-system tradition use the term to describe the establishment and spread of capitalist relations emanating from north-west Europe in the sixteenth and seventeenth centuries (Wallerstein 1979). Others, particularly those in the liberal tradition, are more inclined to identify it with the establishment of multi-lateral trading relationships which emerged in the first half of the nineteenth century, this phenomenon being linked with the productivity leap in manufacturing characterised as the Industrial Revolution (Ashworth 1952; Kenwood and Lockheed 1982). The defining feature of this latter position would normally be expressed in terms of the expansion of multilateral transactions across political boundaries, the resulting matrix of economic relationships operating over a territory in which there was no single public authority or government. There remains, however, some dissatisfaction with this overly literal interpretation of international economy; William Ashworth asserts that the concept implies matters which are 'common to many nations', and views the creation of a world economy as characterising a 'growing similarity of organisation, thought and institutions' (Ashworth 1952: 5).

Ashworth's comment suggests that the establishment of an international market cannot be simply described in terms of exchange relations, but rather that such a system entails an over-arching cultural consensus to which participating countries subscribe. This important point may be explored more fully by a consideration of the role of the nation-state: market transactions are normally identified with individuals and corporate entities, while the nation-state represents a community of transactors defined primarily by geographical boundaries. In this context the nation-state presents a particularly awkward problem for market theorists. In market theory there is no logical reason why the nationality of a transactor should be considered as a relevant dimension in the analysis and, as Haberler rather testily observes, the contrast between the comparative homogeneity of the economic system of an individual country and its isolation or insulation from the economic systems of other countries is 'an effect rather than a cause of the attitudes of statesmen to the distinction between their own country and the outside world' (Haberler 1936: 7).

In essence, writers within the neoclassical tradition present an analysis of international market relations in which the political dimension of economic activity does not exist. This is facilitated by an unspecified assumption, namely, that the inherent logic of the analysis would produce a spontaneous generation of an international order, facilitating mutual, market co-ordinated, co-operation. This neglects the lessons of history, failing to appreciate that with the decline of the idea of universal empire and the emergence of the concept of the nation-state, the principle of national sovereignty has become firmly embedded in international law and international consciousness. This ideological framework provides the basis for the state to mediate in all relationships (economic or otherwise) between nationals and foreigners. One, at least, of the leading neoclassical theorists has been willing to address this problem directly. Lionel Robbins, having described the power, elegance and purity of the theoretically articulated IME observes: 'Unfortunately it involved an assumption that no event in previous history had made at all plausible: namely the assumption that, left to themselves, the various national authorities would spontaneously abstain from interference' (Robbins L. 1976: 156).

A central problem then of sustaining an open market economy operating over a territory in which there is no single public authority is how both to accommodate and to restrain these aspirations for national autonomy. The existence of an economic environment which allows a pattern of specialisation and division of labour according to the principle of comparative advantage implies the existence of a consensual value system or shared perceptions. This limits the scope for the nation-state to mediate in international transactions, thus preventing the emergence of restrictions, bilateral accords or negotiated exchange, which would inhibit the working of market forces. By definition then, state membership of the international market system involves acceptance of some rules of conduct which restrict the state's freedom of action in the sphere of international economic relations. It is in this context that Ashworth's comments appear most germane.

These ideas may be extended further by recourse to the analogy of the national market. Underlying the mechanisms of a market economy is a voluntary rule-based order, which provides a framework for free exchange between economic agents. In the case of the national market, this social and political framework is guaranteed by the state through its monopoly of coercive power. This power is ultimately dependent upon a consensual value system, which provides the legitimacy for state action. The role of the state in this context has two dimensions. First, there is the provision of the public goods necessary to reduce the level of uncertainty, which reduces transaction costs and provides the conditions necessary for the spread of specialisation and exchange (North 1979). Such public goods take various forms, ranging from the maintenance of a legal framework for enforcing contracts and protecting property rights and the provision of a common currency with a stable value, to the enforcement of a system of weights and measures. Secondly, the state needs to concern itself with economic outcomes, i.e. the consequences in terms of economic security and distribution of rewards arising from the working of the system. This dimension has been described most succinctly by Schotter: 'For an economic system to survive, the outcome that it defines must be viewed as fair or justifiable by most of the agents in society' (Schotter 1985: 126). To view the outcomes as unfair leads to a questioning of the legitimacy of the system and, as the state organs are viewed as underpinning the system, of the legitimacy of state organisation also. The two roles become interconnected, in that the state requires legitimacy to exercise the coercive power which is the ultimate guarantor of the framework for market activity. There are two ways in which the state might respond to this challenge. First, it might use its powers to persuade the population of the justness of the outcomes of the system. Secondly, it can intervene to modify rules, thus altering the outcomes through redistributive policies.

The problems of sustaining an international market economy are analogous to those described above. However, in this case there is one serious difference. In the international economy there is no overarching state organisation to provide and enforce a set of common rules. The problems of international system stability may be resolved into three areas of investigation: the political dimension, crucially concerned with the provision and maintenance of the public foundations of the system; the theoretical dimension, associated with the tendency of the system to produce even or uneven development of the constituent parts (more especially the nation-states); and the practical dimension relating to the processes of adjustment, their costs and the degree of resource flexibility.

The question of public foundations itself divides into two elements. What inducements will be effective in persuading countries to comply with the rules of the game and through what agency are such inducements to be provided? These questions have been addressed by Kindleberger, whose thesis may be conveniently described as the 'International Underwriter'. Drawing on the historical experience of the nineteenth-century international economy, and Britain's role within that system, Kindleberger concludes that 'for the world economy to be stabilised there has to be a stabiliser, one stabiliser' (Kindleberger 1973: 305). In his terminology, the maintenance of a liberal international order requires that one country stabilises or underwrites the system by providing others with:

1. Easy access to long-term finance.
2. Rapid and certain access to short-term finance.
3. Free access to commodity markets so that debt repayments and interest can be met by commodity exports.

The above list does not represent an exhaustive account of the features necessary to sustain an open trading system; in particular, it neglects the dimension of security which is a fundamental element of the public foundations for both national and international markets. However, the technical facilities listed above serve to reduce substantially the potential adjustment costs which might be associated with participation in the international market and therefore enhance the positive net gains attainable from participation in an international division of labour.

Kindleberger employs this analysis to explain the break-down of the liberal international order in the inter-war period. He persuasively argues that the decline in system stability in this period arose because of the inability of Britain to continue underwriting the system and the unwillingness of the USA to take on this role. Subsequent development of Kindleberger's thesis, and the application of these ideas to the experience of the post-1945 world order, has produced a complex and subtle theory of hegemonic leadership. However, this will be explored later in the context of post-war system management, and it is important at this stage to relate the 'public foundations' dimension to the connected problems of development and adjustment (Kindleberger 1986).

Market development and system stability

At a fundamental level, the dynamics of development within an international market economy are crucially relevant to the problem of system stability. As I have argued previously, to expand market relations on a transnational scale requires the instrumentality, if not the institutional structures, of super-national power. Such structures (the public foundations) require both a measure of common ideology and the leadership of a dominant nation-state. This 'Gramscian Hegemony', whereby the dominant country generates a framework for co-operative action, is fragile and vulnerable to counter forces which can effectively mobilise antagonistic nationalism in circumstances where instability or other pressures of the market system act adversely on national groups.

The theoretical analysis of the market and the dynamic processes of development being both complex and controversial, I offer a sketched outline of some of the alternative ideas and arguments. The neoclassical position is clear, elegant, but unhelpful. The general equilibrium model as developed by Samuelson and others out of the work of Heckscher and Ohlin, concludes that the extension of specialisation and division of labour to the international economy on the basis of relative cost advantage offers potential gains for all participants. Such gains are once and for all static benefits which, by allowing a more efficient allocation of world productive resources, result in an overall increase in the world product when compared to a pre-trade situation. The analysis of the distribution of these gains is couched in terms of factor price adjustment, the conclusion being that international trade will tend to eliminate factor price differentials that might exist between countries. In addition, the Stolper–Samuelson theory offers some insights regarding the impact on domestic income distribution, concluding that the incomes of the owners of factors used intensively in the production of export commodities will increase absolutely and relatively with the opening of trade. The strength of the general equilibrium trade model is that it takes into account both demand and supply patterns at the same time. Its weaknesses, for policy purposes at least, lie in the large number of highly restrictive assumptions which have to be made in order to deduce the conclusions (see Heller 1973: 125). In particular, it is difficult to incorporate the dynamics of technical change within the structure of the model.

Neoclassical advocates of free trade are willing to recognise that the static benefits are but a small part of the case for linking trade, growth and development. Marshall, the great synthesiser and consolidator of the neoclassical world view, in his *Fiscal Theory of International Trade*, adumbrated the benefits of free trade, not so much in terms of the traditional emphasis on allocative efficiency, but in terms of technological progress leading to monopoly gains progressively eliminated by rapid diffusion of knowledge. This sentiment is echoed by more recent writers in this tradition, such as Johnson, who summarises the essential optimism regarding the diffusion of knowledge thus:

> The mechanism does, however, ensure that, albeit with a possibly very long lag, knowledge created by investment of capital in research and development does become available everywhere and production gravitates towards countries with relatively low labour-time costs, thereby tending to diffuse the process of economic development throughout the world economy (Johnson 1968: 37).

There are, however, major problems associated with the trade-growth nexus and the question of even development, in particular the economic consequences of differential access to knowledge. Some of the most interesting work, and also most disturbing for the ruling neoclassical paradigm, concerns the production and pricing of the commodity knowledge. Arrow (1969), amongst others, has stressed that knowledge is characterised by significant production externalities and is subject to scale economies. What is clear, from empirical investigations of the processes of production and diffusion of knowledge, is that the neoclassical postulate of a symmetrical distribution of knowledge between transactors is extensively violated (O'Brien R. C. 1983). When allowance is made for the persistence of monopoly rents arising from technical innovation, the distribution of gains from specialisation and the spread of the benefits of technical advance becomes problematical. A number of efforts have been made to incorporate technological change and product cycle theories within a general equilibrium market framework. Krugman (1979), in a stylised and highly simplified model, has shown that, with capital mobility and labour immobility and a world divided between innovation and imitation countries, the model yields wage inequality and an associated tendency towards a persistent inequality in the distribution of world incomes.

Much of the work critical of the development optimism of the free trade school may be seen as part of a broad structuralist tradition. This approach, associated particularly with the names of Prebisch, Singer, Myrdal and Lewis, has focused principally on the mechanisms determining the terms of trade between primary and manufactured goods. The debate concerning the validity of this work has been long and somewhat inconclusive (Spraos 1983). Some of the more interesting developments, however, centre on the factors which determine the double factoral terms of trade. Lewis, in an important contribution to this debate, has argued that the relative prices of traded goods are determined from the supply side in terms of an untraded good, food, and that the terms of trade between two regions are therefore determined by the relative labour productivities in food production in them. Differences in labour productivity in the two countries result in a divergence of the double factoral terms of trade from unity. Thus trade generates a structure of unequal exchange or, to put it in another way, exchange values will reflect unequal rewards for labour (Lewis 1969). Other writers, particularly those in Marxist tradition, have developed similar arguments and conclude that the dominant feature of a world market economy is uneven rather than even development, described in terms of 'imperialism of free trade'. If the latter is the case, it clearly presents some considerable difficulty with regard to system stability; while the market mechanism may generate substantial gains in productive capacity, any tendency for these gains to be distributed unequally between the participating states is likely to produce serious problems of legitimacy for the system as a whole.

It might seem that these issues could be resolved by examining development experience in a historical context. Unfortunately, efforts which have been made in this area have produced little in the way of clear or unambiguous evidence for either position. In terms of inter-country comparisons of GNP, most estimates suggest that there has been a marked increase in inequality since the late eighteenth century. Bairoch estimates that, prior to 1800, national disparity in income levels was extremely narrow – probably of the order of 1.0 to 1.6 – whereas in 1977 he estimates the gap between the designated 'developed countries' and less developed countries to be in the order of 1.0 to 29 (Bairoch and Levy Leboyer 1981). When disparities between the developed countries are considered, in particular the ten countries which began development prior to 1860, there would appear to be a process of equalisation. This equalisation process came in two periods, 1860–1913 and 1945–77, both of which are associated with the relative decline of the lead country, the UK in the early period and the USA in the later period (Bairoch and Levy-Leboyer 1981: 9–12). A common explanation of the post-war experience is couched in terms of technical diffusion, income equalisation and ultimate slow-down in the rate of aggregate growth (Cornwall 1977).

A crude aggregative picture of past, present and future trends in per capita income growth is presented in Table 4.1 with the exception of low income Africa, this suggests some narrowing of

Table 4.1   Average annual percentage growth in per capita income

Country Group	1965–73	1973–80	1980–85	1985–90* High	Low
Industrial Countries	3.7	2.1	1.7	3.8	2.0
Developing Countries	4.0	3.2	1.3	3.9	2.0
Low-income Countries†	3.0	2.7	5.2	4.4	2.5
Africa	1.2	−0.1	−2.0	0.8	0.0

* World Bank Projections
† Countries with per capita incomes less than 400$ in 1984
Source: World Development Report 1986. World Bank O.U.P 1986
Table 3.2 p. 45

the income gap between rich and poor. However, such inter-group comparisons mask significant changes in the relative position of individual countries (see Berry A. *et al.* 1983).

Changes in the relative economic position of individual countries introduce an important dimension of international policy. The distinction between relative and absolute gains is essential to understanding inter-state behaviour. However, it represents a dimension which is insufficiently analysed in neoclassical economics, where emphasis is placed on absolute welfare gains or alternatively absolute welfare losses whenever there is a departure from the optimum free market conditions. The problems associated with relative gains are neatly side-stepped by the ubiquitous use of the Pareto Efficiency Principle and the assumed absence of inter-personal comparisons of utility. This allows the assertion of an unambiguous improvement in global welfare provided that the gains for one group are achievable without a deterioration in the absolute position of any other group. Part cause and part consequence of this emphasis on absolute gain is the inability of neoclassical economics to handle the concept of power, a concept which is central to the behaviour of the nation-state. While power is a highly complex concept, it is always relative. If one actor or state achieves an increase in power capability, this necessarily implies a loss of power on the part of another actor or state. Thus politics, seen in terms of power conflict, may be represented as a zero sum game while economics, in contrast, stresses absolute gain and may be represented as a positive sum activity. Unfortunately, given the role of the nation-state within the IME, the two cannot be separated. Granting the not unreasonable assumption that power capability is at least partly a function of economic resources, the distribution of gains from the IME is of crucial concern to the participating states. In this context, the study of international political economy requires a recognition of the potential mercantilist pre-disposition which underlies state behaviour in the inter-national economic sphere (Gilpin 1975; Robinson J. 1977).

This excursion into the question of relative gains serves to focus on the idea that the state can perceive gains and losses incurred in terms of national advantage, of benefits which accrue to a national entity, rather than rewards derived by factor owners from participating in international market exchange. This begs some fundamental issues regarding the nature of the state as a partici-pant in economic transactions. It implies that state actions are determined on the basis of some preference map defined by a mysterious public interest (see Ch. 1). The question of the processes by which a perceived national interest is formed is clearly important, insofar as international economic policy actions are predicated upon such perceptions. Whilst there is a growing body of literature from both economists and political scientists, exploring the underlying forces which shape governments' inter-national economic policies, there is a signal lack of plausible hypotheses which offer a general framework of explanation (Katzenstein 1978).

Returning to the more narrowly economic dimension, it is important to focus on the concept of the balance of payments and the associated monetary and exchange rate framework. This may be represented as a mechanism which, by linking unitary national economies, converts the national into the international market. The balance of payments is pivotal. Historically, it has provided the central focus and trigger for national interventions; this remains true in spite of the work of Hume and others, who effectively criticised the mercantilist idea of policy interventions to secure a balance of payments surplus. In current circumstances, the idea of balance of payments equilibrium as a long-term or medium-term objective has to be set alongside the possibility of structural disequilibria and the associated problems of adjustment. This raises questions which span the issues of constrained or uneven development and adjustment costs. In the context of developing country experience, Linder (1961) pointed out that the necessity to maintain external equilibrium may oblige a country to operate its domestic economy at less than full potential. More recently, writers such as Thirlwall and Kaldor have extended this model to explain the recent economic performance of some developed countries. The combination of changing comparative advantage and struc-tural rigidities leads in some countries to displacement compe-tition, slow productivity growth and structural deficits, serving to constrain economic growth (Thirlwall 1979). This can be further generalised into ideas of virtuous and vicious circles of causation, the former represented by high-growth, payments-surplus economies, the latter being characterised as low-growth, chronic-deficit economies (see Skott 1985).

While arguments concerning structural deficits are frequently dismissed in terms of government-induced inflexibilities in individual national economies (Beenstock 1982), and some variant of the speci-flow mechanism is widely accepted by most economists as a starting point for the analysis of balance of payments adjustment, there is at least a measure of agreement that matters cannot be so easily resolved. There is a need to examine the processes of adjustment and the way in which the associated costs are distributed both within and between countries. Scitovsky has drawn attention to the difficulties of solving the problem at an international level by contrasting it to the ease and smoothness with which it is resolved between regions of the same country. This comparison is used to highlight the importance of the monetary framework in facilitating the adjustment process (Scitovsky 1967). It is worth noting, however, that adjustments at regional level can be just as painful, in terms of structural umemployment, as adjustment at the international level, a crucial difference being that compensatory policies of resource transfer from deficit to surplus regions are both more acceptable and more feasible in a national rather than an international context. Whilst in an absolute sense the costs of adjustment will invariably be borne by the deficit country, the extent and form of this burden will depend in part on the action and reaction of surplus countries. In this context, the rules which govern international economic behaviour are of vital importance in determining the legitimacy of the system. This is a difficult problem in that, given that there is scope for a variety of national responses to external disequilibria, individual countries will seek to adopt policies which both minimise the impact on domestic objectives and, at the same time, limit, where possible, the costs associated with the adjustment process. The latter suggests efforts to transfer as much as possible of the adjustment costs on to someone else. The forms and rules of international payments mechanism need to be carefully examined in terms of the scope and opportunities they provide to minimise, delay or transfer these adjustment costs.

The first section of this chapter represents an attempt to outline the main issues and problems relevant to the establishment and maintenance of an open multilateral trading system, here designated as an IME. It is worth emphasising that both the preceding and succeeding analysis is predicated on the assumption that market structures represent an essential and vital feature of an effective international economic system. The shortcomings of alternative control and co-ordinating mechanisms designed to replace the market have been effectively and comprehensively criticised elsewhere (see Ch. 1 and 2). In the international context, the experience of the 1930s serves to highlight the potential efficiency loss associated with movement towards a system characterised by discrete bilateral transactions between government agencies (Hirschman 1945).

The thesis advanced here is that markets are not spontaneous organisms, a human propensity 'to truck, barter and exchange' (*pace* Adam Smith) not being a sufficient condition for the emergence and continuation of market structures. Such structures depend for their existence and functioning upon a complex of institutional and social constraints which serve to maintain the political legitimacy of the market. These underpinnings are permanently vulnerable to cognitions regarding market processes and outcomes. Consequently and paradoxically, the maintenance of the market may require management and intervention as a means of modifying processes and outcomes to ensure political acceptability. The following section explores and illustrates this position with reference to the experience and the problems associated with efforts to establish an IME in the years since the end of the Second World War. In particular, the questions to be addressed are, in what form and by what means have public foundations been provided for the system? To what extent have such public foundations provided acceptable mechanisms for coping with the problem of adjustment? And, finally, what means are available for dealing with the stresses induced by perceptions of uneven development?

A consciously designed system (1944–71)

The background to the actions which led to the establishment of a post-war IME lies in the experience of the 1930s. The form of the protracted negotiations initiated by the United States, which led to the agreed proposals placed before the Bretton Woods Conference of 1945, was crucially influenced by the perceived consequences arising from the international autarky of the inter-war period. This resulted in a firm commitment on the part of the US administration to the post-war establishment of a fixed exchange rate system and a liberalisation of trading relationships. Additionally, discussion was informed, on the British side, by a conviction that a consciously managed system was a necessary requirement for dealing with the adjustment problems which had undermined the international system in the 1920s (de Cecco 1979). The central problem was to devise a system of exchange rate convertibility which would reconcile the conflicting problems of external adjustment and domestic stability, dirigisme at home and *laissez-faire* abroad.

The British proposals centred upon Keynes' plan for an international clearing union. This represented a radical solution to the problems of adjustment and international liquidity, involving an institutional structure with substantial supernational powers to influence the pattern of exchange rates, and an international clearing mechanism which would encourage countries in surplus, as well as those in deficit, to make the required adjustments. The American position, based upon the White plan, was more modest, envisaging a pooling rather than a creation of international liquidity and, as a consequence, offered much more limited support for countries whose exchange rate came under pressure. Both plans sought to create the conditions under which exchange restrictions on current account could be eliminated and, by the establishment of a multilateral payments network, pave the way for a rapid return to liberal trade policies. Both plans, in their original form, required continuing controls on capital account transactions, both authors being convinced that it was the destabilising influence of short-term capital flows which had destroyed the inter-war exchange standard (Gardiner 1969). In the event, what emerged in 1944 was the International Monetary Fund (IMF) and its sister institution, the International Bank for Reconstruction and Development (IBRD). While these bore a superficial resemblance to the institutions envisaged in the White plan, any commitment to a structure of formal co-operative inter-governmental controls had been eliminated. The articles of association of the IMF allowed member countries limited borrowing facilities to finance short-term current account deficits and provided for limited exchange rate flexibility under conditions of 'fundamental disequilibrium'. In addition, there was a 'scarce currency clause' which allowed countries to impose trade restrictions against a persistent surplus country whose currency had been declared 'scarce' by the fund. There was no mandatory requirement to maintain controls on the capital account, nor was there any requirement for policies to be co-ordinated. In hindsight, the major weakness of the International Monetary System, established under the auspices of the IMF, was that it failed to provide any clear-cut mechanism for dealing with balance of payments adjustment in a world of full employment and expanding economies (Scammel 1980).

In spite of the shortcomings of this exercise in 'a consciously designed International Monetary System' (Williamson J. 1977: 1), the immediate post-war years represented an era of remarkable achievement in international co-operation. However, the gradual establishment of a multilateral trade and payments system between 1948 and 1960 can hardly be attributed to the influence of the IMF and the World Bank; neither institution played any significant role in the reconstruction of Europe which was a vital first ingredient in the movement towards an IME. This required the American initiative of the Marshall Plan, to provide the 'selective incentives' (bribes) necessary to move Europe decisively towards multilateralism. The Marshall Plan was simultaneously an effort to finance the US export surplus, a means of strengthening European resolve to remove trade restrictions, and a policy for ensuring that it remained firmly within the capitalist camp. Under the plan, $17 billion of aid flowed into Europe between 1948 and 1952. Under the prodding of the United States, a Convention for European Economic Co-operation met in April 1948 and proceeded to establish the Organisation for European Economic Co-operation (OEEC) of sixteen (later eighteen) countries, for the purpose of distributing the American funds. In addition, the organisation also provided a forum for policy co-ordination and a means of facilitating trade and payment flows amongst member countries.

The rearming of western Europe, consequent upon the formation of NATO in 1949, provided a means of extending American aid to Europe following the end of the Marshall Plan. The continued high level of assistance was made acceptable to the American taxpayers by the security fears engendered by the Cold War. The rearmament programme had the effect of making the Keynesian policies of deficit finance more acceptable to the conservative interests in American society, thus easing the problems of transition to a peace economy by facilitating maintenance of a high level of domestic demand. This long transition period stands in sharp contrast to the international management of adjustment from war to peace in the ten years following the First World War. There is no argument concerning the central role of the USA in this process; however, it was facilitated by the co-operation of a European political and administrative elite who viewed co-ordinated management as the best means of achieving the agreed goal of a liberal international order (Bowie 1978).

The two prongs of the American drive towards a liberal world economy consisted of the establishment of free currency convertibility and the abandonment/reduction of quantitative and tariff restrictions on merchandised trade. The latter was dependent on the achievement of the former and, aside from the establishment of a set of trading rules embodied in the General Agreement on Tariffs and Trade (GATT), the freeing of trade had to await the establishment of full currency convertibility. Such a system was effectively achieved by 1960; this involved significant currency realignments within Europe, the effect of which was to emerge in the 1960s as an over-valuation of the dollar. As countries progressively removed restrictions on current account transactions, they also gradually relaxed controls on capital and the international movement of bank funds. These latter moves sharply enhanced the degree of interdependence between the capital and money markets of the industrialised countries, thus making the problems of domestic monetary management more complex. The freeing of capital markets, together with the simultaneous development of the Euro-dollar Market, was rapidly to impose strains on the adjustment mechanisms of the international monetary system.

The restoration of currency convertibility was the culmination of sustained American support for the European economies, and it may be represented as the outcome of hegemonic leadership in both the economic and military spheres. The heavy overseas expenditure of the USA during the 1950s had sustained a high level of international aggregate demand, and continued growth of the world economy in the 1960s required a parallel facilitating increase in international liquidity. As the Bretton Woods system did not provide explicit mechanisms for such an increase, the responsibility devolved on the USA as the leading power. The dominant position of the US in the immediate post-war years led to the establishment of the dollar as the major trading currency and the principal reserve asset, which meant that America could expand or contract world liquidity through a variation in the volume of overseas dollar liabilities. The critical shortage of international liquidity in the 1950s was eased in this way: of the $8 billion increase in world reserves between 1949 and 1959, no less than $7 billion were accounted for by an increase in dollar liabilities to foreign monetary authorities (Solomon 1977: 32).

The problem of international liquidity, and its provision by means of reserve currency expansion, was exacerbated by other weaknesses in the international monetary rules, in particular the failure to provide a means of managing and controlling capital flows and the lack of any clear criteria for instituting balance of payments and adjustments. The strains associated with the above began to show in the form of a confidence problem which emerged in response to American payment deficits in the early 1960s. Throughout this decade, the inherent instability of the system was reflected in a succession of financial crises, each of these events triggering a new set of *ad hoc* responses and a succession of temporary expedients, which frequently bypassed the IMF and served simply to paper over the cracks, dealing with the symptoms rather than the disease.

The American response to these problems, which recognised the growing power of the European Community, was the idea of 'Atlantic Partnership'. The mechanisms for achieving co-ordinated management and a shared foreign aid burden was to be the Organisation of Economic Co-operation and Development (OECD). The transformation of the OEEC into the OECD meant the incorporation of the US and Canada as full members and an amendment to the Charter, which was finally agreed in 1961. In addition, the military aspects of the Atlantic Alliance were represented by the evolving structure of the North Atlantic Treaty Organisation (NATO), the American goal being to gain an increase in European spending on conventional forces and a reduction in the US foreign exchange costs. The Atlantic Alliance, and the organisations which supported it, represented an effort by the US to persuade Europe to share the burdens of international leadership. The problem with this initiative, at least from the European point of view, was that the US appeared reluctant to carry the burdens of leadership while determined to retain the benefits. This was reflected in US determination to maintain ultimate control over nuclear weapons in Europe, and in their reluctance to recognise that domestic economic policy had to take account of the wider interests of the international community. This is illustrated by what is known as the '$n - 1$ problem'; in a system with n countries and n exchange rates, there exist only $n - 1$ degrees of freedom. In this environment, US monetary policy had to respond to the consistency requirements if balance of payments conflict was to be avoided. As a variety of critics have noted, the unstated premise of the American initiative was to share the burdens but not the benefits of hegemony within the Alliance; it was to be 'a partnership without equality' (Calleo and Rowland 1973). In spite of these problems, the 1960s are represented as a period of successful developments of the world economy. World trade grew at the historically exceptional rate of an average 7 per cent per annum. The successful completion of the 'Kennedy Round' of tariff negotiations (1967) was a major achievement of the international trade institution (GATT), and brought the average tariff on industrial products down to 10 per cent (Greenaway 1983). Finally, there was a progressive incorporation of the newly independent Third World countries into the IME, and even the East European communist countries, although they remained outside the formal structures of the American-dominated system, increasingly participated in international transactions by means of counter-purchase and barter arrangements (OECD 1983). Strains and tensions emanated primarily from within the small group of lead economies. As may be seen from Tables 4.2 and 4.3 there was considerable divergence in economic performance between these five economies. On the balance of payments, Britain and France experienced recurring deficits while Germany and Japan began to run persistent surpluses; at the same time, the USA's current account surplus, a feature of the 1950s, progessively deteriorated into deficit. National growth rates exhibited similar divergent features, with the UK and the USA experiencing markedly poorer growth performances than the other countries.

It was this feature of divergent economic performance, in particular the lack of a satisfactory mechanism for currency realign-

Table 4.2   Surpluses on current transactions as a percentage of GDP

	1965	1966	1967	1968	1969	1970	1971
USA	0.8	0.4	0.3	0.1	0.0	0.2	−0.1
Japan	1.1	1.3	0.0	0.8	1.3	1.0	2.5
Germany	−1.3	0.2	2.2	2.3	1.4	0.6	0.4
France	0.8	0.1	0.0	−0.5	−1.1	0.1	0.6
UK	−0.4	0.1	−0.9	−0.8	0.6	1.2	1.7

Source: OECD *Economic Outlook* Dec. 1985, No. 38, Table R5

Table 4.3   Growth of real GDP – percentage changes

	1965	1966	1967	1968	1969	1970	1971
USA	6.2	5.8	2.8	4.0	2.9	−0.2	3.1
Japan	5.1	10.6	10.8	12.8	12.3	9.8	4.6
Germany	5.5	2.9	−0.1	5.6	7.5	5.1	2.9
France	4.8	5.2	4.7	4.3	7.0	5.7	5.9
UK	2.3	1.9	2.7	4.1	1.3	2.3	2.7

Source: OECD *Economic Outlook*, Dec. 1985, No. 38, Table R1

ments, which Williamson singles out as the prime cause of the system break-down which came in August 1971: 'the adjustable peg broke down because it did not provide a viable crisis free method of changing exchange rates in an era of capital mobility' (Williamson J. 1977: 51).

During this time, both the liquidity and adjustment problems had been clearly identified and comprehensively explored (Triffin 1960; OECD 1966) but, with the exception of the agreement to create Special Drawing Rights (SDRs) in 1969, no progress was made towards fundamental reform. The history of this period of monetary experience has been extensively documented and the technical issues carefully analysed (Tew 1985; Williamson J. 1977). However, it is important to emphasise the underlying political stance which made solutions so difficult to attain. This derived from the United States' 'basic urge to dominate the monetary system so that external constraints may not limit the American political economy's expansive impulses, at home or abroad' (Calleo and Strange 1984: 114). By the end of the decade, the other major OECD countries were no longer willing to accept or support this view of international monetary management.

An unmanaged system? Issues and problems of the 1970s

The problems of the 1960s have been viewed essentially in terms of the international monetary framework, the systemic structures which made up the fixed exchange rate regime, and which were considered to provide the required pre-conditions necessary to underpin the movement towards unregulated multilateral trans-actions of IME. The issues and the arguments centred on the concerns of the rich, developed countries regarding the control and management of international liquidity, the associated problems of international inflationary pressure, and the mechanisms of exchange rate realignment necessary to cope with differential national inflation and growth rates. The negotiations over system reform, which followed the Smithsonian Agreement of December 1971, while still centring on these issues, were obliged, perhaps for the first time, to recognise the wider dimensions of reform, as articulated by the evolving institutions of Third World opinion (see below).

The emergence of a major grouping of politically independent developing countries determined to participate in the decision-making processes of the IME is a key phenomenon of the 1970s. The post-war period has seen the national membership of the UN grow from fifty-one initial signatories in 1945 to a current membership of 154. Almost the whole of this increase represents newly independent ex-colonial territories of the European powers. To many of these countries, the experience of participation in the post-war IME had led them to conclude that the system was designed and managed in such a way as to serve the narrow interests of the rich, industrialised countries. In institutional terms, the failure to ratify the Havana Charter and establish the International Trade Organisation (ITO), meant that the framework for governing international trade rested upon the General Agreement for Tariffs and Trade (GATT). This organisation, while effectiveiy extending the scope for non-discriminating trade in manufactures, failed signally to further Third World interests in primary product trade. The forum for the discussion of commodity trade was an Interim Co-ordination Committee on International Commodity Agreements (ICCICA) which survived, without achieving any constructive agreement, until it was incorporated into the United Nations Conference on Trade and Development (UNCTAD) in 1965. In those areas of manufactured trade of most interest to the developing countries, negotiations under the auspices of GATT served to restrict rather than to enhance trading opportunities, as in the case of the Multi Fibre Arrangement (MFA). Here, successive re-negotiations have produced a complex network of restrictions on all aspects of trade in textile manufactures, which represent the staple manufacturing exports of many Third World countries.

The developing countries' response to what they conceived of as the inequities of the system was the establishment of a permanent forum to debate the full range of economic issues, money, trade and technology, which were of central concern to these countries. UNCTAD, with a built-in voting majority for developing countries, provided the ideal forum. In its first Secretary-General, Raul Prebisch, it had an economist of international stature, whose drive and commitment to the concerns of the Third World resulted in the rapid establishment of a highly expert and effective permanent secretariat. While UNCTAD provided a 'voice' for Third World demands for economic justice, and a valuable research organisation for monitoring trends and tendencies of the international economy, it lacked the powers necessary to convert ideas into actions (Rothstein 1976). The principal outcome of UNCTAD activities was to place new and radical items on the agenda of world economic reform, culminating in the Declaration on the Establishment of a New International Economic Order, passed by the United Nations on 1 May 1974.

The attempts to achieve system reform had to encompass both the monetary problems of adjustment, liquidity and confidence, which had precipitated the crisis of 1971, and also the, perhaps more intractable, problems associated with Third World perceptions of uneven development. The response of the industrial countries was to try as far as possible to separate these issues and avoid the Third World bargaining ploy of 'issue linkage'. The main vehicle for reform was to be the Committee of Twenty (C20), which was to be charged with the task of formulating a new set of rules to govern the international monetary system. The composition of this committee represented a recognition of the institutional importance of UNCTAD, and of the changing balance of power in the world economy. Its make-up also implied an awareness by the USA that, on key issues, it could no longer automatically rely on OECD support (Williamson J. 1977). The work of C20 centred on monetary issues and the almost universal desire to establish a new system of fixed exchange rates (Williamson J. 1985). Both policymakers and expert advisers viewed system problems principally in terms of international monetary disorder. Solutions were formulated in terms of devising a systemic answer to the liquidity/ confidence problem, identified a decade earlier by Triffin, together with the development of mechanisms which would facilitate symmetrical processes for currency realignment. Given this outlook, why did the world end up with a set of monetary arrangements characterised by the free floating of major currencies, together with some modest amendment of IMF functions, which Williamson dismissively describes as a 'non-system'? (Williamson J. 1977).

The answer to this question is instructive, in that it illustrates the range of factors and circumstances which impinge on policy decisions. A background to this was the growing body of academic opinion advocating freely floating exchange rates, most powerfully represented by Milton Friedman who recommended the move as part of a wider package of monetary responsibility (Friedman and Roosa 1967). In practical terms, world economic events between 1971–74 played an important part in convincing policymakers that a resumption of fixed rate parities, even if this incorporated improved mechanisms of realignment, was not a feasible solution in the light of the dramatic changes in relative prices and the burgeoning and uncontrollable Euro-currency markets. In the end, however, perhaps the most important factor, and that which produced the abandonment of the reform attempts enshrined in the 1976 Jamaica Agreement, was the failure to achieve the necessary agreement on 'monetary sovereignty'.

The problem of monetary sovereignty was the unresolved issue of the late 1960s. It arose from the features of the Bretton Woods system which enabled the USA to operate a domestic monetary policy unconstrained by considerations regarding its external position. This had led to a situation described as 'benign neglect', in which US trade competitors, most notably Europe, were obliged either to inflate their domestic economies or to revalue their currencies in the face of continuing US balance of payments deficits (Kraus 1970). In the event, the failure of the European negotiators in the C20 to persuade the US to accept a measure of international surveillance which would curtail domestic monetary sovereignty, forced them into the position of accepting floating as the lesser evil. As Williamson succinctly describes it: 'floating was seen as providing a release from those constraints that did not require others to accept additional constraints (asset settlement for the USA, limitation on the freedom of reserve composition by the rest of the world)' (Williamson J. 1985: 48).

Experience of the functioning of the modified IME in the decade since 1975 indicates that, while it has not provided permanent solutions to the inherent problems of system stability, it has not resulted in the precipitous decline into autarky that many commentators forecast. A comparison of output and trade indices for the period 1930–38 and 1973–82, two decades characterised by prolonged world depression, shows that in most respects the IME has functioned more effectively in the latter, when compared to the earlier period (see Table 4.4).

Unemployment and inflation experiences in the two periods also shows substantial divergence. Unemployment levels in the OECD have remained significantly below those attained in the inter-war years; however, the 1970s and 1980s have exhibited a continuously rising trend level, from an average of 2.5 per cent in 1973 to 8.5 per cent in 1985. Price experience is markedly different, the interwar years being characterised by falling prices while, from 1972–82, OECD countries exhibited variable inflationary experiences, with an average of 8.5 per cent per annum. This situation has been modified by a gradual decline to 5 per cent per annum in 1985 (OECD *Economic Outlook*, Dec. 1985).

The degree of policy failure in the 1970s bears no comparison with that which occurred in the 1930s, and institutional structures

Table 4.4   Output and trade indices (1930–38, 1973–82)

| | 1930s series (1929 = 100) | | | Post-1973 series (1973 = 100) | |
	16 industrial countries: combined GNP	World export volume		OECD combined GNP	World export volume
1930	94	93	1974	101	105
1931	89	86	1975	101	100
1932	83	73	1976	105	112
1933	84	75	1977	109	117
1934	89	78	1978	114	112
1935	94	82	1979	117	131
1936	102	86	1980	119	133
1937	109	97	1981	120	133
1938	110	91	1982	120	130

Source: CLARE Group, Trade policies: trends issues and influences. *Midland Bank Review*, 1983, Winter

have withstood, more or less successfully, the pressures for increased trade protection. It should be noted, however, that the apparently inexorable growth in surplus capacity and the increasingly under-utilised growth potential within the OECD represents a continuing threat to liberal commercial policies (Strange and Tooze 1981; Greenaway 1983; OECD 1985).

The system proved to be particularly flexible in responding to the oil price shock of 1973 and the associated imbalance in the structure of world payments. It enabled the world economy to avoid, in part at least, the deflationary impulse implied by the massive shift in income from low to high savers. The recycling process, which enabled the Newly Industrialising Countries to maintain high real growth rates through to 1980, was bought at the cost of a new dimension of international instability in the form of the debt crisis of the early 1980s. The important lesson of this experience is that, while the private capital market fulfilled a vital role in balance of payments and development financing, slotting into a gap between the short-term conditional lending of the IMF and the long-term project financing of the World Bank, there is a structural requirement for a 'lender of last resort'. The debt crisis of 1982–84 pinpointed the problem which is created by the absence of an institution which can provide and enforce a framework for co-ordinated decision making.

Returning to the exchange rate dimension, the operation of an international monetary framework within which most of the key currencies have floated against each other has produced a wealth of practical and theoretical insights, 'though only modest progress towards agreement on policy'. The current system has been characterised as 'a form of *laissez-faire* which not only allows the free play of the private market but also allows governments to conduct their policy as they choose, and intervene as they wish in the foreign exchange market' (Corden 1985: 138), a notable exception to this being those countries which joined the European Monetary System (EMS) in 1979. This currency bloc, which represents a strengthening and enlarging of the previous 'currency snake', has enabled member countries to avoid much of the short-term currency variability experienced by countries such as Britain and the United States. The longer-term objectives of internal stability and economic convergence, implied by the currency area policy, remain in the future, but current success has been sufficient to lead some writers to the view that the EMS might be a 'possible first step towards a new international order with reduced currency fluctuations' (Zis 1983).

The optimistic view of floating, that it would allow a measure of policy autonomy and that it would insulate the domestic economy from international monetary disturbance, has been extensively and effectively criticised in the light of recent experience (Dornbusch 1982; Buiter and Millar 1982). The move from fixed to flexible exchange rates has not removed the problem of interdependence or the potential for acute national interest conflicts. The fundamental asymmetry between large and small countries remains, as one writer comments: 'in the floating world dependence on the US dollar has even been strengthened rather than permitting more autonomy' (Wegner 1985: 132). Practical experience over the last twelve years has presented a picture of excessive short-run exchange rate volatility and serious currency misalignment. It is the latter, in particular the problems of persistent currency overvaluation, which are of direct concern with regard to stability of an open trading system. In 1985, Williamson calculated that the dollar was overvalued by 40 per cent. A sustained overvaluation of this magnitude will inevitably generate protectionist pressures from domestic producers, which an administration would find difficult to resist (Williamson J. 1985).

The recent experience of currency misalignment has produced a number of initiatives, most notably the Group of Five 'Plaza Pact' of September 1985, which seeks to develop a co-ordinated strategy towards exchange rate management amongst the OECD countries. Such actions might provide a favourable environment in which to re-activate discussions on currency system reform. United States policy would seem to be moving away from a belief in an unfettered foreign exchange market; the current administration is clearly willing to address the problems of co-ordinated international management which this implies (see the Economic Report of the President 1985).

While the framework of international monetary relations and its possible pathologies has been of dominating concern to the western economies, other concerns have frequently obtruded to complicate the issues. Most notable of these was the Third World demands for fundamental changes, not only in the monetary regimes, but also in the regimes of trade, aid and technology. The demand for a New International Economic Order (NIEO) has been alluded to earlier. It remained a live negotiating issue throughout the 1970s and into the early 1980s to become, at least temporarily, abandoned as a result of the intransigent attitude of the western powers exhibited at the Cancun summit of 1983. Despite the failure of the less developed countries to obtain anything but a small part of the objectives outlined in the NIEO, the demands remain, to represent a serious questioning of system outcomes. Confidence that the IME, as presently constituted, would produce symmetrical benefits for all participants has been effectively undermined. It may well be that failure to achieve desired advances resulted from the decline in the cohesion of the group of Third World countries, overlaid by the emergence of more pressing practical problems associated with the critical area of the debt of Newly Industrialised Countries, but there is no evidence that underlying attitudes and perceptions have changed.

The questioning of market outcomes by Third World countries may be represented as part of a larger 'crisis of confidence' which beset the system in the 1970s. This showed in a concern over ecological issues, population growth and resource depletion. Additionally, the rich countries exhibited increasing concern and uncertainty in the face of accelerating changes in the geographical pattern of world production and division of labour, the latter point arising from the increasing multi-nationality of production, the emergence of direct investment and the associated phenomenon of the Transnational Corporation.

The history of direct investment in the twentieth century would seem to exhibit its own inherent dynamic. Initially such investment served principally as a means of exploiting foreign natural resources. In the 1950s and 1960s it was a vehicle for supplying local markets with goods initially innovated and produced in the home country, and in the 1970s it became a means of establishing global processes of manufacture and product specialisation (Dunning 1979).

From the international perspective, foreign investment tends to create a real benefit by moving resources from less to more productive uses. In the national context, however, the benefit may be less obvious; with the advent of direct investment, a country's comparative advantage in specific sectors of manufacturing has tended to become a somewhat transient phenomenon. Evidence suggests that the Transnational Corporation, endowed with 'ownership specific advantages', will transfer or expand production in the relatively fast-growing markets (Dunning 1979). This can generate a process of cumulative economic deterioration for a structural deficit country which, by adopting slow-growth policies as a temporary expedient, simply exacerbates the problem and generates further uneven development. This argument has been used with some effect to explain the UK experience of the 1960s and 1970s (Panic 1982).

In summary, the problems of international economic relations in the 1970s resolved into two elements. First, the pathology associated with the decline in economic salience of the leading economy, which necessitated modifications of institutional economic structures to take account of the changed hierarchy in the inter-state system. Secondly, the fundamental issues of legitimacy generated by the structural dynamics of the system. The two components interact to produce a complex of destabilising forces. Cox employs the concept of 'Gramscian Hegemony' to analyse the problems and possibilities of system stability, defining the term as follows:

> Hegemony implies a degree of acquiescence by the less powerful in an order guaranteed by the more powerful. To make this possible, the more powerful must act in such a way that their interests have the appearance of a general interest, and they must make such concessions to the interests of the weaker as are needed to retain their consent and to maintain the sense that the system works in some manner to everyone's advantage (Cox 1980: 376).

In terms of the above definition, the 1970s witnessed a serious decline in hegemony. The late 1960s had convinced many of the second-rank powers that the actions of the lead country (USA) were such as to be inimical to the general interests of the wider international community. Consensual agreement (acquiescence) was further undermined by an increasing questioning of the confident assertion 'that the system works, in some manner, to everyone's advantage'. In this context, system maintenance requires system management in both political and economic senses. The form which this management is to take, if the market system is to be sustained into the 1990s, is an immediate and pressing problem.

Conclusion

Present circumstances represent a period of uncertainty both at the level of theoretical speculation and policy response, with regard to scope for market activity and the nature and form of economic management.

At the most obvious level, the debate has focused on the macro policy issue of 'Rules versus Discretion'. This has also been central to the debate concerning the nature and form of the IME. The presentation of the issues is more complex, entailing as it does the added dimension of the nation-state system and the associated problem of sustaining a rule-based economic order; it remains, however, fundamental to the debate on reform. In concluding a perceptive article on the concept of an 'international economic order', Tumlir, director of economic research at GATT, writes: 'rules are, by and large, safer than discretion. But we cannot rely solely on rules. The problem is how to recognise the necessary minimum of discretion, and how to make sure that only the minimum will be exercised' (Tumlir 1981).

For Tumlir, and for others such as Beenstock (op. cit.), the issue is quite clear; what is the minimum element of discretion which would make a system acceptable to nation-states? Following Friedman, there is the presupposition that discretionary intervention, internationally or domestically, leads to a 'politicisation' of the economy which slows the process of structural adjustment. To present this in another way, what Tumlir calls the 'planning ideology', and which he associated with the emergence of Keynesian economics, has resulted in a decline in market demand and supply elasticities, thus inhibiting the adjustment function of the market mechanism. The failure of the international market to adjust to technological advance and changing comparative advantage, the emergence of what Beenstock describes as 'mismatch unemployment', can all be blamed on John Maynard Keynes!

While the above arguments have been both forcefully and skilfully presented, there is an alternative stance, one which has informed the writing of this chapter. The starting point for this view is that the economic order and economic processes are embedded within a social structure, politically and geographically defined by the state. The balance between rules and discretion is an issue of market versus authority, and the form of the relationship will be fundamentally grounded in the social objectives which emerge from the political processes that impart legitimacy to the state. At all levels, the twentieth century has witnessed an increased questioning of the outcomes of unmanaged market processes. Issues of distribution, particularly associated with imbalances in market power, have been central to the demands for intervention. The adjustment processes by which the market responds to exogenous shocks impose substantial costs, the burden of which is not evenly distributed. Social imbalances inherent in dynamic market processes have obliged governments to participate actively in resource allocation and income distribution. Whilst intervention has, on numerous occasions, created more problems than it has solved, it is hardly satisfactory to assert that all politically unacceptable economic outcomes are a consequence of intervention policies.

The stress placed upon the priority of the social and political order over the economic order leads inevitably to a mercantilist perspective on international economic relations. Although this does not imply a rejection of the market or a denial of the efficiency of market mechanisms, it does suggest that, following Robinson, free trade represents one form of mercantilism (Robinson J. 1977). At both the national and international level there is a fundamental need for a rule structure within which exchange activities may take place. These rules rely on a pre-existing framework of political agreement and, consequently, the whole edifice depends upon wide-ranging agreement regarding favourable economic outcomes of the system. The analytical separatability of economics and politics, so essential to free market theorists, cannot be sustained outside the pages of the textbook. Only in exceptional circumstances will the configuration of political power be such as to validate the unmodified outcomes of the free market; under most conditions, the continued existence of market relations depends paradoxically on intervention to modify the outcomes of market processes.

Chapter 5

INDUSTRIAL POLICY
Brian Roper and Grahame Wright

In exploring the rationale for, and experiences of, government economic intervention in the post-war period we take as our backdrop the macroeconomic policy environment portrayed in Chapter 2. Whilst emphasis has shifted as governments have changed, the abiding themes have been the pursuit of growth, the maintenance of external balance, the reduction of unemployment and the control of inflation (see Craven and Wright 1983). The relative primacy of the latter two objectives having been and remaining the issue of greatest contention.

Disaggregating to the micro level, we have seen government economic intervention focusing upon firms and consumers and upon the interaction between them. The explicit policy objectives have included the pursuit of efficiency; the search for structural, sectoral and regional balance; worker and consumer protection; and perhaps most significantly in recent years the promotion of competition and competitiveness and the potential for competition (contestability). A penumbra of policy instruments has been evident. These have taken the form of both selective and global intervention through subsidies, taxation, inducement, encouragement and exhortation, regulation and direct and indirect control.

In the chapter which follows we review some of the major features of post-war industrial policy. Beginning with a historical review, we draw attention to the factors which were instrumental in the development of an ethos which saw a role for government involvement in business affairs. These are seen to be market failure considerations in general and the consequences of monopoly power in particular. We therefore examine the franchise bidding literature, the contestable markets hypothesis and privatisation from the perspective of recent theoretical contributions to the debate about the significance and likelihood of monopoly power being exercised.

Finally, having established that public and private 'firms' face many of the same organisational problems of monitoring and control, we conclude that the 'public versus private' debate is, in reality, a debate over which groups in industrial society should have the power to control.

A political economy of intervention

Surveying some of the major episodes in government economic intervention during the post-war period we must not be too rigid chronologically since industrial policy does not simply mirror the prevailing economic orthodoxy but has within it, at any point in time, vestiges of earlier (and perhaps contradictory) thinking. We share the view that 'the industrial policy landscape is like a hillside on which overlying strata from earlier policy periods outcrop side by side, some eroded, some glaciated, others active' (Morris and Stout 1985: 862).

The Second World War prompted an almost total mobilisation of resources and was the catalyst for increasing collectivism in economic affairs. Even though the tight control by the state over the economy was beginning to relax by 1948, it was never reduced to that which pertained in 1939. The war itself had prompted the increasing involvement of technocrats (businessmen, scientists, and economists, for example) in the affairs of government: their influence was profound and was to remain pervasive. The war also spawned a myriad of tripartite consultative committees comprised of trades unionists, business interests and government. The successors of these (e.g. the National Economic Development Council) continue to operate but their influence has declined.

The objectives set by, and the achievements of, the 1945–51 Labour government remain pivotal in all subsequent discussion of intervention in the mixed economy. Grove has argued that the war had permanently altered the relationship between industry and the state by stimulating corporatism, by promoting the system under which each industry became the concern of a particular government department and, perhaps of most lasting significance, by engendering the assumption that government had an overall responsibility for economic management (Grove 1962). The practical manifestation of this altered relationship between industry and state took the form of general economic planning and the implementation of a nationalisation programme which eventually resulted in a fifth of commercial and industrial enterprises coming into public ownership. The antecedents of these measures are to be found in all-party pre-war discussion (notably in the inter-war period) and are inextricably linked to the debates about social policy which culminated in the consolidation of the welfare state. The extension of public ownership is a key issue for our discussion.

Writing nearer the period, Eckstein (1958) argued that the initial imperative for nationalisation lay in ethical or moral attitudes which gave way subsequently to more practical considerations such as the need to bring strategic or inefficient industries under public control so as to facilitate the government's regulations of the economy. Contemporary commentators referred to the interplay of essentially political and economic reasons for nationalisation. Nationalisation has been practised by both Conservative and Labour governments, although the intrinsic desirability of public ownership is accepted only by the latter (not without some internal discussion). The political arguments for nationalisation arose both from trade union pressure to remove exploitation experienced under private ownership and from the view that it was a means of socialising the means of production and thus the redistribution of wealth and power. The economic arguments are various and have enjoyed differing degrees of emphasis.

First, nationalisation has, periodically, been viewed as an instrument for national planning and control. This partly explains the nationalisation of the 'commanding heights' of the economy through public control of steel, railways and coal. Second, it has been seen as a logical extension of public involvement in the form of both regulation and financial assistance. Examples of this include steel, aerospace and the continuation of municipalisation, with nationalisation being seen as a vehicle for centralisation and rationalisation; economies of scale arguments supporting the nationalisation of gas and electricity. Third, nationalisation has been used as a means of providing assistance for ailing industries usually through re-structuring and capital investment. Examples include coal in 1946 and shipbuilding in the 1970s.

A major spur to nationalisation stems from situations where market imperfections lead to a misallocation of resources. Such imperfections are attributable to the presence of externalities, the need for risky investment on a large scale and the problem of indivisibilities, and the existence of 'natural monopolies' where unit costs are minimised through the concentration of production in one organisation. Once nationalised, however, problems arose over the determination of operational objectives and their accountability to Parliament.

The 1967 White Paper, 'Nationalised Industries: A review of economic and financial objectives' (Cmnd 3437), presaged a new era for the nationalised industries. The purpose was to improve their resource allocation and overall efficiency both by the application of discounted cashflow techniques to investment projects so as to ensure adequate rates of return and by the wider use of marginal cost pricing. Pryke, however, argues that the 1967 White Paper in practice had little effect and goes on to state that:

> Politicians of neither party are interested in devising better pricing structures or seeing that investment projects show a satisfactory rate of return. If they belong to the Labour Party they are . . . instinctively opposed on the grounds that this has nothing to do with Socialism but will, on the contrary, make the nationalised industries more commercial. If they are Conservatives they are wedded to the private enterprise model and believe that those who manage public corporations should, in so far as possible, be left to get on with their jobs (Pryke 1981: 258–9).

This highlights the fact that nationalised industries usually have more than one objective (thus requiring policy trade-offs) which may be in conflict operationally and temporarily. Governments' concern with nationalised industries principally take the form of their profitability and efficiency, their effect on consumer welfare and real incomes and their use as instruments of macroeconomic policy.

Successive Treasuries have been concerned to ensure that nationalised industries efficiently allocate resources, having particular regard to the relationship between prices and costs and the earning of adequate returns on invested funds; conform to macroeconomic objectives with emphasis on their effect on the Public Sector Borrowing Requirement (PSBR); and are internally efficient having regard to the monopolistic or oligopolistic positions which some of them occupy. The framework of control that has been developed is of sufficient generality as to be applicable to all of the nationalised industries. Byatt has described it thus:

> It has, by and large, been a financial framework, but one that has evolved over the years, from an obligation to break even 'taking one year with another' to a complex mechanism involving short-term external financing limits (EFLs), medium-term external financing targets and performance aims. It is likely to develop further in the coming years (Byatt 1984: 67).

In the case of public monopolies, pressure has been building in recent years to find proxies for market forces. Arguing a case for external efficiency audits, Harrison has written that: '. . . pressure exerted through EFLs runs the risk of pushing over onto prices; in the case of loss makers, the pressures are considerable, but the management is inclined to politicise the relationship and concentrate on making the case for more grant, rather than getting on with the job of cutting costs' (Harrison 1984: 102).

This view reflects the liberationist ideology of the 1980s and we will consider it in more detail subsequently. For now we revert to the debates and events of the immediate post-war period.

For most commentators the 1947 fuel crisis, when very cold weather resulted in a severe reduction in coal stocks to the point where electricity supply was threatened, was a watershed for the Labour government. As Smith notes: 'this episode was a serious challenge to the Government's credibility: if it could not successfully plan the energy sector, could it reasonably expect to plan the entire economy?' (Smith T. 1979: 108).

The abandonment of planning following the 1947 fuel crisis has been interpreted by anti-planners (Hayek 1949; Jewkes 1948; Polanyi 1951) as inevitable for both practical and theoretical reasons and by pro-planners as attributable variously to trade union resistance to wage rate manipulation (see Beer 1965), the replacement of Dalton by Cripps at the Treasury (see Winch 1972; Dow 1964) and adverse public, business and civil service opinion (see Smith T. 1979).

Whether anything approaching planning actually occurred has also been called into question. Some commentators have argued that economic policy was ill-formulated, *ad hoc*, piecemeal and unco-ordinated and thus scarcely merited the description 'planning' (see Brittan 1971; Chester 1952). Whilst planning may not have occurred (or been attempted), collectivism had and it was largely unchallenged by the incoming Conservative government of 1951.

By the early 1950s the influence of government on industrial activity was significant. Despite a deceleration in state intervention, selective de-nationalisation, and the lifting of many physical controls, government continued to exercise considerable influence. It had substantial control of the energy utilities and transportation, a major influence through land ownership in the development areas, and domestic purchasing power which could be, and progressively was, used to mould industrial structure in certain key sectors. Perhaps the best reflection of government attitudes towards intervention in the industrial economy in the post-1960 period is to be found in the agencies which it spawned.

The formation of the National Economic Development Council and associated agencies in 1961–62 marked the resurgence of a tripartite approach to planning. The creation of the National Board for Prices and Incomes in 1965 had implications not merely for wage and price controls but raised issues of industrial structure and control.

The Industrial Reorganisation Corporation (IRC) was established in 1966 to facilitate the restructuring of key parts of the private sector. The premise being that production units were too small to compete with large overseas companies. This reflected the view taken in the 1960s that there were untapped scale economies in many British industries which would be released by merger (see Pratten and Dean 1965). One commentator described the government's approach as 'find the most efficient firm in Britain and merge the rest of them into it' (Caves 1968: 321).

The IRC interpreted its role to be restoration of the international competitiveness of manufacturing and processing industries and was a prime mover in the merger activity of the period. In this context it has been described as a 'catalyst, accelerator or steersman' (Young and Lowe 1974: 177). These approaches were directed towards the promotion of efficiency in specific industries in pursuit of the wider objectives of improving productivity, export performance and economic growth.

The establishment of the Department of Economic Affairs (DEA) in 1964, consequent upon the return of a Labour government, saw the extension and elaboration of planning machinery with a recommitment to the establishment of sectoral economic development committees and regional planning agencies, these largely having tripartite membership. The Prime Minister of the day described the DEA thus: 'this new department would be concerned with real resources, with economic planning, with strengthening our ability to export and to save imports, with increasing productivity, and our competitiveness in domestic markets' (Wilson 1971: 3).

Referring to the oft-quoted rivalry between the DEA and the Treasury and the issue of whether it was either possible or sensible to try to keep the Treasury out of economic planning, Leruez has noted that: '. . . it would be wrong to conclude that the Treasury had become subordinated, however briefly, to the DEA. What emerges from documents and speeches of the time is that the DEA and the Treasury were equals, and rivals' (Leruez 1975: 136).

The DEA assumed primary responsibility for microeconomic

policy emanating from the Treasury. A practical manifestation of these events lay in the publication of a *National Plan* in 1965. This was Britain's most ambitious attempt at indicative planning under which government, in conjunction with private industry, formulates consistent objectives which it then attempts to assist private industry to attain via a system of incentives and sanctions. However, as Smith noted:

> . . . it was only a dress rehearsal and not an opening night, still less a long-run hit: the curtain descended very firmly in the form of the July 1966 deflationary measures by which the Government signalled the abandonment of planning, at least on the grand scale. Custom, in the form of the Treasury, the balance of payments and the parity of sterling, had won out . . . (Smith T. 1979: 152–3).

The 1970s saw further and even more vigorous attempts to incorporate dominant interest groups within a tripartite framework focused more directly and immediately upon the realities of economic behaviour. Amongst the outcomes of this orientation were the strengthening of controls on monopolies and mergers (Fair Trading Act 1973), Labour's 'industrial strategy' introduced in 1975, Labour's 'Social Contract' with the TUC which was drawn up in 1972 in opposition and enacted with the repeal of the Conservative's Industrial Relations Act of 1971, and new employment legislation in 1975 and 1976. At the level of intervention in the industrial economy, the Conservatives' acceptance of the principle that public investment had a role to play in supporting vulnerable parts of the industrial private sector was signalled in the Industry Act of 1972.

Labour's 1975 Industry Act can be seen as increasing the tempo of tripartite interventionism by providing a successor to the IRC in the form of the National Enterprise Board (NEB), and by the introduction of tripartite company-level planning agreements, the former being of more lasting significance but both marking a retreat from the more radical ideas of Labour in opposition (see Hatfield 1978). This was scarcely surprising and is confirmed by Harold Wilson's comment that 'contrary to the revolutionary hopes which surrounded the NEB when it was conceived in opposition days, Eric Varley's department . . . ensured that it would not operate like an industrial rogue elephant' (Wilson 1979: 141–2).

The 1975 Industry Act saw the NEB as a new instrument to secure large-scale sustained investment to offset the effects of the short-term pull of market forces. The formation of the NEB reflected a belief that the private sector was inherently myopic in its attitude to investment and risk-taking and thus not capable of sufficiently investing in the 'social interest' and was, therefore, likely to neglect research and development (particularly in high-technology industries) and thus constrain Britain's international competitiveness. By such selective intervention, it was argued, government can and should (temporarily) assist the operation of competitive markets. Within the NEB's constitution can be seen the attempt to harmonise the (conventionally competing) objectives of the achievement of commercial rates of return on public invest-ment and the social objectives of job retention and creation. It was empowered to provide loans at commercial rates and to take equity stakes in private companies. In exercising its powers, the NEB acted as a holding company and had an initial involvement with some of Britain's leading manufacturing firms and served as an instrument for the regeneration of industry by investing in firms having proposals 'which contributed significantly to exports, import substitution, growth of employment or advanced tech-nology' and which encouraged 'the expansion, modernising or restructuring of certain key industries' (NEB 1978).

Novel though it was at its inception, it would be unwise to overestimate the significance of the NEB. Perhaps the fairest assessment of it has been made by Grant who argued that '. . . it did not resemble the instrument of Socialist reconstruction envisaged by its progenitors but rather a state Merchant Bank' (Grant 1982: 50). Other commentators (see, for example, Levacic 1980) have argued that the basic premise of the NEB was funda-mentally flawed. In their view, ample opportunities existed for the market to provide funds for investment in the types of projects funded by NEB. That the market had chosen not to invest was sufficient evidence that the projects were unlikely to generate rates of return considered as acceptable either by the market or under the terms of the NEB enabling legislation. This critical view is, however, predicated on the assumption of a reasonably well func-tioning market which correctly evaluates risk and expected returns and which incorporates a traditional 'neoclassical' view of the objectives and responses of firms, a factor discussed in more detail below.

The 1975 Industry Act also provided for planning agreements which were seen as a means of harnessing companies to the requirements of sectoral and national planning. This concept owed much to the influence of Stuart Holland who maintained that the increasing political influence and economic power of large firms (especially multinational corporations), which constitute a meso-economic sector, comprised a threat to national sovereignty and a barrier to the implementation of Keynesian macroeconomic policies (see Holland 1975). He argued that such firms are not internally inefficient but are socially inefficient in their 'ineffectual response to government policies in such areas as investment, trade, pricing, job creation and regional development. Britain still includes some of the biggest and most efficient companies in Europe and the world but conventional economic policies have failed to harness their massive resources in the public interest' (Holland 1975: 30). This latter phrase, as we have seen in Chapter 1, is not without contention.

For Holland (and Crosland before him) the solution rests on competitive enterprises with dominant firms in oligopolistic industries being taken into public ownership and being so operated as to exert competitive pressure on the industry (see Holland 1975 and Crosland 1956). On the more specific issue of planning agreements there was, and remains, widespread confusion. Only two were concluded (with Chrysler and the National Coal Board). This owed much to a lack of clarity about their objectives, the absence of compulsion on reluctant managements to agree and, to a certain degree, on trade union resistance. In the light of this, it has been noted that '. . . it is surprising that Socialists still place so much faith in them as a centrepiece of Socialist industrial policy' (Grant 1982: 22). That they still do is confirmed by the retention of planning agreements within Labour's *Jobs and Industry* campaign launched at its Annual Conference in 1985, alongside proposals for a National Investment Bank and a joint Labour Party–TUC approach to wages.

Writing in the late 1970s and reviewing the previous twenty years, Smith has noted that '. . . it is abundantly evident that the will to introduce a greater degree of competitiveness into the economy has been exceedingly feeble' (Smith T. 1979: 191). This feebleness has, as noted above, been due in part to a rather ambivalent attitude by governments of either party to the outcomes of increased reliance on market forces, reflecting different views on the nature of the competitive process. On the other hand, institutions such as NEB, IRC and NEDC were predicated on the assumption that market signals are insufficient or inappropriate guides to the (commercially or socially) efficient allocation of resources. Government inducement was thus thought necessary to persuade firms to merge, invest or compete in international markets. In other circumstances, policies have been implemented to moderate the effects of profit-seeking conduct which had resulted in some companies securing powerful market positions through monopolisation, mergers and restrictive practices. The Monopolies and Restrictive Practices Act in 1948 and its subsequent strengthening in 1965 and 1973 reflected the view that society's interests were best served by controlling the extent to which firms with a dominant market share could exploit their monopoly power.

Clearly concern over the possible exercise of monopoly power has been and remains a major reason for government intervention. The underlying rationale for this view comes from what has been referred to as the Structure–Conduct–Performance (SCP) paradigm and it is to this that we now turn our attention.

Monopoly power and regulation

The SCP paradigm is, at its simplest, a belief in a causal relationship between the *structure* of a market (i.e. how many firms and consumers etc.?) and the *conduct* of firms in such markets (e.g. charging prices greater than marginal costs) which, in turn, results in a particular *performance* (i.e. profitability, allocative efficiency). The approach is most easily illustrated (see Table 5.1) with reference to the two polar cases of perfect competition and monopoly.

Table 5.1 The structure–conduct–performance paradigm

	Perfectly competitive market	*Pure monopoly market*
Structure	Many buyers and sellers Free entry/exit	Many buyers and single seller No entry
Conduct	Price equal to marginal cost	Price greater than marginal cost
Performance	No excess profits in long run	Excess profits in long run

The SCP approach has not however been restricted to hypothetical market forms; indeed, its significance springs mainly from its widespread use as a method of categorising actual markets and its influence upon empirical research and its application to policy making. Whole textbooks have been written with the SCP paradigm 'providing both theme and counterpoint for the analysis' (Scherer 1980: 5) of industrial organisation. Although it has been recognised that the causal link between excess profits and high levels of concentration (i.e. small number of firms with high market shares) may sometimes be reversed, the SCP paradigm has been at the centre of UK competition policy both in theory and practice for almost thirty years.

The attention given to market share in monopoly policy stems from the belief that if it exceeds some particular level (currently 25 per cent of the UK market) it is at least *prima facie* evidence that the conduct, and therefore performance, of the firm will be against the national interest. Furthermore, X-inefficiencies may add to resource misallocation according to Leibenstein (1978) because the absence of a competitive 'stick' removes the incentive for managers to ensure that costs per unit of output are minimised. If, however, economies of scale are obtainable through monopolisation, a 'trade-off' exists between efficiency gains and welfare losses (see Williamson O. E. 1968).

This 'trade-off' suggests that some industries would be better served by, a single firm and this has been one of the major theoretical justifications for nationalisation (in the UK) or the severe regulation of private monopolists (in the USA). Unlike the US, monopoly is not ruled out *per se* in the UK. It is recognised that in certain circumstances society may be 'better off' with monopoly power than without it. Consequently some monopolies have been allowed by the Monopolies and Mergers Commission (MMC) to maintain their dominant position. Recent legislation in the UK has however recognised the obverse of this position by acknowledging that a high market share is not a necessary condition for a firm to act anti-competitively. The 1980 Competition Act now allows investigation by the MMC of named firms even if their market share is less than 25 per cent when there are grounds for believing that the firm is acting anti-competitively (see Shaw and Simpson 1985).

A second innovation in the 1980 Act is to allow public bodies to be referred under much the same terms as private firms (see Ferguson 1985). This new feature reflects a growing unease with the traditional view that when the market fails, state ownership can rectify the failure. Many writers, particularly from the Austrian and Chicago School, claim that governments and their agencies are also subject to the same faults and failings as private firms (see Utton 1984 for an assessment of this position). Making state-owned monopolies subject to controls on their conduct has gone some way to satisfying those critics who claimed that 'government failure' was the consequence of attempts to reduce market failure. While the 1980 Act directed attention at the *conduct* of firms to improve competitiveness, a new theoretical approach to the control of monopoly and the regulation of industry has been proposed which questions the need for most anti-monopoly legislation at all. In addition to these developments, a policy of privatisation has been undertaken partly to subject public sector monopolies to the realities of competitive markets. As Sir Geoffrey Howe (the then Chancellor of the Exchequer) proposed in outlining an economic policy for the eighties: 'public utilities and the so-called "natural monopolies" cannot all be allowed to remain without change or challenge in state ownership. Increased competition must be accompanied by progress towards more real public ownership – ownership by the public, not the state' (Howe 1983).

The government sees privatisation then as one method of overcoming the monopoly power of state enterprises while recent theoretical developments have encouraged policymakers to believe that private monopolies need not exhibit the performance predicted by the SCP paradigm. It is to these issues that we now turn.

Privatisation

We have seen then that governments have intervened in the economy in various ways and with numerous objectives, some of which were in conflict (e.g. IRC to encourage mergers, Monopolies Commission to control them). Since 1979, however, intervention by government has largely been enacted through the reversal of previous policies. One might argue that the 1980s have witnessed selective intervention in the public sector designed to restore the 'power of the market' to British industry.

The market is seen by many economists and politicians as the means of reducing the ability of some firms to earn excess profits, or to promote cost-minimising behaviour and reduce the ability of workers and management to function inefficiently. It is 'the market' which will increase competition between firms and ensure that only the fittest survive.

It is argued, however, that for the market mechanism to succeed it is necessary to liberate the competitive spirit. Policies designed to do just that have taken numerous forms but post-1979 they have come to be referred to collectively as 'privatisation'. Though strictly this term is too restrictive as some policies do not involve the sale of public sector assets and/or the creation of a company registered under the Companies Act, it is a convenient shorthand for the whole range of policies introduced as part of the government's 'liberationist' philosophy (see Shackleton 1984; Peacock 1984). It includes such measures as the liberalisation of trade through the deregulation of certain activities (such as allowing private bus companies to compete with the public transport services) or the removal of legally enforced monopolies (e.g. in house conveyancing, solicitors now face competition from other agencies such as banks etc.). The explanation of this policy has been put forward by government spokesmen in the following terms:

> It must be right to press ahead with the transfer of ownership from state to private enterprises of as many public sector businesses as possible . . . the introduction of competition must whenever possible be linked to a transfer of ownership to private citizens and away from the state. Real public ownership, that is ownership by the people, must be and is our ultimate goal (Nicholas Ridley, Financial Secretary to the Treasury, 12 February 1982).

Similarly, it has been stated that:

> The Conservative Party has never believed that the business of Government is the government of business (Nigel Lawson, *Hansard* Vol. 1 (8th series), Col. 440, November 1981).

Academic support comes from advocates such as Beesley and Littlechild (1983) who argue that the aim of privatisation is 'to improve industry performance by increasing the role of market forces'. Such measures as de-nationalisation, the sale of council houses, the introduction of private contractors to supply catering and cleaning services to public sector organisations, and the sale of the government's holding of private sector stock are but some of the many ways in which the principle of privatisation has been invoked. At the heart of the issue is a fundamental debate over the extent to which the market mechanism can be relied upon to generate superior outcomes to any other form of allocative device.

Despite the confidence with which some academics and government spokesmen have accepted the efficiency arguments for privatisation, some writers have remained sceptical. John Kay of the Institute of Fiscal Studies entitled a recent paper written with D. J. Thompson, 'Privatisation: a policy in search of a rationale' (Kay and Thompson 1985). They set out to consider the underlying economic arguments for privatisation; they found however that: '. . . the reality behind the apparent multiplicity of objectives is not that the policy has a rather sophisticated rationale, but rather that it is lacking any clear analysis of purpose or effects' (Kay and Thompson 1985).

Nevertheless, it is important to recognise that privatisation may be supported/rejected on political or ideological grounds and that the particular aspects of a policy promoted by a government may be more the consequence of political expediency than economic imperatives. Revenue-generating (PSBR reducing) privatisations may fall into this category. Indeed, Mr Nigel Lawson (Chancellor of the Exchequer) in his Autumn Statement (12 November 1985), having made passing reference to the efficiency arguments, went on to stress the revenue-generating potential of privatisation, 'the increased pace of privatisation means that the proceeds . . . will rise substantially from £2.5 billion this year to £4.75 billion in each of the next three years' (*The Times*, 13 November 1985).

Structural problems such as monopoly power remain to be resolved. Indeed, the most significant sales of public sector assets to date (other than council houses) have been those with considerable monopoly power. The proposed sale of British Gas (valued at £10 billion) would create another private monopoly to replace the current public monopoly. Recent theoretical developments on the nature of the competitive process and the possible alternatives to the regulation or nationalisation of monopolies are thus central to the operation of the government's proclaimed policy of disengagement from the governance of business.

Alternatives to regulation – franchise bidding

This is an approach to the problem of monopoly power which places emphasis on the possibility of competition even in the case of a 'natural monopolist'.

Suggested by Demsetz (1968) as an improved alternative to the regulation of natural monopolies, the central argument is that the existence of economies of scale, which in an SCP approach implies a single supplier, does not require that there be only one firm wishing to be that supplier. In other words, a distinction is made between competition in supplying the product to the market and competition *for* (the right to be the monopoly supplier to) the market.

If monopoly power is capable of generating excess profits then, according to Demsetz, there will be an incentive for firms to bid for the right to be that monopolist, i.e. to hold the franchise contract for a specified period. Bids will (normally) be in the form of market prices charged to consumers by the bidder if he wins the franchise. Apart from illegal collusion, the successful bid price will tend towards the minimum production cost. Monopoly profits will thus be competed away as rivals will continue to have an incentive to offer lower bids as long as potential profits are attainable. Society benefits through the least cost provision of the product or service without the distortions and inefficiencies of public sector supply or regulation. In the franchise bidding model the role of government is simply to supervise the operation of the bidding process and write the franchise contract.

Superficially franchise bidding offers an efficient alternative to the regulation of natural monopolies for it continues to employ competition as the agent of control despite the monopolisation of the production process. However, this approach is subject to a number of complications, many of which are caused by the costs of contracting.

One of the most fundamental problems with franchising is the need to specify the length of the franchise contract period. Short-term contracts have the advantage that prices can be specified and enforced for the entire period because cost and demand changes are less likely to occur in the short run. The disadvantage lies in the removal of incentives for the franchise holder to invest in new capital equipment because either there is insufficient time to recoup the expenditure or the resale of the equipment at the end of the contract period involves substantial transaction costs. For example, if the fixed assets of incumbent firms are highly specialised, then the 'market' for these assets will be restricted, perhaps to just the successful bidder. A bilateral monopoly is therefore created in which the relative strengths of the parties will determine the outcome. Strategic play by the seller of the assets would be the likely outcome. By refusing to sell to the franchise 'winner', the existing firm could force the new entrant to purchase new equipment which would upset the calculations made when that firm bid for the franchise. Such an outcome would clearly be socially inefficient in such industries as electricity generation.

Furthermore, it is capital-intensive industries which are most likely to be natural monopolies as a consequence of economies of scale generated by high minimum plant size. Also much of this capital will be idiosyncratic and thus a sunk cost. Long-term contracts have the advantage that capital equipment is more likely to be consumed during the contract period (and therefore is fully allocated to the costing process) but their disadvantages are that some system of monitoring cost and demand variations must be undertaken by the sponsoring agency (the government). The longer a firm holds a franchise the easier it becomes for it to control the flow of information to an external monitoring agency. Long contract periods also give the incumbent firm substantial informational advantages over potential rivals.

Another problem, which emerges in cases such as the granting of licences to local independent television and radio stations in the UK (essentially a franchise contract), is that the consumer is not charged a price at all (see Domberger and Middleton 1985). Under these conditions bids are set in terms of the 'quality' of programming; a notion which clearly defies any attempt to rank rival bidders by some objective criterion (see Williamson O. E. 1976).

Finally the franchise bidding literature does not explain the source of the supposed advantage to be gained from competition for a franchise. In the hypothetical example quoted by Demsetz, firms compete for the franchise to be the monopoly supplier of car number plates. But who are these competitors? The first time a franchise is offered it can be supposed that a number of entrepreneurs place competing bids assuming that, if they are the 'winner', then the necessary capital can be purchased and the appropriate labour hired. Once the successful bid is selected, however, what happens to the unsuccessful bidders? It might be argued that they simply enter other markets if they see a profit opportunity or they cease to be entrepreneurs. Whichever is suggested, the question of identity of bidders *at the next round* remains. If it is a firm already undertaking production of some other product, there is no reason to suppose that it will leave the industry in order to enter the franchise industry. It is more likely that the entrepreneur would purchase/hire additional capital and labour but only if he wins the franchise. Remembering that a natural monopoly requires that there be only one supplier of the product or service, i.e. just one location where capital and labour are combined to produce this unique output, it would be surprising if substantially the same workforce and the same physical capital were not used by whichever entrepreneur won the contract. So, after the bidding process was complete and the winner chosen, the successful bidder would have roughly the same workforce and substantially the same capital as the previous entrepreneur. What then is the advantage of change? The only difference between the new supplier compared to the previous firm is the identity of the entrepreneur, but what is the nature of such differences? Arguably entrepreneurs may differ in two respects:

1. the extent to which an entrepreneur makes the 'right' estimates of future cost and demand conditions and thus bids the 'right'

price for the franchise, that is a price low enough to win the franchise but high enough to cover costs; and/or
2. differences in organising capabilities which permit him to use the same capital and labour as his rivals but to do so in a more efficient manner (see Casson 1983).

If the competition to control a natural monopoly (that is competition *for the market*) is in reality a competition between individuals' organising skills or estimating abilities, then why go to the trouble to franchise the enterprise at all? State ownership of the assets would remove the need for frequent exchanges of ownership (and the consequent transaction costs), it could maintain a workforce which had gained all the potential advantages of 'learning by doing', and the competitive element could be injected by competition *for the right to organise* the firm; rival bids being in terms of acceptable salaries. In the UK the recent denationalisation of British Telecom (BT) through the sale of shares to the public gave rise to the problem of control of a (near) natural monopoly. In this case the government have followed the regulatory path rather than franchising. An Office of Telecommunications (OfTel) has been created whose function it is to 'enforce the terms of the licence, monitor anti-competitive practices and advise the Secretary of State' (Littlechild 1983a). Following the work of Littlechild (1983b), BT's ability to generate profits from excessive price rises (and thus quantity reductions) has been restricted. Prices may not rise by more than the rate of inflation less x per cent where x per cent is a value set by OfTel; consequently under present arrangements BT are expected to continually reduce the real price of telephone services for the first five years. As has been observed in another context, it would not be surprising to discover that OfTel will eventually be 'captured' by BT, i.e. the interdependence of BT and a quasi government body such as OfTel produces an incentive for the monitoring agency to minimise public condemnations of poor performance and to 'appreciate the difficulties' faced by the monitored firm. In the UK, franchise bidding has not yet been employed to any great extent. However, many of the criticisms of franchising can also be levelled at the operation of contractual arrangements between public sector organisations (such as the National Health Service) and private suppliers of services such as cleaning or catering. Here problems of monitoring, contract duration, bilateral bargaining over capital replacement/depreciation, and the advantages to the successful bidder of incumbent status, combine with problems associated with the transition from internal public supply to external private contractors.

Wright (1984) has observed that where a 'firm' supersedes the operation of the price mechanism internally through hierarchical control mechanisms, internal pricing if used at all will employ only notional prices. As we explain below, market prices will not be used within a firm because the very existence of 'firms' is due to the relative cost advantage from directing resources through an administrative decision-making process rather than employing the price mechanism. If this were not so, then there would be no firms as we know them, simply transient markets comprised of many independent economic actors buying and selling on the basis of relative prices. As a consequence, regardless of how efficient a firm or organisation might be as a whole, any single part (such as catering services) will be unable to determine precisely the relative prices of the inputs and outputs of that department because at least some will be 'shared' with other parts of the organisation. If they were not, then we would not be dealing with the 'same' organis-ation. Attempts to tender by an internal department for the contract to provide the services which it is currently supplying, in competition with outside catering firms (private or public), will thus be disadvantaged by the lack of appropriate price information and by the lack of experience in the tendering process. Of itself, this may not be signficant except that, for the internal department, this is a 'crucial experiment' (Shackle 1955) because failure results in the internal organisation being wound-up, never to tender again, whereas 'outside' contractors are able to tender for more than one contract and thus can learn from their mistakes. There need be no actual efficiency gain by replacing an internal supplier with an outside contractor although the internal accounting procedure, based on administered internal costing, may show a 'saving'. What then is the purpose of contracting out and similar measures? In practice it seems that two factors are important:

1. the opportunity provided to change the terms and conditions of employment (see Kay and Thompson 1985) for those working in the provision of the service (in catering services most firms re-employ some or all of the 'redundant' internal employees though not necessarily on the same terms); and
2. the organisational skills of the specialist contractor.

Evidence from a recent survey of major contract catering firms suggests that most agreements are undertaken on a management services basis, i.e. the public sector organisation 'buys' manage-ment skills from the contractor while continuing to provide the capital equipment and paying for food. Selection of the appropriate level of capital is left to negotiation between the parties so the contractor determines only one side of the capital/labour ratio (Berry C. 1986).

The contestable markets hypothesis

This 'uprising in the theory of industrial structure' is propounded by William J. Baumol et al. (Baumol 1982; Baumol et al. 1977), and has as its broad conclusion that regulation and state intervention are, in many circumstances, the cause of rigidities in the operation of a market economy and thus the source of barriers to entry which maintain incumbent firms' power to extract monopoly rents.

In this approach the important question concerns the extent to which a market is *contestable*. Baumol's Contestability Hypothesis is essentially theoretical, concentrating on a model of 'perfect contestability' which is acknowledged to be no more than a benchmark. Nevertheless, advocates of this approach have claimed that it has policy-relevant conclusions which undermine the SCP approach: 'thus traditional *per se* indicators of market performance such as concentration, price discrimination, conglomerate mergers, or vertical and horizontal integration do *not automatically* call for government intervention in contestable markets' (Baumol et al. 1982: 465).

The contestable markets thesis should thus be seen as a response to those who have argued that essentially abstract static models of competition are unsuitable for adoption as test criteria by legislators or the courts in determining whether monopoly power is or is not against the public interest. It seeks to provide a rationale for the liberation of industry from regulation and control by demonstrating that efficient outcomes are feasible even in the case of industries comprised of a small number of firms; in the limit just one.

Baumol defines a contestable market as 'one into which entry is absolutely free, *and exit is absolutely costless*' (Baumol 1982). This may seem like a reformulation of the pure competition model but this is not so: 'a perfectly competitive market is necessarily perfectly contestable, but not *vice versa*' (Baumol 1982). Like perfect competition, entry and exit barriers are important but here emphasis is placed on the anticipated exit costs at the time of potential entry as a crucial determinant of contestability. 'Sunk' rather than 'fixed' costs are therefore the important factor in establishing a potential barrier to entry.

A sunk cost is one which, once incurred, cannot be retrieved through resale of the asset or its transfer to an alternative use. A fixed cost, on the other hand, is one which cannot be avoided if the firm is to remain in business, but is not necessarily permanently a sunk cost. The need to purchase expensive capital assets is not therefore seen to be a potential entry/exit barrier so long as (a) such expenditures are a necessary prerequisite for any other entrant (including the incumbent firm) and (b) there exists a resale market for such assets 'since, clearly the less the financial loss incurred in such a transfer, [of assets] the lower will be the costs that are truly sunk and the smaller will be the costs of exit' (Baumol et al. 1982: 469).

If profitable opportunities for entry are believed to exist, then entrepreneurs will enter the market at a lower price than an incumbent firm, extract the surplus profits, then leave the market. Zero entry/exit barriers would thus generate what Baumol et al. have referred to as 'hit and run' entry by rival firms prepared to shave prices until they approach the level of costs. In the case of 'natural monopolies', this lower price results in the entrant totally replacing the incumbent. Where demand quantities exceed the least cost production quantities for a number of firms, then the market will be shared but, in both cases, the only price/quantity combinations sustainable are those which minimise industry costs. In the absence of entry/exit barrier, any price above this will generate entry at a lower price. It follows then that the mere threat of entry becomes sufficient to maintain pressure on an incumbent firm to minimise costs and prices.

Clearly the contestable markets hypothesis is an extreme form of the franchise bidding 'solution' discussed above except that there is within Baumol's analysis no need for government to organise the bidding process. All the government need to do is to ensure that all artificial barriers to entry *and exit* are removed, especially where those barriers are the consequence of state intervention or regulation. Then, as Button (1985) has noted: '. . . public fear of monopoly power vanishes and, indeed, with possible economies from large scale and diverse production, such market forms may offer the most desirable structure for efficient production'.

The theory of contestable markets contributes to the debate over state intervention, deregulation, nationalisation and privatisation, insofar as it suggests that monopoly and oligopoly power are not sufficient conditions for government intervention. However, as Button (1985) also notes, if sunk costs are absent then contestability does not imply the transfer of state-owned assets to the private sector. As long as the threat of entry exists, *even* the publicly owned firm must produce and sell at minimum costs and prices.

In her study of price and productivity changes in the United States, Bailey (1985) argues that regulation tends 'to support cross-subsidy . . . high price/high service . . . artificial boundaries that interfere with the scope of a firm's operations . . . [reduce] incentives for firms to operate on the efficient production frontier'. Her investigations into the unfixing of stock brokerage fees, the deregulation of domestic air fares, and decontrol of price and entry in the road and rail freight industries led Bailey to conclude that, 'the deregulation philosophy which has sought policies that promote contests for markets has thus been highly effective. It has by and large led to enormous productivity improvements in the de-controlled industries' (Bailey E. E. 1985).

A number of theoretical criticisms have been directed at the contestable markets hypothesis however. In particular, Shepherd (1984) bemoans the change of emphasis from studying competi-tiveness *within* markets to an essentially optimistic view of the contest between potential suppliers and the extent to which the threat of potential entry would ensure least cost production and pricing by incumbent firms. While Bailey's results are impressive, there is some doubt as to whether they are supportive of the contestability hypothesis. It is not clear, for example, whether deregulated firms are maintaining prices consistent with minimum costs or whether they are still making excess profits because poten-tial entrants continue to be deterred by numerous other entry barriers which may not lend themselves to empirical observation. Barriers such as informational and 'learning by doing' advantages gained by the incumbent firms or the extent to which potential entrants can assess the level of sunk compared to recoverable costs will give an asymmetrical advantage in the 'contest'.

Advertising, for example, has long been recognised as a possible barrier to entry partly because initial expenditures by a potential entrant will require a substantial budget but also because such expenditure has no 'resale' value. In other words, if the advertising campaign fails, the funds expended cannot be recovered by selling off an asset because the capital invested in the campaign is sunk. The incumbent firm, even if it too originally invested in an adver-tising campaign, gains a first mover advantage just because his costs are sunk (see Waterson 1984: 72).

Perhaps one of the most valuable projects to be undertaken in the UK, the development of the £4.5 billion Channel Tunnel, is a classic example of (literally) a project with sunk costs. Once the capital costs of the tunnel have been incurred, there is no alternative use for the rather large hole under the English Channel. By the year 2020 when The Channel Tunnel Group lose their monopoly rights to be the sole provider of tunnels under the Channel, the possibility of entry is unlikely to deter them from charging prices which generate profits from the monopoly.

Despite the initial appeal of franchise bidding and contestability as a means of allowing market pressures to attenuate monopoly power, it is clear that monopoly power continues to generate problems for the policymaker. While these may be (and have been) ignored, as they have been in such areas as street cleaning or hospital laundries where contracting out (a form of franchise bidding) has been employed despite the problems discussed above, they continue to raise doubts about the notion that the government can withdraw from business affairs. The problem of sunk costs is common to both franchise bidding and to contestability and this implies that: 'policies based upon notions of contestability are not, therefore, automatically consistent with privatisation and reductions in public ownership . . .' (Button 1985).

It should be remembered, however, that the move to disengagement is not solely based on the availability of market constraints on monopolists.

A belief that the public sector is necessarily inferior to the market in finding efficient methods of allocating resources is also a strong influence on the present government's thinking in this area. Even where there are grounds for public involvement (due, for example, to externalities) it is suggested that a market (private firm) solution should be found. Privatisation is seen therefore as providing, of itself, the appropriate environment for stimulating enterprise, efficiency and effort. Yet the justification for such optimism is not made clear.

At the heart of much of this particular debate is the issue of markets versus planning; private firms versus public bureaux. Unfortunately this debate is often diverted from the key issues by a mistaken application of neoclassical theoretical models of firms and markets. There is thus a tendency to use concepts of 'the market process' which are more correctly only applicable to the very restrictive model of atomistic markets where economic agents interact impersonally through price signals. As we show below, however, the reality of firms is very different both in form, organisational characteristics and objectives from the neoclassical model of the firm. Examination of the nature of *real* firms is therefore a necessary prerequisite for any debate over the appropriate domain of markets and planning.

Firms, costs and organisations

The neoclassical 'black box' theory concentrates attention on the role of the firm in the transformation of resources into more highly valued outputs; it is where relative prices of inputs and outputs determine input combinations and output quantities. As these prices are determined within factor and product markets respectively, the theory of the firm is, as Machlup (1967) recognised, simply a hypothetical construct in a theory of markets. It does not, and nor is it supposed to explain, reflect or predict the behaviour of actual firms in particular markets. Indeed, it is questionable whether the neoclassical theory is related to actual firms at all. As has been noted elsewhere (Wright 1984) a computer could perform the role of the neoclassical firm if it were 'connected' to input and output market price data sources.

Firms as we know them have one essential characteristic: they involve people who are directed and organised. Coase (1937) observed that when a real firm wishes to transfer a worker from one department to another the manager simply directs him to carry out his instructions. There is no market exchange with relative prices transmitting the signal that the worker must move to a new task: he goes 'because he is ordered to' (Coase 1937).

In theory, of course, everything which is undertaken by the most complex real firm could be accomplished by atomistic agents acting through the price mechanism; indeed, there are some limited examples where this type of exchange relationship does (almost) exist. Self-employed building workers, some musicians and freelance sales representatives are some of the few employment groups which continue to use market exchange as the direct determinant of their labour supply. According to Coase (1937), the reason why many exchanges take place within firms is because 'there is a cost to using the price mechanism'. These *transaction costs* would be incurred if factors or production responded only to relative price signals. It would be necessary to organise, negotiate and enforce thousands of individual contracts with factor suppliers if firms were to emulate the neoclassical theory.

To reduce these contracting costs, a general contract of employment between workers and the firm is established. This general (implicit) contract replaces the numerous individual ones which would otherwise have been necessary.

Firms are thus organisations within which resources are directed by the owner or managers within the broad limits of the employment contract. To the extent that consumers are 'sovereign', these directions will be in line with consumer interests as ultimately (if rather belatedly) supply must follow consumer demands. Insofar as consumer tastes are determined endogenously, then the planning process would ensure that producer interests are secured. Echoing the argument presented above, Galbraith has recognised that, 'if the market . . . reigned there would be, and could be, no planning. No elaborate organisation would be required' (Galbraith 1969: 50).

Becoming an organisation means that the decision set for the firm must now include an enlarged number of elements concerned with the management of the firm. No longer can we assume that an optimum input–output decision will be made simply on the basis of relative factor and product prices. For once having contracted to employ labour services, the firm needs to find the best method of organising their activities. It is not enough simply to 'leave it to the market' for, as we have seen, the whole rationale for the existence of firms is that they limit the domain of the price mechanism and thus restrict the influence of 'the market'. If workers are to be directed to specific tasks and the organisation is to improve on the operation of an unco-ordinated market, then a major part of the activity of the firm must be in planning. Such planning is the essence of actual firms; or, as Shackle (1970) recognised, the firm is where policy is implemented.

It is through planning that firms attempt to maintain the differential between the costs of organising internally and using the price mechanism with its associated transaction costs. Since other firms are similarly organising internally, each firm must also attempt to administer the production process more cheaply than its rivals. Here then we have an explanation for the origin of firms which also answers the question, what is the role of the entrepreneur? Of course any student of economics could have agreed with Casson that 'an entrepreneur is someone who specialises in taking judgemental decisions about the coordination of scarce resources' but in the black box theory co-ordination was something only required after some disequilibrating shock (Casson 1983: 23, emphasis in original).

Real firms are thus organisations within which the price mechanism is superseded by administrative control. Furthermore, even though one-man firms continue to survive, trade *between* most firms takes on a level of planning and co-ordination not envisaged by the simple textbook models of demand and supply (see Macneil 1978; Williamson O. E. 1979, Richardson 1972). Price changes must be considered by firms within the context of their organisational impact, with managers conscious of the problems of decision making and the implementation of policy changes. So while the long-run effects of price changes will lead to quantity adjustments, short-term movements may be ignored on the grounds that the costs of modifying production plans and organisational procedures exceed the benefits of change, a factor of some significance to macroeconomic policymakers (see Begg *et al.* 1984; Wachter and Williamson 1978). Furthermore, attempts to reduce the costs of transactions between firms can lead to situations where the level of planning and co-ordination between them becomes so great that they merge into a new single organisation.

From this brief discussion of the nature of the firm in neoclassical economic theory, one point at least should be clear: the debate over 'planning' versus 'markets' in the context of industrial policy should not be seen as a debate over whether allocative decisions ought to be left to the market or 'planned' by public sector employees. The rationale for the existence of firms is testimony to the need for planning and administration of resources in the private as well as the public sector. Indeed, there is nothing in the explanation for the origin of real firms as suggested by Coase which implies that they are privately or publicly owned.

Consequently the fundamental issue of public versus private sector firms is, who are to be the planners and over what domain should they exercise their control of resources? Consideration must be given to the extent to which groups of managers should be free to direct resources in their own or their shareholders' interests, or whether the government should directly or indirectly enter the planning arena through state ownership, selective intervention or the regulation of business conduct.

Organisations, objectives and control

If, as we have argued, firms are organisations which supersede the price mechanism through internal organisation, then (*cet par*) as the number of employees increases so the organisational structure of the firm needs to become more sophisticated.

Table 5.2 Average employment per 'firm': UK 1981

Size bands of employment census units*	Number of census units per band	Average numbers employed per size band
1	114 163	1
2	128 901	2
3–4	184 884	3.46
5–10	257 890	6.9
11–24	163 997	15.83
25–49	69 620	34.00
50–99	33 463	69.04
100–199	17 684	138.08
200–499	9 886	301.25
500–999	2 789	688.79
1000–1999	1 166	1 373.65
2000–4999	417	2 924.58
5000+	64	7 502.56

* A 'census unit' is defined as the location where employers hold the pay records of their employees. It is therefore an imprecise measure of the number of firms.

Source: Census of Production 1981. Department of Employment Statistical Branch. Unpublished

One of the most striking features of Table 5.2 is the enormous difference in the size of firms (measured by employment).

Clearly the organisational task varies considerably from firm to firm. At one extreme a one-man firm requires virtually no internal organisation of resources save what the owner 'plans' for himself while at the other extreme the sixty-four firms with, on average, 7500 employees need to have developed sophisticated methods of planning, organising and monitoring the enterprise. Only in the case of the owner-controlled firm will the market directly control the allocation of its resources; in all other cases some form of administrative structure lies between input and output markets.

Examination of the numbers employed by industry groups reveals that over two-thirds of the workforce in the vehicle manufacture and shipbuilding industries are in 'firms' with more than 1000 employees. While in the distribution industry (retail and wholesale) over half the workforce is employed in firms with less than eleven employees. Adjusting for industry groups, the average number of employees by 'firm' size does not differ significantly between the public and private sector.

What then is the difference between public and private sector firms? The conventional answer is their *objectives*, but this too is an oversimplification. It has long been recognised that the separation of ownership from control results in managers being able to secure their own interests subject only to some minimum profit constraint which would ensure that the owners (shareholders) do not dismiss the management. Baumol (1958), Williamson (1963), and Marris (1963; 1964) have each constructed theories which have been collectively described as 'managerial theories' of the firm. Within these models there are two control problems. First, how can managers be induced to operate in the interests of the firms' shareholders and, secondly, how can managers control the operation of the firm to ensure that their own objectives are achieved?

Leibenstein (1966; 1978), while not entering the debate over ownership, has argued that theoretical models of the production process which imply that the least cost combination of inputs will be used is naive. Where competitive pressures are weak (that is the market is not being contested), Leibenstein predicts that firms will have costs above the theoretical minimum; there will be X-inefficiency.

In short, if the usual assumption of self-interested behaviour is accepted then, amongst other things, the performance of firms will depend on the degree of control exercised over and by managers, employees and shareholders. Government, acting in some sense in 'the public interest', may also be party to this control function when acting on behalf of consumers. Performance should rightly be viewed therefore as the outcome of a contest between the conflicting interests involved within firms (see Luffman and Reed 1984).

Significantly, these problems of control and the conflict of interests between owner and manager have also been identified in the case of the public sector bureaux. There is, after all, no reason to believe that managers and employees will have any different goals to those in the private sector. Niskanen (1971) has argued that bureaucrats working to a fixed revenue budget (provided by a sponsoring agency such as government) will have an incentive to overproduce and that 'slack' can build up in the system, generating inefficiencies similar to those identified by Leibenstein. Minford has put the matter more forcibly: 'bitter experience has shown us in Britain that . . . public sector monopolies collude with their workforce to maximise transfers from the taxpayer per unit of output, and that unions act cynically to raise wages and terms of their members, disregarding the severe side-effects on people they do not represent' (Minford 1983).

Both public bureaux and private firms therefore require some mechanism to ensure that only 'legitimate' objectives are attended to by managers and staff. Alchian and Demsetz (1972) have argued that the problem of control within organisations springs from the non-separability of workers' marginal products in 'team' production. Under these circumstances one member of the team is required to monitor his colleagues, but this raises the question: who will monitor the monitor? Alchian and Demsetz suggest that the monitor can be induced to perform his role effectively if he is given the right to some or all of the surplus which effective monitoring generates; a right which he is entitled to sell to another if he wishes. Such they argue is the foundation of the classical capitalist firm but certain activities are inherently difficult to monitor (such as the output of teachers and college lecturers) and this explains why many organisations are 'owned' by the public sector rather than the private sector.

The control problem of real firms and organisations, which Williamson (1963) had recognised in his theory of managerial discretion, prompted him to examine the development of the large corporation: 'most previous treatments of corporate control, including my own, have focused mainly on *external control* forces. What I regard as the distinctive feature of the present theory is that it examines how, through changes in organisational form, the corporation has been able to mobilise the much more powerful forces of *internal control*' (Williamson O. E. 1972: viii).

He recognised that 'substantially the same factors that are responsible for market failures (which led to the creation of "firms") also explain failures of internal organisation' (Williamson O. E. 1973). The costs of organising internally may thus lead to failures of 'firms'.

Because human action takes place within certain behavioural, psychological and neurological limits, economic actors are incapable of pure rational action; rationality is therefore bounded. Human behaviour also exhibits what Williamson refers to as 'opportunism', that is 'an effort to realise individual gains through a lack of candor or honesty in transactions' (Williamson O. E. 1973). Added to these features, economic transactions take place under conditions of uncertainty, often between small numbers of actors, and in situations where information relevant to the exchange is 'impacted', that is, some individuals possess information which is necessary for the other party to gain before a transaction can be undertaken but the information is itself the commodity to be transacted.

As organisations evolved they did so within a unitary structure (U-Form) in which control was exercised from the peak of a pyramid management hierarchy. Williamson has argued, however, that as firms grew the decision-making process became too complex given bounded rationality constraints and the other cost-increasing features of human action. The development of a multi-divisional structure (M-Form) was a significant organisational innovation which permitted firms to economise on transaction costs. In an M-Form structure, decision making is decentralised to 'semi-autonomous operating divisions . . . organised along product, brand, or geographic lines' (Williamson O. E. 1981). Strategic control is exercised by a central office which performs the role of a pseudo-capital market allocating resources to the divisions on the basis of their operating performance. Transaction costs are minimised by concentrating day-to-day decision making within the centralised units.

Although Williamson's work was explicitly directed towards the development of large private sector organisations, 'there is no reason to suppose that his results do not have wider and more general applicability to other types of organisations' (Jackson P. M. 1982: 69); much of it is equally relevant to the growth of public sector bureaux. The importance of this view to the debate regarding the appropriate level of government involvement cannot be overstated. For Williamson's work directs our attention away from the market/non-market debate to a potentially testable thesis regarding the relative effectiveness of different forms of organisation rather than different forms of ownership (see Caves 1980). The approach also leads us to ask what, if any, is the major distinguishing feature of private organisations compared to public sector? Sir Leo Pliatzky, at one time the Permanent Secretary of the Department of Trade, did not see a distinction at least in the possibility of efficiency: '. . . government can, in principle, be as efficient in the management of resources, meaning essentially staff resources, as reasonable comparable private sector organisation' (Pliatzky 1986).

In the United States, however, Rainey's (1983) research revealed that managers in public sector organisations felt constrained by bureaucratic rules from exercising their entrepreneurial talents.

Clearly, in theory at least, the issue of public versus private efficiency is far from being settled in favour of private organisations. Transaction costs, bounded rationality, motivational factors and the need to control are issues common to both public and private 'firms'. There are no grounds therefore for an *a priori* preference for private over public ownership. Unfortunately the empirical evidence available is far from satisfactory as a means of resolving the debate. Nevertheless, Parker's view (1985) is that 'there is no conclusive evidence of lower efficiency in the public sector'.

Fama (1980) argues that the concept of 'the ownership' of firms is irrelevant because 'each factor [of production] in a firm is owned by somebody'. It is, according to Fama, 'the discipline imposed by managerial labor markets [which] resolve potential incentive problems'. Fama acknowledges the argument that a manager may be able to avoid the immediate consequences of 'slacking' or pursuing his own objectives but ultimately his salary and job prospects will be adversely affected by the consequent poor performance of the firm to which he is contracted. Such poor performance would be noted in the managerial labour market and thus reduce his/her perceived value on that market.

Here then is the major difference between public and private sector organisations and firms: ultimately private firms face 'the market test'. Discipline within the firm is thus seen as a response to 'competition by other firms' (Fama 1980) for customers which generates the need to maintain competitive prices and thus competitive costs. Each manager has, therefore, an incentive to monitor his subordinates (and his supervisors) to ensure that *his* prospects are not diminished.

In this approach privatisation and liberalisation of business could be seen to serve the purpose of inducing an efficient monitoring of management by allowing competitive pressures to act on previously 'protected' firms, and by removing the barriers which have led management and workers in public sector firms to believe that their jobs are secure and will not be affected by labour market pressures. There are obvious parallels with the contestability hypothesis applied here to labour (and capital) markets as well as product markets but how far labour markets are, or could be, contestable is open to question. Differences in the initial endowments of skills and marketable talents, access to training and/or funds to facilitate investment in human capital are some of the reasons for doubting that there are no entry barriers to labour markets. Furthermore, human capital investment is, by its very nature, a sunk cost and thus a barrier to entry.

Conclusion

In our review of the British experience of government involvement in business affairs in the post-war period, we have highlighted its emphasis on the competitive process; its predominantly interventionist nature which, whilst stopping short of full planning, has involved a degree of tripartite collectivism and the unavoidable interweaving of political and economic considerations. This serves to remind us that advances in economic theory are not directly translated into policy and that political ideologies are not always fully reconcilable with economic analysis.

In considering the current policy agenda we have focused upon the analytical underpinnings and highlighted the key concept of the firm in the competitive process. We have argued that the recognition of the nature of firms; their role in superseding the price mechanism; their organisational structure; and the control mechanisms they employ, provide a necessary starting point for an assessment of government intervention.

It has been seen that those economists who have an implicit faith in the power of the price mechanism to induce competitive action and thus achieve internal and external control of firms argue for more deregulation, privatisation and reductions in the scope of government intervention. Developments in theory have reinforced these recommendations as they have provided some hope that structural characteristics of markets do not inevitably result in particular types of conduct. Analysis of the contribution of franchise bidding and contestability has not however removed the threat posed by natural monopoly or monopoly power.

We have also questioned the underlying assumption that public sector enterprises will necessarily be less efficient than private firms. It has been shown that public and private 'firms' face similar problems of internal control and that the debate between private and public, market and non-market, is essentially a question of determining the identity and motivation of the key decision makers. Shareholders of private companies, and government in the case of public sector organisations, face the problem of ensuring that management does not merely act in its own interests. Governments must also ensure that, no matter what objectives are pursued by managers of 'firms', the interests of the public are defended.

We therefore conclude that there is a role for government intervention in the affairs of business. Whether this requires public ownership as well as control is not clear. Organisational factors are of central importance in searching for effective control mechanisms. If it is the case that public ownership is desirable, necessary or just unavoidable, policymakers need to ensure that organisational innovation is not stifled. If the role of government industrial policy is the governance of business to ensure efficient outcomes then, whatever the particular objectives set, more attention needs to be placed on organisational structure, monitoring procedures and transaction cost-reducing devices.

Chapter 6

THE LABOUR MARKET
Michael McNulty

In 1986 the projected population of the UK was 56.5 million and as Table 6.1 indicates 26.8 million men and women were in paid civilian employment or seeking it.

Although the term 'labour market' is used throughout this chapter, in reality there are a host of different labour markets employing different types of workers. Since workers are heterogeneous with respect to natural ability, some are debarred from many jobs, others are disadvantaged by lack of human capital, while others may be prevented by restrictive practices from competing for certain jobs. It is a peculiar market in several respects and consideration of it may lead one to conclude that we should not expect it to operate in a similar fashion to other markets (King J. E. 1980).

Table 6.1   Civilian labour force: estimates and projections

	Great Britain		
	Males	Females	Total million
Estimates			
1971	15.6	9.3	24.9
1976	15.6	10.1	25.7
1979	15.6	10.4	26.0
1981	15.6	10.6	26.2
1983	15.3	10.6	25.9
1984	15.5	10.9	26.4
Projections			
1986	15.6	11.2	26.8
1991	15.8	11.5	27.3

Source: Social Trends 1986

Orthodox and institutional approaches

The neoclassical approach views the demand for labour as a derived demand for a factor of production (see Begg *et al.* 1984: Ch. 10). A profit-maximising firm will continue to employ labour until the marginal cost (wage) of doing so equals the marginal value product of the extra worker employed. The supply of labour consists of workers who seek to maximise utility and hence supply more labour in response to higher real wage offers. Equilibrium in the market is achieved through the interaction of supply and demand forces. In competitive markets, wage increases are only justifiable on grounds of increased productivity. The basic Marxist approach emphasises labour as the sole creator of wealth, and profit represents the expropriation of wealth by capital.

Selling labour tends not to be a brief and impersonal transaction, but one in which status is acquired and personal relationships and expectations develop. The wage determination process itself may never operate on the simplistic lines suggested by neoclassical supply and demand analysis, but may be interwoven with custom and practice. Within this complex relationship the worker, in return for certain rewards, may relinquish part of his autonomy and accept the managerial 'right to manage'. Thus the labour process forms an ongoing contract, but one in which little may have been made explicit apart from the wage rate. The 'implicit contract' comprises a bundle of expected behavioural characteristics on each side which may or may not prove to be accurate. Whether key points in the contract of employment are explicit or implicit, wages will tend to be 'sticky' (inflexible downwards). In response to fluctuations of demand, output will often respond more quickly than will wage rates or even product prices (see Okun 1981). Part of the rationale for sticky wages from the viewpoint of employees lies in a concern over relativities (*vis-à-vis* other groups of workers) and the uneven incidence of wage cuts for specific workers as opposed to generalised ones via price rises (see Ch. 3). Where unemployment for some is seen as an alternative to wage cuts for all, then running the unemployment risk with current wages is seen as the preferred option. But the gains from sticky wages need not accrue only to workers. Employers have theoretically the option of varying the wage rate continually as in an auction market to keep employment constant or to offer some implicit contract that will keep money wages constant but allow lay-offs to bear the strain (thus accommodating likely trade union preferences). Neoclassical theory assumes that wage flexibility will be preferred by the employer, but it has been argued by institutionalists that this can prove to be counter-productive (see Thurow 1976). Where training is important, the employer is not likely to adopt a cavalier approach to wage setting following a reduction in product demand. If the labour market is to be efficient in the long run, it must be structured so as to maximise the willingness of workers to pass on knowledge to new employees while minimising their resistance to the acquisition of new skills. It therefore follows that it makes sense to eliminate downwardly flexible wages (or wage competition as Thurow calls it) and give employment security by limiting recruitment to certain 'entry ports'. Both wage and employment flexibility (or insecurity) means employees have a vested interest in resisting technical change which might reduce employment prospects. Thus flexibility which might be the essence of efficiency in a simple static neoclassical model is to be avoided in labour markets where much human capital is gained and transmitted via 'on the job training'. This applies to employment flexibility as well as wage flexibility. The short-run maximisation of profits can sap the morale and co-operation of the workforce. The conditions for static efficiency are short sighted. It may be better that the firm ensure long-run profitability by structuring its labour market to maximise long-run growth; resisting wage and employment flexibility becomes a tool for increasing long-run productivity and dynamic efficiency. In this way lack of wage (and employment) flexibility is not an illustration of a market imperfection that produces inefficiency but represents a functional market adjustment that produces long-run efficiency (Thurow 1983).

Thurow's arguments enable us to understand the phenomenon of internal labour markets, markets at the level of the firm in which both employer and employees have a vested interest in insulating all or part of the workforce from external market forces (see Doeringer and Piore 1971). They are characterised often by substantial training expenditure on the workforce, an incentive to reduce turnover and have limited 'ports of entry', with promotion from within rather than reliance upon external recruitment. Employers will not allow the unemployed to bid themselves back into jobs at lower rates of pay. Even with the relevant skills, institutionally they are disqualified; their bids are rejected. In such a world the predictions of the new classical macroeconomic models are unlikely to be fulfilled. Monetary deflation will lead to unemployment rather than reductions in the rate of inflation. Direct forms of government intervention in wage-setting behaviour in the form of incomes policy will need to accompany monetary restraint in order to avoid the adverse affects that monetary deflation alone will have on employment (see Peston 1980).

Trade Unions

For several important parts of the labour market, worker behaviour is more the result of collective rather than individual action. Although trade unions cover a minority of the workforce, their actions may have serious repercussions on the market as a whole. Trade unions are associations of workers whose main aims are to improve pay and working conditions by collective action (see Metcalfe 1984).

In 1983 in the UK, there were 11 338 000 members (43.7 per cent of the civilian labour force) organised into 393 unions. The recent decline in union membership from 13.2 million in 1979 reflects in part the decline in employment in traditional industries where membership had been concentrated, for example cotton textiles, coal mining, shipbuilding, transport and certain manufacturing industries (see Table 6.2).

The extent of female unionisation is still less than half that of males. However, the total percentage unionised in the UK is some 100 per cent higher than that prevailing in the US, whilst falling far short of the Scandinavian countries.

In competitive markets, pressure by a trade union to shift the supply curve of labour to the left will result in a higher equilibrium wage but increased unemployment. The union rationale does not accept the competitive stance but stresses that the determination of wages without unions allows an employer to use his vastly superior power in the bargaining process. The worker's response is to use countervailing power which becomes an integral feature of the labour market and cannot be regarded as exceptional or exogenous. Competition, as perceived by neoclassical economists, is merely one solution to the power problem.

From a trade union viewpoint, policies designed to curb union power and encourage market forces do not restore competition, but allow the imbalance between individual worker and employer to work to the latter's advantage.

One of the central questions surrounding union activity, then, is the amount of power which they exert and the effects they have on the economy. If in achieving higher wages unions distort the

Table 6.2 Employees in employment: by industry (UK)

	1971	1976	1979	1981	1983	1984 Males	Females (000)	Total
Agriculture, forestry and fishing	432	393	368	352	249	256	84	340
Energy and water supply industries	797	721	721	709	659	547	83	630
Extraction of minerals and ores other than fuels, manufacture of metal, mineral products and chemicals	1 278	1 157	1 143	934	816	642	153	794
Metal goods, engineering and vehicle industries	3 705	3 329	3 372	2 919	2 635	2 054	541	2 595
Other manufacturing industries	3 102	2 794	2 745	2 367	2 154	1 239	889	2 128
Construction	1 207	1 252	1 248	1 138	1 012	864	120	984
Distribution, hotels, catering and repairs	3 678	3 964	4 252	4 166	4 172	1 976	2 348	4 323
Transport and communication	1 550	1 456	1 476	1 423	1 325	1 038	266	1 304
Banking, finance, insurance, business services and leasing	1 366	1 494	1 649	1 740	1 822	968	912	1 881
Other services	5 036	5 975	6 185	6 121	6 106	2 258	3 925	6 183
All industries and services	22 122	22 543	23 157	21 870	21 048	11 841	9 321	21 162

Source: Social Trends 1986

market, then governments may feel justified in attempting to curb their power. But since unions maintain that there exists an imbalance of power under individual bargaining and even often under collective bargaining, in favour of the employer, the issue for them centres around the exploitation of labour (see Hodgson 1984: Ch. 3).

From a Marxist viewpoint, unions are justified in fighting for all the profit of the capitalist. In contrast, the Institute of Directors argue that the growth in the welfare state and employee protection legislation should have reduced the need for unions (see Hoskyns 1985). Do unions have too much power? Is the state justified in intervening in the labour market? The answer to these questions depends upon the political perspective taken, one's view of the operation of the labour market and an assessment of the empirical evidence concerning the effects of union activity on wages and resource allocation (see Friedman 1980: Ch. 8).

Research in the UK (see Stewart 1983a) suggests that on average, unionised workers have been successful in securing up to 10 per cent more than non-union groups. US research suggests that the welfare loss from higher union wages and lower employment is of a very low order, less than 0.33 per cent of GNP (see Hamermesh and Rees 1984). In addition, lower productivity will result if unions resist technological change and attempt to maintain outmoded job/skill demarcation divisions by restrictive practices. Despite such practices, there could still be net advantages for employers in dealing with unions in terms of having a more regimented labour force and easier communication in both directions. Preliminary US research points to this being so, although critics of these findings certainly exist (see Freeman and Medoff 1979).

Firms may view unions more positively where a closed shop is practised. A pre-entry closed shop demands that new employees are already union members; a post-entry closed shop demands they join the union after being hired. Closed shops cover about one-quarter of all employees in the UK and this number has grown in recent years, although it is uncommon in the service sector of the economy. Perhaps what has taken place with respect to closed shops in general is a formal recognition of the need for more orderly relations.

Whilst over half of total employees exercise the right not to join a union or feel that no suitable union exists for them, this right is limited in instances where the closed shop is operated and justified by unions via the free rider argument.

Traditional limitations on the military, police and others in strategic positions to join unions was extended in 1984 to include around 1000 civil servants at the Government Communications Headquarters (GCHQ). The Employment Acts of 1980 and 1982 had already attempted to alter the present distribution of power in the organised labour market in matters relating to the closed shop and strike activity. Present legislation demands an 80 per cent majority with periodic ballots to operate a closed shop. A postal ballot of union members must be held (government finance being available to defray such expenses) prior to any official strike being declared, otherwise a union may be sued for damages arising out of such strikes. Where an official strike takes place, a code of practice suggests that peaceful picketing is limited to only six employees outside the place of work and the picketing of the place of work by employees of other establishments (secondary picketing) is not permissible. Not all legislation is pro employer. The operation of the Health and Safety at Work Act and the Employment Protection Act (1975) may be regarded as giving more power to individual workers and the Advisory Conciliation and Arbitration Service was designed to help both sides where collective bargaining is problematic.

Recent legislative changes may represent a real shift of power back to employers, particularly as they operate against a backcloth of high unemployment. However, recent work on trade union/non-trade union differentials (see Metcalfe and Nickell 1985) somewhat surprisingly shows no narrowing since 1979. Indeed, whereas the period from 1962 until Mrs Thatcher's election was one of relative stability with respect to the earnings differential, her premiership has witnessed the steepest rise for more than a decade, with a 12 per cent gap being recorded in 1983. Further, despite the manufacturing sector bearing the brunt of the present recession, average earnings here continue to rise faster than for the economy as a whole (e.g. 8.5 per cent to 9.0 per cent as against 7.5 per cent average in 1985). It would appear that the actual shift in power may have more to do with the manner and intensity of the policing of the legislation than the legislation itself. Coupled with this is the question of possible lags. Management may not be fully aware of their newly bestowed power or, if it is aware, it may be reluctant to use it.

However, one thing is clear; the textbook representation of a perfect competitive labour market is of little use as a tool to analyse the complex workings of real world labour markets. The concept of the institution is integral to the operation of the biggest labour market and collective bargaining remains the basic mechanism of wage determination. What basically guides government with regard to intervention in such areas is whether they are satisfied with the existing distribution of power, whether they feel the collective bargaining framework is conducive to economic growth and, perhaps in the final analysis, whether it accords with their economic ideology. In this respect, it is clear that the government of Mrs Thatcher has implemented macroeconomic policies which place much faith in the theoretically attractive model of a market-clearing labour market.

Training

A labour force has the dimension of quantity and quality. With regard to the latter we can distinguish between two main settings in which learning takes place, namely training and education. Training is regarded as that setting in which an employer transfers skill to an employee with the express aim that this skill be later used to enhance production; it is very much an internal investment decision which may nevertheless have important effects externally in the labour and product markets. Government intervention in education is considered elsewhere in this book (see Ch. 9). Here we concern ourselves with the special economic problems relating to training and whether experience in the UK suggests that intervention helps or hinders.

Can the market provide supplies of adequately trained manpower in numbers sufficient to deal with varying rates of economic growth, the changing structure of the economy and new technology? Training can obviously enhance the future productivity and income of the trainee as well as the profits of the employer. It is a form of investment in human capital expected to yield a rate of return, depending upon the length of the labour market contract. The more widely applicable the training is to other firms or even other industries, the greater the potential mobility of the trained worker. General training, therefore, can be contrasted with specific training applicable only to the providing firm. In a competitive setting with no constraints on mobility, a generally trained worker will seek the highest post-training wage. Employers will be reluctant to finance training, given the risk of losing trained workers to competitors able to offer a higher wage and who have incurred no training costs. Faced with this labour turnover risk, employers may feel tempted to 'lock in' employees and operate an internal labour market. Here turnover is minimised by offering long-term advantages to those who stay via pension rights and preference in promotion. If training costs have been incurred and output falls, firms will be more reluctant to dismiss the trained workers and trainees than the unskilled. This gives rise to a management rationale for overmanning.

Where a firm provides specific training, the turnover risk is considerably less as the worker must abandon his skill if he wishes to move. Thus a firm may be willing to pay a wage in excess of output during training where there is a good chance of recouping this cost by paying a post-training wage below output value.

This framework of analysis helps us to consider the experience of the UK during the immediate post-Second World War period and into the early 1960s when the country suffered recurrent skill shortages. Industrialists complained that trained workers were 'poached' away by non-training firms, offering more attractive pay packages. This background led to the Industrial Training Act (1964). By 1969, twenty-seven Industrial Training Boards (ITBs) had been established covering 60 per cent of employees. The ITBs were charged with improving the quantity and quality of training and ensuring that the costs of training were spread throughout the sectors concerned. The mechanism was straightforward; a payroll levy was exacted from member firms and this was redistributed in grants to firms undertaking acceptable training. It was hoped that both the quantity and quality of training would increase and that poaching firms would be deterred.

A detailed analysis of the workings of the ITBs lies beyond our discussion, but two areas can be illustrated. Small firms, not particularly geared to training programmes, felt that their freedom to hire skilled workers was suffering and that grants were given out to firms undertaking largely specific training. In other words, the distinction between specific and general training was not fully appreciated. Many employers have little idea of the precise degree of generality of a skill. It is likely, however, that where general skills are relevant, because of imperfect capital markets, workers will be unable to borrow to finance their own training and the employer will be obliged to incur training costs. In 1973 the Act was amended to allow for some exemptions but continued in principle to operate the same mechanism. Skill shortages persisted. Numerous official discussion documents were issued during the 1970s and early 1980s wrestling with the problem of the role of central funding and the future of ITBs (see, for example, *Training for skills*, Department of Employment 1976; *Training for Vital Skills*,

MSC 1976; *Outlook on Training*, MSC 1980; *A New Training Initiative*, MSC 1981).

After a review of the activities of the ITBs in 1981, the Employment and Training Act abolished all but four of them. The new philosophy was to be one of voluntarism. It was argued that there was a tendency for ITBs to become bureaucratic and inefficient whilst there was ample evidence of the desire of employers to go it alone. Certainly there was a desire on the part of government that industry should be responsible for its own training. During the 1970s there had been a strong trend towards increasing government support for the operating costs of the ITBs and a decision to return this responsibility to firms had prompted industry's desire for their abolition (see *Outlook on Training*, MSC 1980). Controversy surrounded the abolition of ITBs. The TUC argued that voluntarism alone would be insufficient and that general (transferable) skills training would again prove unattractive to industry. Voluntarism had proved ineffective prior to 1964 when recession was not a problem and was thus unlikely to be effective in the mid-1980s. With one exception, it was the conviction of ITB chairmen that abolition would prove a retrograde step. The Engineering Industry Training Board (one of the few to be reprieved), despite its own efforts, pointed to a drop in apprentice training from 20 000 in 1979 to only 7000 in 1983, a figure well below that required to secure longer-term future skills. Nationally, apprenticeships fell from 155 000 in 1979 to about 100 000 in 1984.

The ITBs, although important, were however only one part of the training scene. The 1972 Employment and Training Act created the Manpower Services Commission (MSC) which was to be nationally responsible for the public employment services and for training in general. Its history has been one of increasing involvement in the labour market. In addition to its role in co-ordinating ITB work, it was also to be responsible for training in those sectors outside the scope of the ITBs, the transition from school to work, and retraining for adults and the unemployed. The MSC felt it necessary to tackle what can be considered an inherent weakness in the market provision of training. In a recession, training is often sacrificed, leading to severe skill shortages during the recovery. The short-run priorities of firms inevitably result in the underprovision of training. Counter-cyclical training is necessary to counteract this but the market left alone is unlikely to provide it. Cross (1982a) has argued that in a severe recession the deterioration of human capital due to lack of training leads to an increase in the natural rate of unemployment.

The MSC is also involved with the transition from school to work at sixteen. This has been a neglected issue and a source of concern since 70 per cent of sixteen-year-olds leave school. Of these, nearly 60 per cent have no formal qualifications and thus no obvious indicator of ability. From 1985 in selected areas, fourteen-year-olds are offered a four-year full-time programme financed by MSC spanning technical, vocational and general education, including work experience under the Technical and Vocational Education Initiative (TVEI). For which labour markets they are being prepared and whether TVEI actually increases employability remains to be seen. It represents, however, an important example of MSC involvement not only as a facilitator in the labour market but as a non-educational institution having influence on school curricula.

Since training is closely linked with education, it is appropriate that efforts are being made to achieve a closer integration between the world of learning within education and that of training. Efforts in this direction are also being financed by the MSC in the field of adult training. The Open Tech programme is concerned with open learning (flexible study programmes) for adults at technician and supervisory management levels and is intended eventually to be self-financing. Local Collaborative Programmes (LCPs) are designed to help employers define their training needs in conjunction with providers of training and to explore possible ways of meeting them. Meanwhile the Department of Education and Science has launched the Professional and Commercial Updating Programme (PICKUP) to encourage educational institutions to work with employers to develop vocational updating.

Government intervention in training is thus evident but the UK experience in this field can be shown to be woefully inadequate as compared with that of our major trading competitors. A recent comparative training survey puts the UK far behind USA, West Germany and Japan (see MSC/NEDO 1984). British firms spend on average only 0.15 per cent of turnover on training, several times lower than our competitors.

In the UK, 70 per cent of school leavers leave school at the age of sixteen but only 50 per cent receive some form of systematic industrial training as compared with 90 per cent in West Germany. In West Germany, Japan and the USA, training is seen as central to economic success for three reasons. First, anyone in the world can buy in technology but success goes to those who make best use of it. Second, quality products and services demand competence and commitment from the whole workforce; it would appear that UK management has yet to be convinced of this. Third, technical change is occurring at an increasingly faster pace. Our competitors appear to appreciate this but too much of UK industry still regards training as a luxury.

Following this report has come more damning evidence (see *A Challenge to Complacency*, MSC 1985). Not only is the UK backward in training, but there is a complacent attitude towards it in that few employers are found to regard it sufficiently important to place in their corporate strategy. The above report urges three policy themes. Employers should be encouraged to train, and account for it in their annual reports. An Individual Training Credit System should also be introduced whereby employer and employees, with tax relief, pay into a training fund. Finally, employer bodies at local level should be established to oversee and monitor local initiatives, perhaps with legislative backing.

This last point raises again the contentious issue of government intervention. Complacency may yet drive governments into action to increase the quantity and quality of training. The role of government training is therefore unlikely to diminish. The need for greater insight, greater commitment and a fundamental change in attitude on the part of much of industry is still pressing and the importance also of education to the economy may well lead, irrespective of the government in power, to a joint department of education and training.

Wages Councils

The rationale for intervention to revise free market determined pay rests upon the natural imbalance found in unorganised labour markets in favour of the employer. Opponents invoke competitive theory to show that the establishment of legal minimum wages above equilibrium will result in higher wages for some, but unemployment for others (see Begg *et al.* 1984: 59).

In Britain, the agencies developed to deal with low pay are the Wages Councils, which have their origin in the Trade Boards established by Winston Churchill in 1909 and 1914. Wages Councils set legally enforceable minimum rates in certain industries. By 1953 some sixty-six Councils covered about 3.5 million workers. At present there are twenty-six covering 2.75 million workers (11 per cent of the employed workforce) mainly in service industries such as retailing, catering and hairdressing. Two-thirds of these workers are part-time, 80 per cent of them are women, and 5 per cent are under the age of eighteen. Enforcement is undertaken by the

Department of Employment's Wages Inspectorate. Underpayment exists but 1.75 million out of the total 2.75 million workers covered are paid in excess of the minima. The Inspectorate attempts to log 10 per cent of establishments each year. Recent checks show some 6 per cent of workers were underpaid by an average of 10 per cent. The Councils were set up as a means of combating the problems of 'sweated labour' in certain trades where very low pay and excessively long hours had given rise to serious public concern. However, critics argue that modern conditions are far removed from these (see Forrest 1985; and Pond 1985).

In 1985, the Department of Employment suggested options ranging from certain limitations on the operations of Wages Councils to outright abolition (see Department of Employment 1985). The government's aim is to maximise employment opportunities, hence flexibility and freedom of action were essential. It argued that Councils interfered with the freedom of employers to offer, and job seekers to accept, employment at market-determined wage rates. This restricted job opportunities, particularly for young people. It further asserted that a number of studies support the view that statutory minimum rates jeopardise employment.

In a perfectly competitive market, minimum legal rates set below

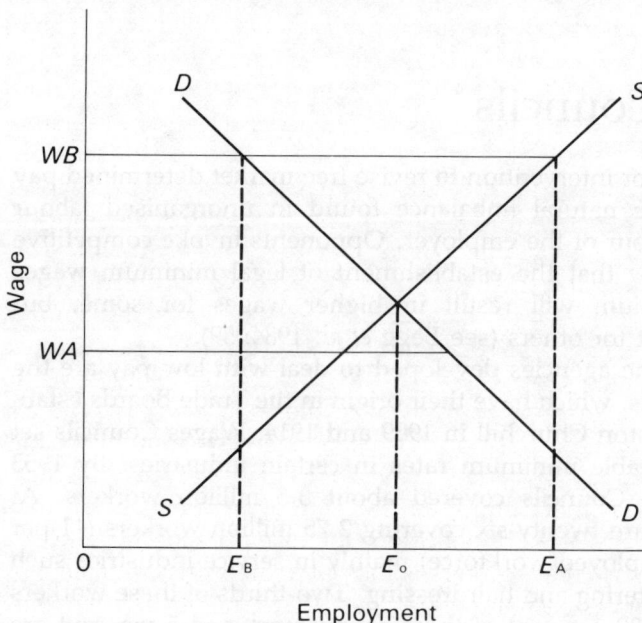

Figure 6.1   Minimum wages in a perfectly competitive labour market

equilibrium e.g. (*WA*) will be superfluous (see Fig. 6.1). However, a legal minimum such as *WB* set above equilibrium will lead to an excess supply of labour and the higher wage is gained at the expense of involuntary unemployment equal to $E_A - E_B$. How much unemployment will depend *ceteris paribus* on the price elasticity of demand and supply for labour (see Begg *et al*. 1984: 237–8).

Is this the relevant framework for analysis? It has been argued that the sectors covered by Wages Councils are typically dominated by small firms in the hotel and catering trade and that these are precisely the sectors where something approaching perfect competition exists. However, the retail trade, hotel industry and licensed trade which together employ more than 2 million of the 2.75 million workers covered by Councils, are dominated by large firms. More than 50 per cent of public house employees covered by the Licensed Non-Residential Wages Council work in managed houses, 66 per cent of which are owned by the six big brewery groups. Thus the small competitive firm argument is not a strong one. Further, since 1.75 million of the 2.75 million workers receive above the minimum, the competitive wage–employment trade-off is irrelevant to the majority, although it could apply to the remaining 1 million (in some trades minima were rarely exceeded).

In the case of monopsony (see Fig. 6.2) where there is only one employer and the profit-maximising wage (*WA*) paid is less than the marginal revenue product of (MRP) labour, it is possible for a legal minimum wage (*WC*) set equal to the competitive equilibrium to have a positive effect upon employment (see Salvatore 1986: 491–501). While this may be uncharacteristic of the UK, proponents of Wages Councils argue that legal minima provide a base for the low paid without greatly affecting employment levels. This is refuted by abolitionists (see Begg *et al*. 1984: Ch. 10).

The Bow Group (on the left of the Conservative Party), the TUC, the Low Pay Unit (a pressure group for the low paid) and a number of academics have argued that no substantive evidence exists that Wages Councils have so blocked job creation as to warrant the loss of protection given to those on low pay who are in a weak bargaining position. This has been confirmed by Craig and Wilkinson (1984). They argue that increases in consumer demand were far more important for employment expansion than are reductions in wages. In addition, the case for abolition is based on the hypothesis that workers could solve their own problems by pricing themselves back into jobs. This places the onus of reducing unemployment on to those who have already been relatively disadvantaged by relative wage change movements since 1979. The

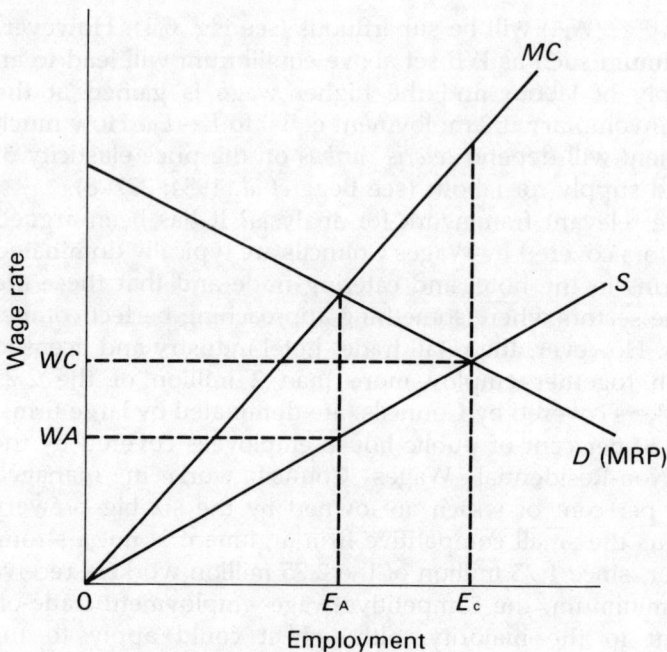

Figure 6.2   Minimum wages under monopsony

burden of real wage adjustment is more appropriate for the higher echelons of the labour market. The CBI (against abolition but in favour of reform) argued that it would be costly for small firms to negotiate wages individually instead of through the Councils and that employees, stripped of Council protection, might flock to join militant unions. This might result in higher wage increases being won from strong firms and an attempt to spread these to weaker ones. In addition and, perhaps from the CBI's point of view, worst of all, abolition might lead to less scrupulous employers treating workers harshly, producing agitation for a national minimum wage, which could destroy many jobs.

Critics of the Wages Councils have marshalled their arguments on competitive lines. Forrest and Dennison (1985) argue that on the basis of US evidence, minimum wages do cause a limitation of employment opportunities and that the burden of proof lay on defenders to argue that market forces do not operate in the UK. Others attempted to estimate the extra jobs likely to be created by abolition. These range from 70 000 to 300 000 (see Lipsey D. 1985).

In view of such arguments or perhaps in spite of them, abolition did not take place in 1985. Under-twenty-ones were removed from

Wages Council regulations and a single minimum hourly rate and overtime rate remain. A new procedure was proposed whereby the government could abolish Councils on a pragmatic basis. In addition, it was intended to deratify the International Labour Organisation Convention No. 26 whereby member states are obliged to create or maintain the fixing of minimum rates in trades where wages are exceptionally low and no effective collective bargaining arrangements exist.

The removal of the under-twenty-ones from Wages Councils' coverage affects some 500 000 workers. The government estimated that this would create 100 000 more jobs, as it was convinced that pay for young people had in general been fixed too high. Youth pay relative to adult pay is higher in the UK than in European countries. However, the relatively low youth unemployment in Germany compared with the UK and their relatively low wages compared to adults, largely reflects the large training component in their employment.

Special employment measures

The workforce has changed enormously over the last twenty years in the UK. There are 1 million fewer people in work compared to the early 1960s. Some 3 million jobs have been lost from manufacturing alone in the period 1970–85. At the same time the numbers seeking work increased greatly from 23.8 million (1961) to 26.3 million (1982). Married women active in the labour market increased by 70 per cent. These changes, combined with the general recession, have produced over 3 million officially registered as unemployed. Two out of five unemployed workers are under twenty-five years of age. This incidence of youth unemployment is in marked contrast to West Germany where it is argued that it is much lower than the adult rate because young workers are very much in demand, having received the most recent training. New jobs in the UK tend to be part-time and are often taken by married women who are not on the register. If unemployment is to be reduced to 2 million by 1990, 2.7 million more jobs need to be created (see Metcalfe and Richardson 1984). Special governmental schemes for the unemployed, some under the auspices of the MSC, have been introduced since 1975. Are such schemes cost effective with lasting positive effects on the economy or do they introduce distortions which make the task of creating real jobs much more difficult?

The Youth Training Scheme (YTS) with a budget of around £1 billion was set up in 1983 to guarantee twelve months' training to some 400 000 otherwise unemployed sixteen-year-olds. An annual sum is paid to the sponsors which means that they can use the trainees at no net cost to themselves while trainees themselves qualify for a weekly allowance. The scheme could represent the first real integrated system of education, work experience and training for under-eighteens. From the trainee's view it can best be judged by the extent to which it leads to better or at least some form of permanent work. Over 0.75 million have passed though it since inception but most leave after thirty-five weeks of their year's course. Critics regard it not as a training scheme but a response to high unemployment. The quality of training also varies enormously depending on the particular scheme. In addition, YTS has attracted criticism for the low allowances paid to trainees and its poor record on industrial safety and failure to address the type of training required. Nevertheless, by 1990 it is hoped that the new scheme will raise to 100 per cent the number of seventeen-year-olds in full-time training or education from the low figure of only 30 per cent in 1981. With this expansion and with further refinements such as training certificates on completion, government spokesmen regard the new YTS as a quantum leap.

It is possible that YTS will become the norm for sixteen-year-olds leaving school and thus form the recognised link between school and the world of work. This approach could have much to recommend it, particuarly if YTS trainees can thereby make a much more informed decision about career choice, so reducing search costs. It is difficult, however, to envisage how trainees will be attracted into completing a two-year programme when the drop-out rate on the one-year scheme is already disturbingly high. It appears vital therefore to effect a change in structure and quality for the success of the new scheme.

Of fundamental importance, especially if YTS becomes the only route for sixteen-year-olds to enter into employment, is the *de facto* acceptance by government that the financing of initial training is not something to be left to industry. The co-operation of industry is vital for its success, and so long as finance is mainly borne by the MSC, then government largely finances training for the first two years for those who would have been regarded as normal trainees by industry. This represents a major and perhaps a necessary intervention in the labour market.

The Community Programme (CP), introduced in 1982, subsidises totally public sector job creation programmes for adults (over twenty-five) unemployed for over one year and for the eighteen to twenty-five age group unemployed for over six months. Over 0.25 million have now gone through the programme but this represents only a small proportion of the target group. On completion, some 70 per cent return to unemployment and about 50 per cent do not consider their job chances have been enhanced (see Department of Employment 1985). It has the effect of recycling the long-term unemployed and offers only a temporary substitute for real job creation.

The Job Splitting Scheme (introduced in 1983) is calculated not to raise total demand for labour but to share out the existing demand while reducing unemployment figures. The Job Release Scheme (introduced in 1977) offers elderly workers an allowance until pensionable age if they make way earlier for the younger unemployed, hence total labour supply is reduced.

In 1986 a scheme designed to help the 1.4 million long-term unemployed (over twelve months) commenced whereby a £20 taxable allowance is paid directly to the worker for six months if full-time work of less than £80 per week is accepted. Filling unattractive low-paid vacancies and so increasing a flexible approach on the part of workers is the initial aim; thereafter it is designed to enhance their overall job prospects, once back in employment. Such a scheme could be very cost effective but it is hardly likely to change significantly the magnitude of the unemployment problem.

Job subsidies have several effects on employment. The deadweight effect results from a subsidy being claimed for jobs which would have been created anyway. The substitution effect results from the subsidy encouraging the recruitment of subsidised workers at the expense of non-subsidised ones, while the real job effect considers the number of extra jobs, net of any substitution effect. The displacement effect attempts to capture the effect on jobs where the output of firms receiving the subsidy competes with the output of non-competing firms and the latter suffer a reduction in their demand for labour. The net result of these factors means that the fall in numbers registered as unemployed is less than the number of participants on the schemes. A recent study from the Institute of Manpower Studies (IMS) showed that the real job effect, net of substitution, for schemes has varied between 10–40 per cent, which means that for every 100 jobs within such schemes only ten to forty owed their existence to them (see Rajan 1985). For the Young Workers Scheme (1982–86) (a straight subsidy to employers who hire youths) the figure was 20 per cent, i.e. five such jobs have to be fashioned to achieve one genuine creation. However, one has to compare the relative effectiveness of the schemes as job creators with the cost of other policy options designed to reduce unemployment.

The IMS estimates that the Public Sector Borrowing Requirement per job is around £2500. This should be seen in the light of the average net cost per unemployed person which is currently well over twice that amount. In pure monetary terms, then, subsidies, despite often involving a large deadweight effect, can be seen as very cost effective. Other job-creating policies via various forms of reflation present a much more expensive (and different in nature and quality) method costing between £15 000 to £10 000 per job (see Rajan 1985).

The rationale of job subsidies has to do with the perceived political need to alleviate unemployment in the short term. It recognises too the constraints associated with demand reflation, while at the same time accepting the difficulty of expecting unemployment itself to lead to labour market adjustments in the form of downwardly flexible wages. Although reflation involves important trade-offs with inflation and the balance of payments, the role of these special measures must remain secondary in nature. They extend to less than 20 per cent of the total of registered unemployed.

Discrimination in labour markets

Unequal treatment can arise in the employment of individuals having a common characteristic such as sex, ethnic origin, colour, marital status or religion. In the UK, inequalities between the sexes are most obvious. Women comprise some 44 per cent of the total employed labour force, but are disproportionately represented in low-paying occupations. Women on average earn only some 60–70 per cent of male earnings. Even among higher-paying occupations, women are crowded into the less well-paid positions. Part-time employment, an increasingly important phenomenon in the last decade, is almost entirely confined to married females.

Inequality may involve genuine unjust treatment. Alternatively, unequal treatment may be explained by 'natural' economic forces of supply and demand and not constitute discrimination.

The term discrimination is at times loosely applied to certain areas of inequality. For example, a police force may 'discriminate' against applicants of diminutive stature. In an economic analysis of a labour market, however, the term is confined to those situations in which unequal treatment is accorded groups with respect to terms or conditions of employment despite equal productivity. The discriminating characteristic, whether religion, colour, sex or ethnic background, is generally easily identifiable and unconnected with productivity potential. Thus insofar as the police regard height as a proxy for ability to deal with criminals, then diminutive stature is a negative productivity characteristic.

To what extent do males and females have different characteristics which could lead to unequal treatment in the labour market? One may largely discount differences in physical strength as in so few jobs is this factor of prime importance. What is of great importance are two interrelated factors, participation in further education and subsequent labour force experience. Although the married women's participation rate in the labour market has increased dramatically over the last few decades, women often leave the market to have children. The human capital they have acquired depreciates during absence and on return they may require further training. *Ceteris paribus*, the return on human capital will therefore be less for females. This provides one rationale for the fact that in the early 1980s more than twice as many men in the labour market had degree or equivalent qualifications than women. An alternative reason is of course that women, in investing less in human capital, are simply reacting rationally to discrimination they know is a feature of the labour market. This may explain why they have tended to concentrate on school subjects better suited to low-status occupations. Discrimination may exist prior to entry into the labour market by pressure exerted within the education system, causing the concentration of women into certain occupations. The situation with respect to education appears to be changing, however. In 1985, while women formed 42 per cent of the workforce, they formed 40 per cent of students in higher education.

Another observed factor within their labour market experience is that in nearly all occupations and industries women display higher turnover rates. This, together with withdrawal for family formation, may lessen employer incentive to finance female training. There is also some evidence of the concentration of women in smaller plants and firms and these tend to pay lower wages and offer fewer prospects. Small firms are less likely to employ unionised labour and women in general are less likely to be union members. Insofar as unions raise wages, then women are less likely to benefit.

One would expect to observe some labour market inequality between the sexes based upon their differing economic characteristics. At the same time, it is also clear that some discrimination is practised and contributes to the gross observed earnings differential, but the precise role of discrimination is difficult to identify clearly. Attempts to quantify the role of the economic characteristics and their part in explaining the differential, treat discrimination as a residual, but there are several problems. Generally discrimination is perceived as being practised by employers; it arises on the demand side of the labour market. However, differences in pay can arise through differences in the supply conditions of the two groups of workers. These may be the result of straightforward differences in preferences for certain types of work or years of socialisation within education, marriage and the labour market which emphasise the subjugation of women. Marriage and a career may go hand in hand for a man; for a woman they may compete. Where the sexes are equally productive but differing elasticities of supply allow a profit-maximising employer in an imperfect market to pay women less, this may not be regarded as discriminatory by the employer but is according to our definition.

Why is discrimination practised (see Pike 1984)? The neoclassical 'taste' theories emphasise that discrimination represents non-profit-maximising behaviour. As such, this behaviour causes a misallocation of resources and a lower national income than could otherwise be achieved (see Becker 1971). Monopoly theories emphasise the exploitation of weak groups. Employers gain monopoly profits which they may share with favoured workers. No discrimination would mean a change in relative earnings in favour of women. But can men be said to gain as a whole at the expense of women? Since most adults marry and agree to share family income, there seems little point in a husband discriminating against his own wife in the labour market. Perhaps what is sought is not economic gain but a desire for status (see Thurow 1976). Radical theories differ again in seeing discrimination as part of the capital–labour conflict. Capitalist employers divide and rule and so attain lower wages for both men and women (see Roemer 1979). However, the glaring sex inequalities which also exist in non-capitalist countries would tend to support approaches which stress male dominance irrespective of the economic system. Finally, statistical discrimination theory asserts that employers treat sex or colour as a convenient proxy for negative productivity characteristics. If an employer believes that women are less interested in training or more likely to leave, he will treat all as if they possess this characteristic and they will continue to be hired at less favourable rates and perhaps not considered for promotion. Where this is not the case, such discrimination is erroneous, but the employers do not know this. They feel no need to engage in search costs and continue to discriminate.

What role is there for government intervention in this area? It should be remembered that the state is the prime provider of education and as such is in a key position to address the issue of pre-entry labour market discrimination. The pattern of educational provision between the sexes, attitude formation, careers advice and work preparation all play a crucial part in forming supply characteristics of females. The state is also the biggest single employer and is therefore in a powerful position to influence the behaviour of others.

Legislation in the UK has taken the form of the Equal Pay Act 1970, fully operative from 1975, and the Sex Discrimination Act of 1975. The first requires women to receive equal treatment to males in matters of pay and conditions when employed on the same or broadly similar job, or a job different to, but of equal value with, male jobs. The Act is generally credited with narrowing the hourly male/female earnings differential for full-time workers, but has had relatively less effect on part-time female workers since there tends to be no comparable male rates.

It will be recalled that one argument against high minimum wages was that they cause higher unemployment in competitive conditions. Should we not have seen a rise in female unemployment? The situation is clouded by changes in the industrial structure which have favoured female employment. Allowing for this, there is some evidence of a negative relationship between relative pay and the relative employment of females (see Metalfe and Richardson 1984). With rises in the relative cost of employing females, one could expect an increasing preference for males. The Sex Discrimination Act forbids this; an employer cannot base any recruitment, training, promotion or dismissal decision even partially on grounds of sex. Backing up the Act is the Equal Opportunities Commission (EOC) set up to promote equal opportunities for women. Discrimination nowadays is confined largely to a reluctance to promote or recruit women into higher positions rather than being a matter of paying them less for the same or similar valued work.

So far we have considered some aspects of sex discrimination but much of the analysis can also be applied to the question of race. In 1984 Great Britain had an estimated total of 2.4 million people

Table 6.3   Population by ethnic origin, Great Britain 1984

Origin	'000
White	50 844
West Indian	526
Indian	805
Pakistani/Bangladeshi	206
Other states (e.g. Arab, Chinese)	619
Not stated	829

Source: Department of Employment 1985

of ethnic origin (see Department of Employment 1985). This corresponded to about 4.5 per cent of the total population (see Table 6.3).

The vast majority are economically active. As such, racial discrimination cannot be viewed as existing on the same scale as sex discrimination, although it is clear that it does exist. Non-white male workers display slightly lower activity rates than do white males and earn some 17 per cent less after standardising for age, marital status, years of schooling and experience. This differential is taken as a residual to imply discrimination (see Stewart 1983). Ethnic groups tend to cluster around certain conurbations in the South East, West Midlands and the North West and display higher unemployment rates than do whites, even if born in the UK and having attained similar qualifications. Thus employment discrimination appears to exist as well as that with respect to promotion. For UK-born black workers the picture is even worse than for their overseas-born counterparts with an unemployment rate double that of first-generation immigrants. This suggests that discrimination may well be increasing as the proportion of UK-born black people rises. Other evidence shows white people to be nearly four times more likely to be offered work than black interviewees in retail work in Leicester (see Commission for Racial Equality 1985). Similarly, research carried out over the same period in London, Birmingham and Manchester showed that at least 33 per cent of employers discriminated against black job applicants (see Policy Studies Institute 1985). Comparison with research carried out by the PSI in 1973 and 1974 shows no decrease in the level of discrimination. Such findings should be viewed against a succession of Race Relations Acts (1965, 1968 and 1976) designed to prevent such behaviour.

The rationale for government intervention in this field may be viewed from several perspectives. The taste (neoclassical) approach views legislation as attempting to change employer preferences in an imperfect labour market. The monopoly approach sees the use of law as an attempt to remove the monopoly profit previously enjoyed by the discriminating groups, while the statistical or erroneous approach would regard legislation as bringing about a fundamental change in attitudes forcing employers to allow the discriminated groups to compete on equal terms. It is permissible for an employer, in defence, to show that the productivity of a particular female is lower than that of a male (where discrimination is alleged) but not to justify action based on broad generalisation concerning women.

The effectiveness of policy leading to a change in attitudes may take several decades to show results. Changes in attitudes within the family may be necessary, allowing role reversal (e.g. in matters of child care) if the wife has superior labour market potential. Were this the norm, in the long run, males would be concentrated in low-paid and part-time occupations without discrimination being practised. The evaluation of such policy may require a whole generation to pass through the labour market before widespread success may be claimed. In the meantime, other policies may be suggested to complement or hasten change, for example subsidies (or taxes) on employers who employ (or fail to employ) the discriminated group, special employment and training programmes designed to lessen the crowding effect of women in certain areas of the labour market.

The effectiveness of legislation to counter forms of labour market discrimination by insisting on fair practice from all parties involved cannot be said to have been a resounding success in Britain. If the monetary or psychic costs of compliance are greater than any gains from upholding the law, then transgressions will continue. The attractiveness of violation in turn depends upon the efficiency of policing, which may prove much easier if legislation were to take the form of quotas, whereby employers were compelled to hire proportions of the relevant groups. This is a practice used in the USA but which has failed to find support in this country. It could lead to difficulties where supplies of certain grades of quota workers are inadequate or where the uneven geographic spread of ethnic groups meant a blanket quota would prove to be too crude an instrument to effectively increase opportunities.

Economic policies may prove ineffective to bring about major changes in social attitudes and less inequality in the labour market. If the heart of sex discrimination lies within past and current family power structures, it is asking rather a lot to expect the laws on equal pay and opportunity to combat this (see Millett 1977). Yet neither greater aggregate demand nor the introduction of new education and training initiatives designed especially to help those discriminated against are any more guaranteed of success than legislation. The aggregate demand approach carries with it all the well-known inflationary problems, while the education and training approach is essentially long run and may still fail to eradicate discrimination.

Policies for incomes

It is the effect that money wages may have on the general price level that has caused more controversy than any other aspect of the operation of the labour market. Monetarists have pointed to the connection in the long run between increases in the money supply and inflation while others attribute a central initiating role to trade unions operating in an imperfect labour market (see Jackson D. *et al.* 1972). With a fixed money supply, wage push by unions would result in unemployment (see Trevithick *et al.* 1981). To avoid this consequence, governments in turn feel obliged to increase the money supply. In brief, there is little agreement amongst economists as to the root cause of inflation (for a fuller consideration of this issue, see Ch. 3).

Faced with the danger of inflation, contributed to by trade unions, few governments feel that they can simply let imperfect market forces take their course. Government is, given the size of the public sector, an extremely important employer. Hence the pay settlements arrived at in the public sector will inevitably influence those in the private sector. But government is expected to steer the economy towards a steady growth of increasing living standards, a healthy balance of payments and full employment. Given these objectives, the general level of pay settlements falls within a government's responsibilities. Dissatisfaction with the effectiveness of demand management policies in dampening the inflationary pressures of the 1960s and 1970s led to the adoption of incomes policies as an alternative (see Blackaby 1972; 1978). In the 1980s the current government has rejected this approach and favours instead policies designed to change the structure of the labour market.

The history of incomes policies is much older than many imagine (see Schwettinger 1976). They are basically of two types: either legislative control or exhortation, and one or other of these forms has been frequently used in the UK since the early 1960s, at least until 1979. They all attempted to relate money wages increases to productivity growth so as to reduce inflation. On the political front, an incomes policy also provided a specific opportunity to help the low paid, via flat rate increases to all, and so effect a redistributive aim of government (see Fallick 1982).

The case against incomes policies maintains that they prevent the market from playing its allocative role (Brittan and Lilley 1977). Short-run shifts in supply and demand do occur but the lack of wage flexibility does not allow labour markets to clear. The market becomes even more imperfect and inefficiency is caused by government interference. Monetarists also argue that however well-intentioned incomes policies might be, they have not, and could not, work (see Friedman 1980). Constrictions on the labour market, in the form of maximum percentage wage increases, will either be evaded or, if they were adhered to, would simply negate themselves, given the eventual and inevitable relaxation of policy. Gains would be seen to be essentially of a temporary nature, any wage restraint being undone with the passage of time. In opposing incomes policies, free marketeers join forces in a strange alliance with the far left. They, however, stress the basic right of trade unions to bargain for maximum wages for their members. More fundamentally they assert that the working class should not restrain their incomes and bear the brunt of a fundamental weakness of the capitalist system (see Nuti 1969).

What has been the experience of incomes policies in the UK? While policies were in force, wage increases appear to have been lower than one would otherwise have expected but, following the relaxation of policy, wages have tended to restore themselves to levels that they would have reached had the policy not existed. In that sense, they may be said to have failed, yet the accuracy with which one can estimate what would have otherwise happened is problematical. Comparing a 'policy on' period with a 'policy off' period immediately afterwards may point to the policy's ineffectiveness, but equally may point to the policy not being applied for long enough (see Parkin and Sumner 1972: Ch. 4). This last point may be of great importance where the underlying aim of the policy is not the strict adherence to a numerical norm but a change in attitudes towards lower money wage increases. The failure of demand management to deliver the goods with respect to the simultaneous achievement of full employment and price stability suggests the need for an additional instrument (see Robinson D. in Morris (ed.) 1985). It must be admitted that most incomes

210 THE LABOUR MARKET

policies have been tried in the UK when labour markets have been tight. But the fundamental problem is in how to achieve success while coping with particular cases of inflexibility (the special case). It is difficult to see how this can be easily resolved. Following the imposition of an incomes policy, there will invariably be some group which is unhappy with, and intent on effecting some change in, the existing occupational or industrial wages structure (Snowdon 1983).

Post-Keynesian proponents of incomes policies see progress in terms of the establishment of a permanent policy. Temporary policies have been more akin to panic measures to avoid crises, whereas what is needed is governmental commitment to an overall economic policy of expansion within which incomes policy plays an integral part (see Cornwall 1984). But the problem of relativities would remain.

Is a consensus feasible in this area? The potential for a tripartite approach by employers, unions and government is great, yet so are its attendant problems (see Grant and Nath 1984). These range from the bargaining concerned with the prioritisation of goals, to the lack of a strong centralised collective bargaining system conducive to policy being carried out (as exists in the Scandinavian countries) and the fundamental need to establish a workable mechanism to facilitate changes in relative wage rates. But the UK does have some tripartite experience on which to build. While not incorporated into the formal structure of the major institutions as is the case in Austria, there are specific examples of tripartism at work within the MSC and the Commission for Health and Safety (although here government participation is indirect). Tripartism of a more direct nature exists in the National Economic Development Council and the forty-five Economic Development Committees (Little Neddies). It remains to be seen whether one can build on such experience for more fundamental purposes (see Cassels 1985).

This tripartite approach has recently been taken up again by Labour Shadow Chancellor Roy Hattersley in arguing for a 'National Economic Assessment'. This would involve unions (and the CBI if willing) agreeing with government a set of desirable targets for public spending, money supply and the exchange rate. Within this context, agreement would be reached concerning the wage increases that would enable increased aggregate demand to be translated into real job creation. The policy would not be statutory. The problem of gaining compliance from individuals would of course remain. The price of non-compliance, however, would be that unemployment would not decline as fast as desired. This proposal broadens the debate on incomes policies and reflects more the broad Swedish tripartite experience of recent decades.

The advocates of statutory policies have not given up their fight. They argue that what has been lacking from earlier policies was any real incentive to comply. Such an incentive, albeit negative, could be provided by a tax levied on employers paying above the norm, but the most profitable firms may still be able to buy themselves out of compliance (see Jackman and Layard 1982).

We have earlier referred to the general arguments used by the free marketeers against incomes policies *per se*. But this is not to say that governments of this type do not have policies which restrain wage increases. The broad aims of the current Conservative government have been to master inflation by control of the money supply, to increase individual incentives by increasing (post-tax) disposable income, to restore collective bargaining to a market setting and to return to the private sector certain areas of public ownership (see Ch. 5). The success of the monetarist experiment is questionable. The money supply has proved very difficult to control, but the government has succeeded in deflating aggregate demand by reducing public borrowing at a time when the world economy was also in recession. The determination of cash limits for areas of public spending has acted as a form of incomes policy for the public sector. Given the limits imposed, jobs can only be preserved by very restrained pay increases. Current government policies can therefore be regarded as incomes policies under another name and deflation is one way of altering the balance of power in the labour market so as to favour employers (see Kalecki 1943; Kaldor 1982).

Whatever its title, official terms of reference or mode of operation, it seems clear that governments will continue to have some form of policy for incomes. Market forces have proved to be no more efficient than previous direct attempts to effect significant change in wage bargaining. The choice is between which set of imperfections and consequences we would prefer to live.

Conclusion

This chapter has attempted to give an insight into some areas of concern in the UK labour market. It has stressed that the labour market is never perfect, that it has special peculiarities which make normal market analysis less than appropriate and that dissatisfaction with its operation has caused governments to effect policies designed to alter the distribution of power between the parties involved. Conservative governments since 1979 have made special effort to return the labour market to a more natural (free market) setting, with changes in trade union law, abolition of Industrial Training Boards, amendments to Wages Councils and various privatisation schemes, part of philosophy of which is to encourage more flexibility of wages (see *Youth Aid* 1983). Paradoxically, the Conservative government's fight against inflation in a time of deepening recession, with resultant serious rises in unemployment, has necessitated major interventions of a different kind. MSC initiatives have involved major spending programmes to alleviate unemployment and provide 'training' for young people (see Davies B. 1984). However, alarming numbers do not gain jobs after such 'training' and are forced back on to state benefits.

It is debatable whether YTS is a training scheme which significantly increases employability for the vast majority. The period 1979 to 1986 has seen DHSS social security spending rise by 33.7 per cent and the Department of Employment's spending rise by 67.2 per cent, this latter rise being the highest for any central government department over the period. It can, of course, be argued that schemes like YTS are part of the government's philosophy to achieve a flexible labour market. An alternative perspective based on apprehension views such efforts as a desperate response to street riots, rising crime and rocketing unemployment.

Ironically, with over 1 million workers on MSC programmes of one kind or another (and the prospect of social security being denied those who refuse YTS places) this may appear to some as manipulation of the market and experimenting with the direction of labour. Such programmes, it will be remembered, have been and are effected in the name of market freedom by governments resolutely opposed to state intervention.

Chapter 7

HOUSING
Philip Holmes

Introduction: past progress, current problems

The British housing system is particularly complex with government involvement taking many forms. During the twentieth century the housing system has been subject to considerable change, one aspect of which is demonstrated in Table 7.1.

Table 7.1 Dwellings and households 1951–81, England and Wales (millions)

	1951	1956	1961	1966	1971	1976	1981
Dwellings	12.5	13.7	14.6	15.8	17.0	18.1	19.2
Households	13.3	14.0	14.7	15.9	16.8	17.6	18.3
Balance	−0.8	−0.3	−0.1	−0.1	+0.2	+0.5	+0.9

Source: 1951–1976: DoE Housing Policy: A Consultative Document, Annex B, Table 3, 1977; 1981: Households: DoE Housing and Construction Statistics 1970–1980, Table 142 (projection); Dwellings: DoE Housing and Construction Statistics 1974–1984, Table 9.1

Anyone examining that table might well be led to believe that housing policy has been one of the major success stories of post-war British social policy. Indeed, the transformation of the housing balance from a situation where there was a 'crude deficit' of some 800 000 houses in 1951 to a 'crude surplus' of 900 000 thirty years later is indicative of the considerable advances which have taken place in the sphere of housing during this period.

The 1985 Inquiry into British Housing acknowledged the progress to date:

huge strides have been made since the end of the last war. Overcrowding has been dramatically reduced; the number of properties lacking amenities has fallen rapidly; for many their goal of homeowner-ship has been attained; and in many areas crude housing shortage no longer persists. The great majority of people are housed in decent accommodation (Inquiry into British Housing 1985: 4).

These successes have been achieved within a housing system which has significant sectors which are subject to market forces but which is also characterised by considerable, and varied, govern-ment intervention. It might appear, therefore, that a market-government mix has been very effective in the housing field.

However, despite the gains made, Britain still faces severe housing problems: '. . . out of sight of the majority, a minority of the population are suffering very badly'(Inquiry into British Housing 1985: 4).

The apparent surplus of 900 000 dwellings in 1981 undoubtedly presents a false scenario, for a number of reasons. First, the figure relates to England and Wales as a whole and takes no account of 'local shortages' in some areas. The fixity of dwellings and the rela-tive immobility of many households mean that housing shortages can exist in one locality at the same time as there are surplus houses in other areas.

A second factor which needs to be considered is that just as the market for labour is characterised by frictional unemployment, so the housing market requires that at any one time there will be some vacancies (i.e. unemployed housing). After taking account of vacant dwellings, Lansley (1984) calculates that the crude surplus of dwellings for 1981 is reduced to a deficit of about 13 000 and when second homes are taken into account he estimates a deficit of almost 200 000 dwellings.

Thirdly, the figures given in Table 7.1 for the number of house-holds is almost certainly an understatement of the true position. The number of households is not independent of the number of available houses and the figures in Table 7.1 make no allowance for 'concealed' households (e.g. single-parent families, adult chil-dren, aged parents living with another household). The Depart-ment of the Environment estimated that in 1981 there were approximately one-third of a million such households in England and Wales, with about half of them wanting their own accom-modation (figures reported in the Inquiry into British Housing 1985: 23).

Another important consideration is that the figures given in Table 7.1 give no indication of the quality of the housing stock, nor of the suitability of that stock in terms of types of dwellings (size, age, number of rooms, bathroom facilities etc.) compared to household types (pensioner/non-pensioner, number of children etc.). In relation to quality and suitability, three points should be considered: the fitness of the stock; the number of houses lacking basic amenities; and overcrowding. It must be acknowledged that the definition of what constitutes an unfit dwelling is to some extent subjective and may be regarded as a relative, as opposed to absolute, concept. Nevertheless, the Department of the Environment estimated that in 1981 the number of unfit dwellings in England exceeded 1.1 million, although this represented a fall of almost 50 000 on the comparable 1976 figure (DoE 1982).

The number of dwellings deemed fit but which lack one or more basic amenities fell significantly between 1976 and 1981 from almost three-quarters of a million to less than 400 000 houses (DoE 1982). However, while the number of dwellings considered unfit or lacking basic amenities has fallen in recent years, the condition of the housing stock has undoubtedly deteriorated in another very important respect. In the period 1976–81 the number of houses in England judged to be fit but in need of repairs costing in excess of £7000 (at 1981 prices) increased by some 45 per cent from under 400 000 to almost 600 000. Furthermore, approximately 2.5 million houses required repairs costing between £2500 and £7000 (DoE 1982).

This increase in the degree of disrepair is not confined to any one tenure type. Doling *et al.* (1985: 44) point out that '. . . increasing numbers of owner-occupiers . . . are experiencing financial difficulties which are often exacerbated by their status as owner-occupiers and which manifest themselves in a number of ways which directly affect their ability to maintain their homes and their status as owner-occupiers'. In particular, they point out that 'the state of repair of the average owner-occupied house deteriorated' between 1976 and 1981.

As far as overcrowding is concerned, in the twenty-five years from 1951 the number of overcrowded households in England and Wales fell from over 660 000 to 150 000 (DoE 1977).

In addition to these problems, many households live in accommodation which could be considered inappropriate to their requirements (e.g. families with small children living in high-rise flats, elderly or disabled people in accommodation which makes little or no allowance for their special requirements).

Clearly, then, in spite of the considerable advances which have been made since 1945, it would be wrong to believe that post-war British housing policy has resulted in there no longer being a serious housing problem. There remain housing shortages in some areas with resulting problems of homelessness, disrepair has increased in recent years, overcrowding persists (albeit on a smaller scale) and some households live in accommodation unsuitable for their needs.

Suggested solutions to these problems range from a complete withdrawal of government intervention from the housing system to allow the market to act 'unhindered', to calls for much greater governmental control and planning of the system. Having outlined the current major problems in the housing system, the remainder of this chapter considers the competing arguments of the marketeers and interventionists to try to discover a suitable 'way forward'.

In the next section some basic concepts relevant to housing markets will be introduced, followed by a discussion of some of the attributes of the 'good' (housing) which could lead to market failure and the possible need for government intervention. Past and current government intervention will then be briefly reviewed, with emphasis being placed on the failure of this intervention to solve housing problems. The marketeers' case will then be reviewed and the concluding section will suggest some changes which, it is believed, will help to tackle some of the housing problems in Britain.

Housing markets: important concepts

The first contact which most economics students have with studies of market structure is analysis of the limit case of perfect competition. One of the fundamental assumptions underlying this model is that the market is concerned with one completely homogeneous product. When we move away from perfect competition to more 'real world' market conditions it is often necessary to drop this assumption of homogeneity. In attempting to analyse housing markets (the need to talk in terms of a number of markets, not just one market is discussed below) it must be recognised that housing is a particularly heterogeneous commodity. Houses can vary in many ways, e.g. size, location, number of rooms, heating systems, gardens, neighbourhood environment, etc. Clearly this causes difficulty when attempting to define and measure a unit of housing (see Robinson R. 1979: Ch. 1).

More important perhaps, in view of the problems discussed above, is the fact that the fixed location of dwellings creates a series of local markets. This is important both in terms of the problems it raises and in considering possible solutions. As Charles points out:

> . . . the fact that houses are geographically fixed means that identical houses in different areas are not good substitutes. It is thus quite possible for a situation of excess demand to exist in one area alongside another in a state of excess supply . . . movement . . . to low-priced excess supply areas in response to price differentials . . . is not likely to be significant compared to the pull of employment opportunities (Charles 1977: 17).

Clearly national 'surpluses' mean little in this context and consequently national solutions are likely to be equally meaningless unless the localised nature of the problem is fully considered. In deciding on possible solutions it is therefore necessary to consider the needs of particular localities.

In addition to physical and locational differences, housing can vary in terms of its tenure type. People wish to purchase the flow of housing services associated with houses (which are an asset or a stock) and can do so either by purchasing the asset itself or by renting it. In Britain, rented housing is further divided into that owned by the public sector (mainly local authorities) and that owned by the private sector. There is therefore a choice of three tenure types: owner-occupation, privately rented, or publicly rented. The changing distribution over time of the housing stock in England and Wales by tenure types is shown in Table 7.2.

Table 7.2   England and Wales housing stock by tenure type 1914–83 (percentages)

	1914	1938	1960	1975	1983
Owner-occupied	10.0	32.5	43.8	55.0	62.1
Publicly rented	—	9.6	24.7	28.9	26.2
Privately rented	90.0	57.9	31.5	16.1	11.7

Source: 1914–75: DoE Housing policy, technical volume 1, Table 1.23, p. 38, 1977; 1983: DoE Housing and construction statistics 1974–1984, Table 9.3

It can be seen that there has been a marked shift away from privately rented accommodation in favour of owner-occupation and renting from the public sector. Some of the reasons for these changes are discussed below.

The existence of different tenure types creates distinct, but inter-related, markets for housing. Changes in conditions in one market, say a rise in the cost of renting publicly owned accommodation, will have an impact in other sectors of the housing system, perhaps an increased demand for owner-occupation. However, the effect is likely to be limited, since mobility between the various tenure types is limited.

Despite the interrelationship between the different housing markets, the method of allocation within each sector is largely determined by market forces, although there is government inter-vention (see below). As far as publicly rented accommodation is concerned, allocation is largely an administrative matter. Within the privately rented sector government intervention in the form of rent control has led to there being excess demand for this type of accommodation (as indeed there is for publicly rented dwellings) and allocation tends to be on a 'first-come, first-served' basis. It is not possible in this chapter to give a fuller discussion of the allo-cational mechanisms and the determinants of demand and supply within each sector. For a straightforward, but relatively compre-hensive discussion of these issues see Charles (1977). However, two points should be mentioned in more detail. The first relates to the supply of new dwellings. Given the durability of housing, the total stock of dwellings is very largely determined by the stock inherited from previous periods. New buildings only represent 1–2 per cent of the total stock each year. Furthermore, the supply of new buildings tends to be relatively price inelastic with the result that increases in demand have little impact on increasing new supply. This has important implications for government policy which will be discussed later.

The second point worthy of note is that it is necessary to distinguish between housing demand and housing need.

> Housing need may be defined as the quantity of housing that is required to provide accommodation of an agreed minimum standard and above for a population given its size, household composition, age distribution, etc., *without taking into account the individual household's ability to pay for the housing assigned to it* . . . need is sometimes described as a 'social' concept which is independent of economic considerations (Robinson R. 1979: 55–6).

While Robinson goes on to say that this definition of need is not strictly correct as total housing requirements and standards are partly determined by economic factors, it does demonstrate the major distinction between demand and need. Housing services tend to be consumed in excess of need. This distinction is important when considering the arguments of marketeers and interventionists.

This section has briefly discussed some of the concepts considered important for an understanding of the major market versus intervention arguments. The next section takes some of these points further in considering the attributes of housing which, it is argued, have led to market failure, and a need for government intervention.

The housing system and market failure

The case for government intervention in any market mainly rests on the belief that imperfections exist in it. In particular, there may be informational or transactional imperfections, externalities may be evident or the good in question may be a public good. Clearly, housing cannot be considered to be a public good, but the other two arguments in favour of government action have been suggested as reasons for government intervention in housing markets. It appears that the arguments which have been put forward most forcibly have been based on externality considerations, and in particular on merit good arguments. However, before discussing these views there will be a brief review of the other imperfections which, it is argued, exist in the housing system.

As was mentioned in the previous section, houses are long-lived assets and of the total stock only a fraction is available for purchase or rent in any one period. These points, together with the relatively small increases in stock from new building, mean that existing house owners will have some market power, and quantity adjustments to changes in market conditions, say an increase in demand for a particular type of house, are necessarily slow. This problem is exacerbated by the length of time it takes from first deciding to build a house to its completion. Balchin (1981) points out that the private sector housebuilding industry is predominantly speculative. Housebuilding firms start to build houses with the expectation of being able to sell them within a short period of completion. However, by the time of completion it is quite possible that market conditions will have changed. Since much of the speculative building is undertaken by relatively small firms, the industry is particularly susceptible to changes in the economic environment and to shifts in government economic policy.

The whole of the housebuilding process tends to be characterised by considerable uncertainty (see Balchin 1981) and the supply of housing is relatively inelastic. As a result, changes in demand are most likely to affect prices rather than the quantity supplied. This of course does not mean that the market fails to reach equilibrium but is important when considering housing need rather than demand (see below).

Further problems in housing markets arise because most participants enter these markets only rarely. Given the heterogeneity of the commodity and the search costs involved in acquiring relevant information, all participants will act on incomplete information and will almost invariably seek expert advice (e.g. from estate agents, surveyors, solicitors, building societies). Charles (1977) points out that experts are likely to have two effects on housing markets. First, she points out that since they are involved in price setting, their views will affect both behaviour and prices. Secondly, acquiring expert advice raises the transaction costs associated with entering housing markets and this in turn will 'provide a disincentive to frequent movement, which implies low personal adjustment to economic variables' (Charles 1977: 15). It is therefore likely that there will be slow adjustment on both the demand and supply sides of housing markets.

The problems of slow adjustment are likely to be increased by the fact that many participants are on both sides of the market at the same time, that is they are contemporaneously buying and selling housing services. While another consequence of costly information could be the use of price as an indicator of quality which may lead to some people making incorrect decisions, this should be limited by the role of experts in the markets.

Imperfect capital markets, particularly as far as individuals are concerned, and contractual problems between landlords and tenants arising from housing being both an investment and a consumption good, will further impair the workings of housing markets.

While all of these problems cause housing markets to function somewhat less than perfectly, the major justification for government intervention appears to be based on the externality argument. Housing is not a public good, but while some marketeers would argue that housing is a private good, it appears that it lies somewhere between the two. This view recognises that while many of the benefits associated with housing accrue privately, there does exist an interdependence of utility functions with respect to housing consumption.

Perhaps the most obvious and most basic externality associated with housing consumption derives from the fact that housing conditions can affect many aspects of an individual's life which will in turn affect others, e.g. health, attitudes to society's values (e.g. education and crime), educational attainment (e.g. the effectiveness of an individual's private studies is likely to be partially determined by housing conditions), fire risks.

In addition to any general desire for higher standards of living for the population at large, these factors cause both consumption–consumption and consumption–production externalities.

Poor housing conditions may lead to an increase in the spread of infectious diseases which could clearly affect people other than those living in the poor conditions. Similarly, any increase in crime resulting from poor housing conditions will impact on other people. In a society which 'publicly' provides health care and policing, these effects are even more widespread. Furthermore, ill-health and poor educational achievement will adversely affect production.

In addition, externalities result from the value of any one property being affected by the state of the neighbouring environment, i.e. neighbourhood externalities. Any person who improves the state of repair (particularly externally) of an individual property will at the same time marginally increase the value of surrounding properties. However, if surrounding properties are in a bad state of repair, improving an individual property may have little impact on the value of that one property. The owner may therefore decide against improvement. If all owners behave in the same way, no property will be improved because it is not a worthwhile investment for any one owner. However, if all owners were to invest in their properties it is quite possible that they would all benefit. As Robinson points out, 'atomistic behaviour is likely to prevail and to lead to an inefficient outcome' (Robinson R. 1979: 103). Without intervention, the effect of neighbourhood externalities may be to slowly extend slum areas.

A final, and in this context particularly important, set of externalities are altruistic externalities, which can be considered in terms of the broader merit good argument. 'Housing is a merit good if society believes that all members of the community should consume housing of at least a given standard whatever the income or other attributes of the individual' (Whitehead 1984: 119). The merit good argument appears to have been a major reason behind much of the government intervention which has taken place. Intervention occurs because society's minimum standard (its estimate of need) is not being achieved through the market mechanism. Supply and demand may be in equilibrium, but the market is not leading to an equating of supply and 'need'.

Successive British governments do appear to have intervened in housing markets because of a perceived shortfall from a minimum standard. 'A decent home for every family at a price within their means' has been a stated objective of British governments of all political persuasions for many years. While this is a fairly vague aim it suggests a desire to remove local as well as national housing shortages, to maintain and improve the state of repair of the housing stock and to deal with problems of overcrowding and people living in accommodation unsuited to their circumstances.

In view of the emphasis on need and the discussion of inelastic supply above, it would seem appropriate for government policy to be directed towards increasing the supply of housing. Unfortunately much of government policy has been targeted on the demand side with the result that the problems outlined in the first section still remain. This will be discussed more fully in the next section.

With respect to the merit good argument it should finally be noted that the present government appears to view owner-occupation as a merit good. As such it has pursued policies specifically aimed at extending owner-occupation, e.g. sale of local authority housing. Since owner-occupation is difficult to achieve for low-income groups it is questionable how far it can be extended (see Doling *et al.* 1985).

A final reason why British governments have intervened in housing markets has been in the pursuit of wider policies of redistribution of income and wealth. Since housing typically accounts for a large part of the family budget (e.g. in 1982, 52 per cent of all local authority households in England and Wales paid rent equal to 10 per cent or more of their household income (DoE, *Housing and construction statistics 1973–1983*: Table 12.8)), assistance with the purchase of housing services (either through ensuring house costs are below market prices, or through subsidies to demand, e.g. mortgage interest tax relief, housing benefit assistance) is an important means of redistribution.

In conclusion, while housing may be regarded as principally a private good, a number of justifications have been given for intervention in the housing system. In particular, the imperfections and externalities suggest that leaving housing provision solely to the market would lead to a situation where the consumption of housing services would be far less than optimal from a social point of view. The next section will briefly review how governments in Britain have attempted to avoid this under-consumption.

Government intervention – government failure?

Although British governments have been involved in housing since the nineteenth century when minimum standards were laid down for health reasons, direct intervention in the system has grown substantially only since the First World War. However, despite there having been direct government involvement for some seventy years, it appears that at no time has an overall policy been devised to co-ordinate the different forms of intervention. Short-term 'solutions' and political considerations have been given priority, with little or no attempt having been made to define objectives and devise long-term policies to achieve them.

There are basically three ways in which a government can inter-vene in any market: it can directly provide a good or service; it can lay down regulations for provision; or subsidies can be given. All three types of intervention have taken place in the British housing system. For example, public sector housing is directly provided by the state, rent control legislation regulates the levels of rent which can be charged in the private rented sector, and housing benefit (formerly rent and rate rebates and allowances) subsidises housing costs for the relatively less-well-off.

Much of the intervention which has taken place has aimed to reduce the cost of housing. Even within this general aim there has been no co-ordinated policy, but rather a whole range of measures have been introduced, seemingly without much consideration of equity or of their impact on specific housing problems.

For owner-occupiers there are three factors which should be discussed when considering government's cost-reducing measures. First, the interest paid by a mortgagor is deductible from an owner-occupier's personal income in determining taxable income. Tax relief on interest paid on loans for non-business purposes is only given on money borrowed for house purchase or improvement. The rationale for this tax relief was that up until 1963 the imputed income from owner-occupation was taxed and as with other forms of income any interest charged on loans relating directly to that income was tax deductible. The abolition of the tax on imputed income in 1963 represented the second cost-reducing measure. While the abolition of the tax might have been expected to lead to the end of mortgage interest relief, this did not happen for what appear to be largely political reasons. However, Robinson (1979) has shown that the effective subsidy to owner-occupiers is equal to the tax which would be paid if imputed income was still taxed, rather than the mortgage interest relief. Finally, unlike other assets, owner-occupied housing is not subject to capital gains tax on sale.

Although these measures do appear to reduce costs for owner-occupiers, their effects are questionable. One effect of these subsidies is to raise disposable incomes, which in turn would be expected to increase the demand for housing services. Given inelastic supply, prices will rise so that the net effect of the subsidies on purchasers may be negligible.

In the private rented sector, measures to reduce the cost of housing have centred on rent control. This has taken different forms over the years but basically has sought to keep rents below their market level by limiting the rents which landlords could charge. It has been suggested that rent control was largely to blame for the decline in the private rented sector. While it has undoubtedly been a contributory factor, Charles (1977) believes that this sector would have declined even without this form of intervention (see Robinson R. 1979 for a full discussion of rent control).

The publicly rented sector has largely set rents on the basis of administrative decisions rather than market forces with the result that council house rents have typically been below market rents. However, this policy has been reversed to some extent in recent years by the Conservative government's introduction of a new housing finance scheme and the abolition of the rule that local authorities could not make a profit on their housing revenue accounts.

Finally, the housing benefit system gives subsidies to low-income households which reduces their net rent payments, and mortgage interest payments may be paid in respect of owner-occupiers in receipt of supplementary benefit.

In addition to the fact that when taken together these policies tend to be regressive in nature, the whole approach is highly questionable in a situation of inelastic supply. Increased purchasing power does not necessarily lead to increased housing consumption; rather the price of housing services may simply rise.

Subsidies to supply have been much less common than have

those to demand, and have been subject to far more changes in policy direction. The major form of intervention on the supply side has been through the building of houses for the publicly rented sector, although more recently there has been an increase in joint ventures between the public and private sectors, e.g. building for sale, rather than for public renting. However, the building of public sector housing tends to be greatly affected by central government's macroeconomic policy, with the housing programme frequently bearing the brunt of any public expenditure cutbacks and deflationary policies.

Post-war peaks for housing starts (a housing start is when the building process commences) in Britain came in 1964 for the private sector with almost 248 000 houses started and in 1967 for the public sector with 214 000. Since then, however, there has been considerable variation in the number of houses started (see Table 7.3 for post-1970 figures).

The private sector is clearly affected by macroeconomic policy, but the impact on the public sector is much more marked. The 1981 figure for the public sector is less than half of that for two years earlier and just over 17 per cent of the post-war peak. Obviously, the housebuilding industry is subject to considerable cyclical variations, yet successive governments have tended to ignore these problems when determining macroeconomic policy, in spite of the housing objectives set and the apparent need for policies to increase supply.

Table 7.3   Houses started, Great Britain, 1970–84 (thousands)

	Private sector	Public sector	Total
1970	165	154	319
1971	207	137	344
1972	228	123	351
1973	216	113	329
1974	106	146	252
1975	149	174	323
1976	155	171	325
1977	135	132	267
1978	157	107	265
1979	144	81	225
1980	99	56	155
1981	117	37	154
1982	141	53	193
1983	170	48	217
1984	154	40	194

Source: DoE *Housing and Construction Statistics 1970–1980*, Table 7.2 and *1974–1984*, Table 6.1

Before concluding this section on government intervention, housing rehabilitation will briefly be discussed. This has largely been a post-war phenomenon, with improvement grants for private owners being introduced in the Housing Act of 1949. Rehabilitation increased in importance as it was recognised that improving the existing stock could be a much more cost-effective method of achieving desired standards than is the provision of new building. Rehabilitation policy has taken a number of forms (see Balchin 1985) but in general has involved both the public and the private sectors. Rather than concentrating only on the public sector stock or on the purchasing of private housing by the public sector in order to improve that housing, emphasis has been placed on encouraging private owners to carry out improvements, e.g. by the provision of improvement grants and by the public sector improving the general environment of particular areas.

Undoubtedly, post-war UK housing policy has led to a generally much higher standard of housing, but despite seventy years of government intervention problems persist in the housing system. Post-war governments have consistently emphasised cost-reducing measures rather than attempting to increase supply. As such they have failed to take account of some of the most fundamental characteristics of the housing system, including factors which have led to intervention in the first place. Most notably, they have largely ignored the problems caused by inelastic supply which can mean that adequate housing will still not be obtained by poorer households even if their purchasing power is increased. This apparent lack of understanding on the part of policymakers of basic economic concepts has led some economists to argue that the problems which still exist are due to intervention (e.g. see Harrington 1972; Stafford 1976). The marketeers' response has been to call for the withdrawal of government from the housing system. This view will now be considered.

Solutions through the market?

Just as with almost any other social policy problem there are economists who argue that housing problems are much more likely to be solved by allowing market forces to act unhindered. Indeed, there are some who argue that housing problems are largely the result of intervention, thus 'if government had set out to create chaos in the housing market it could not possibly have done a better job. The real problem of housing is, essentially, created and perpetuated by government' (Stafford 1976: 7).

Supporters of market solutions argue that while housing markets are far removed from the economist's model of perfect competition, free market forces will nonetheless lead to the most efficient outcome. It is argued that the imperfections which do exist are not sufficient to justify government intervention with its associated 'distorting impact'. In addition, marketeers argue that housing is essentially a private good with the purchaser of housing services receiving almost all of the benefits once a very low minimum standard of housing has been achieved. Therefore, externalities are largely non-existent. This, of course, gives little or no weight to altruistic or caring externalities.

Before going on to discuss the ways in which marketeers believe housing problems could be solved, there will be a brief review of their criticisms of government intervention. The argument against government intervention takes two forms. First, that intervention is a bad thing *per se*; and secondly, criticisms of the types of intervention which have actually taken place. The first argument revolves around the notion that market forces allocate resources on the basis of individual consumers' and producers' expressed preferences leading to an efficient and equitable allocation. Within such a view, government intervention will infringe on individual liberty and will coerce people to consume housing services of a type and quantity which would not otherwise be demanded. For example, in building public sector housing minimum requirements for living space, storage space etc. were set down (Parker-Morris standards). These minimum standards may well be above those which would have been demanded in a free market system. However, it should be remembered that while economic individualism is undoubtedly widely accepted, it is nonetheless a value judgement. In some cases there is clearly a case for putting social choices above individual preferences. Given that housing is a long-lived asset, it needs to be recognised that while free markets in housing may lead to appropriate standards at the time of building, these standards may be inadequate at a later date, say if living standards in general are rising. Furthermore, allocation within a free market will partly be determined by the distribution of income and wealth, the results of which may be viewed by society to be unsatisfactory.

Criticisms of the forms of intervention which have occurred in Britain are based on the belief that 'Social and political objectives have been pursued with an almost complete disregard of the basic laws of economics, and with little concern for the serious ultimate repercussions' (Stafford 1976: 6). In particular, it is argued that government intervention has failed to recognise the inelasticity of housing supply, has largely been the cause of the decrease in the supply of private rented accommodation and, by laying down such strict standards for public rented dwellings, has led to coercion in housing consumption and less houses being built for a given investment. While these criticisms undoubtedly have some foundation (see previous section), they do not necessarily lead to the conclusion that governments should not intervene in housing markets; rather they suggest that if intervention is to take place the constraints imposed by the characteristics of the markets need to be fully considered before policy decisions are taken. However, the two strands of the case against intervention have been used to support the belief that no interference should take place and marketeers have suggested ways in which they believe housing problems can be solved.

Advocates of the market have suggested that some of the housing problems discussed in the first section would be overcome by allowing market forces to work freely, with the result that a 'filtering' process would be set in motion. This view recognises that most housing problems occur at the lower end of the system, but holds that with rising living standards and a consequent demand for bigger and better accommodation at the top end of the system, benefits will be transmitted downwards. It is believed that the demand of high-income groups will lead to superior accommodation being built. This will lead to the vacation by this group of their property as they move up-market and slightly lower income groups will in turn move up-market into this accommodation. This process continues down the housing system until those in the worst housing move to slightly better accommodation and their dwellings are either occupied by previously homeless people or are demolished. Filtering involves declining prices for housing services and changes in occupancy, but is seen as a solution to both homelessness and the existence of slum property.

However, the effectiveness of this process is highly dubious. First, it is likely to be very slow. Not only do nearly all households have to be extremely mobile for the process to work but also, as noted above, the annual addition to stock represents only a small percentage of the total. At the same time as new dwellings are being built, older houses are deteriorating further, and new households will be being formed. Secondly, the relative prices of the existing stock must fall, and fall faster than the decline in quality if households are to increase the consumption of quality-adjusted housing services. In a system where prices have tended to be inflexible downwards and where the adjustment process is slow, the filtering solution appears unlikely to succeed. Further, as dwellings move down the income range it is likely that they will be converted (say from houses into flats) and that poor quality will persist.

An alternative solution to housing problems put forward by proponents of the market who recognise that some government intervention is required is to issue housing vouchers (i.e. a voucher of a given monetary value which can be spent only on housing). The rationale underlying voucher schemes is to subsidise demand, but to leave supply to be determined by the market. Advocates of vouchers believe that they bring about the least possible intervention with the market mechanism given that some intervention is necessary. While vouchers may limit intervention, there is no reason to suggest that they would be any more effective than other subsidies to demand in housing markets. Inelastic supply remains a major obstacle, thus '. . . subsidies will increase prices before they affect output and will therefore be of main benefit to existing home owners, landlords and land owners' (Lansley 1979: 34). If intervention is designed to achieve a minimum standard of housing consumption for all, then it would appear that housing vouchers will not provide the solution.

Another suggestion has been put forward by supporters of the market who believe that there is a role for government in the housing system. While recognising that there are market imperfections which necessitate state intervention, they argue that this does not justify public provision. Traditionally the public sector has been dominated by non-market decisions. Rents have been set and allocation determined by administrative decisions with considerable differences in policy between different areas. In recent years, however, more pro-market policies have been implemented by central government. In particular, local authorities have been pressed into increasing rents towards levels which would be more likely to prevail in a free market, and council house sales have been encouraged with tenants being given a 'right to buy'. However, the extent to which the encouragement of public sector sales is concerned with increasing the role of market forces has been brought into question by the inducements offered to tenants to buy their homes. For example, the 1980 Housing Act gave public sector tenants of three or more years' standing the right to 'discounts' on the market price ranging from 33 to 50 per cent for someone resident in the public sector for twenty years or more. In addition, tenants were given a right to a council mortgage. It appears that 'most of the encouragement of the owner-occupied sector is thus little to do with privatisation *per se* but rather a promotion of one form of market provision rather than another' (Doling *et al.* 1985: 44). This suggests, to an extent, that owner-occupation is being viewed as a merit good, although it should be noted that a similar 'right to buy' does not exist for tenants in the private rented sector.

In terms of the more general housing objectives, council house sales have almost no effect, or possibly even a negative impact. The sales do nothing to increase the total stock of dwellings and reduce the range of houses available within this sector. A policy whereby money raised from sales was used to increase public sector building would be more likely to help to achieve these general objectives.

It would appear from the preceding discussion that market-oriented policies would be unlikely to solve housing problems. Although marketeers argue that government intervention has replaced one evil with another, by raising quality but failing to avoid shortages, the evidence of the pre-intervention housing system suggests that free markets result in unsatisfactory housing conditions (see, for example, Rowntree 1902). Filtering is unlikely to prove successful, housing vouchers fail to deal with the problem of supply inelasticity, and council house sales have little to do with the objective of 'a decent home for every family at a price within their means'. It therefore appears that intervention of some sort is required. The question is: 'What type of intervention is likely to be successful?'

What sort of intervention?

The previous sections have analysed the arguments of marketeers and interventionists and have demonstrated three points. First, while there is no doubt that the benefits of housing accrue largely to the individual consumer, there appears nonetheless to be a need for intervention if a social optimum is to be achieved. This need arises because of the characteristics of the good and the nature of housing markets. The second point which has been demonstrated is that in deciding on the policies to be implemented it is necessary to take full account of the characteristics of housing markets. Full-scale planning is not being suggested as a feasible alternative.

What is being advocated is some limited intervention within the overall framework of a market-oriented system. Since market mechanisms will have a large role to play, it is essential that policymakers recognise the constraints and opportunities which exist in the housing system. In particular, it is an absolute necessity that any policy should acknowledge the limitations imposed by inelastic supply and the considerable uncertainty which characterises the building industry.

Finally, there is a need for policymakers to clearly set out the problems which exist, define their objectives and devise co-ordinated policies to achieve those aims. In other words, problem-based solutions are required, rather than vague objectives and piecemeal intervention.

The main problems which exist in the housing system are local shortages, increasing disrepair and housing mismatch in terms of accommodation being unsuitable for particular household needs (including overcrowding). The specific target of removing (or at least substantially reducing) these problems is a reasonable interpretation of the much vaguer objective of 'a decent home for every family at a price within their means'. It is this target which I take to be the aim of intervention. This ignores, but does not preclude, intervention to achieve what is considered to be a more equitable allocation of housing. If policies are implemented to deal with the supply side problems, then subsidies to demand are much more likely than at present, to help solve the problems faced by low-income families. However, it appears that the supply side problems must be tackled first.

In order to adequately deal with the problem of housing shortages it is necessary not only to have information on the extent of the current shortfall but also to have estimates of future housing needs. This will require forecasts of household formation based on demographic data, together with some attempt to estimate future household types so as to minimise problems of mismatch. Having estimated current and future shortfalls, a timetable can be drawn up to try to eliminate the problem of housing shortages. The fact that shortages are localised will make forecasting difficult and policies must be flexible enough to take account of subsequent re-estimation. Such a forecasting system is not new. The 1977 Housing Green Paper (DoE 1977) estimated that in order to take account of an increase in households and to deal with some existing housing problems, 300 000 houses would have to be built each year up to 1986. Table 7.3 shows that this figure had not been achieved.

Clearly, forecasting future building needs does not solve the problem; it is only the first stage of the process. If the estimated building requirements are to be met, then it appears that it is necessary to reduce uncertainty in the building industry and to try to lessen the cyclical fluctuations in housebuilding. It seems that this can only be achieved by the public sector taking a strong lead and undertaking to build the majority of the estimated requirements at a consistent annual rate of production. This does not necessitate a large increase in the share of the housing stock owned by the public sector. Some provision could be on a joint private/public basis along similar lines to the current Urban Development Grant scheme. Alternatively, the public sector could undertake to build houses with the sole objective of selling the dwellings on completion. The public sector seems much better equipped to deal with cyclical problems because it is not as constrained as the private sector by the short-run cash-flow problems associated with falling demand. This is particularly true given the speculative nature of much of private sector housebuilding. At the same time the public sector is more able to ensure adequate standards and give consideration to the environment of the neighbourhood. The major problem with such an approach is that in times of public expenditure cutbacks, long-term capital projects tend to be vulnerable. As with all social policy issues, the extent to which objectives can be achieved will depend on the political importance attached to the problem. However, undertaking more public sector building appears to be necessary if shortages are to be reduced and problems of mismatch alleviated. If the state of repair of the housing stock is to be improved, it again appears that government intervention is required. The increasing disrepair of recent years has taken place within a framework largely dominated by market forces. Policies to improve the general environment of an area can encourage house owners to carry out improvements. In other words, the process which leads to the extension of slum areas can be reversed. In addition, it needs to be recognised that disrepair is worst among low-income households. Clearly these are the households least able to deal with the problem. If the disrepair of the houses of this group is to be reversed, then it will be necessary for government to give assistance, for example, in the form of improvement grants.

Conclusion

There can be no doubt that vast improvements in housing conditions have taken place in post-war Britain. However, severe problems do persist for a significant number of households. While the private sector appears to be incapable of solving these problems on its own, government intervention in its current form, with its emphasis on increasing real purchasing power by reducing the cost of housing, is also unsatisfactory. If the problems which remain are to be adequately dealt with, intervention must take place on the supply side of the system. It must be recognised that increased purchasing power does not ensure suitable housing for low-income households. Despite its successes, British housing policy has been dominated by short-term palliatives. What is required is a more thoughtful and long-term approach to housing problems.

Chapter 8

HEALTH CARE
Arthur Walker

Introduction

Throughout the period since 1948 the overwhelming proportion of
health care in the UK has been provided by the National Health
Service (NHS). Most of the NHS care has been provided free at the
time of use and the funding has come largely from general taxation
(charges together with NHS contributions (the 'health stamp') have
only provided between 23 per cent (1962–63) and 9 per cent
(1974–75) of the NHS budget). This system of care has come under
attack from critics who would prefer a much greater reliance upon
the market mechanism. This chapter evaluates the economic arguments of the pro-market and pro-NHS lobbies. Before moving to
an evaluation of these arguments, a short section is included which
outlines the major features of possible systems of organisation and
finance of health care to provide some detail of the systems which
are being compared in the market versus state (NHS) debate. In
Table 8.1 the major possible financial and organisational arrangements for health services are outlined. Variations in the arrangements for hospital care, hospital finance, doctors' employment,
doctors' reimbursement, access to doctors and overall method of
financing care are considered. The characteristics of the health care
system which have been selected do not provide a complete
description of a health service (many more subdivisions of rows
and columns could be suggested) but they are those which are
central to the market/state (NHS) debate as they are the major
determinants of the scale and pattern (input mix and output mix
including where the care is provided) of health care provision and
the distribution of its costs and benefits. Doctors play a central role
in the health system providing care directly by their own labour
and also determining to a large extent which other services are

Table 8.1 Systems for the organisation and finance of health services

Pattern of hospital organisation	Method of funding hospitals	Pattern of Doctor employment	Method of paying doctors	Patients' initial right of access to a doctor	Overall method of finance of care
1. State production	1. Fixed budget (from state)	1. State employees	1. Salaried	1. To a general practitioner only	1. General taxation
2. Private non-profit-making (charitable/voluntary)	2. Capitation fees† (pre-payment)	2. Employee of private organisation	2. Capitation fees† (pre-payment)	2. To general practitioner and some specialists	2. Compulsory insurance (payroll tax)
3. Private for profit	3. Fee per item of service	3. Self-employed	3. Fee per item of service	3. Free choice by patient using general practitioner or specialists	3. Voluntary insurance and charity

In each column the description in the first and third rows represents the state and market variants for that aspect of the health service, the second row represents an organisational form between the extremes but these sometimes lie closer to the state, sometimes closer to the market end of the spectrum and therefore do not together constitute a consistent system.
† A capitation fee involves a payment in advance of the need for any care to a doctor or hospital (probably on an annual basis) in return for which the doctor (or hospital) will provide any care the individual requires. The doctor or hospital is thus bearing the risk (although they may themselves be able to reinsure).

provided for a patient. The organisation of hospitals is of concern because of their dominant role in the cost of modern health services.

As a generalisation it is reasonable to say that the defenders of the UK health system are defending a system which corresponds fairly closely to the first row of Table 8.1. Those of a free market persuasion are supporting a system that combines the features of the third row. In the remainder of the chapter it is essentially these two positions that are compared.

The UK system departs from the first row model in a number of ways although quantitatively these departures are mostly small, and are partly the result of the historical evolution of the NHS, and partly a pragmatic response to the difficulties of a wholly administered system. The NHS combines state production of hospital services and mainly salaried hospital doctors with funding mostly from general taxation. However, general practitioners are self-employed and are reimbursed mainly by a form of prepayment, and NHS hospitals employ some agency nurses. Catering, cleaning and laundry services in hospitals are as a result of the present government's privatisation policies being supplied to an increasing degree by private contractors tendering for NHS contracts. Alongside the NHS there exists a private medical care service which draws upon NHS doctor labour on a part-time basis and to a limited extent on NHS facilities (mostly through the so-called 'pay beds' system). This small private sector is discussed towards the end of this chapter. On the boundaries of the health care system, a great deal of the care of the elderly and infirm takes place outside of the state-administered system although often with the aid of state financial support, and a large number of mostly minor episodes of illness are dealt with by individuals by self-prescription of drugs and other treatments purchased mainly from pharmacists' shops. Free marketeers have shown considerable interest recently in Health Maintenance Organisations (HMO) as suppliers of health care. These have been growing in popularity in the United States but involve prepayment for care.

The only other organisational feature of a health system that might be considered of comparable importance to those included in the table is the organisation of the production of drugs.

The drug industry raises an additional set of policy questions, particularly relating to research and development, and examination of these questions would require more space than is available in this chapter. In the UK the government has practised limited regulation (in terms of prices and profitability) of the drug industry which is comprised mainly of large multinational companies. More recently much tighter restrictions have been imposed upon the brands of drugs which can be prescribed by general practitioners on behalf of the NHS.

It is clearly impossible in a chapter of this length to consider all of the departures which have been made from a wholly adminis-tered (planned) system in the UK or which might be made from a purely market system if one were adopted. It is the view of the author that a political choice must be made about the broad type of system and that any departures of detail from that system should be justified on the grounds that they improve the attain-ment of health service objectives.

The market versus the state in health care

The argument between the pro-market and pro-state lobbies in this field of health care has been about three issues (or sets of issues), the issue of rights, the issue of distribution and the issue of efficiency. These issues are not completely independent of one another but it is convenient for the purposes of exposition to treat them sequentially, indicating the links as the discussion proceeds. For the most part the political debate which has gone on since the NHS was founded has involved the market lobby attacking the NHS on grounds of infringement of individual rights and inefficiency (citing usually excessive bureaucracy and waiting lists for treatment) while the NHS lobby have counter-attacked by emphasising the unfairness of a system of health care based on ability to pay in contrast to the fairness of the NHS.

This political debate has to a considerable extent been uninfor-mative about 'real world' health service problems as the claims of both sides have been based upon a comparison of an idealized version of the system they support with the much less attractive real world version (or sometimes a caricatured version) of the system they oppose. It will be argued that the marketeers' view of rights ignores the reality of the position of the consumer in modern health care, and their view that markets lead to greater efficiency also ignores some particular difficulties of health and health care. On the other hand, the anti-marketeers' view that the distribution of health care would be severely unequal under a market system (or indeed any non-NHS system) overstates both the difficulties of redistribution in a more market-oriented system and the extent of the achievement of the NHS.

The market

The marketeers' view of rights is an individualistic one. The individual should have the right to offer his labour and spend his income (earned and property income) as he wishes subject to the constraints of the set of prices facing him in the market (including the price of labour) with the exception of a contribution which he must make to the provision of public goods. In practice, which goods are public goods and the scale of their provision is the subject of debate among marketeers, but as a minimum would include in the health field some public health spending (sewerage, clean water, immunisation against communicable diseases). That there is a role for the state in these areas is taken to be uncontentious between marketeers and non-marketeers although there would certainly still be disagreement about the pattern of organisation of production of these public goods (the marketeers preferring private contractors wherever possible). This view of rights is based upon two propositions. First, that individuals are the best judges of their own welfare and, second, that they are best able to represent their interests by voluntary exchange in markets. Voluntary exchange has the further attraction of the 'invisible hand' proposition, that the well-being of society as a whole is best achieved by individuals pursuing their own interests through the market (see Ch. 1).

If the marketeers are prepared to adopt a stance over individual rights in which ensuring the rights they have identified takes precedence over any efficiency or distributional considerations, then the NHS can be opposed because it inevitably involves a degree of coercion in either its finance or in the type of provision it offers.

The weakness of this extreme position, at least as far as health care is concerned, becomes apparent when we examine whether individuals are the best judges of their own interests when it comes to taking care of their health. Some individuals may not be in a position to make choices because of accident or severe illness. However, even for those who are there are severe problems of uncertainty and lack of information about the occurrence and recognition of illness and its treatment. This leads to perverse behaviour about health by at least some individuals because of exaggerated fears about illness or its treatment, or unwarranted optimism about possible future treatment if they fell ill. More significantly, the individual's ignorance gives a vitally important role to his doctor acting as his agent (that is the power to make important decisions is in effect handed to someone else). How well the agent's decisions reflect the patient's best interest is open to debate. It seems unlikely that the agency relationship is perfect. A perfect agent would make the same decisions as the patient would if the patient were able to weigh the medical information of the doctor alongside all his other circumstances. In practice, the doctor is focusing mainly on the patient's medical condition and is only imperfectly aware of all the other circumstances facing the individual.

The imperfection of the agency relationship seems likely to be worse when the doctor has a financial interest in the treatment provided (this problem is discussed further below). Although the patient is protected from unscrupulous behaviour by a code of medical ethics there is, in almost any doctor–patient contact, considerable scope for discretion within ethical constraints in the number of examinations, tests, additional visits and even in the type of treatment prescribed. Medical ethics also focus overwhelmingly on doing everything medically possible for a patient and doctors may feel compelled to take action (additional surgery for a terminally ill patient) which patients might, if they could be fully informed, prefer to avoid.

The second area of weakness of the extreme position on rights concerns the notion that individuals can best represent their interests through voluntary exchange in markets. This is a proposition that relies on two factors, first that the individual can choose as much health care as he wants when he wants subject to his budget constraint and health care prices, but second it assumes that a market for health care delivers value for money. It seems unlikely that individuals would be enthusiastic about giving an overwhelming weight to the right to choose if what they get in return was poor value for money. This raises the question of the efficiency of markets in health care and there are three particular areas of concern, the problem of monopoly, the problems of insurance as a means of finance and the agency relationship and its interaction with the method of finance. The weakness of a general case in favour of markets on efficiency grounds (a general case built on solid theoretical and empirical foundations rather than merely faith and casual empiricism) has been indicated by Hahn (1982a) and Sen (1983). The weakness lies in the very restrictive assumptions needed for this success: complete markets, absence of market power, an auctioneer or his equivalent. In health care these assumptions are seriously violated.

In health care there are a number of potential sources of monopoly power. The insurance industry and the pharmaceutical industry tend to be dominated by a few large organisations probably because of the existence of substantial economies of scale in these sectors, in the former because of the need to pool large numbers and often large risks and in the second because of indivisibilities in research and in marketing activities. Limits on patient travel distance mean that hospitals and other health facilities are quite likely to be local monopolies. Finally, it must be noted that governments in many nations have created an additional source of monopoly power in health care by granting regulatory power to groups of health professionals who use these powers mainly for the benefit of the professional group rather than for the benefit of society as a whole. In the health field this has involved restricting entry to the medical profession, usually by raising the level of training needed to qualify. The medical profession have also opposed medical audit (evaluation of existing practitioners) usually by arguing that there is need for clinical freedom even if this means that some incompetence/bad practice is concealed from public view. The pro-market lobby do usually grant the state the role of restricting the abuse of monopolistic power but, in practice, mainly because of information and expertise requirements this role is difficult for the state to fulfil. In the case of professional monopoly it is difficult to see how some regulatory control to ensure quality of doctors can be avoided and difficult to know how to prevent the capture of the regulatory body by the profession.

Central to any debate about the efficiency of markets in health care is the role and problems of health insurance. The economic literature on health insurance has developed largely from the contribution by Arrow (1963) which clarified some of the theoretical issues and raised many further questions for study. Although many theoretical issues have not been fully resolved and empirical evidence lags far behind the theoretical developments, it is clear from the work carried out to date that private insurance has severe problems as a method of finance for health care.

The importance of insurance rests upon the fact that it offers the individual or organisation operating in a world full of risks a means of reducing the scale or number of these risks. Following Arrow, an individual faces two types of risk: the risk of becoming ill, and the risk of whether recovery will be total or incomplete or delayed. The individual faces the possibility of financial losses (costs of medical attention and loss of income from lost working time) and psychic losses (feeling ill). The sort of health insurance contract normally offered allows the individual to mitigate the financial consequences of ill-health.

The willingness to buy insurance indicates a desire on the part of the purchaser to shift a risk, implying that a certain loss of income (the premium) is preferable to the uncertain prospect of loss without the insurance. The premium the individual is willing to pay will be larger than the expected loss if the individual is risk averse. The seller of the insurance contract is prepared to accept the risk usually because he is able to pool a large number of risks and the total amount he has to pay out in compensation and administration is less than the income from premiums.

Having indicated that it is possible for insurance to yield gains to voluntary participants in such trade, it is then necessary to ask how much insurance should be available and at what price and whether real world insurance markets are likely to offer this desirable price and quantity combination. For an ideal competitive market under uncertainty (in which a Pareto optimal outcome could come about) all risks must be insurable and the insurance must be sold in markets where both insurers and insured are price takers. These are very restrictive conditions and for a number of reasons real world insurance markets are unlikely to approach this theoretical ideal. The problem of monopoly power in the insurance field has already been noted. Two other factors that restrict real world insurance markets, 'moral hazard' and 'adverse selection', arise from the insurer having insufficient information about the insured. There is an incentive for the insurer to invest in the acquisition of additional information but the costs of this rise rapidly and information costs are an important part of the 'transaction costs' involved in insurance markets. Significant transaction costs result in a degree of insurance coverage that is less than complete.

Moral hazard has received considerable attention. There is, however, still no fully developed theoretical discussion and the empirical work on the extent of the problem lags far behind existing theoretical work. Important contributions to the literature have come from Arrow (1963), Feldstein (1973) and Pauly (1968; 1983).

Moral hazard is a problem of resource misallocation which arises because the insurance contracts that are normally offered are inadequately specified and cannot be policed with the information available to the insurers.

The nature of moral hazard associated with health insurance can be appreciated by considering how it arises. This can be illustrated by describing a set of conditions under which moral hazard will not arise and then showing how different are the circumstances in the health insurance case. Moral hazard will not arise if the event which is insured is entirely beyond the control of the insured party or any agent of the insured, if the occurrence of the event is clearly observable, and if the extent of occurrence varies this is also clearly observable and compensation can be determined accordingly. The conditions facing the insurer offering cover for health care expenses are in practice very different. Let us for the present assume that the insurer agrees to cover all health care expenses arising in a given period together with income lost from work, in exchange for a fixed premium. Modifications of this basic contract are discussed later.

The first problem with insuring against ill-health is that some illness is within the control of the individuals. The individual can affect the probability of occurrence and the severity of illness by his actions. If the individual is insured he may be more inclined to take risks with his health.

The second problem for the insurer is that the occurrence of ill-health is not always easily observed. The insurer normally relies on the insured person's doctor, but even doctors have to accept some disorders on the word of the patient, for example, most low back pain is in this category. Even more serious for the insurer is the problem of monitoring the extent of illness. Once again the role of the doctor is important and the insurer will normally be liable for whatever he decides to order for his patient. The liabilities of the insurer are thus dependent on the actions of the insured and his doctor. While there is clearly a potential for moral hazard in the health insurance case, there remains a question of whether the insured or their doctors will behave in a way which leads to a misallocation of resources. Unfortunately, the incentives in the circumstances outlined make a misallocation of resources extremely likely. When the insurance policy covers all the costs of illness, the price of care to the individual is effectively zero and consumption of care will be extended beyond the economically efficient level (marginal cost of care equals marginal value of care – the rate of utilisation beyond which an individual spending his own income would not increase his consumption). This is illustrated in Fig. 8.1. If the individual has full insurance cover for health expenses, he

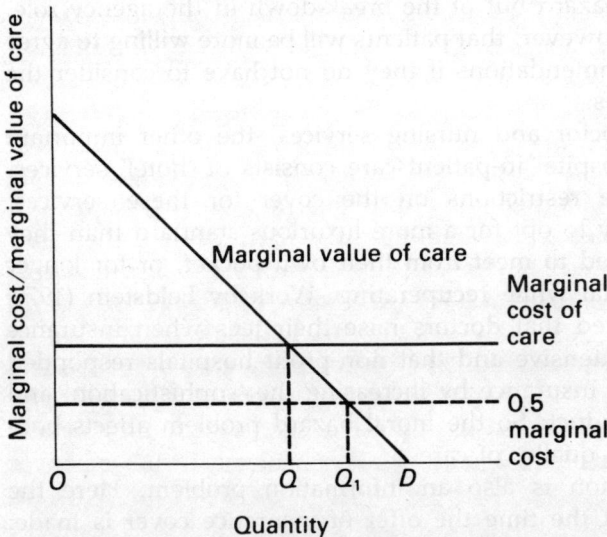

Figure 8.1 Insurance and the consumption of health care

will consume quantity of care *OD*, whereas if he were meeting the expenses out of his own pocket he would consume only *OQ* of care. Increasing the liability of insurers leads to higher premiums, making it less attractive to be insured.

This is a familiar problem of a conflict between individual and collective rationality. For any individual patient it is rational to consume care paid for by insurance until the marginal value is zero. The individual cannot guarantee that restraining his own consumption will lead to similar action by others and hence lower premiums. A collective agreement to restrain consumption would lead to lower premiums and improved efficiency, but such an agreement is unlikely to hold, especially when the number of individuals involved is large.

In the discussion of Fig. 8.1 it has been assumed that the individual makes the decision about the consumption of care. The role of the doctor 'agent' adds a further significant complication. It may be that the doctor will act as a near-perfect agent and the outcome will be similar to *OD*. But it might be that the doctor's financial interest in the amount of care the patient receives will lead to a more serious break-down of the agency relationship, with care being provided that is not justifiable on medical grounds (supplier-induced demand). To the extent that patients would be prepared to go along with the doctor's recommendation in the absence of insurance, the problem of misallocation of resources is not the result of moral hazard but of the break-down in the agency role. It seems likely, however, that patients will be more willing to agree to doctor's recommendations if they do not have to consider the cost consequences.

Apart from doctor and nursing services, the other important component of hospital in-patient care consists of 'hotel' services. Unless there are restrictions on the cover for these services, patients are likely to opt for a more luxurious standard than they would be prepared to meet from their own pocket, or for longer periods in hospital while recuperating. Work by Feldstein (1970; 1971) has indicated that doctors raise their fees when insurance becomes more extensive and that non-profit hospitals responded to the growth of insurance by increasing the 'sophistication' and price of their product. So the moral hazard problem affects both the price and the quality of care.

Adverse selection is also an information problem. Here the problem arises at the time the offer of insurance cover is made: when individuals fall into different risk groups (that is, groups who are likely to impose different liabilities on the insurer) and are aware of this, but the insurer has no effective way of identifying low- and high-risk individuals. Premiums are thus based on the average experience of the whole group and will be too high for the low-risk individuals and too low for the high-risk. It is quite possible that unless the low-risk group are extremely risk averse they will find insurance unattractive at the premium offered and withdraw; this will lead to higher premiums and eventually only high-risk individuals and those who are extremely risk averse will purchase insurance. Unless a way can be found of identifying lower risk individuals, this group will cease to be insured or will be paying excessive premiums and thus suffering welfare losses.

The type of insurance policy considered in the discussion so far involves the insurer reimbursing the individual for the full cost of medical care, together with income lost from work because of the illness.

There are three common methods of modifying an insurance policy to try to limit the problems outlined: ceilings on the level of payments to the insured, deductibles and co-insurance. There are also two other types of insurance policy: prepayment and indemnity according to a fixed schedule.

Ceilings on the level of payment are very unsatisfactory from a welfare perspective. They limit the insurer's liability but they do nothing to reduce moral hazard up to the ceiling; beyond that ceiling individuals are un-insured, but it is precisely these larger risks that individuals who want insurance most want to avoid.

A deductible is the exclusion from insurance coverage of a fixed amount of the expense, for example, the first £X of expense for each episode of illness. It is fairly clear that significant deductibles will simply lead individuals to seek supplementary insurance to achieve full cover.

However, Keeler et al. (1977) suggest that the demand for supplementary insurance in the United States to cover moderate deductibles ($200 per annum) would be negligible, for large deductibles where there would be some supplementation but full supplementation would not be sought. If supplementary insurance is sought, this recreates the moral hazard problem.

Co-insurance involves the insured person in paying some fraction of the cost of care, and the co-insurance rate refers to the fraction to be paid by him. Again taking the simplest care, in terms of Fig. 8.1, if the individual faces a 50 per cent co-insurance rate, effective marginal cost of care is $0.5\,MC$ and the individual will consume OQ_1 of care. Higher co-insurance rates will move the individual still nearer to OQ. Clearly the greater the elasticity of demand the greater the impact of co-insurance on the demand for care. By reducing the extent of moral hazard, co-insurance may encourage more people to take out insurance. It should be noted that if individual demands differ, the optimal extent of co-insurance will differ for different individuals but no fine adjustment of insurance contracts is possible in practice.

Feldstein (1973) made some empirical estimates of the efficiency gains that would accrue from raising the co-insurance rate in the United States. For what Feldstein regards as the more plausible values of the parameters in his model, the estimates indicated that there were large gains to be had from reducing insurance coverage.

Apart from insurance against costs, two other forms of health insurance have emerged: prepayment, and indemnity according to a fixed schedule. Prepayment involves paying to the providers of medical services a sum of money in return for which they agree to provide all medical services required in a given period, usually a year. Indemnity according to a fixed schedule involves establishing a list of the services to be covered by the insurance policy and the size of the payment which will be made for each service. Arrow (1963) notes that in perfect markets all three forms of insurance would be equivalent. The indemnities against a fixed schedule would be equal to the market prices of the medical services, so the value to the insured would be the same as if the insurance covered the costs of care. In turn, these would be equal to a sum paid in advance for services free at the time of use. Arrow points out, however, that insurance against full costs and prepayment both offer protection against uncertainty about the price of medical services as well as against uncertainty about the need for them.

Prepayment has not usually been popular with physicians mainly because the physician is effectively forced to bear the risk. It has been used in the UK as the basis for general practice remuneration, but here the risks are limited by an ability to refer a patient to hospital for further care at no cost to the general practitioner. An advantage of prepayment is the incentive it provides for cost-minimisation by the suppliers of medical care. One disadvantage of prepayment is the restriction it places on patient's freedom of choice of doctor at the time of illness. It should be noted, however, that a consequence of insurance against costs is that the patient no longer has any incentive to shop around to find the best combination of cost and quality of care.

With indemnity according to a fixed schedule, the services covered and the fees schedule inevitably become a matter for negotiation between insurers and providers of care, with the result dependent upon the relative power of the two groups.

Both prepayment and indemnity according to fixed schedule will have some impact upon moral hazard arising from price distortion or unscrupulous behaviour by doctors. In the case of prepayment, the onus is upon the providers of care to restrict wasteful use and they probably have more specific information about patients than the insurance companies, which will enable them to do this. In the case of a fixed schedule of fees and services, the extent of moral hazard is limited in that fees above the agreed level are only partially covered and the patient is not insured at all for services not on the agreed list. This may have the undesirable consequence that patients use more costly and perhaps medically less satisfactory treatments because they are covered by insurance while more economical and medically appropriate treatments are not on the agreed list. For example, in the United States some patients appear to receive costly hospital inpatient care because outpatient care is often not covered in health insurance policies. Some degree of moral hazard will thus still exist within the bounds of the fixed schedule.

None of the devices discussed so far do much to deal with the problem of adverse selection. One way of attacking the problem is to collect more information, but the cost of collecting this will have to be added to premiums and it may be less costly to tolerate some adverse selection. The major consequence of adverse selection is that some low-risk individuals choose to remain uninsured and thus also cause the price of insurance for the remainder to rise. One widely canvassed solution to the problem is to make insurance compulsory and hence make the experience of the whole group the basis for premiums. This clearly cannot be defended within the marketeers' voluntaristic framework of analysis if there are individuals who would not freely insure at the premiums offered. It has not been possible to arrive at an empirical estimate of the magnitude of the problem of adverse selection in systems of private health insurance.

As a conclusion to this discussion of the efficiency aspects of health insurance it is worth noting the argument of Arrow (1963) that the limitations on the operation of the market mechanism have created social institutions in which the usual assumptions of the market are contradicted and which correct or at least mitigate the consequences which would flow from reliance upon purely market processes. Arrow places considerable emphasis on the trust relationship between doctor (as agent) and patient; he notes also that the doctor is relied on as an expert in certifying the existence of illnesses and injuries for various legal and other purposes. Society expects that his concern for the correct conveying of information will, when appropriate, outweigh his desire to please his customers. The suitability of the doctor for this role is partly assured by the rigid and high entry requirements for medical school. Arrow acknowledges that these are far from perfect checks (medical ethics place an almost overwhelming emphasis on duty to the patient) but they may go some way towards limiting the extent of moral hazard. In a more limited way the role of the doctor will help to reduce adverse selection in that they will not normally conspire with patients to mislead the insurance company about the patients' true riskiness.

On the basis of the preceding discussion it seems, even after allowing for co-insurance or other modifications of insurance contracts, that a market for health care is inevitably going to fall some way short of the idealised performance of markets held out by the pro-market lobby.

The weakness of the efficiency case for markets does not deter all of the pro-market lobby, some of whom argue that the preceding discussion is based upon a static or at least an equilibrium notion of efficiency whereas the real benefit of markets is their contribution to dynamic efficiency. In the view of 'Austrian' economists, the world is characterised by pervasive uncertainty, and disequilibrium is the normal state of affairs. Information – about preferences, costs (which are subjective) – is widely scattered among individuals, the virtue of the market is that it provides a mechanism by which the decisions of different individuals can become better matched, disequilibria provide opportunities for entrepreneurship and successful entrepreneurship yields welfare improvements. In the Austrian view (see Ch. 2) it is impossible for the planner to acquire enough information to achieve a performance as good as that which will be achieved by individuals acting in a market context. That markets do behave in this beneficent way in the context described by the Austrian economists or that the government planner would perform worse cannot be demonstrated at the present time by methods which would satisfy the majority of economists. Like the extreme position on rights discussed earlier with which it is quite closely associated, the Austrian view of dynamic efficiency provides an unanswerable case in favour of markets to those who accept it but to most economists to adopt this position as a basis for policy would be to take a huge leap in the dark.

In this evaluation of markets for health care there remains the question of the consequences of and for the distribution of income. Marketeers appear to be agreed that the distribution of income arising from the free play of market forces following upon some initial endowment of wealth and talents is unlikely to be perfectly satisfactory; they acknowledge in particular that some people's incomes are likely to be unacceptably low. The marketeers are divided, however, as to the appropriate course of action to deal with this problem. One possible approach is simply to rely upon private charity. Many marketeers (e.g. Friedman 1962) have argued that the existence of a caring externality is fairly widespread within the society but that charitable activity is a public good and therefore reliance upon private charity is subject to the free rider problem and hence likely to be sub-optimal. This justified a role for government which for most marketeers would involve a system of cash transfers (see Friedman and Friedman 1980) to deal with the problem of low income. No attempt to ensure that the poor spent the money transferred on health insurance rather than other goods would be justifiable in the eyes of most marketeers. This position appears to be a useful counter to the argument of the pro-NHS lobby that the poor would be badly exposed by a move towards a market-based system of health care. There are potentially some problems in relying upon income transfers with no restriction upon how they are spent by the recipients. Guaranteeing the patients' ability to demand care may be costly if nothing is done to tackle the supply side problems in medical care, already outlined. To ensure comparability with the present position under the NHS would require an indexing of the income transfer according to the price of a health insurance contract.

There is also a problem that some individuals may spend the money for other purposes and when they fall ill be unable to pay for care. The suffering of these individuals may be regarded as a just desert for being foolhardy with their income, but the income transfer alone will not have successfully internalised the 'caring externality'. It would seem likely that only some restriction such that the transfer be spent only on health (a health voucher) would appropriately deal with the externality. Finally, some individuals are uninsurable with the private sector: those already chronically sick, the elderly infirm, the mentally ill and the mentally handicapped. For most of these groups the cost of their present care would rapidly eliminate any private resources they possessed, leaving the state to meet the full cost of their care as it does at present. This section of the population already absorbs a significant proportion of the health service and social security budgets so it cannot be assumed that the scale of income transfers involved would be small unless a much less generous level of provision for these groups is contemplated than is available under the NHS at present. In the longer term some, but by no means all, of these cases will be shifted to insurance companies but with a consequent rise in premiums.

While state-organised income transfers are a useful device to rebut claims that a market system of health care is inevitably inequitable, Sugden (1982) has presented an argument which undermines the public good theory of philanthropy which many economists thought provided the justification for such transfers. Sugden demonstrates that the public good theory of philanthropy is inconsistent with certain well-established observations. The important implication of his work is that we can no longer assume that private philanthropy will necessarily result in underprovision of charitable activities. A demonstration that private philanthropy would fail in the health care case, or a new general theory of philanthropy would appear now to be needed if most marketeers are to be convinced of the need for state-organised income transfers.

More recently Sugden (1984) has proposed a different theory of philanthropy which he calls the 'theory of reciprocity'. This theory suggests that the free-rider problem can be solved, but not necessarily; it is thus consistent with observations of the success of private philanthropy in some circumstances and its failure in others. On the basis of reciprocity theory, Sugden conjectures that the more homogeneous a community is in respect of tastes and incomes the more likely it is to successfully produce public goods through voluntary activity. However, even in a society of identical individuals it is possible to get locked into an equilibrium in which no one contributes anything towards a public good. If the UK can be regarded as diverse in terms of incomes and tastes then, on the basis of reciprocity theory, it would seem unlikely that private philanthropy will adequately deal with the 'caring' externality, but the case for state-organised income transfers is for the present somewhat insecure.

The National Health Service

Assessment of the performance of the NHS can also be conveniently divided into issues of efficiency and of equity.

Two criticisms of the NHS which are frequently held up as examples of its inefficiency are that there has been a rapid growth in the number of administrators and that there are often long waiting lists for some surgical procedures to deal with mainly non life-threatening disorders (cold surgery). Marketeers (for example Green D. G. 1984) also cite the lack of consumer sovereignty under the NHS, emphasising two effects: first that patients are severely restricted in their choice of doctor and second that some treatments are not offered to some patients who could benefit from them and who under a market system would willingly pay for and receive this care. Finally the NHS, particularly the hospital service, may be criticised because the key medical decision makers, the consultants, are salaried with a job for life and subject to few restrictions on their performance and thus appear to lack incentives to behave efficiently.

Many people assume that administrators are too remote from patients to have a significant effect upon the output of health care, viewing expenditure on their salaries as almost deadweight loss. The fact that between 1973 and 1977 (the years following the major reorganisation of the NHS) the number of administrative and clerical staff increased by 28 per cent led to popular press statements identifying a 'problem' of over-administration which was becoming worse, with scarce funds being diverted away from health care. This negative view is probably seriously misleading.

The Royal Commission on the NHS (1979) felt that it was unfair to criticise the number of administrators when there had been no research which could enable the right number to be determined. If we consider the growth in NHS administrators from 1973–77, over 600 administrative staff were recruited to service Community Health Councils which were designed to allow a greater community representation in the running of the service. The introduction of ward clerks and appointments and records clerks has released nursing staff from clerical work. Better management of services may also lead to resource savings and to improved patient care.

More significantly, when we consider the NHS in comparison to more market-oriented systems we must also consider the administrative costs of the method of finance. For example, in a private insurance system there are the costs of collecting premiums and of reimbursing the claimants. In 1977 the OECD published a study of the administrative costs attached to the co-ordination of the health care system, and the cost of operating the social security element in terms of collecting premiums and making reimbursements. The UK, because of its tax-financed system, fell among the group of countries with very low administrative costs in this OECD study, spending 2.6 per cent of total health expenditure on general administrative costs. The comparable figures for countries with greater emphasis on insurance (private or social) and on private suppliers of care were: West Germany 5.0 per cent, the United States 5.3 per cent, Switzerland 8.7 per cent, and France 10.8 per cent (OECD 1977).

A better focus for the criticism of administrators and of doctor decision takers in the NHS is that for too long the NHS information base has been inadequate to allow proper planning and monitoring of services. Information is not routinely available on the costs of treating particular disorders in different hospitals or on the use of different treatment methods. Information of this sort which does exist has had to be constructed by special study. There is no routine monitoring of the performance of consultants, the number of patients they treat, lengths of stay, re-admission rates, incidence of post-operative infections and mortality rates. What evidence there is suggests that consultants vary quite widely in the techniques they use but there has been little or no systematic evaluation in many areas of health care to determine what is 'best practice' (see Cochrane 1972). The absence of such information is not just a problem for the NHS: Maynard (1983) noted similar problems in the United States and in Australia. Decision makers do not have the relevant information to manage their health care systems.

There is growing recognition of the importance of such information with an increasing emphasis on performance indicators. Those indicators introduced in the NHS to date concentrate upon use of inputs and throughputs (patients treated) rather than the output indicators which are needed for a proper assessment of efficiency. Nevertheless, clear progress is being made on this front. It should be noted that the collection of information to improve efficiency may in the short run at least involve more spending on administration.

One particular criticism of administration which the Royal Commission on the NHS found had some basis was that decision making was often slow. A series of changes bearing upon this problem have been instituted, culminating with the implementation of the recommendations of the Griffiths Report (1984) for the introduction of general managers at all levels of the NHS (hospital, district, region and nationally) to streamline decision taking.

The problems of waiting lists within the NHS is extremely complex, and attempts to explain them in terms of simple supply and demand analysis are not convincing. Thus marketeers' claims that what is needed is a positive price to ration the scarce resources (Seldon 1967) or the early Ministry of Health view that lists could be run down by short bursts of increased effort on the supply side (Ministry of Health 1963) or by improved efficiency on the supply side, must be dismissed as too simplistic. Feldstein (1964) and Culyer and Cullis (1975; 1976) found no evidence that waiting lists fell as supply increased, in fact over the period investigated they were remarkably stable. This almost certainly reflects the role of doctors as both suppliers and demanders (as agents) of care, consultants who determine who from the patients they see in outpatients goes on the waiting list, while general practitioners are likely to refer more or fewer patients to consultants according to how quickly they believe they will be treated.

Two aspects of waiting lists may be problematic. First, the lists could be manipulated by consultants seeking a larger share of health service resources. Second, the main demand for private medicine in the UK is for non-emergency ('cold') surgery and it is this type of care for which NHS waiting lists are long. The presence of a waiting list clearly provides an incentive to patients to 'go private' and jump the queue. The doctors who provide the private care are to a large extent the consultants who place patients on NHS waiting lists.

The extent to which waiting lists are a problem can only be assessed with more information than is currently available. Culyer (1976) points out that NHS decision makers should give systematic attention to waiting time and the costs of waiting (to patients and to the health service) rather than the length of lists, and also to the criteria (medical and social) used to place patients on waiting lists and select those for treatment.

The welfare loss occasioned by the loss of consumer sovereignty under the NHS is difficult to quantify but, as has been indicated, consumer sovereignty in a market for health care is severely restricted by the information inequalities between doctors and patients. Under existing NHS arrangements, patients can change their general practitioner and have a right to a second opinion in specialist care, to the extent that there is a problem it is mainly because these options are not exercised frequently enough. The likely reasons for patients failing to exercise their options are that they are unaware of their rights or are afraid to assert them. It does not seem likely, as marketeers frequently assert, that people do not shop around because they are not spending their own money: NHS care has a time price even if there is no money price and patients are not indifferent to the care they receive.

That some patients do not receive care under the NHS which they would be prepared to pay for in market systems points up a more fundamental difference between the two systems. In the NHS, rationing of some health care is carried out largely on the basis of clinical judgement (hopefully of the likely benefits of the care) while in the market care is available on the basis of ability to pay with all the attendant risks of overprovision because of supplier-induced demand. The marketeers, however, are deluded if they believe that no one goes without treatment from which they could significantly benefit: in market systems the poor (uninsured) are the ones excluded or receiving second-rate care. The task for the NHS should be to evolve an adequate system for monitoring the decisions of consultants on the allocation of care.

It is worth noting that more care could be provided by the NHS if its budget was increased. The health service in the UK receives a low proportion of GDP (5.2 per cent) by international standards while Australia, Canada, West Germany, France, Sweden and the USA spend between 6.5 and 7.4 per cent (all figures for 1974 or near date, OECD 1977).

Finally there is the issue of inefficiency on the part of medical decision makers who lack incentives to behave efficiently. The need for more information on differences between best practice and actual practice has been noted. A different approach to this problem which has been the subject of experiment in the NHS is clinical budgeting (Wickens and Coles 1985). In essence this involves a decentralisation of decision making within the NHS and with it hopefully a shift in emphasis away from accounting for inputs towards trying to maximise output from a given input. Under the present system a large proportion of resources are held in common (e.g. X-ray or laboratory facilities) in hospitals, and individual consultants simply draw on them until they are used up even though their marginal valuation of the use for their patients may be very small. Clinical budgeting would involve consultants becoming budget holders (the budgets may be notional) allocating the budget to areas of care which bring the greatest benefit to their group of patients, as an incentive part of any savings from the budget might be allowed to the consultant for spending on new equipment or the development of new treatments.

Innovations such as clinical budgeting and improvements in NHS information systems will enable the NHS to increase its efficiency. When the NHS was founded it was intended that it should be an egalitarian service delivering care according to need rather than ability to pay. The equality objective was not specified in a precise operational way and thus greater equality was not pursued systematically in the NHS in its first two decades but was achieved only as a by-product of attempts to improve services for all patients across the whole of the UK. Over the last twenty years a considerable amount of evidence has been presented suggesting the existence of several types of inequality in the NHS.

Geographical inequality was explored in some detail by Cooper and Culyer (1970; 1972) who showed, for example, that the Metropolitan (now Thames) regions and the Oxford region were better provided than the Sheffield (now Trent) region on every single one of a large number of indicators of provision of care and better provided than most regions on the majority of these indicators. Some of the inequalities were very large and there was evidence that inequality within regions was also very large.

The first systematic attempt to reduce geographical inequality came in 1970, but the task has been tackled much more systematically since the work of the Resource Allocation Working Party (RAWP) in 1976 (with similar work being carried out in Scotland, Wales and Northern Ireland). RAWP recommended that revenue funds should be allocated according to relative need for care with no account being taken of previous allocations. The RAWP formula used population, adjusted for age and sex, and marital status as well as standardised fertility ratios and mortality ratios as the basic measures of need. Further adjustments were made for cross-boundary flows of patients and for the costs of medical education. The formula having been applied, the DHSS was then committed over the period of a decade to make corrections to the distribution of resources. Given the wide differentials in resource provision identified in the early 1970s, the application of RAWP has been fairly controversial and this has been especially the case over recent years when the growth in resource provision to the NHS as a whole has slowed. The RAWP approach has been subject to a great deal of criticism but it nevertheless represents a clear and systematic commitment to geographical equality.

The most comprehensive catalogue of evidence of social class inequality in health and care provision was provided by the Black Report in 1980. This reviewed evidence on inequalities in mortality, morbidity and use of health services. The Black Report and evidence compiled by Le Grand (1982) on the use of health services shows that individuals in social classes IV and V have a lower life expectancy and report more ill-health than those in social classes I and II and they use health services less, relative to need, than the better-off groups. The need to reduce this inequality was seen by Black as one of the major changes facing the NHS. Le Grand (1985) has recently argued that the most useful framework for developing policies to tackle this inequality is that provided by Grossman (1972). The Grossman approach emphasises that the individual's health is determined by an initial stock of health which depreciates over the life cycle, but this depreciation can be offset by health-producing activities such as exercise, good diet and health care; on the other hand, depreciation might be increased by activities such as smoking or bad diet. The approach emphasises individual choice and therefore policies must be constructed which shift the balance of incentives in favour of health-producing activities and against health-reducing activities. An important implication of the approach is, however, that some of the determinants of inequality are beyond the control of the NHS or any health service but are rooted in the wider range of inequalities in society. Thus there are limits to the possibility of attaining equality of health or even of health care (relative to need) as long as these inequalities in society remain.

The final area of inequality within the NHS concerns the treatment of different illness groups. The Royal Commission on the NHS (1979) noted that the care of the elderly, the mentally ill and the mentally handicapped had received less resources than those allocated to other patient groups. Since 1976 these groups, together with children, have been regarded as priorities for additional spending within the NHS; there is also a stated intention to shift the care of these groups away from large institutions and into the community. Shifting priorities within the NHS is a slow process, particularly when the growth in funds available for all care is very small, nevertheless improvements will occur in the care of these groups. It is difficult to believe that these groups would be better placed in a more market-oriented system.

Private health care in the UK

As has been indicated, private medicine and private health insurance have existed alongside the NHS since its inception. Over the years 1979–81 the annual growth in the number of subscribers to private health insurance was 16 per cent, 26 per cent and 14 per cent respectively, but since then the rate has fallen to around 3 per cent per annum. Despite this rapid growth, it remains small in comparison to the NHS; although about 7 per cent of the population are covered by private health insurance, expenditure is only about 2 per cent of that of the NHS. The reason for the divergence between the figures for coverage and expenditure is that for the most part private insurance is used to cover non-emergency ('cold') care. Almost two-thirds of the expenditure finances about thirty surgical procedures including hernias, haemorrhoids, varicose veins and minor gynaecological surgery, which are mostly disorders for which there are NHS waiting lists and indicates that private insurance is used heavily as a means of 'queue jumping' with the privately insured reverting to NHS care for emergency care or chronic illness (long-term care for mental illness or acute disorders such as kidney failure are not covered in most insurance policies).

The supply of medical labour to provide private care was increased in 1980 when a change in contracts allowed even full-time NHS consultants to earn up to 10 per cent of their income from private care. The demand increase of the late 1970s and early 1980s was chiefly the result of a growth in occupational and group schemes with individual subscriptions growing much more slowly.

In recent years the industry has suffered from rapidly rising costs, partly from moral hazard and partly because of adverse selection as the group and occupational schemes have drawn in higher risk groups. Although premiums have been raised significantly in the 1980s the proportion of income paid out in benefits has continued to rise. BUPA, the largest carrier, has placed some expensive hospitals out of bounds and has sought to negotiate a scale of fees with consultants. At the end of 1985, Private Patients Plan (the second largest carrier) announced a new policy to replace its main health insurance policy to combat rising costs. The new policy has more exclusions and contains an option for deductibles. Meanwhile BUPA has announced a further substantial price rise (11 per cent in January 1986).

It seems extremely unlikely that private insurance will play a significantly larger role in health care in the near future unless the government takes further action to stimulate its growth.

Conclusion

This chapter has indicated some of the problems of markets in health care: the weakness of the consumer sovereignty model, monopoly, moral hazard and adverse selection connected with the insurance mechanism, supplier-induced demand, and finally the lack of agreement among marketeers about the means of ensuring equity. Some of the criticisms of the efficiency of the NHS were also found to be at least partly valid and the NHS has still some way to go to achieve the egalitarian aspirations of its founders.

In the view of this author, a market system in health care appears to be fundamentally flawed and belief in the eventual success of such a system is a matter of faith not logic. The UK private sector already exhibits some of the flaws in market systems identified in this chapter and does not look capable of providing a challenge to the NHS. It would therefore require a major political initiative in favour of markets to significantly change the balance of provision of care.

Whilst it is easy to be overly complacent about the performance of the NHS, it should be viewed as a successful system capable of further improvement. The means by which further improvements in performance can be achieved have, as has been indicated, been developing over the last decade and further encouragement should be given to the systematic collection of data to evaluate and to monitor the health care system. The NHS is the system in place, it is popular, it can be improved and it would appear totally unreasonable to replace it with an entirely different system the merit of which in the long term is in doubt and any shift would in the short term involve significant adjustment costs.

Chapter 9

EDUCATION

Barrie Craven, Brian Dick and Barry Wood

Introduction

Education is almost impossible to define. Whilst there is a formal education system, generally state run, most commentators would widen the definition to include apprenticeships, pre-school nurseries, even private study of a particular interest and possibly hobbies. In Britain state education expenditure as a percentage of GNP has increased from 3.6 per cent in 1960/61 to 5.3 per cent in 1984/85. This has partly displaced previous forms of education but more generally has been focused on increasing the human capital of the population in response to an increasingly complicated mode of production.

The historical explanation or justification of this public sector growth is that private markets fail. Most commonly it is argued (see Ch. 6) that firms are only prepared to provide specialist training for their particular needs with the result that, if left to firms, individuals would have few basic skills which they could utilise over their lifetime. Individuals may be prepared to finance their own (or their children's) education, but education has commonly been seen as a merit good and in consequence this route has been considered as unacceptable. Strictly speaking this merit good argument (which implies that people undervalue the returns to education) justifies compulsory general education with possibly a 100 per cent subsidy to eliminate distributional problems, but it is arguable that the growth of state supply has been produced by a bureaucratic wish to standardise and expand rather than as a consequence of market failure.

Today the historical arguments have come full circle. The private sector of education is substantial and thriving and the traditional public sector bureau (the DES) is under pressure (from parents, employers and even youngsters) to change and is even faced with competition, particularly from the Manpower Services Commission (MSC). In 1984/85, for example, the MSC spent £1414 million on training of which the expanding Youth Training Scheme received £758 million.

The failure of public provision is perceived in three main areas. First in access to education. One of the arguments used by the proponents of state-provided education is that such a system effectively eliminates inequality in access to education. While in the

Table 9.1 Students* attending university or college: by socio-economic group of father,† 1981–82

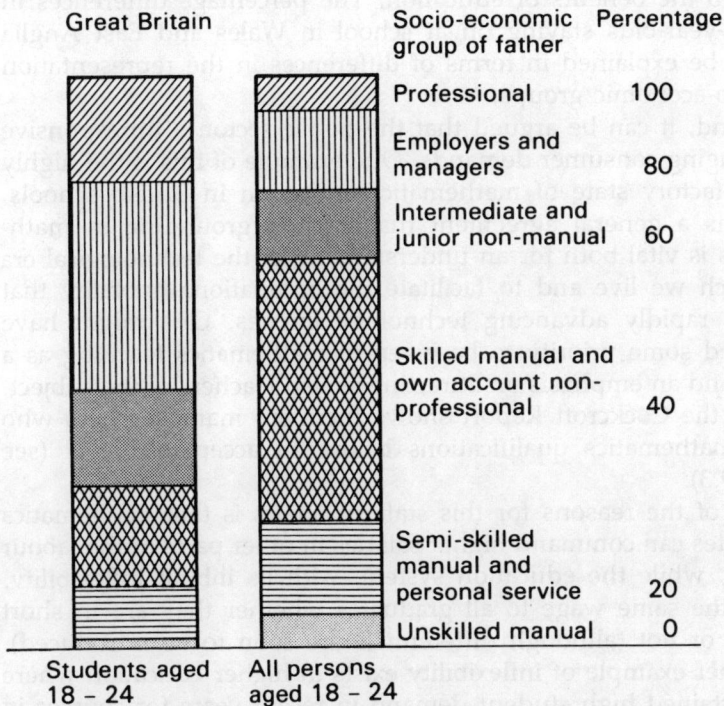

Great Britain		Socio-economic group of father	Percentage
		Professional	100
		Employers and managers	80
		Intermediate and junior non-manual	60
		Skilled manual and own account non-professional	40
		Semi-skilled manual and personal service	20
		Unskilled manual	0
Students aged 18 – 24	All persons aged 18 – 24		

1 Full-time and sandwich course students aged 18 – 24, studying at universities, polytechnics, or colleges of further education (including colleges of education in Scotland and Northern Ireland).

2 See Appendix, Part II: General Household Survey. People whose fathers were members of the armed forces, full-time students, or had never worked are excluded from the sample.

(*Source: Social Trends* 1984)

compulsory sector (five to sixteen-year-olds) there is some truth in this argument there is no doubt, as Table 9.1 indicates, that families in which the father has a professional or managerial occupation provide the support that ensures that their children have a far greater likelihood of entering higher education and consequently of obtaining better-paid jobs. Inequality persists (see Table 9.1) not despite the compulsory system but because of it; some parents can and do exploit it for the benefit of their children.

Further inequality exists between regions as Table 9.2 shows.

The evident regional differences in sixteen-year-olds remaining in education may partly be explained by an uneven distribution of socio-economic groups but they are also influenced by social attitudes to the benefits of education. The percentage differences in sixteen-year-olds staying on at school in Wales and East Anglia cannot be explained in terms of differences in the representation of socio-economic groups.

Second, it can be argued that the public sector is unresponsive to changing consumer demands. One example of this is the highly unsatisfactory state of mathematics education in British schools. There is a general agreement that a good grounding in mathematics is vital both for an understanding of the technological era in which we live and to facilitate the occupational mobility that such a rapidly advancing technology implies. One might have expected some priority to be given to mathematics teaching as a result and an emphasis on attracting skilled teachers of the subject. But as the Cockcroft Report shows there are many teachers who have mathematics qualifications below an acceptable level (see Table 9.3).

One of the reasons for this state of affairs is that mathematics graduates can command higher salaries in other parts of the labour market, while the education system, with its inbuilt inflexibility, offers the same wage to all graduates whether they are in short supply or not (although differentials are soon to be introduced). A further example of inflexibility exists in higher education where the sustained high student demand in recent years for courses in accountancy and law has not resulted in a dramatic shift in supply; rather the problem has been solved by rationing places out to those with exceptionally good 'A' levels.

Third, the education system may be described as inefficient. Ten years ago universities and polytechnics argued that it was impossible for them to become more efficient and that consequently their staff/student ratio of 1 : 7.5 (approximately) could not be increased without a real reduction in the quality of education. Today, with

Table 9.2 Young people staying on at school or going to further or higher education*

Academic year 1982/83 (percentages)

| | Total‡(000) | Population aged 16 years | | | |
| | | Staying on at school‡ (A) | Going to non-advanced further education§ | | |
			Full-time (B)	Part-time¶ (C)	(D) = A + B + C
North	51.6	23.3	17.7	11.8	52.8
Yorkshire and Humberside	82.5	25.2	18.6	9.4	53.2
East Midlands	63.7	24.6	22.6	22.6	56.9
East Anglia	30.5	23.9	17.6	6.4	47.9
South East	276.3	31.9	16.4	6.0	54.3
South West	72.8	23.2	22.1	7.0	52.3
West Midlands	88.1	23.7	22.8	9.0	55.5
North West	108.2	24.0	21.1	12.3	57.4
England	773.7	26.8	19.2	8.4	54.4
Wales	46.0	31.6	20.0	8.1	59.7

* By region of residence
† DES estimates of population in age group at 31 August 1982
‡ Enrolment at 1 January 1983, excluding privately funded pupils in independent schools
§ Enrolment at 1 November 1982
¶ Excludes evening only

Source: Regional Trends 1985

Table 9.3   Mathematics qualifications of teachers

	% of mathematics teaching qualifications of staff			
	Good	Acceptable	Weak	Nil
432 schools in sample:				
Comprehensive				
13/14–18	45	28	12	15
11/12–18 large	38	29	17	16
medium	36	24	17	22
small	32	28	14	25
11/12–16	23	34	20	23
10/11–14	17	20	24	38
Modern	17	33	16	35
Grammar	59	28	8	6
Sixth-form college	61	27	7	5
Estimated total for all secondary schools (excluding middle)	33	29	17	21

Source: *The Cockcroft Report*, 1982, Table 15, p. 258

the university sector approaching ratios of 1 : 10 and the polytechnics aiming for 1 : 12, it is quite clear that efficiency gains have been made: we know of no evidence that the quality of education has fallen (see Craven *et al.* 1986). Inefficiency may have been reduced but this process has been slow and subject to much resistance, not least from academics with whose self-interest these pressures may conflict.

In the school sector the problem is even more worrying. As Table 9.4 shows, pupil–teacher ratios have been falling in recent years making the education system even more costly on a per pupil basis.

There is little incentive for teachers, local authorities or parents to reorganise the school system on a more cost-effective basis. In the long run, given the educational funding mechanism in Britain, rising education costs may cause local and national politicians to

Table 9.4   Pupil–teacher ratios in British schools 1973–83

	1973	1974	1975	1976	1977	1978	1979	1980	1981	1982	1983
Nursery	25.1	23.9	22.2	22.1	21.8	22.5	22.1	21.6	21.5	21.6	21.8
Primary	25.6	24.9	24.2	23.8	23.7	23.4	22.9	22.4	22.3	22.3	22.1
Secondary	16.9	17.3	17.0	16.8	16.8	16.7	16.5	16.4	16.4	16.4	16.2
Special	10.5	9.9	9.3	8.9	8.5	8.3	7.9	7.6	7.5	7.4	7.3

Source: *Annual Abstract of Statistics* 1985 (HMSO)

demand change. There must, however, be few taxpayers who regard the political process, as a vehicle for change, as being as quick or effective as the profit motive.

The economic analysis of education

Education is considered by economists as an economic activity similar in principle to the production and consumption of all other goods and services. Consumers buy (possibly at a zero price) the service because the utility derived from either the consumption or investment facet of education is at least as great as its cost. In a world of shorter working time and high unemployment, the consumption element may not be unimportant but it is necessary to note that the distribution of educational expenditure may not be egalitarian. More particularly, in post-compulsory education the existence of academic entry restrictions results in an income redistribution from taxpayers to qualified students. Given the tax system in the UK and the predominance of students (in this sector) from families with higher than average incomes, the redistribution effect may even be regressive.

Economists have tended to concentrate on the investment characteristics of education. It is conventionally assumed that those in education pay, at least, a price in terms of forgone earnings though this may be offset by maintenance grants. Figure 9.1 illustrates the analysis for undergraduates. Area A represents lost income, mainly between the ages of eighteen and twenty-one, while area B represents the higher income generated by the superior marketable skills of graduates.

Discounting the future anticipated earnings enables a private rate of return to the individual to be calculated. It is important to note that this analysis can be extended to the schooling of children. During the last century both employers and parents objected to compulsory education being extended up to the age of fourteen as the child lost many years of 'productive and rewarding' work. Even part-time education can be considered in these terms for here leisure time is curtailed in the anticipation of future benefit from education. In recent years (at least in some parts of the country) employment opportunities for young people at the end of statutory schooling (at age sixteen) have rapidly declined. A new range of courses involving formal education and practical work experience have been developed. The youngsters' displeasure with these courses is not surprising for in comparison to traditional employ-

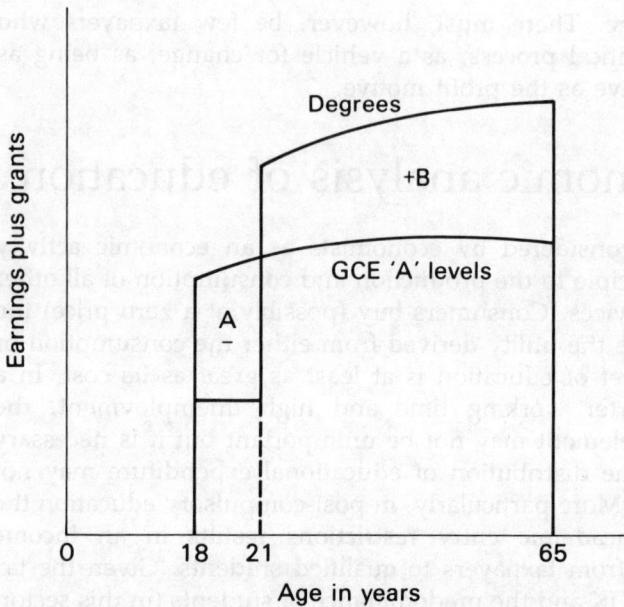

Figure 9.1   Qualifications and income

ment/training the income forgone is considerable and the future returns unlikely to be substantial. However, young people are realistic: in comparison to the actual alternative available which is unemployment, the income forgone (unemployment pay minus YTS income) is generally negative and future prospects are slightly enhanced and so they attend the courses.

Measures of rates of return on this type of human capital are now widely available. Ziderman (1975) showed that in the UK part-time technical qualifications generated the greatest returns (20 per cent plus) while those for post-graduate qualifications were generally low (less than 5 per cent). In principle, educational resources could be reallocated on the basis of rates of returns (i.e. maximising human capital). It is important to note, however, that such calculations depend on cross-section studies of earnings differentials between qualified and unqualified workers. This raises two questions: first, what proportion of the earnings differential has been generated by education rather than natural ability, hard work, perseverance etc; and secondly, is it likely that earnings differentials will remain the same despite the steadily increasing number of qualified persons and the common observation that they are filtering down the labour market, taking jobs previously open to those with fewer qualifications?

The above problems flaw the human capital approach as a viable public policy instrument. Proxies for long-term rates of return do exist, namely, unemployment rates for different types of graduates, first wage levels, private employer projections and government/employer requirements (see Tarsh 1982).

Many economists recognise that education is primarily a private good and therefore in principle support private market solutions. In practice, government intervention is commonly justified by economists in the following terms:

1. That children are too young to make adequate decisions and that their parents may neglect their duties.
2. That there is ignorance on the part of parents of the benefits of education.
3. That there are income distribution problems.
4. That there are difficulties in predicting returns.
5. The presence of externalities.

Parental neglect and ignorance can be overcome by making education compulsory with poor parents being helped by a system of vouchers, financed out of taxation. Here there may be a justification for state intervention and control but there is no case in terms of points 1–3 for state supply. Given the long-term nature of returns, prediction is inevitably difficult. This may justify state supply of certain types of education and a reduction in others on the grounds that the government knows better than the individual. Whether government, with its short electoral horizon, does know best lies, like beauty, in the eye of the beholder.

Externality arguments provide the strongest economic justification for state intervention. In Fig. 9.2, externalities raise social returns SD_1 above private returns (PD), shifting the equilibrium from A to B and the quantity of education from OD to OE.

The only way of ensuring that consumers buy OE however is to reduce the price to zero, i.e. a 100 per cent subsidy BE. A further problem arises if social returns are represented by SD_2. Here consumers will only buy the optimal quantity OF if the price is negative (e.g. income supplements as well as a 100 per cent subsidy in higher education) or if they are obliged to consume it by law (e.g. five to sixteen-year-old compulsory education). What are these externalities? Those usually attributed to education include a more thoughtful and caring society, a more efficient public and private sector because they can rely on basic literacy and numeracy, an inter-generational effect as educated mothers and fathers raise the educational skills and expectations of their

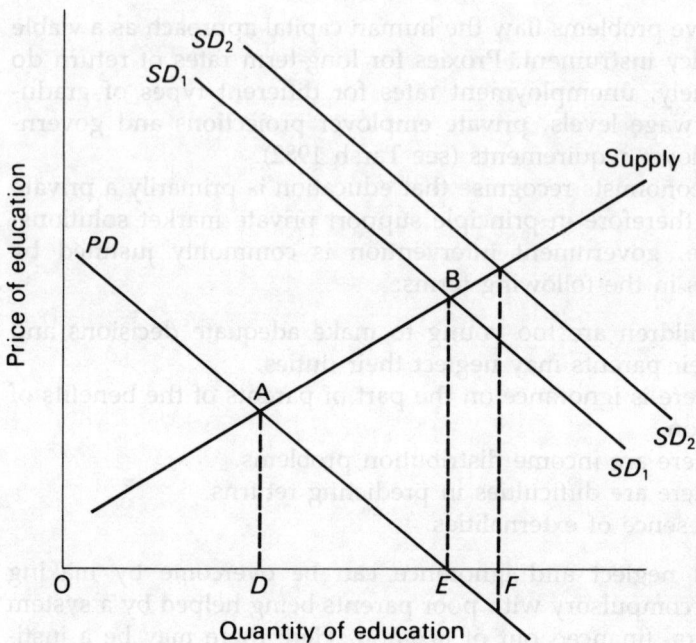

Figure 9.2   Externalities and education

children and a rise in productivity of non-educated/trained workers due to the guidance of skilled labour.

Economists' views on the value of externalities vary from the significant (Vaizey 1972) to the sceptical (Blaug 1972). While there are obvious difficulties in measuring the extent of externalities and consequently the optimal degree of subsidy, there is no doubt that a 100 per cent subsidy creates further difficulties. Most importantly, as education is a multi-discipline product, consumers have to make a choice of courses, modes of study and so on. Zero (or negative) priced education provides consumers with little incentive to choose the most beneficial course (there is no financial cost) and, equally, producers have few incentives to be responsive to changing consumer tastes. Course provision will be determined by education bureaucrats and costs are therefore unlikely to be as low as they would be in a competitive market. Put another way, a zero-priced education system is unlikely to be responsive to market signals.

A radically different economic explanation of the role of education is provided by the filter (or screening) hypothesis. Arrow (1973) argued that education could be considered as a filter, separating the more able from the less able, rather than a process of training people in 'useful' skills. It is important to understand that the filter theory does not deny the human capital theory; it is entirely consistent with it in that the more highly skilled receive higher earnings. It is, however, the explanation of the higher earnings that is different. In human capital theory the skilled worker has a higher marginal productivity and hence earns more, while in the filter theory the firm employs more educated workers because they have more potential to be productive especially after the firm has trained them. Neither Arrow nor other filter theorists would deny that education generates some human capital return, but they do argue that the filtering function is also important.

The filtering function of education becomes more significant if a radical view of wage determination is accepted. Thurow (1976) argues that jobs and their associated rates of pay come first and firms seek the most able candidates for the position. People at the highest levels of the job queue obtain better-paid jobs because the firm perceives that they can be trained to be more productive and not because of knowledge previously acquired (in the education system). A person's position in the labour queue is determined partly by age, sex, race, religion, marital status and the like but most importantly by education which provides unique and independent evidence on the individual's potential productivity.

Acceptance of the filter theory as at least a partial explanation of the role of education leads to two problems. First, if education is a good filter, then it will provide an independent objective measure of an individual's ability. Tests should ideally measure the skills, personal motivations and other work-relevant abilities of the individual. Whether education fulfils this role is of course highly debatable and certainly firms do not always accept educational qualifications as sufficient information, but may use them as an initial screening device. A further issue here is whether an effective filter could be provided more cheaply. Do firms use educational qualifications as a filter because it is costless to them? If firms had to pay the full cost of the filter directly, would they find a cheaper alternative?

Secondly, because education is a significant variable in determining a person's position in the labour queue it is an obvious route by which the individual can improve his job prospects. It is interesting to note here that while education can be the path by which the individual achieves upward earnings mobility, the job competition model predicts that the national distribution of income will be unaffected by education. In this model, jobs come first and with these come the associated rates of pay which have been determined by the character of technical progress, the sociology of wage determination and the distribution of training costs between employers and employees. More education of the poor and disadvantaged, perhaps the most persistent and long-lasting cry of the social engineers of the 1960s, only works if the poor become as equally productive as the middle classes and if wages are determined on the basis of productivity. If the job competition model is correct, then the national income distribution is pre-set and can only be changed by direct government intervention on wage levels and/or tax rates.

The opposing view can be clearly seen in operation in higher education. A graduate of mechanical engineering may enter a manufacturing firm and his acquired skills (and of course his life-time experience) may allow him to be more directly productive and thus enable him to earn higher wages. Alternatively, a graduate of medieval history may enter the managerial profession. There his acquired knowledge is of little direct use; the firm employs the graduate because of his potential. Historically British education has been biased towards the latter type of course (see Weiner 1981). But recent changes such as youth training schemes and continued support for science and engineering in advanced higher education (see HMSO, Cmnd 9524) can be interpreted as a move towards the former.

The medieval history type of course may be a good filter but the question of work relevance cannot be ignored. However, a course which involves 'training' may be an equally good filter but have the additional advantage of generating greater productivity. Indeed, it can be argued that trained manpower (engineers, scientists) are an important aspect of technological change and thus a determinant of economic growth (see Solow 1957).

Other explanations of the role of education

Economic factors are not the only justification for education provision and this section considers other major justifications for it which have been proposed. Each is considered in terms of three crucial criteria: resource allocation methodology, efficiency and public intervention implications.

The educationalists' perspective

Many educationalists take the view that the purpose of education is to enrich the individual; that education is *ipso facto* 'a good thing', that educationalists are the best judges of what constitutes 'good education' and that education should be supplied free by the state. The educationalists' objectives are imprecise and pluralistic and are well expressed by Peters who suggests that the criteria implicit in the concept of education are:

1. That education implies the transmission of what is worthwhile to those who become committed to it.
2. That education must involve knowledge and understanding of some kind of cognitive perspectives which are not inert.
3. That education at least rules out some procedures of transmission, on the grounds that they lack wittingness and voluntariness on the part of the learner (Peters 1967: 12).

Such criteria are so wide ranging that the study of anything to anyone could be justified simply by an educationalist saying it is worthwhile. This approach fails to consider the costs of providing educational resources and consequently fails to provide resource-allocation criteria in a world of limited resources upon which there are competing demands. Similarly, no consideration is given to the efficiency with which educational resources are utilised. Finally, and perhaps most importantly in the context of this book, state supply is justified by assertion.

The social perspective

This concept is derived from an interpretation of education within the cultural context of society. It represents the view that much of educational provision (in terms of objectives and philosophy) can be explained by historical analysis.

The connections between culture, education, resource allocation and the state of the British economy has recently been articulated by Weiner (1981). In his thesis, the historical development of education, reinforcing (as Williams R. 1965 also explains) the elite culture, has for Britain resulted in too many educational resources being directed towards 'individual enrichment' and too few towards 'vocational training'.

This has resulted in oversupply of, for example, arts and

social/liberal studies students, unsuited to and loath to take employment in manufacturing industry. The dominant preferred culture which has emerged favours the professions, public service and the service industries and discriminates against production and manufacturing. Thus:

> The politicians, civil servants, churchmen, professional men and the publicists who did so much to shape modern British political opinion and policy moved in a climate of opinion uncongenial to the world of industry . . . Political calls for economic growth went against the grain of the values and style of life actually believed in by most politicians and civil servants as well as by the rest of the elite (Weiner 1981: 79).

This theme is elaborated upon and reinforced in numerous references from writings in literature, poetry, song, history, economics, politics and sociology. Weiner suggests that culture largely determines economic potential. To change the economic order, education should move away from individual enrichment and towards vocational training. Here is a clear recognition that there is an economic side of education and that the traditional view of educationalists essentially leads to educational justification by force of assertion. 'At the end of the day, it may be that Mrs Thatcher will find her most fundamental challenge not in holding down the money supply or inhibiting government spending, or even fighting the stewards, but in changing this frame of mind' (Weiner 1981: 166).

Resource allocation here depends upon history and culture. As cultural norms change so will our expectations of the education system. While the impact of culture on education cannot be denied, this approach is incapable of providing resource-allocation judgements. Furthermore it says little about efficiency or the role of the state.

A Marxist interpretation

Marxists see the purpose of education in capitalist economies in largely functionalist terms. Education supports not only the *status quo* class divisions (by passing on its culture and values) but also the capitalist economic system. Indeed, welfare services generally are state provided in this context, not as a result of a compassionate and caring society but as a state response to a decaying and crumbling economic system. This system, Marxists claim, is incapable of producing its own adequate levels of health care, social services, housing and education. Marxists may well be able to generate resource-allocation criteria in a Marxist society but such issues are irrelevant to Great Britain in the late 1980s. Marxists do, however, emphasise one point of significance which is commonly overlooked in conventional studies of education, namely the distribution of the benefits of state education expenditure. It is by no means certain that state supply generates a more equitable distribution of income.

The corporatist approach

Galbraith argues that education has an important function in his corporatist explanation of modern economic activity. Technologically advanced corporations require educationally qualified labour. Education (other than at the primary level) is not necessary for skilled and unskilled blue-collar labour, but it is necessary for managers, engineers, salesmen and accountants. Galbraith suggests that as growth in productivity and automation lessens the demand for the former, so the demand for the latter rises.

The role of further and higher education is therefore to provide adequate supplies of qualified manpower for the needs of industry. In essence, education should be for industry rather than about industry.

> But unemployment also reflects the cultural development of the system. It will be smaller, at any given level of demand, the better the cultural accommodation to the needs of the industrial system. If this accommodation is good, there will be a smaller core of functional illiterates who cannot be used at all. And there will be a larger number of people not only to fill the vacancies calling for Higher Education but also with the added mobility between occupations and regions that goes with education (Galbraith 1969: 285).

Galbraith provides some guidance on the resource-allocation criteria question. He argues that resources should be directed towards the need of employers. Neither state subsidy nor supply is prescribed by the corporatist view, for if there were private markets, firms would have to pay more for skilled labour (or else labour would not undertake the investment in its own human capital), but firms would also be compensated by lower taxation.

Education as job creation

An analysis of welfare services by Gould (1981) argues that the Salaried Middle Classes (SMC) are consumers and producers of welfare and concludes 'that the benefits to them are so great that we ought to consider the possibility that they constitute an independent class capable of pursuing and realising their own interests in competition or in collaboration with capital or labour' (Gould 1981: 409).

Gould suggests that Marxists have become too concerned with the distributional shares going to either labour or capital (the only beneficiaries of capitalism) and have neglected the importance of the SMC. Of course it is conceded that labour has gained (after a century of struggle) something from the welfare services but capital has also gained.

'Where evidence is found of a poor return to the workers, it is assumed that capital benefits; where there is no obvious advantage to capital, it is a victory for organised workers' (Gould 1981: 410).

In the case of education, Gould argues that thirty years of post-war expansion have left unchanged the social inequalities faced by working-class children. Education has resulted in qualification inflation and the diploma disease (see Dore 1976) which has benefited neither labour nor capital but mainly administrative, professional and technical workers. Gould points out that the greatest expenditures per head in education are upon sixth-form and higher education, the overwhelming beneficiaries being the SMC and the wealthy. 'If there was the political will to devote such enormous resources to education, how come the will was lacking when it came to those areas from which the working class could really have benefited?' (Gould 1981: 410.)

The late H. G. Johnson considered that for academic staff in universities there was a substantial element of consumption in their employment. 'This includes good public facilities for themselves, common rooms, lounges, refectories and bars, supply of current newspapers and magazines, inexpensive tea, coffee and pastry and good facilities in the form of individual offices, secretaries and reproduction facilities, and imposing buildings in which to house them' (Johnson 1973: 45).

Whilst this may smack of X-inefficiency (see Ch. 1), it hints too at the thesis that higher education serves not society (Williams R. 1965) nor the needs of industry (Galbraith 1969) except coincidentally, but the needs of the employees of education.

To put the preceding argument in stark economic terms, a considerable part of the income received by the SMC in education is a partial transfer payment. In addition, there may be a substantial proportion of economic rent.

Resource allocation here is determined by the benefits to the SMC, efficiency is positively discouraged by the employees of education and state intervention is justified by assertion.

Social cohesion

The concept of social cohesion means different things to different people. It is held that education can be important in smoothing social, ethnic and cultural differences in cosmopolitan cities, and in this sense promotes and creates social cohesion through the seeking of common values. Ziderman (1985) considers that in so doing, educational policy may, especially in highly developed societies, because of the emphasis placed on the desirability to conform and 'stay in line' promote the opposite effect. Blaug stated that 'the fact of the matter is that education of young children to some extent does amount to 'brain washing' in that it serves to internalise socially accepted attitudes and norms of conduct' (Blaug 1972: 204). The objective of social cohesion provides no clear answers to our original questions of resource-allocation criteria, efficiency and the role of the state.

There is no doubt that the issues considered in this section have all had a degree of influence on the size, scope and structure of our educational system. In comparison with the economic criteria previously outlined, their collective failure is obvious. In particular, they fail to provide any resource-allocation criteria and only generate an unsupported claim for more resources. Given our awareness of the bureaucratic nature of a state educational supply, it is not surprising that such cries are commonly ignored. Increasingly the government, employers, parents and the public look towards economists to provide the means of assessing the 'success' of the education system, as new (and sometimes not so new) issues come to the fore. As is shown in the next section, it is the economists' criteria which are beginning to dominate the agenda.

Persisting issues in the education debate

We are concerned in this section with whether education resources are better deployed by markets than organised by governments and how far market principles and pricing can be introduced into the provision of education by government. To that end we will concentrate on a few important and persisting practical issues in the education debate. Seldon has written: 'it is a fallacy to suppose that all services which, for whatever reason or accident of history, have become 'public services' are what the economist in a more technical sense describes as 'public goods' that should or must be provided by government and financed out of taxes' (Seldon 1975: 9).

Loans versus grants

The economist's approach to resource allocation in education with its emphasis on costs and benefits is nowhere better illustrated than in the debate on the size and composition of the higher education sector. In the UK higher education is provided on the basis that all with the basic qualifications for entry will be allowed access to it and will not be constrained by lack of income. Recently the imposition of additional quotas on student numbers (over and above minimum GCE 'A' level requirements) and the reduction in the real value of (state-funded) student grants have restricted automatic access. Subsidies to institutions through the UGC and the local authorities together with a system of non-repayable grants to students (albeit on a sliding scale related to parental income) plus all tuition fees still facilitates the minimisation of financial cost to be borne by students. The imposition of quotas on student numbers has been a response to the desire by government to cut public spending generally and to the competing demands for resources by other government departments.

As already noted, the private benefits of higher education are substantial and accrue to its consumers in the form of higher life-time earnings; the opportunity cost to an individual consumer is relatively small and consists largely of forgone earnings during the period of education. State provision and financing is justified on the grounds that there are significant positive externalities to the rest of society in the form of increased economic growth with associated benefits such as increased individual living standards, higher levels of employment and lower levels of inflation, not to mention such immeasurable externalities as increased social cohesion.

Market economists question the significance of the externality effects and argue that the adoption of loans in place of grants and the dropping of quotas will lead to a change in the size and nature of the higher education sector that will at least be more economically efficient.

Arguments in favour of loans

The first argument in favour of the repayment by the student of part or all of the cost of higher education is advanced in the name of distributional equity. It can be regarded as conflicting with redistributive objectives that the potentially affluent student should receive subsidies from a society the majority of whose members have lower incomes than the beneficiaries of higher education. An additional 'distributive' argument is that a full-cost 'free' grant leads to a pattern of educational provision unresponsive to market signals and not necessarily in the national economic interest (as opposed to some wider social or cultural interest). A third argument in favour of loans is that they would widen access to higher education if they were combined with the removal of quotas on student numbers. A fourth argument is that under a system of loans the growth or decline of institutions and subjects within higher education would depend upon their success in attracting students (and research funding) rather than on the deliberations of a small group of politicians and establishment academics. The abandonment of quotas would be a pre-condition if the full effect of this was to be felt by inefficient producers. A final advantage suggested is that a loan system would be much cheaper for governments even after allowing for higher administrative costs.

Types of loans

If a loan scheme was adopted in the UK it could take any one of a variety of forms. It may, for example, be decided to make loans which would cover the full cost of a course including capital costs, loan repayments at market rates of interest and indexed to allow for inflation. Such a scheme would recognise the important benefits that accrue to individuals from education. Other loan systems may link repayments to the income tax system, a proportionate tax over a specified income threshold. In such a system graduates who fail to complete their degree or find no market for their qualifications will pay little or nothing whereas those with high incomes will pay a high rate of tax. Furthermore some combination of grant and loan systems might be adopted.

Extensive use of loan schemes is made in a number of European countries as well as in Canada, the United States, South America and Japan.

Problems in using loans

Perhaps the major practical problem is concerned with funding. Who would finance the loan? There is currently in Britain only a tiny market in the provision of loans to finance human capital. A number of proposals have been made such as the government itself borrowing and then making the loans and thus acting as a human capital bank and local authorities being allowed to develop their own schemes. Opponents of such ideas raise a number of problems. They argue that government expenditure would be greatly increased because the government would have to borrow now whereas repayments and thus savings would come only much later and then may not be as great as anticipated if there were significant defaulting or increased emigration of graduates.

But other proposals see the government guaranteeing loans and encouraging the private banking system to advance them. This latter scheme is particularly interesting because it would allow cuts in public expenditure by diverting the burden of student finance to the commercial banks, although tuition fees would have to be part of the loan if the effect on government spending was to be significant. A further advantage of this scheme is that it may be more economically efficient in the sense that if students are financing their own courses they may be motivated to work harder and if institutions of higher education are dependent on student preferences they in turn may be encouraged both to innovate and be relevant.

A second major issue that arises is the effect of loans on the demand for education. Loans would raise the lifetime opportunity cost of higher education and could therefore be expected to reduce the demand for it. They may also imply a change in the pattern of demand for subjects as prospective students shift from courses with low private rates of return (e.g. some humanities courses) to those with higher private rates of return (e.g. some science and non-graduate vocational courses). But such a shift in demand may be argued to be an economically efficient use of resources and to the extent that it conflicts with other objectives, for example a university's alleged need to provide a multi-subject curriculum, then the government may offer a subsidy that recognises that social need.

A third problem is that some poorer members of society will be inhibited from entering higher education because they will be less willing to incur debt than those with higher incomes.

Currently the evidence is that the full grant does not cover all of a student's costs and as a consequence the poor are already discouraged. There is therefore no reason to believe that grants are necessarily superior to loans in encouraging the poor to enter higher education. The argument also implies that the poor are incapable of making rational decisions. In particular, it suggests that they are unaware of the benefits of education and do not value the opportunity to exercise choice in education. There is no conclusive evidence to support this view.

A fourth problem focuses upon the effect on women. It is some-times called the 'negative dowry' argument. It is suggested that women would be inhibited from entering higher education because the need to repay a loan would interfere with the desire to have a family and thus (usually) withdraw from the workforce. It may also make qualified women less desirable as marriage partners if there was a danger that the husband may have to take on her debt. The various loan schemes recognise this problem and pose different responses to it. If repayment were delayed until after a child reached some minimum age, for example, there would be an incentive for expensively educated women to delay having a family and to return sooner to the workforce after a family. No such incentive exists under the present system and society bears the cost.

Further problems occur with the actual implementation of a loans scheme and may be summarised as cross-subsidisation effects. For example, if only incomes above a particular threshold are taxed at a percentage rate, then the higher earner will subsidise the lower earner and the private returns to education will be reduced. This has implications for the allocation of resources, not least through the narrowing of income differentials, and there is the associated practical problem of selecting the appropriate tax rate.

There is also the question of the rate of interest to be levied on loans. In most of the countries using loans schemes the rate is well below the commercial rate. The question must be, do we wish to subsidise human capital at the expense of other investment?

But despite the problems (which are surmountable) the bulk of current expenditure on higher education could be derived from consumers, most of whom by investing in higher education will be fitted for the better-paid and more interesting jobs and who in consequence should receive public support only in the form of loans but with generous and flexible terms of payment. The public interest in the 'transmission of a common culture and common standard of citizenship' (Robbins Report) could be recognised in explicit subsidies to support those subjects which fulfil that aim but which would not otherwise survive in the market place. Furthermore, 'the uncovenanted benefit to society from fundamental research would be recognised by government financial support for research on a contract basis' (Peacock 1984: 21).

Vouchers

Just as loans may be a more efficient way of determining the size and composition of the higher education sector, so a system of education vouchers may be a more efficient way of achieving objectives with respect to nursery, primary and secondary education. Evidence (see Tables 9.1 and 9.2) that the education system is doing little to reduce inequality and that the lowest income groups continue to be relatively deprived are almost without exception met by proposed solutions that would operate within the present institutional structure of state provision.

It would be possible to tackle the inadequacies of the educational system by changing its structure, in particular by devolving power to parents away from central and local government. It can be argued that giving parents real choices concerning the nature of their children's education will lead to an institutional arrangement that would be more responsive to the demands of parents than the present system. And such a solution would be allocatively more efficient if the market (consumer choice) is superior to bureaucratic dictate.

The educational voucher is the mechanism by which this change could be wrought. Here parents would be issued with a voucher for each child of school age which would come from the central or local government and equal the average cost of education.

Parents would present these vouchers at the school of their choice at the beginning of the school year. Schools would cash the voucher with the government. 'Good' schools (as perceived by parents) would receive a disproportionate number of vouchers and thus cash and 'poor' schools would receive little or none. Good schools would as a result be able to buy more and better educational resources whilst poor schools would either have to close or adapt their behaviour and performance to that of good schools. Educational provision in the form of curriculum and methods of teaching would become responsive to market pressures (parental wishes) and much less to the preferences of bureaucrats and teachers.

As Peacock said:

> The general proposal [for vouchers] implies far reaching changes in educational provision. These changes include:
> (i) turning state schools into 'profit' or at least 'cost' centres;
> (ii) making all schools derive the bulk of their current income from consumers who would be free to present vouchers to schools of their choice so that schools at present in the state sector need no longer be owned and operated by centrally financed local authorities;
> (iii) requiring schools to expand and contract in response to market forces; and
> (iv) radically altering, in consequence, the whole structure of local government finance (Peacock 1983: 113).

Types of vouchers

It is a common error on the part of the opponents of the educational voucher system that there is only one type of voucher whereas the literature considers a variety of forms (see Blaug 1984: 113–15). Thus, for example, there is the voucher whose value equals the average cost of a school place in an area and which is accepted in 'approved' schools as a full payment for education. It is the type of voucher that was used in California in the Alum Rock experiment and is associated with Jencks *et al.* (1970). This is a fixed price voucher and parents are not allowed to top it up by drawing on private income. Proponents of this kind of voucher do suggest a supplementary voucher inversely related to parental income which means that poorer families will have a disproportionate effect on school revenues: schools with many poor children will have more resources per pupil.

Yet another kind of voucher associated with Friedman (1962)

makes its value the same for each child; the voucher can be spent in any 'approved' school, private or state, but the school can charge whatever level of fees they wish. Friedman suggested no supplementary voucher which means that any difference between voucher value and school charges has to be met from family resources. This particular form of voucher has a number of implications. The total amount spent by government on education may rise because parents of children in private schools would qualify for vouchers but increased state expenditure on education may in fact accord with parents' wishes. In the present UK education system, parents of children in private schools have no incentive to lobby for increased expenditure. The actual fees charged by schools may exceed, by a significant margin, the average cost of provision of education and thus the voucher value. Whether or not parents could meet the difference would then depend both upon family income and their valuation of the benefits to be received from education expenditures as opposed to other expenditures.

With regard to this second point, although Friedman did not propose a supplementary voucher, he did propose a negative income tax. Low-income families would therefore have cash transfers and be better placed to augment the minimum purchasing power of the voucher. A number of variants of the above approaches to vouchers have been developed. One elaborated by Peacock and Wiseman (1964) aims to protect those on low incomes. It aims to make the voucher value greater for those on low incomes by making it subject to income tax. As they argue, considerable distributional effects in terms of education resources could be achieved by manipulating the size of the voucher and rates of taxation in favour of the less well off.

Whatever the form of voucher chosen, the objective is to transfer decisions that determine the extent and nature of education in schools away from bureaucrats and teachers to those who consume the product, namely parents acting in the best interests of their children. Even considerable imperfections in the distribution of incomes do not provide a case for government provision as opposed to regulation (minimum school-leaving age, examination regulations and so on), as parental purchasing power can be manipulated through taxes, subsidies and improved flows of information, though there would be a case for government intervention in circumstances where competition between educational establishments would be difficult to achieve, for example in isolated rural areas.

As noted above, it may well be that if a voucher system was

adopted, more resources would be allocated to education. At present, decisions about how much to spend on education as opposed to health care, defence, industrial policy etc. are made indirectly through the political process. A direct expression of preferences through vouchers may well demonstrate a greater demand. There certainly appears to be no good reason to believe that those on lower incomes are less able to judge the benefits of education than those on high incomes nor that they are less likely to supplement the voucher proportionally from private means.

A voucher scheme is about parents making choices. Informed choices about where to spend the voucher can only be made if parents have full information about the educational objectives of the different schools in the area. Parents will need to know about teaching methods used, curriculum content and achievement rates. Providing this kind of information (inherent in whatever form of voucher is used) not only benefits the consumer but the producer also has to specify objectives unambiguously and explain achievements or lack of them and thus justify the effectiveness of teaching methods. Improved information flows of this sort have important implications for cost effectiveness.

Although educational vouchers do seem to have many advantages, they also have disadvantages. The criticism most commonly advanced relates to the supply of places. What happens if the demand for places at some favoured school outweighs the supply of places? This raises questions about anticipated shifts in demand and about the responsiveness of supply to those shifts. There is evidence from the recent partial relaxation of restrictions on school catchment areas that initially at least there may be sharp shifts in demand. County councils in the UK do report excess demands already for some schools and distributing pupils between schools to even out demand is often done on the basis of geographical proximity, 'the nearest get in first' (Durham County Council 1985).

A similar mechanism would have to be employed initially with a voucher scheme (perhaps 50 per cent on the basis of proximity and 50 per cent selected at random), but if the voucher was really to reflect parental preferences, then supply would have to be able to respond. Once initial changes had taken place it might be expected that shifts in demand would not be large and erratic. The major constraint on the supply side would be classroom space. Much classroom space is non-specific, that is it can be used for any teaching function unlike, for example, a chemistry laboratory. Shifts in demand could be met by the use of demountable classrooms. All county educational authorities have these and so long as parental preferences are expressed early enough in the year they can relatively easily and cheaply be moved to meet marginal changes in demand. Demographic changes leading to falling school rolls since the 1970s have created surplus capacity in many schools and would make an experiment with vouchers a real possibility.

But it is not only the supply of capital facilities that would be a problem. An education system dependent upon the expression of parents' preferences may require geographical mobility on the part of the teacher as demand shifts occur and it may also imply shifts in demand for particular subject specialisms. Both of these implications of the education voucher scheme have consequences for teacher tenure. At present in the UK many authorities transfer teachers from schools with falling numbers to others where there are vacancies. This is relatively easy at primary school level but much less so at secondary school level where teacher skills are more specific. An unfortunate side effect of no redundancy agreements and transfers of this kind is that square pegs may get pushed into round holes, at least at the margin, with predictable results on standards, and the external recruitment of new blood in education authorities is inhibited. A voucher scheme, where curriculum content would have to respond to market signals, may encourage teacher retraining and the taking of refresher courses, but satisfactory response to shortages of skills, for example mathematics and sciences skills may require that schools be allowed to pay teachers with skills in short supply higher salaries to attract them from alternative employment. At present teachers receive the same salary independent of the demand and supply conditions for their skill. This may be satisfactory for a humanities graduate for whom relatively few alternative opportunities exist to practice their skills but it does little to attract mathematicians for whom, at present at least, many well-paid alternatives exist.

Teacher tenure may also be affected if the voucher as a full expression of parent preference is to operate unfettered because schools would want to make distinctions between teachers on the basis of quality as well as scarcity. At present, in the UK state system, it is virtually impossible to dismiss an inefficient teacher. Attempts by government in the 1980s to discriminate in favour of good teachers (of whatever subject discipline) have been frustrated by teacher unions. Within a state-provided system of education, quality increments could be paid if agreement could be reached with the unions about what constitutes quality. Once this has been done, teachers could be employed on formal contracts. Such a development may ultimately occur in the UK state system. At present the inability to adequately reward quality may be inhibiting education provision and it would continue to do so under a voucher system.

Vouchers would encourage greater equality of opportunity than the present system of state-provided schooling because they would allow poorer families to buy themselves out of poor schools.

According to West, it is the inability to do this in the present scheme that is the major cause of inequality, and adds:

> Indeed, paying respect to the preference of the vast majority of parents could be justified on much stronger grounds of equity . . . Vouchers, even if available to the rich as well as to everybody else, would improve the quality of the schooling available to the rich hardly at all. Choice has long been exercised by the highest income groups. In contrast, vouchers would improve the quality to the lower income class to an enormous extent. And this would apply, moreover to most children within this class . . . (West 1982: 17).

Opponents respond to these arguments by emphasising the inability or unwillingness of many parents to make choices or by singling out a particular variant of voucher for criticism. Thus some argue that if topping up of vouchers was permitted and private schools were included, then the private sector of education would grow and the gap between it and the state sector would widen with serious implications for social cohesion.

Teacher unions see vouchers as a threat to teachers' jobs. Any system which is concerned to allow the working of market forces implies change and in particular rewards to the successful and failure and loss of jobs to the unsuccessful.

Could vouchers work?

Whether or not vouchers could work is difficult to say. There has been one trial in the United States in the Alum Rock area of California and there has been a feasibility study in Kent (Kent County Council 1977/78). The Conservative government elected in Britain in 1979 seemed keenly interested in the idea. The Department of Education and Science was considering in 1982 a scheme where parents were to be given a means-tested voucher worth the annual cost of an average place for a maintained school (£800 for primary schools, £1100 for secondary schools and £1600 for sixth-form colleges) cashable at any maintained or independent school but for day places only. What provision was to be made for the financing of transportation to distant schools is unclear but loans were to be made available to help popular schools to expand. The idea now seems to have been abandoned (for the present at least) largely due to cost. As Blaug writes: 'the biggest cost . . . would be the subsidy to children already going to independent schools, not to mention the subsidy to additional children switching from maintained to independent schools. Even if the full value of the voucher were added to taxable income . . . the additional cost to the Exchequer might be as much as half a billion pounds' (Blaug 1984: 175–6).

Peacock, writing on the same topic, said: 'some kind of experiment, perhaps in one area of the country is now mooted. This is the wrong approach. An experiment which is conducted on the assumption that the Government has no long-term commitment to a voucher scheme is almost certain to fail' (Peacock 1983: 115).

It is difficult to evaluate the results of the Alum Rock experiment which ended in 1977. North and Miller write that: '. . . the federal government found it difficult to find a school system that would try the experiment. The little district of Alum Rock in California, however, was in poor financial condition and its superintendant felt that any experiment could not help but ameliorate the multiple problems he faced' (North and Miller 1983: 209), and in discussing the results of the experiment they concluded that:

> First of all, by and large parents did not exercise much more choice than before. The power of school administrators and professionals emerged undiminished and, indeed, may have increased. On the other hand there is no doubt that the experiment promoted diversity among schools and encouraged further experimentation. Nevertheless, the entrenched position of teacher and administrator groups led the experiment far from the original intention of those who wished to improve the conditions of the market on the school system (North and Miller 1983: 210–11).

What little evidence there is available in other words suggests that if a voucher scheme is to be undertaken it has to be undertaken wholesale and with vigour. The perception has to be on the part of those involved in the scheme (pupils, parents, teachers, bureaucrats) that it is being pursued with conviction. Again the little evidence that is available from Alum Rock in the USA is that the main stumbling block to implementation, in addition to cost, will be the vested interests of teachers and bureaucrats. A voucher system of school education provision is possible in the UK but it will not be easy. Blaug does not sound hopeful when he writes:

> I would hold that the stupifying conservatism of the educational system and its utter disdain of non-professional opinion is such that nothing less than a radical shake-up of the financing mechanism will do much to promote parent power. And, in the final analysis parent power is what the entire debate is all about (Blaug 1984: 175).

Teacher contracts

The issues related to teacher contracts raised in the previous section and the prolonged industrial dispute in the school system in Britain during 1985/86 should serve to emphasise the importance of teacher contracts.

Before considering the current issues, however, it is worth noting the characteristics of teacher contracts in private education systems. First, teachers are paid a sufficient wage to attract suitably qualified and experienced candidates to the post. If private schools have to pay a higher wage to attract some skills (say mathematics), then they pay the appropriate wage whereas others, in more plentiful supply, are offered lower wages. Secondly, teachers' pay is related to the quality of their teaching, which is not an inevitable function of years of experience, but rather relative to some loosely defined set of educational objectives. What are these? They are invariably dominated by examination successes but also include objectives that many parents perceive to be highly important, namely, appropriate values, respect for parents and authority, encouragement of hard work, neatness in appearance and so on. While these objectives are difficult to define and parents and school may consequently misjudge the teacher's effectiveness, this is a problem that is inherent in a whole range of service industries. After all, a parent who dislikes a doctor can choose to change, irrespective of the 'true' qualities of the doctor, so why should the same parent not have at least an element of choice in the teacher that his/her child is entrusted to? Thirdly, teacher contracts are for limited periods and may not be renewed.

These three characteristics of teacher contracts allow teachers to be paid on the basis of relative scarcity and also to have a continuing incentive to be 'good teachers' in terms of the goals of the school (which are strongly influenced by parents).

In the public sector in Britain today the debate about teachers' earnings in comparison to others is a typical public sector dispute about relativities. It is certainly difficult to attract graduates of some disciplines into the teaching profession whilst it is clear that the supply of others at current wage rates is more than adequate. As long as wage differentials are not influenced by market forces, this problem is inevitable. During 1985 the issue of quality assessment and out-of-school activities has come to the fore. Once again this is a typical problem of the public sector, for while the vast majority of teachers may well perform to a highly acceptable standard there is almost no method for either encouraging the unsatisfactory nor any penalty that may frighten the lazy. Once again we see that the problem (teacher contracts) is very substantially the result of public provision – that is, a case of public sector failure.

Manpower planning

One justification for state intervention in the education process is to facilitate effective manpower planning. Attempts to predict changing manpower requirements in the UK have not up to now, however, proved successful. Given the long gestation period for skilled labour (from school subject selection at about fourteen years of age to work experience after graduation) it is possible for manpower imbalances to persist for a considerable length of time before market pressures correct them. It is argued that if manpower planners can identify future shortages/surpluses, then it is possible that educational planners can direct extra/reduced resources into these areas. A number of problems arise in practice however: forecasting labour demand depends annually on correctly forecasting each sector's growth rate; the accuracy and stability of incremental labour/output ratios is highly uncertain; the relationship between occupation and educational qualifications is not fixed; and whilst educational planners may provide opportunities for training, in the absence of labour direction, students may not take up the places (see Gannicott and Blaug 1977: 130–6).

In the UK all of these issues came to the fore in the Zuckerman (1961) and Jackson (1965) Committees' reports on the shortage/surplus of scientists, technologists and engineers in Britain in the 1960s. Forecasting such labour demand and supply which is naturally a prerequisite of any policy proposal was undertaken by triennial surveys in educational establishments, government departments and a sample of firms. Employers were asked how many people they employed, what their original subject disciplines were, the type of work upon which they were currently engaged and the number they would like to employ in three years' time given that the required numbers of persons were available. In principle, the use of employers' estimates is attractive in that firms should be the best judge of how to solve their own problems of changes in composition of demand, in productivity and in the substitutability of labour that comes with technical progress.

Unfortunately employers' estimates have a poor track record and Sir Solly Zuckerman, in evidence to the Robbins Committee on Higher Education 1963, concluded 'we discovered in our successive inquiries that one of the least reliable ways of finding out what industry wants is to go and ask industry' (HMSO, Cmnd 2154, Evidence Volume B, p. 432).

Despite this and other criticisms of the manpower requirements predicted in the Zuckerman Committee's reports, the later Jackson Committee used the same predictive device to generate forecasts of shortages of scientists and engineers by the late 1960s. On the basis of these forecasts, sweeping changes were proposed in schools and colleges that were in part implemented.

Crucial omissions were made by the Jackson committee in two areas, first the stocks of employees in any given occupation varies in age, skill and experience. Simple totals of employees mask these important differences and are therefore very misleading when predictions are derived. Secondly, the Jackson Committee appears to have assumed that labour is used for a narrow range of occupations and is not transferable despite the widespread evidence to the contrary.

The possibility of errors in their forecasts was ignored by the Jackson Committee and indeed Gannicott and Blaug (1977) argue that they accepted as axiomatic in all their work that industry 'needed' more scientists and engineers. The economist's concept of labour demand was completely ignored.

The Committee's predicted shortages had a considerable impact on the policy debate. More resources for the education and training of scientists and engineers were provided (reluctantly) by the University Grant Committee (see UGC 1968). The swing away from science in the schools generated much concern and 'a more relevant' syllabus. The university sector was criticised for weaning off the most talented science and technology graduates into further research.

By the end of the 1960s the facts became clear. Unemployment amongst scientists and engineers approached and eventually passed the national average. The UGC on the basis of manpower predictions had acted counter-cyclically and actually oversupplied the market, thus worsening job opportunities. The swing away from science in the schools identified in the Reports may well have been a natural response to students' awareness of the increasing lack of employment opportunities in the sciences and the pursuit of post-graduate qualifications could be interpreted quite simply as an effort on the part of those with scientific qualifications to further differentiate themselves as products thus improving their declining employment opportunities.

Quite clearly the Jackson Committee's use of need rather than the economist's concept of demand was in error but it is now clear that accurate estimation of demand is very difficult. This example of failure in manpower planning does not necessarily imply that government could never use the technique though at present the use cannot easily be justified by past experience.

Conclusion

The state education system in the UK can be considered, at least in part, as a case of public sector failure. More resources would help: they could be used to satisfy more parental desires within the existing educational structure, to attract scarce specialist teachers or to ensure increased grants for students in higher education. But resources are not free and education does not have a right to demand more and more of them. Increasingly the taxpayer and the government seem intent on better value for money.

We take the view that the most appropriate approach to the problem would be a radical change towards a more market-oriented educational system. Parents, pupils and students would in such a system have their ability to influence the system by their democratic political vote reduced, but gain far greater control through the economic democracy of the market place. In this way it may be possible to redirect the educational system to better meet society's demands in the 1990s and beyond.

Chapter 10

REDISTRIBUTION AND THE TAX-BENEFIT SYSTEM

Nicholas Terry

Introduction: some political and economic background

This chapter is concerned with the rationale for the redistribution of income (flow) and wealth (stock) as a government policy objective. It will examine the use government makes of taxation and certain transfer payments ('benefits') as the instruments by which it tries to achieve changes, considered desirable by political decision takers, in the existing distribution. Such policy tools will be presented as the measures introduced by the state (hence the term 'state benefits') to effect marginal adjustments to the pattern of incomes and the holdings and rate of accumulation of wealth resulting from the ruling mechanism of resource allocation. As the discussion here is drawn from the experience of the UK, in applying the tax-benefit system to redistribution the institutional arrangements involved with resource allocation will be taken as being predominantly market based. This means that the ability of economic agents (individuals, households and firms) to make claims upon resources for consumption (production and investment) will be directly related to their ability to pay those prices demanded for resources by the set of markets comprising the economy. The exercise of such market power is, therefore, a function of the economic agents' income and wealth.

Government, however, may view the existing pattern of market power, and hence the resulting distribution, to be, at the margin, inappropriate for meeting the perceived requirements of individuals, households and firms. For example, the income return to certain units of the factor labour, as determined by either marginal productivity theory or wage relativity or both, could be considered inadequate to fulfil the expenditure 'needs' of the household into which the income flows. These needs can be defined according to the minimum income required to provide a household with a bundle of goods and services which would maintain the members at or above a hypothetical 'poverty level' of consumption. So that if the household income is assessed to be below the poverty level, then the state would supplement their income by making transfer payments. Conversely, those individuals and households in possession of certain physical and financial assets (capital), or those earning incomes which are considered sufficient to render these groups capable (without, at the margin, significantly affecting their consumption levels) of contributing to the support of others. The nature and extent of this support can be the result of the calculation of a liability for taxation based on different definitions of capital and incomes, and the setting of threshold and band limits for tax payments. Thus, the existence of imperfections in the ruling distribution provides political decision takers with a rationale for redistribution by attempting to 'correct' imbalances in the market-determined distribution. Such a policy objective can be defended by appealing to the moral acceptability of notions of justice, fairness or equity. The need to command the general agree-ment of the electorate may also explain the method chosen to achieve redistribution which appeals to the apparently simple notion of taking from the 'rich' and giving to the 'poor'. That is, it involves confiscating income through taxation and supplementing incomes through benefits. The way the system operates may be illustrated diagrammatically as in Fig. 10.1.

Economic theory offers a justification for government action to redistribute income and wealth on the grounds of the possible desirability of augmenting the concept of Pareto efficiency with considerations of equity. A Pareto-efficient distribution of income and wealth would be that which results from the satisfaction of the first-order conditions for efficiency in exchange and efficiency in production, and the second-order condition for the optimal mix of utility. Government distributional preferences are normally measured by the form and content of a collective utility function, known as a social welfare function (SWF) (see Ch. 1). Following Bergson (1938), this concept exists to determine in a precise form the value judgements required for the derivation of the conditions for maximising collective economic welfare, where collective welfare may be influenced by both efficiency and equity. The effect, *ceteris paribus*, of confiscating and supplementing income will be to transfer income, via government, from well-off to less

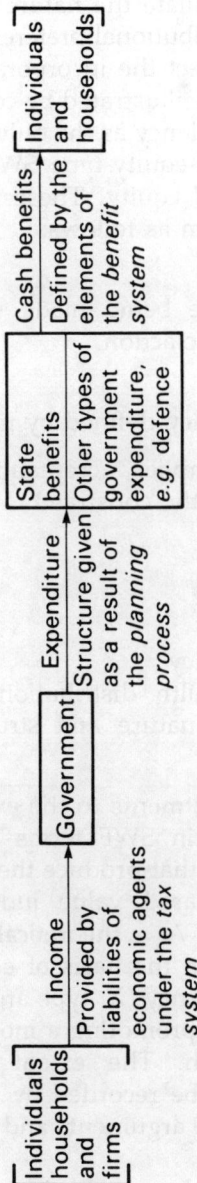

Tax income *less* Social security cash benefits = Net payments to government or net payments to beneficiaries

Figure 10.1 The two-way flow principles of the UK tax-benefit system

well-off individuals, so that such action is prefaced by a value judgement about the desirability of such reallocations. The SWF can, therefore, be used to articulate the nature of the subjectivity of political decision takers' distributional preferences. The different forms that a SWF can take reflect the incorporation of any distributional preferences and may be illustrated by comparing a Pareto-type SWF, which considers efficiency as the only criteron by which to judge policies, and a Pareto-equity-type SWF, which includes an assessment of efficiency *and* equity. These two types of SWF may be stated in functional form as follows:

Pareto-type SWF:

   $W = f(X_1)$, subject to no one being made worse off by any proposed economic action. [10.1]

where W = social welfare
      X_1 = economic efficiency defined by market power

And where maximising W implies acceptance of the existing income distribution because of the constraint.

Pareto-equity-type SWF:

   $W = f(X_1, X_2)$ [10.2]

where W = social welfare
      X_1 = economic efficiency
      X_2 = income and wealth distributional preferences as defined by the nature and structure of the tax-benefit system.

The pursuit of marginal adjustments to the existing distribution can, therefore, be interpreted in SWF terms as an attempt by decision takers to make choices that produce the maximum advantage consistent with the declared value judgements; that is, maximise W in equation [10.2]. At a theoretical level, the formulation of distributional policy on the basis of equation [10.2] will imply sacrificing economic efficiency (X_1 type arguments) in return for gains measured in terms of promoting a more equitable distribution of income and wealth. The extent of this so-called efficiency–equity trade-off will be recorded by the emphasis that decision takers attach to X_2-type arguments and may be illustrated diagrammatically as in Fig. 10.2.

In Fig. 10.2 *PP* represents the production possibility (transformation) curve which shows the alternative combination of commodities A and B that are technically feasible to produce. Its distance from the origin O is assumed to reflect that resources are

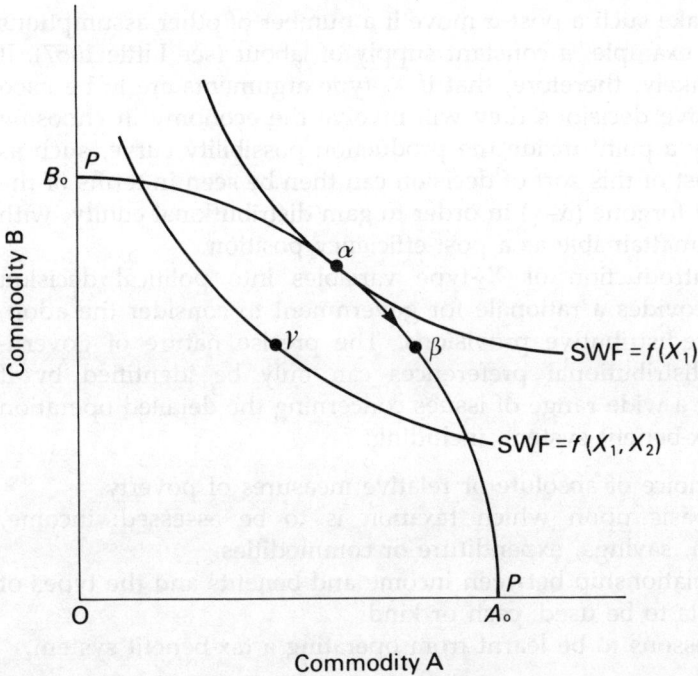

Commodity A

Figure 10.2   The equity–efficiency trade-off

being fully utilised with maximum efficiency. Its overall (concave) shape indicates the conventional case of diminishing returns so that as the output of A is reduced from A_0 (where all resources are devoted to A) by small, equal amounts, the increases in B get smaller and smaller; and similarly if the output of B is reduced from B_0 (all resources devoted to B). Producing at points beyond *PP* are ruled out because this would require more resources or greater efficiency than are currently available; and producing at points below *PP* would violate the efficiency assumption. A SWF containing only efficiency (X_1-type) arguments would, therefore, translate decision takers' preferences into a resource allocation point somewhere *on* the production possibility curve, say point α. It has been argued that it may be possible to redistribute (using taxes, for example), without forgoing any efficiency; by attempting to move the economy along its existing production possibility curve from point α to, say, point β which is preferred to α on distributional grounds but where full efficiency exists at both points. This is, in effect, an extension of Hotelling's (1938) misguided case for marginal cost pricing, as it would only be possible to make such a post-α move if a number of other assumptions held; for example, a constant supply of labour (see Little 1957). It is more likely, therefore, that if X_2-type arguments are to be used in allocative decisions they will involve the economy in choosing to occupy a point inside the production possibility curve, such as γ. The cost of this sort of decision can then be seen in terms of the efficiency forgone (α–γ) in order to gain distributional equity, with β being unattainable as a post-efficiency position.

The introduction of X_2-type variables into political decision taking provides a rationale for government to consider the adoption of redistributive provisions. The precise nature of government's distributional preferences can only be identified by it resolving a wide range of issues concerning the detailed operation of the tax-benefit system, including:

1. The choice of absolute or relative measures of poverty.
2. The basis upon which taxation is to be assessed: income, wealth, savings, expenditure or commodities.
3. The relationship between income and benefits and the types of benefits to be used: cash or kind.
4. The lessons to be learnt from operating a tax-benefit system.

Just how much 'correction' to the market-determined distribution is deemed desirable by decision takers will, therefore, be related to these issues, particularly the level of tax and benefit targeted and achieved.

The design of the tax-benefit system is only one of a number of diverse questions facing centralised decision takers; the answers to which normally emerge from the 'planning process'. According to Kornai (1979), this comprises a set of mechanisms and agencies by which collective objectives are formulated and methods of implementation decided. This process may be summarised as an attempt to maximise the following functional form:

$$\text{(Max.)} \quad W = f(X_1, X_2, X_3, \ldots, X_n) \qquad [10.3]$$

where

$X_3, \ldots, X_n$ represent all those factors, other than economic efficiency and distributional preferences, considered significant by decision takers.

Examples of X_3-type variables would be the objective of government of raising revenue and maximising the tax 'take' to fund non-distributional expenditures, and using tax policy to influence the pattern of personal and corporate financial behaviour. The effects that such diverse aims have upon the use made of fiscal instruments, such as taxation and social benefits, may well bring them into conflict with their efficacy as redistributive tools.

The literature on distribution can be divided into that which considers the distribution of income among individuals and that which examines the distribution of income among the factors of production such as land, labour and capital. Given the importance of the distribution between factors, for both economic theory and the formulation of public policy, it is surprising that most of the empirical work concerning redistribution has emphasised the distribution between individuals or households. This discussion about redistribution therefore concentrates upon individuals rather than factors.

The alternative aims of government redistribution policy

The objectives of government redistribution policy will be outlined here according to the following likely concerns: the elimination of poverty; the reduction of inequalities in the distribution of income and wealth (and any associated incentive effects); and the promotion of greater equality in the spread of specific goods and services, including education and medical care.

The main problem with analysing poverty is not that there is disagreement about the need to do something about eliminating it, rather its definition can vary depending upon whether an absolute or relative measure is adopted. Absolute measures of poverty are usable at all times in all economies, for example, the level of income needed for subsistence living. Relative measures attempt to compare the living standards of the worst off with those that exist elsewhere in the same economy; for example, the poor could be defined here as those whose income levels prevent them from engaging in the consumption behaviour normally associated with a particular economy (see Townsend 1979). The various measures generated by both definitions, however, are troublesome since it is difficult to establish an absolute measure that is unrelated to social norms, and it is unclear how a consensus about normal consumption activities can be reached.

A justification for pursuing the equality of incomes can be provided by that branch of moral philosophy called Utilitarianism associated with Bentham, Hume and Mill, which requires that government policy should achieve 'the greatest happiness of the greatest number'. In terms of economic theory, this is equivalent to saying that the sum of individual utilities should be maximised, and when this is combined with the self-evident truth (Pigou 1920) that different persons can be treated as if they have similar temperaments, the following (redistribution) proposition emerges: '. . . it is evident that any transference of income (by, say, the tax system) from a relatively rich man to a relatively poor man (until their incomes are equal) of similar temperament, since it enables more intense wants to be satisfied at the expense of less intense wants, must increase the aggregate sum of satisfaction' (Pigou 1920: 89).

This conclusion is reached because the utility of the rich is reduced by less than the increase in the utility of the poor. The proposition and its policy implication can be, however, challenged on a number of premises. First, it assumes that utility is measurable in such a way as to render different individuals' utility levels comparable. Such a reliance upon the concept of cardinal utility (see Majumdar 1958) and the legitimacy of inter-personal comparisons of utility has been heavily criticised (see Robbins 1935). Second, it assumes that all individuals have similar tastes so that the marginal utility of money income curve is the same for every individual – although those with different money incomes occupy different points on such a curve. This creates several theoretical difficulties, including the requirement to estimate the elasticity of the marginal utility of income (see Theil and Brooks 1970). Third, it implies that social utility is a sum of individual utilities, which gives rise to the so-called 'aggregation problem' (see Green H. 1976). Fourth, it ignores the possibility that taxing the rich and giving money to the poor may give both rich and poor less incentive to work thus reducing aggregate output and hence social utility (subject to the form of the aggregate production function). And fifth, it excludes other arguments that might be used to support continuing some degree of inequality; for example, that income should be apportioned according to need or deservingness.

What makes an individual need higher levels of consumption (and hence greater utility) varies according to the ethical notions of those using it to further the interests of a particular cause; for example, what underpins the inclusion of a specific parameter in a decision taker's objective function. Arguments about worth depend upon identifying features (such as actions or qualities) that separate individuals or groups within an economy, which make them worthy of higher shares of income and wealth; for example, that the most talented individuals should receive some economic rent. This approach has tended to create the view that income resulting from individuals' own efforts is justified (and should not be totally confiscated) whilst that which results from influences outside their control, such as inherited wealth, is not justified (and should therefore be confiscated). An extension of this notion can be seen in arguments regarding 'equality of opportunity' (see Letwin 1983) and 'procedural justice' (see Nozick 1974). Under the former concept, a particular distribution of income is equitable if it is the result of a set of economic arrangements where everyone has the same opportunity to be either rich or poor. The latter concept views any given income distribution as the result of a process of rules: if everyone regards the rules as fair, then the resultant distribution is just.

Several writers, however, have rejected need or deservingness as a basis for justifying unequal shares, and argue instead that inequality is necessary for broader moral reasons, in particular safeguarding individual liberty (see Hayek 1978b). They consider that egalitarian policies involve varying degrees of individual coercion and are hence unacceptable. Thus, taxation would be viewed as restricting freedom of choice over consumption, investment and bequests. In addition, other economists have emphasised that egalitarian policies may have hidden costs in terms of the possible disincentive effects on work effort and savings propensity, and hence economic activity and capital formation (see Okun 1975; Harberger 1964). The net result of equality of incomes would, therefore, be lower economic growth and a smaller amount of social utility available for universal distribution. Most attention in this area of debate has focused on the relationship between taxation and its effects upon labour supply, although both the theory and evidence have yielded ambiguous results. Economic theory divides this effect into the 'income effect' and the 'substitution effect' and the aggregate (net) result will be dictated by the relative strength of these effects. The empirical studies have been constrained by the need to use stylised work–leisure choice models (see Deaton and Muellbauer 1980). One result of this specification problem is that sample survey and econometric-based studies have tended to exclude non-pecuniary explanations (self-esteem and status) for labour supply levels and individuals' responses to change such as taxation. An exception to this can be found in the income maintenance experiments carried out in the USA (see Godfrey 1975). Despite the uncertainty of the evidence, there does seem to be some substitution at the margin, leisure for work, implying that the greater the amount of redistribution the greater the disincentive effect. This, in turn, has led to the suggestion that an appropriate social objective might be the achievement of the maximum degree of income inequality compatible with a given rate of economic growth. The problem here is a practical one of measuring precisely the disincentive effect in different sectors of the economy. A refinement of this approach would be to support inequality if it works to the advantage of the least well-off individual (see Rawls 1972). Thus, if some difference in incomes is needed to encourage individuals to increase aggregate output, and if as a result the incomes of the poor are improved, then the original income inequality is justified. The conclusion to be made here is that an economy should allow those unequal shares which maximise the benefits to the worst off. The main drawback with this principle is that it assumes indifference as between varying degrees of inequality, which would imply variations among the well-off, and it assumes that the least well-off individual is easily identified. An interesting corollary of this so-called maximum objective is that once made operational its repeated application could eventually produce total equality of incomes; that is, either the improvement of every post-change worst-off individuals, or a position at which no further redistribution to the worst off could occur without violating the output constraint.

An alternative to redistributing money incomes, as a mechanism for achieving egalitarianism, is to redistribute specific goods and services, that is, to supplement or replace market supply by subsidies or earmarked vouchers. Casual evidence suggests that individuals are concerned less with the income or utilities of other people than with their consumption of specific commodities. As Buchanan has argued:

> What liberarian backers of such proposals (like negative income tax) do not fully appreciate is the lack of interest on the part of the public in real income distribution as such. One must search diligently to find much 'social' concern expressed for the prudent poor whose lives are well-ordered and stable. The evidence seems to indicate that general redistribution of purchasing power, or even general change in relative levels of well-being, is not generally desired. Instead members of the public want, and express through their behaviour, relief for specific spending patterns (Buchanan 1968).

If, therefore, taxpayers prefer their tax revenues to be spent on goods and services for the poor (because of distrust that the money will be spent 'wisely'), then redistribution in kind may be considered more efficient than redistribution in cash simply because altruism on this basis may be more forthcoming. The difficulty with this argument is that redistribution in cash appears to be easier, more effective and morally more attractive than redistribution in kind. It offers freedom of choice, to the recipient, and implies the abolition of subsidies and vouchers. Moreover, in its simplest form it requires only one instrument, redistributive income taxation (see Collard 1978).

The nature and effects of the UK tax system

What matters in understanding any given tax regime in relation to redistribution policy is where, on whom and how often the burden of particular taxes occurs, and the aggregated rate of tax this burden produces. The analysis of such influences is usually referred to as the 'incidence' of taxation. To achieve a meaningful insight into the incidence of the UK tax system, its main characteristics will be described here according to its treatment of: personal income, company income and employment; expenditure; and investments and capital. Having outlined how each of these three groupings of different aspects of the tax system operate, their redistributive effects will be examined according to the extent of their influence upon poverty, inequality and incentives.

Personal income, company income and employment

The UK personal income tax system operates on the basis of three variables: tax rates, allowances and reliefs. The tax rates comprise a 'basic rate' (currently 29 per cent) and a number of so-called 'higher rate bands' (currently 40, 45, 50, 55 and 60 per cent); liability for one or more of these rates is a function of individuals' annual taxable income. Any positive taxable income is charged at the basic rate up to a certain income limit (currently £17 200 per annum), beyond which the higher bands apply according to total taxable income. Taxable income calculated by taking the difference between individuals' total income in any given tax year (in the UK this means from April to March) and their personal allowances plus any other appropriate tax-deductible items, known as 'reliefs' (see Bertram and Edwards 1985: Part 1). In the UK, personal income taxes are collected by either the pay-as-you-earn (PAYE) scheme, which is based on a system of codes assigned to individual employees depending on their taxable income, directly from employers, or on a scheme of annual retrospective assessment. The retrospective scheme is used mainly to calculate the income tax bill of the self-employed (e.g. partnerships) but is also used to calculate any additional (to PAYE) tax liability for those individuals whose annual income does not simply comprise their weekly or monthly wage or salary.

The UK corporation tax system operates on the basis of the following considerations: corporation tax rates, advanced corporation tax, capital allowances and reliefs. The 1984 Budget provided for the phased reduction of the main rate of corporation tax from 50 per cent for the tax year ended 1984 to 35 per cent by the tax year ended 1987, and thereafter. There also exists a different rate of corporation tax (currently 29 per cent) for companies earning profits not exceeding a certain limit (currently £100 000), known as the 'small companies rate'. Advanced corporation tax (ACT) is the tax paid by companies on their dividends (distributed profits) to shareholders. It is levied at the basic rate of income tax and in the hands of the shareholder it represents the 'tax credit' on the dividend. This credit may be used by shareholders to offset their personal tax liability on dividends. Therefore, part of the corporate tax liability on distributed profits is 'imputed' to the shareholders, which explains why the system of corporation tax currently used in the UK is known as the 'imputation system' (see King M. 1977). The company is able to offset ACT against its corporation tax liability for the year in which it pays the dividend, up to a maximum (currently 30 per cent) of its taxable income (see Scrimgeour 1984). Capital allowances can also be used to reduce liability for corporation tax, and are granted on the basis of a proportion of the cost of such items as plant and machinery as being tax deductible. One of the main reliefs available to companies is the deductibility of interest payments made to holders of fixed interest debt issues, for example, debentures and loan stock (see Hardman 1985).

In addition to income tax, which is payable on both personal and business income, the UK tax system defines a liability for additional payments to be made to government by employed and self-employed individuals, and employers. This payroll tax is called National Insurance (NI) and the level of contribution is dependent on both the amount of earnings and by upper and lower thresholds. There are four 'classes' of contribution which vary in their scope (see Kay and King 1983). The argument often put forward in support of the NI scheme is that it 'finances' state benefits, particularly pensions, and this idea will be discussed later.

This grouping of taxes does very little to take individuals out of poverty (see Le Grand and Robinson 1984b). To trace the distributional impact of company taxation (optimal tax theory) requires an incidence model of such complexity that discussion about its specification and use lies outside the scope of this chapter (see King M. 1977). In order to comment upon the effect of personal taxes (including NI) on inequality and incentives it is necessary to examine the proportion they take as income increases; that is, the average tax rate.

Table 10.1 indicates that the system of personal income taxes is overall progressive up to the middle-income groups; after that it is broadly proportional. A progressive tax system is one where the proportion of tax increases as income rises, whereas a proportional tax is one in which the proportion is constant, regardless of income. The top three-fifths of the population face almost the same average tax rate: approximately 20 per cent. This surprising conclusion arises because of the difference between marginal and average rates of tax. Marginal income tax rates can be high (60 per cent) but these individuals can use tax-avoidance methods (which are legal, as distinct from tax evasion which is not) to reduce their total tax bills.

The effect of income taxation on labour supply depends on the relative strength of the income and substitution effects. High marginal tax rates do not necessarily reduce labour supply; only

Table 10.1 Average income taxes actually paid, 1984

Group	Gross income (£)	Income tax* and employees' NI contributions (£)	Percentage of gross income
Top fifth	20 350	4 740	23.29
Next fifth	12 010	2 430	20.23
Middle fifth	8 260	1 380	16.71
Next fifth	4 880	330	6.76
Bottom fifth	3 240	−10[†]	—
All individuals	9 750	1 770	18.15

* After tax relief at source on mortgage interest and life assurance premiums.
† Negative average tax payments result largely from imputed tax relief on life assurance premiums paid by those with nil or negligible tax liabilities.

Source: Central Statistical Office 1985: Table A, p. 99

if individuals substitute leisure hours previously spent working will labour supply fall. Conversely, increases in average tax rates may induce individuals to work harder to maintain their post-tax income levels. What is clear, however, is that the empirical evidence on incentives does not provide support for the strong case that is often made (by politicians) for reducing taxes as a means of releasing frustrated work effort and increasing occupational mobility (see Godfrey 1975).

Expenditure

The instruments used in the UK to tax spending on commodities and services include a general tax called valued added tax (VAT), and special taxes on specific commodities such as tobacco, alcholic drinks and petrol and diesel fuel. VAT is an *ad valorem* tax applied at each stage of exchange of commodities and services from primary production to final consumption. It is levied on the difference between the sale price of items (outputs) to which tax is applied, and the cost of items (inputs) acquired for use in their production or distribution, hence it is sometimes known as an input–output tax. At each stage of exchange, the trader is responsible for the payment of tax included in the (higher) customer price but reclaims a refund of any VAT included in the prices charged by the traders' suppliers. The rate of VAT can be varied according to different commodities and industries but the UK presently uses a standard rate (currently 15 per cent) for all commodities and services, other than those that are either zero-rated (e.g. books, electricity, gas and exports) or exempt (e.g. the provision of finance, insurance and funerals). The difference between these two categories of goods and services is that only zero-rated ones can be the subject of a refund (see Bertram and Edwards 1985: Part 1).

The efficacy of taxing expenditures as a redistributive tool (with regard to poverty and inequality) is crucially dependent upon the incidence of this type of taxation. Economic analysis distinguishes between the nominal incidence (formal liability) and the effective incidence (actual liability). In the case of VAT, the nominal incidence rests with the trader or manufacturer (who are in reality tax collectors), whilst it is the final consumer that pays the tax because they are at the last stages of exchange. In order to examine the actual burden of commodity taxation, and hence its true redistributive effect, requires the estimation of the relevant demand elasticities (see, for example, James and Nobes 1983). In practice, these are difficult to measure although the Treasury does attempt this for the purposes of estimating the likely tax take from any given budgetary provision or change. It is usually assumed that most commodity taxes are passed on (this is known as 'tax shifting') entirely to consumers. This is tantamount to accepting that the demand for such commodities is perfectly inelastic. Table 10.2 gives estimates of the redistributive impact of commodity taxes based on this assumption.

Table 10.2 shows that the percentage of disposable income paid in tax (which includes other taxes on commodities, see CSO 1985) is very close to being regressive (where the proportion of tax falls as income rises) with the bottom income group paying 23.38 per cent of their disposable income in tax as compared with 23.70 per cent for the top income group. The main explanation for this is that the better off tend to have higher marginal and average propensities to save, so that expenditure (and hence tax) takes up a smaller proportion of their income than it does for the less well off.

Table 10.2   Average rates of commodity taxes, 1984

Group	Disposable income (£)	Indirect taxes (£)	Tax as a percentage of disposable income
Top fifth	15 610	3 700	23.70
Next fifth	9 580	2 490	25.99
Middle fifth	6 880	1 890	27.47
Next fifth	4 550	1 300	28.57
Bottom fifth	3 250	760	23.38
All individuals	7 980	2 030	25.44

Source: Central Statistical Office 1985: Table A, p. 99

It is often argued that an alternative to reducing income tax rates, as a means of improving work incentives, is to switch the burden of taxation away from income and towards commodities. This would work, however, only if individuals were subject to a sort of 'fiscal illusion'; that is, if they were less aware of commodity taxes than income taxes. For if the tax take remained the same in each case, then the actual incidence of taxation would also remain the same. The hypothesis, however, requires empirical investigation.

Investment and capital

The income generated by financial assets is added to individuals' total income for the assessment of income tax. Investment income is, therefore, charged at the same rates as personal income tax. Although until the 1984 Budget there was an additional rate of tax (15 per cent at the time of its abolition) payable on an investment income, which meant that the highest marginal rate of income tax was 75 per cent. This was known as the 'investment income surcharge'. Different forms of investment, however, are treated differently for tax purposes. For example, dividend receipts by ordinary shareholders are deemed to have borne tax at a 'rate of imputation' (currently 29 per cent) so that basic rate taxpayers face no further tax liability on such investment income. Shareholders with a zero tax liability can claim a tax rebate of an amount equivalent to the tax already paid by the company. Those with higher rates pay tax on their dividends at a rate which is the difference between their highest marginal rate and the basic rate. (If, for example, a shareholder faces 50 per cent tax rates on other income, the rate payable on his dividends is 50 per cent minus 29 per cent, which is 21 per cent.) Hence the maximum rate payable on investment income for holdings of ordinary shares is 31 per cent. There are also special rules governing deposits held at banks and building societies (the composite rate system); offshore funds; 'deep-discount' securities and relief based on the purchase of shares in certain designated companies or businesses in 'eligible trades' (the Business Expansion Scheme).

In the UK, liability for capital taxes arises not on the holdings of wealth (and income tax payable on the income they produce) in asset form, rather on the disposal, transfer and acquisition of such assets (e.g. shares, family businesses and land). In each case, there exists a separate form of taxation: capital gains tax for disposals; capital transfer tax; and stamp duty for acquisitions. Capital gains tax (CGT) is payable at a single rate (currently 30 per cent) on all gains realised above an annual exemption limit (currently £6300 for individuals). The 1982 Budget provides for the indexation of these annual exemptions based on the rise in the retail price index and an 'indexation allowance' for CGT, which allows for the effect inflation has on capital value so that CGT liability is calculated on the 'real' rise in the asset's capital value from the time of acquisition to disposal. Prior to March 1986 capital transfer tax (CTT) was paid by individuals on the chargeable value of assets, over a certain limit, at different rates depending upon when the transfer occurred. If it took place on or within three years of death, then the rate of CTT payable ranged from 30 to 60 per cent depending on the amount of chargeable value. If the transfer occurred at any other time, known as a 'lifetime transfer', the same chargeable bands applied but the rate charged was half that for the death rate. The 1986 Budget, however, abolished CTT on lifetime gifts to individuals and introduced a tapered charge for gifts made within seven years of death. From now on CTT is to be renamed Inheritance Tax. Stamp duty is an *ad valorem* tax charged on acquisitions of shares, land and other property (as from October 1986, payable at either ½ or 1 per cent). For most property (a 1 per cent charge) but excluding shares and marketable securities (½ per cent), stamp duty is only payable if the value of the property acquired exceeds a certain amount (currently £30 000); otherwise it is charged on the whole value (see Bertram and Edwards 1985: Part 2).

The effectiveness of these capital and investment taxes may be seen by looking at recent trends in the revenue they raise. As a percentage of total Inland Revenue receipts, the revenue raised during the ten-year period prior to 1983/84 has declined from 3.9 per cent to 1.2 per cent (CTT) and 3.0 per cent to 1.3 per cent (CGT) (see Byrne 1984). Moreover, the real value of their receipts has more than halved during the same period. Such figures suggest that neither CTT nor CGT are likely to have been particularly effective in reducing inequality of whatever type, and the new style Inheritance Tax is even less likely to have any redistributive effect. In terms of their incentive effect, the main issue is whether they impede the propensity to save or invest or both. The relationship between capital taxes and saving is, however, analogous to that between income tax and labour supply. There may be a substitution of consumption for saving, or an incentive created for individuals to save more to preserve post-tax capital values. As noted earlier, there has been little empirical research on this question (but see Sandford 1973). The differences in the CGT treatment of alternative investment vehicles may provide the basis for following an investment strategy specifically designed to exploit particular tax advantages. In addition, stamp duty can be treated as a transaction tax and may act as a disincentive (even at its reduced rate) to holding certain assets, such as company shares. It has been argued, therefore that the structure of such taxes is related to non-distributional government objectives (see Terry 1985). An investment selection process based on tax factors may well have an effect upon savings incentives or influence revenue-raising tactics by government or both. In practice, the operation of CTT suggests that individuals are prepared to spend time and money (for advice) to avoid paying tax; for example, giving over wealth in anticipation of death and the setting up of sophisticated tax-avoidance trusts (see Seager 1984). This will also be true of Inheritance Tax because it will operate very much like Estate (death) Duty which preceded CTT.

The nature and effects of the UK benefit system

Most transfer payments made by government are either income-based benefits, which include all forms of social security, or commodity-based benefits, such as subsidies to medical care, education and housing. Having described briefly how these two parts of the benefit system operate, their redistributive effects will again be examined, by reference to their influence upon poverty, inequality and incentives.

Income-based benefits

One approach to describing this part of the benefit system would be to employ the concepts of 'insurance' and 'assistance' which featured in the Beveridge Report (Beveridge 1942). This report, which is normally seen as the basis of the current system, defined national insurance under which individuals paid contributions into an insurance fund that would make payments if they became ill, elderly or unemployed, and national assistance which would provide support for the unemployed not eligible for the insurance benefit. The present system, however, bears little resemblance to Beveridge's scheme with one of the principal changes being to rename national assistance 'supplementary benefit', although much of the administrative structure and notation remains. National insurance benefits received have little relationship to National Insurance contributions made (although the latter do affect eligibility) and are now partly funded from general taxation. The level of national insurance benefit has never been generous enough to have had much impact on poverty so that low-income groups have become reliant upon supplementary benefits. A variety of other measures have been introduced such as child benefit and family income support that do not fall readily into the original insurance or assistance categories. This distinction, therefore, is not the most helpful available and will not be followed here.

The UK income benefit system will, instead, be outlined according to categorical and means-tested types of benefits. The former are received by all those who fall into a specific category; for example, the unemployed, the sick, the elderly and families with children. Eligibility and the amount of such benefits received are usually independent of income, with the particular classification of an individual being the decisive factor. Means-tested benefits can have some categorical element (such as being confined to the unemployed) but their most significant feature is that both eligibility and the level of benefit are dependent on income. Table 10.3 indicates the main social security programmes and their associated cost.

As Table 10.3 indicates, the principal categorical benefits are retirement pensions, child, invalidity and unemployment benefits. Before the retirement pension can be received (by women over sixty and men over sixty-five, certain contributions have to be paid; and the full benefit cannot be paid unless contributions have been made over a specified period. In 1978, a state earnings-related pension scheme (SERPS) was introduced designed to mature fully after twenty years of contributions when the retirement pension will comprise the basic pension, plus additional earnings-related

Table 10.3 The main social security programmes, 1984

Programme	Cost (£m)	Percentage of total government spending
Categorical:		
Retirement pensions	15 620	10.7
Child benefit	4 670	3.2
Invalidity	2 010	1.4
Unemployment benefit	1 530	1.0
Sickness benefit	780	0.5
Other*	1 580	1.1
Means-tested:		
Supplementary benefit	6 460	4.4
Other†	1 730	1.1

* Includes widows, maternity and disablement allowances
† Includes family income supplement and war pensions

Source: Central Statistical Office 1985: Table 1, p. 105

pension. Employers can 'contract out' their employees from the scheme, provided the occupational pension they offer matches the benefits of the state-run scheme. Child benefit is paid at a flat rate per child up to the age of sixteen, or nineteen if in full time secondary education. The amount received is independent of national insurance contributions and an extra benefit is paid to single parents. Invalidity and sickness benefits are payable to those off work through injury or sickness for specified periods or on a permanent basis. Unemployment benefit is payable, for a specified period, to those involuntarily unemployed. The amount received under these last three benefits depends on certain contributions being met (see Smith and Rowland 1985).

The main types of means-tested benefits are supplementary benefit and family income supplement. Any individual aged sixteen or over who is not in full-time employment or education and who is considered to have insufficient income from other sources (including categorical benefits) is entitled to supplementary benefit. As there are no contribution conditions, the amount of benefit received is calculated according to the difference between an individual's income and 'needs' as defined by the system. Family income supplement is available to families whose head is in full-time employment and have at least one dependent child. The benefit level is half of the difference between the family's income and an 'allowance' level determined by the family's circumstances (see Cohen and Lakhani 1986).

In terms of its influence on poverty, the social security system can be considered a success. Estimates of its impact on the total amount needed to raise the incomes of all less well-off people to at least as much as the supplementary benefit level (the so-called 'poverty gap', see Hemming 1984) show that in 1974–76, for example, the effect of the system was to reduce the poverty gap from 3.5 per cent of GNP to 0.2 per cent (see Beckerman and Clark 1982).

With respect to promoting greater equality, however, it becomes necessary to discover how much the system also helps the better-off. For when, in helping the less well-off, it simultaneously benefits the better-off, there is likely to be little impact on overall inequalities. According to Beckerman and Clark, this can be assessed by calculating the 'vertical expenditure efficiency' (VEE) of the system; that is, the proportion of the benefits that accrue to households who would have been below the supplementary benefit level without them. Hence a system with, for instance, 90 per cent VEE would be very effective as a redistribution instrument, since nearly all its benefits would be received by the less well-off. Conversely, a system with a 10 per cent VEE would be largely ineffective, since most of its benefits would go to the non-poor. Beckerman and Clark demonstrate that overall the system bordered on the effective side, with a 57 per cent VEE in 1974–76; that is, 57 per cent of its benefits were received by the less well-off. There was considerable variation, however, by type of programme, ranging from 6 per cent VEE for sickness benefit and 13 per cent for child benefit and family income supplement, to 60 per cent for supplementary benefit and 68 per cent for pensions. For the categorical benefits, such as sickness and child benefits, this is unremarkable since these go to all those in the relevant category regardless of income, although it is curious that a similar outcome was not observed for retirement pensions. Conversely, the means-tested supplementary benefit could be expected to have a high VEE.

An alternative test of the efficacy of the social security system as a means of reducing inequalities is to examine the subsidy received as a proportion of income. Such figures are presented in Table 10.4 below and indicate that the system is highly effective with the bottom group receiving almost of all its gross income (original income plus cash benefits) from social security, while the top group receives very little.

Table 10.4   Income subsidies as a proportion of income, 1984

Group	Income subsidies as a percentage of gross income
Top fifth	2.95
Next fifth	6.74
Middle fifth	13.80
Next fifth	49.18
Bottom fifth	96.60

Source: Central Statistical Office 1985: Table A, p. 99

Individuals on social security usually face a loss of benefit if they take employment or, if they already have a job, lose benefit if they work longer hours; therefore, these programmes raise individual marginal tax rates. This will induce a substitution effect, leisure for income; however, there is no possibility of an income effect to offset this possible discouragement of work effort. Social security benefit recipients have to work less hard to maintain their incomes, not harder as with the income tax, because the benefits are paid by the state. This means that the income effect reinforces the substitution effect in discouraging work effort.

Commodity-based benefits

Many goods and services are provided either free at the point of consumption or at subsidised prices. Most attention has been directed towards examining the distributional impact of medical care, education, housing and public transport. The relative importance of these benefits in kind is shown in Table 10.5.

Table 10.5   Selected benefits in kind, 1984

Programme	£m	Percentage of total government spending
Health services	15 800	10.8
Education	15 680	10.7
Housing subsidies	1 380	0.9
Travel subsidies	1 480	1.0

Source: Central Statistical Office 1985: Table 1, p. 105

The nature of these subsidies is described elsewhere (see Ch. 7, 8, 9). Following Le Grand (1982) it may be possible to gain an insight into how effective these services are as a redistributive tool by classifying them as either 'pro-poor' or 'pro-rich'.

Table 10.6 provides a summary of the effect of commodity subsidies by expressing the expenditure on such benefits as a ratio comprising the best-off and the worst-off quintile income groups. If a ratio has a value of larger than 1, then the greater the benefit of the subsidy to the best-off group; and if it is smaller than 1, then the greater the benefit to the worst-off income group. The figures given in Table 10.6 indicate that most services are either distributed almost equally, but post-sixteen forms of education accrue mainly best-off (a value of much higher than 1), with the exception of housing programmes, concentrating on council tenants, which help mainly the less well-off. Expenditure on the National Health Service (NHS) is equally distributed in the sense that the average poor person receives roughly the same as the average rich one, although this fails to recognise that the poor tend to need more health services. State spending on pre-sixteen education is spread almost equally, but post-sixteen forms of education accrues mainly to the better-off. Public transport also has a pro-rich distribution of government expenditure, with rail subsidies being the most unequal of those given in Table 10.6. Of all current spending on

Table 10.6 Income subsidies as a proportion of income

Service	Ratio of expenditure per person in top fifth to that per person in bottom fifth*
Pro-poor:	
Council housing	0.3
Primary education	0.9
Secondary education – under 16	0.9
Pro-rich:	
National Health Service	1.4
Secondary education – over 16	1.8
Non-university higher education[†]	3.5
Bus subsidies	3.7
Universities	5.4
Rail subsidies	9.8

* For the details of computation, see Le Grand 1982
† Polytechnics, colleges of education and technical colleges

Source: Le Grand 1982

the social services, it can be estimated that only about one-fifth is directed mainly at the less well-off. The rest is either spread equally or towards the better-off.

It can be deduced, therefore, that commodity subsidisation has failed to promote egalitarianism. An explanation for this lies in distinguishing between programmes with 'universal' subsidies and those with 'means-tested' ones. The former are those where everyone eligible is offered the particular service either free or at a subsidised price, for example NHS medical care and public education. Means-tested programmes are those where the amount of benefit received depends on individuals' income, for example, medical prescriptions and student grants. Usually, it is the universal programmes that tend to favour the better-off, and the means-tested ones the worse-off. Clearly, if a service is provided at a subsidised price to all who wish to use it then, unless it covers an inferior good, the better-off will buy more of the commodity. This is also true if the service is provided 'free', since there are always likely to exist costs associated with using it, for example, transport costs involved in getting to where the service is available, and these costs will be a heavier burden on the poor than on the better-off. Thus universal services are likely to be consumed more by the better-off, who will also receive relatively more of the government subsidy.

The fiscal system as a whole: conclusions and future reforms

It has been shown that the principal instruments of redistribution used in the UK are fiscal ones: the tax and benefit systems, and subsidies to finance services, such as medical care, education and housing. Before drawing any conclusions about their overall success in reducing inequalities, it is necessary to consider the effect of the system as a whole by comparing the distribution of different kinds of income: original, gross, disposable and final. Original income is that before any taxes are paid or subsidies received; gross income (as used in Tables 10.1 and 10.4) is original income plus the value of income subsidies; disposable income (as used in Table 10.2) is gross income minus income taxes (including NI contributions); and final income is disposable income plus the value of commodity subsidies less commodity taxes. Table 10.7 presents the basis for the relevant comparisons by showing the percentage share of each type of income received by different income groups.

Table 10.7   The effect of taxes and benefits on inequality, 1984 (percentage share of total)

Group	Original income	Gross income	Disposable income	Final income
Top fifth	49	42	40	39
Next fifth	28	25	24	24
Middle fifth	18	17	18	18
Next fifth	6	10	12	12
Bottom fifth	0.3	5.6	6.7	7.1
Gini coefficient	0.499	0.369	0.334	0.324

Source: Central Statistical Office 1985: Table B, p. 100

Table 10.7 indicates that the top income group received nearly half of the total original income but less than 40 per cent of final income; while the share of the bottom group increased from less than half of 1 per cent to just over 7 per cent. It also provides a summary statistic measure of the degree of equality in the distribution of income called the 'Gini coefficient'. The possible values that the Gini coefficient can take lie between 0 and 1: a value moving closer to 1 indicating greater inequality; a value closer to zero signifying greater equality; and at its limits complete equality (0) and complete inequality (1) (see Atkinson 1983). For 1984, this measure of equality had a range of from just less than a half to just less than a third. Possibly the most remarkable aspect of Table 10.7 is that most of the changes of the shares of each group and in the Gini coefficient occur between original income and gross income. As the difference between these two is accounted for by income subsidies, this suggests that social security is an effective redistributive tool. Conversely, direct taxes, indirect taxes and benefits-in-kind have very little impact. The lessons to be learnt, therefore, appear to be as follows. First, government should extend means-testing and thus make the social security system more effective. Means-tested services, however, often have low take-up and they are often regarded as stigmatising and socially divisive. Second, the failure of commodity subsidisation to achieve equality does not necessarily imply that these subsidies should be removed. They may have other functions, for example, public sector health and education may be seen as a way of discouraging a segregation of medical care and education between rich and poor. The promotion of equality may not, therefore, be the only goal of the social services.

After nearly forty years since its introduction, the UK social security system is about to be significantly altered (see HMSO 1985b). These changes are intended to be a recasting of the entire welfare system but in place of any central philosophy, as with Beveridge, they have four loosely connected aims. First, to redistribute the entitlement benefit (categorical and means-tested) by such measures as replacing family income supplement, which is paid directly to households, with a 'family credit', to be paid through wage packets. Second, to eliminate those circumstances where an individual who tries to escape poverty by taking a job or working harder at their existing one find themselves as badly off or worse off than before because of the loss of all or some benefits. The former case is known as the 'employment trap', the latter case the 'earnings trap', and together they make up what is usually termed the 'poverty trap' (see Hemming 1984). This is to be achieved by relating the new tax credit to disposable income rather than original income, which will probably avoid marginal rates of income tax exceeding 100 per cent which causes the poverty trap. Third, to simplify the system of partly discretionary supplementary benefits by such measures as replacing supplementary benefit with a system of income support which will be means-tested and consistent with the family credit. Fourth, to encourage private retirement pensions by such measures as reducing benefits payable under the SERPS and providing extra (tax) incentives for occupational pension schemes. These proposals are, however, marginal adjustments (although they represent adjustments of a kind and degree not previously considered) to the social security system, rather than an attempt to modernise.

The UK tax system is also likely to be reformed in the near future with major changes expected in its current structure, particularly in the operation of personal reliefs. This pressure for change, however, is prompted by the government's concern over avoiding what it sees (misguidedly as was noted previously) as the disincentive effect created by income taxes, rather than a recognition of the failure of tax policy to either eliminate poverty or significantly reduce inequalities.

The disappointing performance of government redistribution policy can be traced back to two characteristics of the way in which the fiscal system has been directed towards redistributive concerns: first, the absurdity of the two-way flow principle (see Fig. 10.1); and second, the principle of 'universality' (that is, equal benefits and equal contributions). The idea of taking from individuals/households via tax and national insurance, and then paying to them cash benefits, under two essentially separate systems, is usually defended using a timing or cash-flow argument. That is, while tax is collected on an annual basis, benefits for poor families require a much more frequent assessment (say, weekly or monthly). This argument, however, is based largely on an illusion because those borderline families that are net recipients (benefits > tax) are, in effect, being treated *as if* there was a negative income tax; whilst those families who are sometimes net recipients and net taxpayers (tax > benefits) could elect the basis upon which they wish to be assessed. The tax-benefit systems should be integrated. This would provide for greater simplicity and comprehension by those involved which would, in turn, ease the psychological burden of taxation and generate cost savings in administration which could be used as benefits. An integrated system is illustrated in Fig. 10.3.

An integrated tax-benefit system will not, itself, produce a great impact upon redistribution unless the existing pattern of taxes and

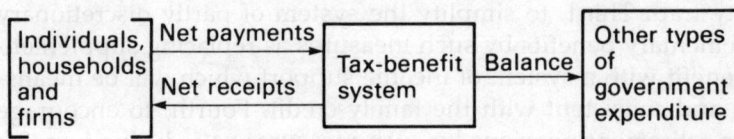

Figure 10.3 The principle of integrating the tax-benefit system

transfer is changed. This can probably be best achieved by abandoning the notion of universality and adopting a full-scale negative income tax system. The attraction to government decision takers of the former notion is that it is likely to satisfy, at the same time (but for different reasons), both the poverty and middle-rich pressure groups. For the poverty lobby it might appear to guarantee entitlement whilst for the middle-rich it creates the illusion that net taxpayers are, at least, getting something out of 'the system'. It is unlikely, however, to target benefits where they are genuinely required. The highest absolute number of recipients under the present system, for example, are those who receive child benefit and retirement benefit which means that the non-poor get quite a lot but the poorest do not get enough. Many of the so-called non-poor recipients must include the middle-income groups and the wealthy who (arguably) should be doing the redistributing. Child benefit and pension benefit account for well over half of the social security budget (see Table 10.3) and a reallocation of part of this sum could reduce poverty. What is needed, therefore, is greater selectivity within the system. The system of universal child benefit, which is a straight transfer via the tax system, makes the assumption that families cannot provide for their own life-cycle means and that horizontal transfers have to be made to individual families. It is based on out-dated fears about declining birth rates and nutritional defects among the young. The call for greater selectivity in pensions would be challenged on the assertion that they are self-financing through NI contributions. This has produced the expectation amongst contributors that the state pension is an entitlement for which they have forgone consumption during their working years. This perception of a pension as of right, however, is misplaced because the actuarial evidence indicates that most lifetime contributions would be inadequate to finance the requirements of present pension fund benefits.

Under the existing structure of (positive) income tax there is an allowance level below which no tax is paid; income above this is taxed at varying proportions of the difference between actual income and that level in tax. A negative income tax system would make this arrangement symmetric. Thus if an individual has income below the allowance level, then a certain proportion of the difference between income and the allowance level should be paid to the individual, a negative tax payment. This would provide an additional mechanism for attaining selectivity in the fiscal system, thus increasing its redistributive impact. Such a tax scheme would also eliminate the poverty trap because some of any extra earnings are retained and incomes can thereby be increased by working (see Atkinson 1983).

This chapter began by arguing that dissatisfaction with the spread of income and wealth resulting from a market-based system of resource allocation provided the rationale for government to attempt redistribution. Subsequent discussion showed that whilst particular aspects of governments' main policy instrument, the fiscal system, has had an effect upon distribution, mainly on the mitigation of poverty by income subsidies, other parts, income and commodity taxes and benefits-in-kind, have had much less impact. If, therefore, the existence of such a government policy is taken as reaction to market failure with respect to its treatment of distributive issues, then the above conclusion about the effectiveness of the fiscal system would suggest an element of government (policy-making or planning) failure. It is difficult, however, to measure the extent of this failure without intimate knowledge of the X_2-type variable contained in the SWF described earlier by equation [10.2]; for example, what weighting is given to, say, poverty, inequality and incentives. What is clear is that the tax-benefit system features elsewhere in government management of the economy strategy, not least as a means of raising revenue. Indeed, the impetus behind the current debate over the future fiscal system indicates that there has occurred a shift away from concern about creating a more equitable distribution of income and wealth, and towards other (essentially political) goals. These include producing higher levels of individual financial independence (independent, that is, of the state) and to secure so-called 'value-for-money' in the supply of public and merit goods. The lesson that remains, as illustrated by the fact that a negative income tax system has been ignored by government, is that the fiscal system can have a substantial impact on distributional issues provided it is designed and operated in a way wholly consistent with the stated objectives of redistribution.

Chapter 11

MARKETS, INTERVENTION AND PLANNING; SOME CONCLUDING REMARKS
Brian Roper and Brian Snowdon

In this book we have examined the issue of government intervention in a variety of contexts. It is our view that the most
fundamental issue underlying disagreements between economists
on matters of policy is the question of the proper role of government in the economy. Ultimately the choice of economic policy
may be made on political rather than economic grounds although
the choice will usually be justified by reference to some economic
theory (or 'defunct economist'). Undoubtedly, political considerations underlie economic arguments and vice versa; the domains
of economics and politics overlap. We have seen that economic
analysis provides a rationale for government intervention in a
market economy by identifying a number of areas where markets
can fail. We have also recognised that governments too can fail.
However, it is a political decision as to how much intervention
should take place in practice (see Culyer 1985: Ch. 36).

The differences which exist between economists are not purely
technical. Ideological elements are inextricably bound up in economic controversy. The late Joan Robinson went so far as to argue
that:

> In short, no economic theory gives us ready made answers. Any theory
> that we follow blindly will lead us astray. To make good use of an econ-
> omic theory we must first sort out the relations of the propagandist and
> the scientific elements in it then by checking with experience, see how
> far the scientific element appears convincing and finally recombine it
> with our own political views. The purpose of studying economics is not
> to acquire a set of ready-made answers to economic questions, but to
> learn how to avoid being deceived by economists (Robinson J. 1960: 17).

That economists disagree over the desirable balance between the public and private sectors, over the forms of intervention and the choice of instruments, over the relative efficiency of markets, intervention and planning is inevitable. The extent and desirability of the government's role in an economy has always been a major concern of economists and some of the most influential thinkers in economics have developed fundamentally different views of the capitalist system (see Cole *et al.* 1983).

Friedman's vision shows the capitalist system in a very favourable light. In his view the market system has remarkable power in raising living standards if only government would refrain from interfering with the economic machine. For Friedman, all that is necessary is for governments to provide law and order, to enforce contracts, to establish a stable monetary environment and to protect the citizen from external aggression. From such a perspective, economic difficulties are seen not as the result of unfettered free enterprise but rather the inevitable outcome of inappropriate and unnecessary government intervention. Health care, housing and education can best be provided through the market; competition is the most effective form of consumer protection; labour unions damage the interests of workers; and Keynesianism is synonymous with monetary mismanagement. A universal system of free markets is the best way of raising the living standards of all members of society (see Friedman 1980). In addition, Friedman argues that the preservation of economic freedom is an essential pre-requisite for the survival of political freedom. In this respect, his vision corresponds to that originally expressed by Hayek (1944) in *The road to serfdom* (see Hayek 1979).

Keynes presents us with a different vision. He criticised capitalism in order to defend and improve it. Whilst Keynes had no sympathy with central planning and was notoriously blind to Marxism, he did accept a significant role for the government in terms of economic management. In his view *laissez-faire* capitalism was dead. He was convinced that economists should direct their attention to finding new instruments and policies which could 'adapt and control the working of economic forces' without interfering with 'contemporary ideas as to what is fit and proper in the interests of social stability and social justice' (Keynes 1972: 300–6).

The Galbraithian perspective is similar to Keynes' in that an important role for government is recognised and supported. However, Galbraith is concerned that Keynes' vision was too limited and that in an 'Affluent Society' additional problems would be created requiring further government action. In particular, in a world dominated by giant corporations, consumer wants would be manipulated in a 'revised sequence' so that an imbalance between the public and private sectors, in favour of the latter, would be an inevitable outcome. The long-term result would be a system characterised by 'private affluence' amidst 'public squalor'. This is encapsulated in the following extract from Galbraith's *The Affluent Society*.

> The family which takes its mauve and cerise, air-conditioned, power steered, and power-braked automobile out for a tour passes through cities that are badly paved, made hideous by litter, blighted buildings, bill boards, and posts for wires that should long since have been put underground. They pass into a countryside that has been rendered largely invisible by commercial art . . . They picnic on exquisitely packaged food from a portable icebox by a polluted stream and go on to spend the night at a park which is a menace to public health and morals. Just before dozing off on an air mattress beneath a nylon tent, amid the stench of decaying refuse, they may reflect on the curious uneveness of their blessings. Is this indeed, the American genius (quoted in Breit 1984).

Hirsch, in developing a similar theme, has concluded that 'the prime economic problem now facing the economically advanced societies is a structural need to pull back the bounds of self advancement' (Hirsch 1977: 170). For such writers the capitalist system is characterised by an increasingly intense distributional struggle, a zero sum game, which cannot be resolved by free market forces (Thurow 1980).

The Marxist vision of the market system is of course quite different. Here capitalism is presented as a chaotic system which must ultimately collapse, destroyed by its own internal contradictions. Government is far from being an independent arbiter in the economic system. Its activities are seen to be directed towards the needs of capitalist accumulation (see Burden and Campbell 1985; Green and Nore 1977).

Some writers have argued that the politico-economic systems of the world are converging as the process of increasing industrialisation leads to a broadly similar type of economy in all countries, both capitalist and socialist. The theory was initially expounded by Tinbergen (1961) but has subsequently been developed by Van den Doel (1971). The modified convergence theory articulated by Van den Doel is based on four assumptions (see Ellman 1980). First, there exists an optimal economic system. Second, each economic system operates in a similar environment. Third, in time actual economies move gradually towards the optimum. Fourth, different economic systems have different objectives. This latter assumption is the crucial modification made by Van den Doel to Tinbergen's original theory. It is the difference in objectives which prevents the total convergence of the systems. Partial convergence is held to be inevitable as each society strives to reduce inefficiencies.

What of the future? Can capitalism survive? Are we witnessing a revival of *laissez-faire* capitalism? Intervention in capitalist market economies has become a major preoccupation of their governments especially since 1945, often for reasons concerned with distributive justice. The mitigation of inequality without damaging the efficiency of the system is the great social democratic compromise. However, as Scitovsky has pointed out 'capitalism works when it's flexible, but self destructs when it is not' (Scitovsky 1980: 2).

To those who have faith in market forces, intervention, in its many forms, leads to the fragmentation of the economy and represents the most important source of inflexibility leading to inefficiency. Such artificial rigidities impede the ability of the system to generate rising living standards in a world characterised by constant change. Adaptability is seen to be the key to economic success, and the price mechanism is seen as the only efficient mechanism for transmitting relevant information to the economic actors.

Dirigiste critics point out that the Smithian vision, which is currently enjoying a renaissance, is outdated and does not correspond to modern capitalist systems which are riddled with powerful monopolies, externalities, interdependencies, and individual actors who increasingly measure their welfare in relative as well as absolute terms.

It is our view that the mixed economy will survive and that for a variety of theoretical, practical and political reasons, governments are likely to continue to play a significant role in capitalist market economies. Adjustments to the 'mix' are likely to take place but there will be no return to nineteenth-century capitalism.

We are mindful that 'the political problem of mankind is to combine three things; economic efficiency, social justice, and individual liberty' (Keynes 1972: 311).

Which combination of markets, intervention and planning achieves the best balance of these objectives? In seeking an answer we should keep an open mind for, as Phyllis Deane reminds us:

The lesson that we should draw from the history of economic thought is that economists should resist the pressure to embrace a one-sided or restrictive consensus, there is no kind of economic truth which holds the key to fruitful analysis of all economic problems, no pure economic theory that is immune from changes in social values or current policy problems . . . the right answers are unlikely to come from any pure economic dogma (Deane 1983: 11–12).

REFERENCES

Alchian A A, Demsetz H 1972 Production, information costs and economic organisation. *American Economic Review* 62(1): 777–95.

Aldcroft D 1984 Unemployment patterns in the 1930s and 1980s. *The Economic Review*: 30–2.

Alt J E, Chrystal K A 1983 *Political economics*. Wheatsheaf Books.

Armstrong H, Taylor J 1985 *Regional economic policy and its analysis*. Philip Allen.

Arrow K J 1951 *Social choice and individual values*. John Wiley, New York.

Arrow K J 1963 Uncertainty and the welfare economics of medical care. *American Economic Review* 53(5): 941–73.

Arrow K J 1969 Classificatory notes on the production and transmission of knowledge. *American Economic Review* 59: 23–35.

Arrow K J 1973 Higher education as a filter. *Journal of Public Economics* 2: 193–216.

Arrow K J, Hahn F H 1971 *General competitive analysis*. Oliver and Boyd.

Ashworth W 1987 *A short history of the international economy, 1850–1950*. Longman

Atkinson A B 1983 *The economics of inequality* 2nd edn. Oxford University Press.

Atkinson A B, Stiglitz J E 1980 *Lectures on public economics*. McGraw Hill Book Company.

Bacon R, Eltis W 1976 *Britain's economic problem: too few producers*. Macmillan.

Bailey E E 1981 Contestability and the design of regulatory and antitrust policy. *American Economic Review* 71 May: 178–83

Bailey E E 1985 Price and productivity change following deregulation: the US experience. Paper presented to the Royal Economic Society: London: 5 June 1985 and published in *The Economic Journal* 1986.

Bailey R, Snowdon B 1982 Free markets or seige economy. In Elcock H (ed.) *What sort of society*. Martin Robertson.

Bailey S K 1967 The public interest: some operational dilemmas. In Friedrich C I (ed.) *Nomos v the public interest*. Atherton Press, New York.

Bairoch P, Levy-Leboyer M 1981 *Disparities in economic development since the industrial revolution*. Macmillan.

Balchin P N 1981 *Housing policy and housing needs*. Macmillan.

Balchin P N 1985 *Housing policy: an introduction*. Croom Helm.

Ballard L V 1936 *Social institutions*. Appleton Century, New York.

Barber A 1985 Ethnic origin and economic status. *Department of Employment Gazette* Dec. 1985.

Barker K *et al*. 1985 Macroeconomic policy in Germany and Britain. *National Institute Economic Review* No. 114 Nov. 1985: 69–89.

Barker T 1980 The economic consequences of monetarism: a Keynesian view of the British economy 1980–90. *Cambridge Journal of Economics*: 4 No. 4 Dec. 319–36.

Barry N P 1983 The New Liberalism. *British Journal of Political Science* 13(1).

Bauer P T 1981 *Equality, the third world and economic delusion*. Harvard U.P., Harvard, Massachusetts.

Baumol W J 1958 On the theory of oligopoly. *Economica* 25: 187–98.

Baumol W J 1982 Contestable markets: an uprising in the theory of industry structure. *American Economic Review* 72(1): 1–15

Baumol W J Bailey E E, Willig R D 1977 Weak invisible hand theorems on the sustainability of multiproduct natural monopoly. *American Economic Review* 67: 350–65.

Baumol W J, Panzar J C, Willig R D 1982 *Contestable markets and the theory of industrial structure*. Harcourt Brace Jovanovich, San Diego.

Becker G 1971 *The economics of discrimination* 2nd edn. University of Chicago Press.

Beckerman W, Clark S 1982 *Poverty and social security in Britain since 1961*. Oxford U.P.

Beenstock M 1980 *A neoclassical analysis of macroeconomic policy*. Cambridge U.P.

Beenstock M 1982 *World economy in transition*. Allen and Unwin.

Beer S H 1965 *Modern British politics*. Faber.

Beesley M, Littlechild S 1983 Privatisation: principles, problems and priorities. *Lloyds Bank Review* No. 149: 1–20.

Begg D 1982 *The rational expectations revolution in macroeconomics*. Philip Allen.

Begg D, Fisher S, Dornbusch R 1984 *Economics* British edn. McGraw-Hill Books Ltd.

Bergson A 1938 A reformulation of certain aspects of welfare economics. *Quarterly Journal of Economics* 52: 310–34.

Berry A, Bourguignon F, Morrison C 1983 Changes in world distribution of income between 1950–1977. *Economic Journal* 90(370): 331–50.

Berry C B 1986 The economics of contracting out with reference to the catering services at Newcastle Polytechnic. Unpublished undergraduate dissertation, School of Economics, Newcastle Polytechnic.

Bertram D, Edwards S 1985 *Comprehensive aspects of taxation, parts 1 and 2, 1985–86 edition* 37th edn. Holt, Rinehart and Winston.

Beveridge W 1942 *Social insurance and allied services.* Command Paper No. 6404, HMSO.

Beveridge W 1944 *Full employment in a free society.* Allen and Unwin.

Bird R 1971 Wagner's law of expanding state activity. *Public Finance* **26**: 1–26.

Black D 1980 *Inequalities in health report of a research working party chaired by Sir Douglas Black.* London: Department of Health and Security. (An edited version is in Townsend *et al.* 1982.)

Blackaby F T 1972 *An incomes policy for Britain.* Heinemann.

Blackaby F T 1978 Incomes policy. In Blackaby F T (ed.) *British Economic Policy 1960–74.* Cambridge U.P.

Blaug M 1972 *An introduction to the economics of education.* Harmondsworth Penguin.

Blaug M 1978 *Economic theory in retrospect* 3rd edn. Cambridge U.P.

Blaug M 1984 In Le Grande J, Robinson R *Privatisation and the welfare state.* Allen and Unwin, pp. 160–76.

Bleaney M 1985 *The rise and fall of Keynesian economics.* Macmillan.

Bootle R 1981 How important is it to defeat inflation. *Three Banks Review* No. 132 Dec. 1981: 23–47.

Bosanquet N 1983 *After the new right.* Heinemann Educational Books.

Bowie R R 1978 The basis for post-war co-operation. In Kaiser K, Schwartz P H (eds) *America and Western Europe: problems and prospects.* Lexington Books.

Breit W 1984 Galbraith and Friedman: two versions of economic reality. *Journal of Post Keynesian Economics* **iii**(1): 18–29.

Brimmer A 1983 Monetary policy and economic activity: benefits and costs of monetarism. *American Economic Review* **73** No. 2 May 1983: 1–12.

British United Provident Association, Private Plan, Western Provident Association 1983 *Provident scheme statistics 1981: an overview.* BUPA, PPP, WPA, London.

Brittan S 1971 *Steering the economy.* Penguin.

Brittan S, Lilley P 1977 *The delusion of incomes policy.* Temple Smith.

Bronfenbrenner M 1969 *Is the business cycle obsolete?* John Wiley and Sons, New York.

Brown A J 1985 *World inflation since 1950 an international comparative study.* Cambridge U.P.

Brown C, Gay P 1985 *Racial discrimination: 17 years after the act.* Report 646 of the Policy Studies Institute.

Buchanan J M 1968 What kind of redistribution do we want? *Economica* **35**: 185–90.

Buchanan J M, Burton J, Wagner R 1978 *The consequences of Mr Keynes.* Institute of Economic Affairs.

Budd A 1978 *The politics of economic planning.* Fontana.

Buiter W H 1980 The macroeconomics of Dr Pangloss: a critical survey of the new classical macroeconomics. *Economic Journal* **90** March: 34–50.

Buiter W H, Miller M 1982 Real exchange rate overshooting and the output cost of bringing down inflation. *European Economic Review* **18**.

Burden T, Campbell M 1985 *Capitalism and public policy in the UK.* Croom Helm.

Burton J 1982 Varieties of monetarism. *Three Banks Review* No. 134 June: 14–31.

Butler E 1985 *Milton Friedman: a guide to his economic thought.* Temple Smith/Gower.

Button K J 1985 New approaches to the regulation of industry. *The Royal Bank of Scotland Review* No. 148: 18–34.

Byatt I C R 1984 The framework of government control. In Smith J G (ed.) *Strategic planning in nationalised industries.* Macmillan.

Byrne D 1984 A relief for the wealthy. *Low Pay Review* No. 17: 12–21.

Cagan P 1956 The monetary dynamics of hyperinflation. In Friedman M (ed.) *Studies in the quantity theory of money.* University of Chicago Press.

Cairncross A 1971 *Essays in economic management.* Allen and Unwin.

Calleo D P, Rowland B 1973 *America in the world political economy: Atlantic dreams and national realities.* Indiana U.P., Bloomington and London.

Calleo D P, Strange S 1984 Money and world politics. In Strange S (ed.) *Paths to international political economy.* Allen and Unwin.

Cassels J S 1985 Can tripartism compete? *Three Banks Review* No. 146.

Casson M 1983 *The entrepreneur: an economic theory.* Martin Robertson.

Caves R F 1968 Market organisation, performance and public policy. In Caves R F (ed.) *Britain's economic prospects.* Allen and Unwin.

Caves R F 1980 Corporate strategy and structure. *Journal of economic literature* **18**: 64–92.

de Cecco M 1979 The origins of the post war payments system. *Cambridge Journal of Economics* **3**.

Central Statistical Office 1985 The effects of taxes and benefits on household income 1984. *Economic Trends* No. 386: 99–115.

Chamberlain E H 1933 *The theory of monopolistic competition.* Harvard U.P., Cambridge, Massachusetts.

Charles S 1977 *Housing economics.* Macmillan Studies in Economics.

Chester D N 1952 Machinery of government and planning. In Worswick G, Ady P (eds) *The British economy 1945–50.* Oxford U.P.

Clower R W 1965 The Keynesian counter-revolution: a theoretical reappraisal. In Hahn F, Brechlin F (eds) *The theory of interest rates.* Macmillan.

Coase R H 1937 The nature of the firm. *Economica* **4**: 386–405.

Coase R H 1960 The problem of social cost. *Journal of Law and Economics* **3**: 1–44.

Coates D, Hillard J (eds) 1986 *The economic decline of modern Britain.* Wheatsheaf Books, Harvester Press.

Cochrane A L 1972 *Effectiveness and efficiency: random reflections on health care.* Nuffield Provincial Hospitals Trust.

Cockcroft Report 1982 *Report of the Committee of Inquiry into the teaching of mathematics in schools* under the Chairmanship of Dr W H Crockcroft. HMSO.

Coddington A 1983 *Keynesian economics. The search for first principles.* Allen and Unwin.

Cohen R, Lakhani B 1986 *National welfare benefits handbook* 15th edn. Child Poverty Action Group, London.

Cole K, Cameron J, Edwards C 1983 *Why economists disagree. The political economy of economics.* Longman.

Collard D 1978 *Altruism and economy.* Martin Robertson.

Commission for Racial Equality 1985 *Report of a formal investigation into the Beaumont Shopping Centre.*

Cooper M H, Culyer A J 1970 An economic analysis of some aspects of the NHS. In Jones I (ed.) *Health services financing.* British Medical Association.

Cooper M H, Culyer A J 1972 Equality in the NHS: intentions, performance and problems in evaluation. In Hauser M M (ed.) *The economics of medical care.* Allen and Unwin.

Corden W M 1985 *Inflation exchange rates and the world economy* 3rd edn. Clarendon Press.

Cornwall J 1977 *Modern capitalism: its growth and transformation.* Martin Robertson.

Cornwall J (ed.) 1984 *After staglation. Alternatives to economic decline.* Basil Blackwell.

Coutts K *et al.* 1981 The economic consequences of Mrs Thatcher. *Cambridge Journal of Economics* 5: 81–93.

Cowling K, Mueller D 1978 The social cost of monopoly power. *Economic Journal* 88 Dec.: 727–48.

Cox R W 1980 The crisis of the world order. *International Organisation Journal* xxxv: 370–95.

Craig C, Wilkinson F 1984 *Pay and employment in four retail trades.* Department of Applied Economics Labour Studies Group. University of Cambridge.

Craven B M, Dick B, Wood B 1986 The behaviour of a resource reducing bureau: a case study of an English Polytechnic. *Applied Economics* 18(1).

Craven B M, Wright G A 1983 The Thatcher experiment. *Journal of Macroeconomics* 15(1): 21–40.

Cripps F, Godley W 1978 Control of imports as a means to full employment and expansion. *Cambridge Journal of Economics* No. 3 Sept.: 327–34.

Crosland C A R 1956 *The future of socialism.* Jonathan Cape.

Cross R 1982a *Economic theory and policy in the UK.* Martin Robertson.

Cross R 1982b The Duhein–Quine thesis, Lakatos and the appraisal of theories in macroeconomics. *Economic Journal* 92 June: 320–40.

Crossman R 1975 and 1976 *The diaries of a cabinet minister.* Hamish Hamilton and Cape, vols I and II.

Culyer A J 1971 The nature of the commodity 'health care' and its efficient allocation. *Oxford Economic Papers* 23: 189–211.

Culyer A J 1976 *Need and the National Health Service.* Martin Robertson.

Culyer A J 1985 *Economics.* Basil Blackwell.

Culyer A J, Cullis J G 1975 Hospital waiting lists and the supply and demand of inpatient care. *Social and Economic Administration* 9(1): 13–25.

Culyer A J, Cullis J G 1976 Some economics of hospital waiting lists in the NHS. *Journal of Social Policy* **5**(3): 239–64.

Dalton G 1974 *Economic systems and society*. Penguin.

Davies B 1984 Thatcherite visions and the role of MSC. *Youth and Policy* **2**(4).

Davies G 1985 *Governments can affect employment*. Employment Institute.

Deane P 1983 The scope and method of economic science. *Economic Journal* **93** March: 1–12.

Deaton A, Muellbauer J 1980 *Economics and consumer behaviour*. Cambridge U.P.

Demsetz H 1968 Why regulate utilities? *Journal of Law and Economics* **11**: 55–65.

Demsetz H 1969 Information and efficiency: another viewpoint. *Journal of Law and Economics* **12** April: 1–22.

Demsetz H 1982 *Economic, legal and political dimensions of competition*. North Holland, Amsterdam.

Department of Employment 1976 *Training for skills*. HMSO.

Department of Employment 1983 Consultative paper on wages councils. HMSO.

Department of the Environment 1977a *Housing policy: a consultative document*. HMSO.

Department of the Environment 1977b *Housing policy: a consultative document, annex B*. HMSO.

Department of the Environment 1977c *Housing policy, technical volume 1*. HMSO.

Department of the Environment 1981 *Housing and construction statistics 1970–1980*. HMSO

Department of the Environment 1982 *English house condition survey*. HMSO.

Department of the Environment 1984 *Housing and construction statistics 1973–1983*. HMSO

Department of the Environment 1985 *Housing and construction statistics 1974–1984*. HMSO

Dixit A 1982 Recent developments in oligopoly theory. *American Economic Review* **72** No. 2 May: 12–28.

Dixon R, Thirlwall A P 1975 A model of regional growth rate differences on Kaldorian lines. *Oxford Economic Papers* **27** No. 2 July: 201–14.

Doel J van den 1971 *Convergence and evolution*. Assen, The Netherlands.

Doeringer P B, Piore M J 1971 *Internal labor markets and manpower analysis*. Heath, Lexinging, Texas.

Doling J, Karn V, Stafford B 1985 How far can privatisation go? Owner-occupation and mortgage default. *National Westminster Bank Review*: 42–52.

Domberger S, Middleton J 1985 Franchising in practice: the case of independent television in the UK. *Fiscal Studies* **6**(1): 17–32.

Dore R 1976 *The diploma disease*. Allen and Unwin.

Dornbusch R 1982 Flexible exchange rates and interdependence. *National Bureau of Economic Research* (*Working paper No. 1035*).

Dornbusch R 1985 *Sound currency and full employment*. Employment Institute.

Dow J C R 1964 The management of the British economy 1945–60. Cambridge U.P.

Downs A 1957 *An economic theory of democracy*. Harper and Row, New York.

Dunning J H 1979 Explaining changing patterns of international production: in defence of the eclectic theory. *Oxford Bulletin of Economics and Statistics*.

Durham County Council 1985 Minutes of the Education Committee.

Eatwell J 1982 *Whatever happened to Britain*. Duckworth.

Eckstein H 1958 *The English health service*. Harvard U.P., Cambridge, Massachusetts.

Ellman M 1978 The fundamental problem of socialist planning. *Oxford Economic Papers* **30** No. 2: 249–61

Ellman M 1980 Against convergence. *Cambrige Journal of Economics* **4**: 192–210.

Fallick J L 1982 Incomes policies. In Artis M *et al*. *Demand management supply constraints and inflation*. Manchester U.P.

Fama E F 1980 Agency problems and the theory of the firm. *Journal of Political Economy* **88**(2): 288–307.

Feinstein C H 1972 *National income, expenditure and output of the UK, 1855–1965*. Cambridge U.P.

Feldstein M S 1964 Hospital planning and the demand for care. *Bulletin of the Oxford University Institute of Economics and Statistics*.

Feldstein M S 1970 The rising price of physicians' services. *Review of Economics and Statistics* **52**(2): 121–33.

Feldstein M S 1971 Hospital cost inflation: a study of non-profit price dynamics. *American Economic Review* **61**(5): 835–72.

Feldstein M S 1973 The welfare loss of excess health insurance. *Journal of Political Economy* **81**(2 part 1): 251–80.

Feldstein M S 1977 Quality change and the demand for medical care. *Econometrica* **45**(7): 1681–1702.

Ferguson P R 1985 The Monopolies and Mergers Commission and economic theory. *National Westminster Quarterly Bank Review* Nov.: 30–40.

Fine B, Murfin A 1984 *Macroeconomics and monopoly capitalism*. Wheatsheaf Books.

Foley D K 1978 State expenditure from a Marxist perspective. *Journal of Public Economics* **9**: 221–38.

Forrest D 1985 Minimum wages, unemployment and poverty. *The Economic Review* **3**(1): 34–7.

Forrest D, Dennison S R 1985 Low pay or no pay. *Hobart Paper 101*. Institute for Economic Affairs.

Freeman R, Medoff J 1979 The two faces of unionism. *Public Interest*. Fall.

Frey B 1978 *Modern political economy*. Martin Robertson.

Friedman M 1948 A monetary and fiscal framework for economic stability. *American Economic Review*: 245–64.

Friedman M 1956 The quantity theory of money – a restatement. In Friedman M (ed.) *Studies in the quantity theory of money*. University of Chicago Press.

Friedman M 1962 *Capitalism and freedom*. University of Chicago Press.

Friedman M 1968 The role of monetary policy. *American Economic Review* **58**: 1–17.

Friedman 1970 A theoretical framework for monetary analysis. *Journal of Political Economy* **78**: 193–238.

Friedman M 1975 *Unemployment and inflation*. Institute of Economic Affairs.

Friedman M 1983 A monetarist reflects. *The Economist*; 35–7.

Friedman M, Schwartz A 1963 *A monetary history of the United States*, 1867–1960. Princeton U.P.

Friedman M, Roosa 1967 The balance of payments: free versus flexible exchange rates. *American Enterprise Institute*. Washington DC.

Friedman M, Friedman R 1980 *Free to choose*. Penguin.

Galbraith J K 1978 *The affluent society*. Hamish Hamilton.

Galbraith J K 1969 *The new industrial state*. Harmondsworth, Penguin.

Galbraith J K 1974 *Economics and the public purpose*. Andre Deutsch.

Gannicott K, Blaug M 1977 Scientists and Engineers. In Baxter C, O'Leary P J, Westoby A *Economics and Education Policy: A Reader*. Longman in association with The Open University Press.

Gardiner R N 1969 *Sterling/dollar diplomacy*. McGraw Hill, New York.

George K 1982 Monopoly and merger policy. *Fiscal Studies* **6**(1): 34–48.

Gilpin R 1975 *Power and the multinational corporation: the political economy of foreign direct investment*. Basic Books, New York.

Godfrey L 1975 *Theoretical and empirical aspects of the effects of taxation on the supply of labour*. OECD, Paris.

Gomes G 1982 Irrationality of rational expectations. *Journal of Post Keynesian Economics* **v**(1): 51–65.

Gordon R 1981 Output fluctuations and gradual price adjustment. *Journal of Economic Literature* **19**: 493–530.

Gough I 1979 *The political economy of the welfare state*. Macmillan.

Gould A 1981 The salaried middle class in the corporatist welfare state. *Policy and Politics* **9**(4): 408–18.

Gowland D 1985 *Money inflation and unemployment. The role of money in the economy*. Wheatsheaf Books.

Grant W 1982 *The political economy of industrial policy*. Butterworth.

Grant W, Nath S 1984 *The politics of economic policymaking*. Basil Blackwell.

Green D G 1984 Doctors versus workers. *Economic Affairs*, Supplement to Oct.–Dec. 1984.

Green F, Nore P 1977 *Economics an anti-text*. Macmillan.

Green H A J 1976 *Consumer theory* (revised edn). Macmillan.

Greenaway D 1983 *International trade policy*. Macmillan.

Griffin K 1978 *International inequality and national poverty*. Macmillan.

Grossman 1972 *The demand for health: a theoretical and empirical investigation*. Columbia U.P., New York.

Gujarati D 1972 The behaviour of unemployment and unfilled vacancies: Great Britain 1958–71. *Economic Journal*: 195–204.

Haberler G von 1936 *The theory of international trade with its applications to commercial policy* (English translation). William Hodge.

Hadjimatheo G, Skouras T 1979 Britain's economic problem: the growth of the non-market sector. *Economic Journal* **89**: 392–401.

Hahn F 1980 Unemployment from a theoretical viewpoint. *Economica* **47**: 285–98.

Hahn F 1982a Reflections on the invisible hand. *Lloyds Bank Review* **144**: 1–21.

Hahn F 1982b *Money and inflation*. Basil Blackwell.

Hamermesh D S, Rees A 1984 *The economics of work and pay*. Harper and Row.

Hansen B 1969 *Fiscal policy in seven countries 1955–1965*. OECD, Paris.

Harberger A 1954 Monopoly and resource allocation. *American Economic Review* **44**: 7–8.

Harberger A 1964 Taxation, resource allocation and welfare. In *The role of direct and indirect taxes in the federal reserve system*. Princeton U.P.

Harberger A 1971 Three basic postulates for applied welfare economics. An interpretative essay. *Journal of Economic Literature* **9**: 785–97.

Hardie C J M 1985 Competition policy. In Morris D (ed) *The Economic System in the UK* (3rd edn). Oxford U.P.

Hardman J P 1985 *On tax in business.* Gee and Company.

Harrington R L 1972 Housing – supply and demand. *National Westminster Bank Review*, May: 43–54.

Harrison A J 1984 Monitoring performance. In Smith J G (ed.) *Strategic planning in nationalised industries*. Macmillan.

Hatfield M 1978 *The house the left built*. Victor Gollancz.

Hayek F A 1945 The use of knowledge in society. *American Economic Review* **XXXV**(4).

Hayek F A 1973 *A tiger by the tail*. Institute of Economic Affairs.

Hayek F A 1975 *Full employment at any price*? Institute of Economic Affairs.

Hayek F A 1978a *New studies in philosophy, politics, economics*. Routledge and Kegan Paul.

Hayek F A 1978b *The mirage of social justice*. Routledge and Kegan Paul.

Hayek F A 1979 *Road to serfdom*. Routledge and Kegan Paul.

Hayek F A 1983 The Austrian critique. *The Economist*: 45–8.

Heald D 1984 *Public expenditure. Its defence and reform*. Martin Robertson.

Heller R 1973 *International trade: theory and empirical evidence* (2nd edn). Prentice Hall, Englewood Cliffs, New Jersey.

Hemming R 1984 *Poverty and incentives: the economics of social security*. Oxford U.P.

Hicks J 1937 Mr Keynes and the classics. *Econometrica* **V**: 147–59.

Hicks J 1974 *The crisis in Keynesian economics*. Basil Blackwell.

Higham D, Tomlinson J 1982 Why do governments worry about inflation? *National Westminster Bank Review*: 2–13.

Hines A G 1971 *On the reappraisal of Keynesian economics*. Martin Robertson.

Hirsch F 1977 *The social limits to growth*. Routledge and Kegan Paul.

Hirschman A O 1945 *National power and the structure of foreign trade* (reprint). University of California Press.

Hirschman A O 1970 *Exit, voice and loyalty*. Harvard U.P., Cambridge Press, Massachusetts.

HMSO 1961 *Report of the Advisory Council on scientific policy, Committee on scientific manpower*. Cmnd 1490.

HMSO 1963 *Higher education: report of the Committee under the chairmanship of Lord Robbins*. Cmnd 2154.

HMSO 1965 Cmnd 2806 *Committee on manpower resources for science and technology. A review of the scope and problems of scientific and technological manpower policy* (The Jackson Report).

HMSO 1967 Cmnd 3437 *Nationalised industries: a review of economic and financial objectives*.

HMSO 1979 Cmnd 7615 *Royal Commission on the National Health Service*.

HMSO 1985a Cmnd 9524 *The development of higher education into the 1990s*. Green Paper.

HMSO 1985b *The reform of social security, programme for action*.

HMSO 1986 *Social trends* **16**.

Hodgson G 1984 *The democratic economy*. Penguin.

Holland S 1975 *The socialist challenge*. Quartet Books.

Hoover K D 1984 Two types of monetarism. *Journal of Economic Literature* **22**: 58–76.

Hoskyns J Sir 1986 Report of Annual Convention February 1986. Institute of Directors.

Hotelling H 1938 The general welfare in relation to problems of taxation and of railway and utility rates. *Econometrica* **vi**: 242–69.

Howe Geoffrey Sir 1983 Agenda for liberal conservation. *Economic Affairs* **3(2)**: 71–83.

Hume D 1752 *Of money*. Reprinted in Walters A A (ed.) *Money and banking*. Penguin.

Inquiry into British Housing 1985 *Inquiry into British housing: report*. National Federation of Housing Associations.

Jackman R, Layard R 1982 An inflation tax. *Fiscal Studies* **3**: 47–60.

Jackson 1965 Committee on Manpower Resources for Sciences and Technology, *A Review of the Scope and Problems of Science and Technology with Manpower Policy* HMSO Cmnd 280c.

Jackson D, Turner H A, Wilkinson F 1972 *Do trade unions cause inflation?* University of Cambridge, Department of Applied Economics, Occasional Paper 36.

Jackson P M 1982 *The political economy of bureaucracy*. Philip Allan.

James S, Nobes C 1983 *The economics of taxation* (2nd edn). Philip Allan.

Jencks C et al. 1970 *Education vouchers: a report of financing elementary education by grants to parents*. Centre for the Study of Public Policy, Cambridge, Massachusetts.

Jensen M C, Meckling W H 1976 Theory of the firm: managerial behaviour agency costs and ownership structures. *Journal of Financial Economics* 3: 305–60.

Jewkes J 1948 *The new ordeal by planning*. Macmillan.

Johnson H G 1968 *Theory for a developing world economy* (Wicksell Lecture). Almquist and Wicksell, Stockholm.

Johnson H G 1971 The Keynesian revolution and the monetarist counter-revolution. *American Economic Review* 61: 1–14.

Johnson H G 1973a The monetary approach to balance of payments theory. In Johnson H G *Further essays in monetary economics*. Allen and Unwin.

Johnson H G 1973b The university and social welfare. *Minerva* 1: 30–52.

Kahn R 1974 On re-reading Keynes. In *Proceedings of the British Academy*. Oxford U.P., vol. LX, pp. 361–91.

Kahn R 1978 Some aspects of the development of Keynes' thought. *Journal of Economic Literature* 16: 545–59.

Kaldor N 1959 Economic growth and the problem of inflation. *Economica* 26: 287–98.

Kaldor N 1970 The case for regional policies. *Scottish Journal of Political Economy* 17: 337–48.

Kaldor N 1972 The irrelevance of equilibrium economics. *Economic Journal* 82: 1237–55.

Kaldor N 1982 *The scourge of monetarism*. Oxford U.P.

Kaldor N 1983 *The economic consequences of Mrs Thatcher*. Duckworth.

Kalecki M 1943 Political aspects of full employment. *Political Quarterly* 14: 322–31.

Katzenstein P 1978 *Between power and policy*. Maddison University of Wisconsin Press.

Kay J A, King M A 1983 *The British tax system* (3rd edn). Oxford U.P.

Kay J A Thompson D J 1985 Privatisation: a policy in search of a rationale. Paper presented to the Royal Economic Society. London: 5 June 1985, printed in *The Economic Journal* March 1986.

Keegan W 1984 *Mrs Thatcher's economic experiment*. Penguin Books.

Keeler E B, Merrow D T, Newhouse J P 1977 The demand for supplementary health insurance, or do deductibles matter. *Journal of Political Economy* 85(4): 789–801.

Kent County Council 1977/78 *Education vouchers in Kent: a feasibility study for the Education Department of Kent County Council*.

Kenwood A G, Lougheed A L 1982 *The growth of the international economy 1820–1960*. Allen and Unwin.

Keynes J M 1926 *The end of laissez-faire*. Reprinted in *Essays in persuasion*. Macmillan, vol. IX *Collected works* 1972.

Keynes J M 1933 National self sufficiency. *The Yale Review* 22: 755–69 (reprinted in Keynes J M 1973a p. 243).

Keynes J M 1943 The objective of international price stability. *Economic Journal*: 185–7.

Keynes J M 1972 *The collected writings of John Maynard Keynes Vol XI. Essays in Persuasion*. Macmillan.

Keynes J M 1973a *The collected writings of John Maynard Keynes, vol VII. The general theory of employment interest and money*. Macmillan.

Keynes J M 1973b The general theory of employment. Reprinted in *The collected writings of John Maynard Keynes Vol. XIV, the general theory and after part II defence and development* ed. by Moggridge D. Macmillan.

Keynes J M 1973c *The collected works of John Maynard Keynes. The general theory and after part I preparation* ed. by Moggridge D. Macmillan.

Keynes J M 1982 *The collected writings of John Maynard Keynes Vol XXXVIII, social, political and literary writings* ed. by Moggridge D. Macmillan.

Killick T 1976 The possibilities of development planning. *Oxford Economic Papers*: 161–84.

Kindleberger C P 1973 *The world in depression 1929–39*. Allen Lane.

Kindleberger C P 1986 International public goods without international governments. *The American Economic Review* **76**(1): 1–13.

King J E (ed.) 1980 *Readings in labour economics*. Oxford U.P.

King M A 1977 *Public policy and the corporation*. Chapman and Hall.

Kirzner I M 1973 *Competition and entrepreneurship*. University of Chicago Press.

Kornai J 1971 *Anti-equilibrium: on economic systems theory and the tasks of research*. North-Holland, Amsterdam.

Kornai J 1979 Appraisal of project appraisal. In *Economics and human welfare*. Academic Press, New York.

Koutsoyiannis A 1979 *Modern microeconomics*. Macmillan.

Kraus L 1970 A passive balance of payments strategy. *Brookings Papers on Economic Activity*. Brookings Institution, Washington DC.

Kristol I 1983 *Reflections of a neoconservative*. Basic Books, New York.

Krugman P 1979 A model of innovation, technology transfer and the world distribution of income. *Journal of Political Economy* **82** (2): 253–66.

Laidler D 1975 The end of demand management. In Friedman M *Inflation and unemployment*. Institute of Economic Affairs.

Laidler D 1981 Monetarism: an interpretation and an assessment. *Economic Journal* **91**: 1–27.

Lall D 1981 The case for free trade. *The Business Economist* **13**(1): 6–17.

Lall D 1983 *The Poverty of Development Economics*. IEA London.

Lange O, Taylor F 1938 On the economic theory of socialism. As reprinted in Nove A, Nuti D M *Socialist Economics*. Penguin.

Lansley S 1979 *Housing and public policy*. Croom Helm.

Lansley S 1984 *Right to a home*, ed. Labour Housing Group Spokesman 9–19.

Larkey P, Stolp C, Winer M 1981 Theorising about the growth of government: a research assessment. *Journal of public policy* **1**: 157–220.

Lawson T 1985 Uncertainty and economic analysis. *Economic Journal*: 909–27.

Lawson T, Kirkpatrick C 1980 On the nature of industrial decline in the UK. *Cambridge Journal of Economics* **4**: 85–102.

Lees D S 1962 The logic of the British National Health Service. *Journal of Law and Economics* **5**: 111–18.

Le Grand J 1982 *The strategy of equality*. Allen and Unwin.

Le Grand J 1985 *Inequalities in health and health care.* Nuffield/York Portfolio 5, Nuffield Provincial Hospitals Trust.

Le Grand J, Robinson R (eds) 1984a *Privatisation and the welfare state.* George Allen and Unwin.

Le Grand J, Robinson R 1984b *The economics of social problems.* Macmillan.

Leibenstein H 1966 Allocative efficiency versus x-efficiency. *American Economic Review* **56**: 392–415 (June).

Leibenstein H 1978 X-inefficiency Xists – reply to an Xorcist. *American Economic Review* **68**: 203–11.

Leibenstein H 1979 A branch of economics in mining: micro-micro theory. *Journal of Economic Literature* **17**: 477–502.

Leijonhufvud A 1968 *On Keynesian economics and the economics of Keynes.* Oxford U.P.

Leruez J 1975 *Economic planning and politics in Britain.* Martin Robertson.

Letwin W (ed.) 1983 *Against equality.* Macmillan.

Levacic R 1980 Selective intervention. Unit 15, Course D324. *Business Economics.* The Open University.

Levacic R 1985 Keynes was a monetarist. *Economic Affairs* **4**(3): 19–21.

Levacic R, Rebmann A 1982 *Macroeconomics: An introduction to Keynesian–Neoclassical controversies.* 2nd ed. Macmillan London.

Lewis W A 1969 Aspects of tropical trade 1883–1965 (*The Wicksell Lectures*). Almquist and Wicksell, Stockholm.

Lindbeck A 1977 *The political economy of the new left.* Harper and Row, New York.

Lindblom C E 1965 *The intelligence of democracy.* The Free Press, New York.

Lindblom C E 1977 *Politics and markets. The world's political–economic systems.* Basic Books, New York.

Linder S B 1961 *An essay on trade and transformation.* Wiley and Co, New York.

Lipsey D 1985 *The Sunday Times*, 31 Mar.

Lipsey R G 1960 The relationship between unemployment and the rate of change of money wage rates in the UK 1862–1957: a further analysis. *Economica* **27**: 1–32.

Lipsey R G 1978 The place of the Phillips curve in macroeconomic models. In Bergstrom A R (ed.) *Stability and inflation.*

Lipsey R G 1983 *Positive economics* 6th edn. Weidenfeld and Nicolson.

Lipsey R G 1984 After monetarism. In Cornwall J (ed.) *After stagflation alternatives to economic decline.* Basil Blackwell.

Little I M D 1957 *A critique of welfare economics* 2nd edn. Oxford U.P.

Littlechild S 1983a Deregulation of telecommunications: some economic aspects. *The Economic Review* November: 29–34.

Littlechild S 1983b *Regulation of British Telecom profitability.* Department of Trade.

Llewellyn D T 1984 The British monetarist experiment: a preliminary assessment. *Economics* 20, Spring: 15–22.

Lucas R E Jnr 1972 Expectations and the neutrality of money. *Journal of Economic Theory* **4**: 103–24.

Luffman G A, Reed R 1984 *The strategy and performance of British industry 1970–80*. Macmillan.

Machlup F 1958 Equilibrium and disequilibrium: misplaced concreteness and disguised politics. *Economic Journal*: 1–24.

Machlup F 1967 Theories of the firm: marginalist, behavioural, managerial. *American Economic Review* **57**(1): 1–33.

Maclennan D 1982 *Housing economics*. Longman.

Macneil I R 1978 Contracts: adjustment of long-term economic relations under classical, neoclassical and relational contract law. *North Western University Law Review* **72**.

Macrae D C 1977 A political model of the business cycle. *Journal of Political Economy* **85**: 239–63.

Maddison A 1979 Long run dynamics of productivity growth. *Banca Nazionale del Lavoro* 1979: 3–44.

Maddison A 1980 Western economic performance in the 1970s: a perspective and assessment. *Banca Nazionale del Lavoro* **33**: 247–89.

Maddison A 1984 Origins and impact of the welfare state. *Banca Nazionale del Lavoro Quarterly Review* **37**: 55–87.

Majumdar T 1958 *The measurement of utility* (revised edn). Macmillan.

Malthai J 1984 Rethinking scarcity: neoclassicism neo Malthusianism and neo Marxism. *Review of Radical Political Economics* **16**: 81–94.

Manpower Services Commission/National Economic Development Office 1984 *Competence and competition*. NEDO Books.

Manpower Services Commission 1985 *A challenge to complacency*.

Marris R 1963 A model of the 'managerial' enterprise. *Quarterly Journal of Economics* **77**(2): 185–209.

Marris R 1964 *The economic theory of managerial capitalism*. Macmillan.

Marshall A 1920 *Principles of economics*. Macmillan.

Masson R T, Shaanon J 1984 Social costs of oligopoly and the value of competition. *Economic Journal* **94**: 520–35.

Mayer T et al. 1978 *The structure of monetarism*. Norton.

Mayer T 1980 David Hume and monetarism. *Quarterly Journal of Economics* **95**: 89–101.

Maynard A 1983 Privatising the National Health Service. *Lloyds Bank Review* **148**: 28–41.

Maynard A, Williams A 1984 Privatisation and the National Health Service. In Le Grand J, Robinson R (eds) *Privatisation and the welfare state*. Allen and Unwin.

Meltzer A 1981 Keynes' general theory: a different perspective. *Journal of Economic Literature* **19**: 34–64.

Metcalfe D 1984 Unions and pay. *The Economic Review* **2**(1): 24–7.

Metcalfe D, Nickell S 1985 Jobs and pay. *Midland Bank Review*, Spring.

Metcalfe D, Richardson R 1984. In Prest A R, Coppock D J (eds) *The UK economy* 10th edn.

Miliband R 1982 *Capitalist democracy in Britain*. Oxford U.P.

Mill J S 1981 *Autobiography*. University of Toronto Press. Routledge and Kegan Paul.

Mill J S 1985 *Principles of political economy*. Routledge and Sons.

Millett K 1977 *Sexual politics*. Virago Press.

Minford P 1983 Agenda for liberal conservatism: comment. *Economic Affairs* 3(2): 94–8.

Minford P et al. 1983 *Unemployment: cause and cure*. Martin Robertson.

Ministry of Health 1963 *Reduction of waiting lists, surgical and general*. HM (63) 22.

Mises L von 1920 Economic calculation in the socialist commonwealth. As reprinted in Nove A, Nuti D M (eds) *Socialist economics* 1972 Penguin.

Mises L von 1949 *Human action: a treatise on economics*. Hodge and Co.

Modigliani F 1977 The monetarist controversy or should we forsake stabilisation policies. *American Economic Review* **67**, May: 1–19.

Moore B, Rhodes J 1973 Evaluating the effects of British regional policy. *Economic Journal*: 87–110.

Moore B, Rhodes J 1976 The relative decline of the UK manufacturing sector. *Cambridge Economic Policy Review* March.

Morgan B 1978 *Monetarists and Keynesians*. Macmillan.

Morris D J, Stout D K 1985 Industrial policy. In Morris D (ed.) *The economic system in the UK* 34th edn. Oxford U.P.

Mosley P 1984 *The making of economic policy*. Wheatsheaf Books, Harvester Press.

Mueller D C 1979 *Public choice*. Cambridge U.P.

Mullineux A W 1984 *The business cycle after Keynes*. Wheatsheaf Books.

Murrell P 1983 Did the theory of market socialism answer the challenge of Ludwig von Mises? A reinterpretation of the socialist controversy. *History of Political Economy* **15**(1).

Muth J 1961 Rational expectations and the theory of price movements. *Econometrica* **29**: 315–35.

Myrdal G 1957 *Economic theory and underdeveloped regions*. Duckworth.

McFarlane B 1984 Economic planning: past trends and the new prospects. *Contributions to Political Economy* **3**: 1–13.

McLachlan G, Maynard A K (eds) 1982 *The public/private mix for health*. Nuffield Provincial Hospitals Trust.

National Enterprise Board 1978 *Annual Report and Accounts for 1976/7*. HMSO.

Nelson R R 1977 *The moon and the ghetto: an essay on public policy analysis*. W W Norton & Co Inc, New York.

Niskanen W A 1971 *Bureaucracy and representative government*. Aldine-Atherton, Chicago.

Niskanen W A 1973 *Bureaucracy: servant or master*. Institute of Economic Affairs.

Nordhaus W 1975 The political business cycle. *Review of Economic Studies* **42**: 617–43.

North D C 1979 A framework for analysing the state in economic history. *Explorations in Economic History* **16**: 249–59.

North D C, Miller R L 1983 *Economics of public issues* 6th edn. Harper and Row, New York.

Nove A 1983 *The economics of feasible socialism.* Allen and Unwin.
Nove A, Nuti D M (eds) 1972 *Socialist economics.* Penguin.
Nozick R 1974 *Anarchy, state and utopia.* Basic Books, New York.
Nuti D M 1969 On incomes policy. *Science and society* **33**: 415–25.
O'Brien D 1984 Say's law. *The Economic Review* **2**: 27–8.
O'Brien R C (ed.) 1983 *Information, economics and power: the North–South dimension.* Hodder and Stoughton.
O'Connor J 1973 *The fiscal crisis of the state.* St Martin's Press, New York.
OECD 1966 *The balance of payments adjustment process.* Paris.
OECD 1982 *Historical Statistics.* Paris.
OECD 1977 *Public expenditure on health.* Studies in Resource Allocation No. 4, Paris.
OECD 1981 *East–West trade: recent developments in countertrade.* Paris.
OECD 1985 *Co-operation and recovery.* Economics Outlook (38): vii–xviii. Paris.
Okun A 1975 *Equality and efficiency: the big trade-off.* Brookings, Washington DC.
Okun A 1981 *Prices and quantities. A macroeconomic analysis.* Basil Blackwell.
Olson M 1965 *The logic of collective action.* Harvard U.P., Cambridge, Massachusetts.
Panic M 1982 International direct investment in conditions of structural disequilibrium: UK experience since the 1960s. In Black J, Dunning J H (eds) *International capital movements.* Macmillan.
Pappas J L, Brigham E F, Shipley B 1983 *Managerial economics* UK edn. McGraw-Hill.
Parker D 1985 Is the private sector more efficient? A study in the public v private debate. *Public Administration Bulletin*: 2–23.
Parkin M, Sumner M T (eds) 1972 *Incomes policy and inflation.* Manchester U.P.
Pauly M V 1968 The economics of moral hazard: comment. *American Economic Review* **58**(3): 531–7.
Pauly M V 1983 More on moral hazard. *Journal of health economics* **2**(1): 81–5.
Peacock A T 1983 Education voucher schemes: strong or weak? *Economic Affairs* January.
Peacock A T 1984 Privatisation in perspective. *Three Banks Review* No. 144.
Peacock A T, Shaw G K 1978 Is fiscal policy dead? *Banca Nazionale del Lavoro Review* **31**: 108–22.
Peacock A T, Wiseman J 1964 *Education for democrats.* Hobart Paper 25. Institute of Economic Affairs.
Peacock A T, Wiseman J 1967 *The growth of public expenditure in the UK.* Allen and Unwin.
Peaker A 1974 *Economic Growth in modern Britain.* Macmillan.
Peston M 1980 Monetary policy and incomes policy: complements or substitutes. *Applied Economics* **12**.
Peters R S 1967 *Ethics and Education.* Glenview: Scott Foreman and Company.

Peterson W, Estenson P 1985 The recovery: supply side or Keynesian. *Journal of Post-Keynesian Economics* 7(4): 447–62.

Phelps E S 1967 Phillips curves, expectations of inflation and optimal unemployment over time. *Economica* 34: 254–81.

Phelps E S (ed.) 1973 *Economic justice*. Penguin.

Phillips A W 1958 The relation between unemployment and the rate of change of money wage rates in the UK 1862–1957. *Economica* 25: 283–99.

Pigou A C 1912 *Wealth and welfare*. Macmillan.

Pigou A C 1920 *The economics of welfare*. Macmillan.

Pigou A C (ed.) 1925 *Memorials of Alfred Marshall*. Macmillan.

Pike M 1984 Female discrimination in the labour market. *The Economic Review* 1(5): 3–7.

Pliatzky L 1986 Can government be efficient? *Lloyds Bank Review* No. 159: 22–32.

Polanyi M 1951 *The logic of liberty*. Routledge.

Pond C 1985 The Case for Minimum Wage Protection. *The Economic Review*: 1–5 No. 1 September 31–34

Pratten C F 1985 *Applied macroeconomics*. Oxford U.P.

Pratten C F, Dean R M 1965 *The economics of large scale production in British industry*. Cambridge U.P.

Pryke R 1981 *The nationalised industries: policies and performance since 1968*. Martin Robertson.

Rainey H G 1983 Public agencies and private firms. *Administration and Society* 15(2): 207–43.

Rajan A 1985 *Job subsidies. Do they work?* Institute of Manpower Studies.

Rand A 1967 *Capitalism: the unknown ideal*. New American Library, New York.

Rawls J 1972 *A theory of justice*. Oxford U.P.

Richardson G B 1971 Planning v competition. *Soviet Studies* XXII(3): 433–47.

Richardson G B 1972 The organisation of industry. *Economic Journal* 82: 883–96.

Robbins L C 1935 *An essay on the nature and significance of economic science* 2nd edn. Macmillan.

Robbins L Lord 1976 *Political economy: past and present. A review of leading theories of economic policy*. Macmillan.

Robinson D 1985 The economic system in the UK. In Morris D (ed.) 3rd edn. Oxford U.P.

Robinson J 1933 *The economics of imperfect competition*. Macmillan.

Robinson J 1960 *Collected economic papers vol II*. Basil Blackwell.

Robinson J 1971 *Economic heresies*. Macmillan.

Robinson J 1977 What are the questions? *Journal of Economic Literature* 15(4): 1318–39.

Robinson J, Wilkinson F 1977 What has become of employment policy. *Cambridge Journal of Economics* 1: 5–14.

Robinson R 1979 *Housing economics and public policy*. Macmillan (Studies in Planning).

Roemer J E 1979 Divide and conquer: microfoundations of a Marxian theory of wage discrimination. *Bell Journal of Economics* 10(2): 695–705.

Rothbard M N 1970 *Man, economy and state*. Nash Pub., Los Angeles.

Rothbard M N 1976 Ludwig von Mises and economic calculation under socialism. In Moss L S (ed.) *The economics of Ludwig von Mises*. Sheed and Ward.

Rothbard M N 1978 *For a new liberty*. Collier Macmillan.

Rothstein R L 1976 Foreign policy and development policy. Non-alignment to international class war. *International Affairs* 52: 598–616.

Rowley C K 1973 *Antitrust and economic efficiency*. Macmillan.

Rowley C K 1983 Unemployment, is government macroeconomic policy impotent? *Journal of Economic Affairs* 3: 109–12.

Rowntree B S 1902 *Poverty: a study of town life* 2nd edn. Macmillan.

Sahlins M 1972 *Stone age economics*. Tavistock Publications.

Salvatore D 1986 *Microeconomics: theory and applications*. Collier Macmillan.

Samuelson P A, Solow R M 1960 Analytical aspects of anti-inflation policy. *American Economic Review* 50: 177–94.

Sandford C T 1973 *Hidden costs of taxation*. Institute of Fiscal Studies (6).

Santomero A M, Seater J 1978 The inflation unemployment trade-off: a critique of the literature. *Journal of Economic Literature* 16: 499–544.

Sargent T, Wallace N 1976 Rational expectations and the theory of economic policy. *Journal of Monetary Economics* 2: 69–183.

Saunders P 1985 Public expenditure and economic performance in OECD countries. *Journal of Public Policy* 5(1): 1–21.

Scammell W 1980 *The international economy since 1945*. St Martins Press, New York.

Scherer F M 1980 *Industrial market structure and economic performance* 2nd edn. Rand McNally, Chicago.

Schotter A 1985 *Free market economics: a critical approach*. Macmillan.

Schultze C L 1968 *The politics and economics of public spending*. The Brookings Institution, Washington DC.

Schweltinger R L 1976 *The Illusion of wage and price control*. The Fraser Institute. Vancouver

Scitovsky T 1967 The theory of balance of payments adjustment. *Journal of Political Economy* 75: 523–32.

Scitovsky T 1980 Can capitalism survive? – An old question in a new setting. *American Economic Review* 70: 1–9.

Scrimgeour J L 1984 *Accounting for UK company taxation*. Longman.

Seager K M 1984 *A guide to capital transfer tax*. Whitechurch Securities, Teddington.

Seldon A 1967 National or personal health services. *Lancet*.

Seldon A 1975 Experiment with choice in education. In Maynard A *Hobart Paper 64*. Institute of Economic Affairs.

Sen A K 1981 *Poverty and famines: An essay on entitlement and deprivation*. Clarendon Press.

Sen A K 1983 The profit motive. *Lloyds Bank Review* No. 147.

Sen A K 1985 The moral standing of the market. In Paul E F, Paul J, Miller

F D (eds) *Ethics and economics.* Basil Blackwell.

Shackle G L S 1955 *Uncertainty in economics and other reflections.* Cambridge U.P.

Shackle G L S 1970 *Expectation, enterprise and profit.* Allen and Unwin.

Shackleton J R 1982 Economists and unemployment. *National Westminster Bank Quarterly Review* Feb. 1982: 13–29.

Shackleton J R 1984 Privatisation: the case examined. *National Westminster Bank Quarterly Review* May: 59–73.

Shand A 1984 *The capitalist alternative. An introduction to Austrian economics.* Wheatsheaf Books, Harvester Press.

Shaw R, Simpson P 1985 The monopolies commission and the process of competition. *Fiscal Studies* 6(1).

Sheffrin S M 1983 *Rational expectations.* Cambridge U.P.

Shepherd W G 1984 Contestability vs competition. *American Economic Review* **74**(4): 572–87.

Singh A 1977 UK industry and the world economy. *Cambridge Journal of Economics* **1** No. 2: 113–36.

Skott P 1985 Vicious circles and cumulative causation. *Thames Papers in Political Economy.*

Smith A 1976 *An enquiry into the nature and causes of the wealth of nations.* General eds Campbell R H, Skinner A S. Textual ed. Todd W B. Clarendon Press.

Smith K 1984 *The British economic crisis.* Penguin.

Smith R, Rowland M 1985 *Rights guide to non-means-tested social security benefits* 8th edn. Child Poverty Action Group.

Smith T 1979 *The politics of the corporate economy.* Martin Robertson.

Snowdon B 1981 Phillips curve or trade off curve. *Economics* **XVII**: 103–5.

Snowdon B 1983 *Inflation government and the role of incomes policy.* Anforme.

Snowdon B 1985 The political economy of the Ethiopian famine. *National Westminster Bank Quarterly Review* Nov.: 41–55.

Snowdon B, Wynarczyk P 1984 Have the Keynesians been vanquished? *Economic Affairs* **5** No. 1, Oct.–Dec.: 53–60.

Solomon R 1977 *The international monetary system, 1945–76: an insider's view* 1st edn. Harper and Row, New York.

Solow R 1957 Technical change and the aggregate production function. *Review of Economics and Statistics* **39**: 312–20.

Solow R 1980 On theories of unemployment. *American Economic Review* **70** March: 1–11.

Spraos J 1983 *Inequalising trade?* Oxford U.P.

Stafford D C 1976 Government and the housing situation. *National Westminster Bank Quarterly Review* Nov.: 6–19.

Stafford D C 1978 *The economics of housing policy.* Croom Helm.

Stein J 1976 *Monetarism.* North Holland, Amsterdam.

Steiner P O 1977 The public sector and the public interest. In Haveman R H, Margolis J *Public expenditure and policy analysis.* Markham Publishing Co, Chicago.

Stewart M 1983a Relative earnings and individual trade union membership. *Economica* **50** May.

Stewart M 1983b Racial discrimination and occupational attainment in Britain. *Economic Journal* **93** Sept.

Stigler G J 1974 Free riders and collective action. *Bell Journal of Economics* **5**: 359–65.

Stigler G J 1975 *The citizen and the state*. University of Chicago Press.

Stigler G J 1983 Nobel lecture: the process and progress of economics. *Journal of Political Economy* **91**(4).

Strange S, Tooze R (eds) 1981 *International politics of surplus capacity*. Allen and Unwin.

Struthers J J 1984 Rational expectations: a promising research program or a case of monetarist fundamentalism? *Journal of Economic Issues* **18** Dec.: 1133–54.

Sugden R 1982 On the economics of philanthropy. *Economic Journal* **92**: 341–50.

Sugden R 1984 Reciprocity: the supply of public goods through voluntary contributions. *Economic Journal* **94**: 772–87.

Tarschys D 1985 Curbing public expenditure: Current trends. *Journal of Public Policy* **5**(1): 23–67.

Tarsh J 1982 The labour market for graduates. *Employment Gazette*.

Taylor J 1972 The behaviour of unemployment and unfilled vacancies: Great Britain 1958–71. An alternative view. *Economic Journal* **82**: 1352–68.

Terry N G 1985 The 'big-bang' at the Stock Exchange. *Lloyds Bank Review* April, 156: 16–30.

Tew B 1985 *Evolution of the international monetary system 1945–84* 3rd revised edn. Hutchison Education.

Theil H, Brooks R B 1970 How does the marginal utility of incomes change when real income changes? *European Economic Review* Winter: 218–40.

Thirlwall A P 1974 The panacea of a floating pound. *National Westminster Bank Quarterly Review* August: 16–28.

Thirlwall A P 1979 The balance of payments constraint as an explanation of international growth rate differences. *Banca Nazionale del Lavoro Quarterly Review* March.

Thirlwall A P 1981 Keynesian employment theory is not defunct. *Three Banks Review* Sept.: 14–29.

Thirlwall A P 1982 *Balance of payments theory and UK experience*. Macmillan.

Thomas R E 1981 *The government of business* 2nd edn. Philip Allan.

Thurow L C 1976 *Generating inequality*. Basic Books, New York.

Thurow L C 1980 *The zero-sum society: distribution and the possibilities for economic chance*. Basic Books, New York.

Thurow L C 1983 *Dangerous currents. The state of economics*. Oxford U.P.

Tinbergen 1961 Do communist and free economies show a converging pattern? *Soviet Studies* **12**, No. 4

Tobin J 1977 How dead is Keynes? *Economic Enquiry* **15** Oct.: 459–68.

Tobin J 1981 The monetarist counter-revolution today – an appraisal. *Economic Journal* **91**: 29–42.

Tomlinson J 1983 Does mass unemployment matter? *National Westminster Bank Quarterly Review*: 35–45.

Tomlinson J 1986 *Monetarism: is there an alternative?* Basil Blackwell.

Townsend P 1979 *Poverty in the United Kingdom*. Penguin.

Trevithick J 1975 Keynes, inflation and money illusion. *Economic Journal* 85: 101–13.

Trevithick J 1980 *Inflation: a guide to the crisis in economics*. Pelican.

Trevithick J, Mulvey C, Jackman R 1981 *The economics of inflation*. Martin Robertson.

Triffin R 1960 *Gold and the dollar crisis, the future of convertibility*. Yale U.P., New Haven, Conn.

Tullock G 1976 *The vote motive*. Institute of Economic Affairs.

Tumlir J 1981 Evolution of the concept of international economic order 1914–80. In Cairncross A (ed.) *Changing perceptions of economic policy*. Methuen.

University Grants Committee 1968 *University development 1962–67*. HMSO Cmnd 3820.

Utton M A 1984 *The political economy of big business*. Martin Robertson.

Vaizey J 1972 *The political economy of education*. Duckworth.

Van der Hass 1967 *The enterprise in transition*. Tavistock Publications.

Vaughn K I 1980 Economic calculation under socialism: the Austrian contribution. *Economic Inquiry* **XVIII**.

Vaughn K I 1981 Introduction to T J B Hoff's *Economic calculation in the socialist society*. Liberty Press.

Wachter M L, Williamson O E 1978 Obligational markets and the mechanics of inflation. *Bell Journal of Economics* 9(2): 549–74.

Wallerstein I 1979 *The capitalist world economy*. Cambridge U.P.

Waterson M 1984 *Economic theory of the industry*. Cambridge U.P.

Webb M 1976 *Pricing policies for public enterprises*. Macmillan.

Wegner M 1985 External adjustments in a world of floating: different national experiences in Europe. In Tsoukalis L (ed.) *The political economy of international money*. Sage Publications (for Royal Institute of International Affairs).

Weiner M J 1981 *English culture and the decline of the industrial spirit 1850–1980*. Cambridge U.P.

Weintraub E R 1974 *General equilibrium theory*. Macmillan.

Weintraub S 1961 *Classical Keynesianism, monetary theory and the price level*. Chilton, Philadelphia.

West E G 1982 Education vouchers – evolution or revolution. *Economic Affairs*.

Whitehead C 1983 Housing under the Conservatives: a policy assessment. *Public Money* 3(1): 15–21.

Whitehead C M E 1984 In Le Grand J, Robinson R (eds) *Privatisation and the welfare state*. Allen and Unwin, pp. 116–32.

Whynes D 1983 *Invitation to economics*. Martin Robertson.

Wickens I, Coles J 1985 *The ethical imperative of clinical budgeting*. Nuffield/York Portfolio 10, Nuffield Provincial Hospitals Trust.

Wildavsky A 1966 The political economy of efficiency: cost-benefit analysis, systems analysis and program budgeting. *Public Administration Review* 26(4): 292–310.

Williams R 1965 *The long revolution*. Pelican.

Williams R M 1951 *American society: a sociological interpretation*. Knopf, New York.

Williamson J 1977 *The failure of world monetary reform 1971–74*. Thomas Nelson.

Williamson J 1985 The exchange rate system. *Institute for International Economics, Policy Analysis in International Economics* Sept. 1983 (revised June 1985).

Williamson O E 1963 Managerial discretion and business behaviour. *American Economic Review* 53: 1032–57.

Williamson O E 1968 Economics as an antitrust defense: the welfare tradeoffs. *American Economic Review* 58: 18–36.

Williamson O E 1972 *Corporate control and business behaviour*. Prentice-Hall, New York.

Williamson O E 1973 Markets and hierarchies: some elementary considerations. *American Economic Review* 63(2): 316–25.

Williamson O E 1975 *Markets and hierarchies: analysis and antitrust considerations*. Free Press, New York.

Williamson O E 1976 Franchise bidding for natural monopoly. *Bell Journal of Economics* 7 Spring: 73–104.

Williamson O E 1979 Transaction-cost economics: the governance of contractual relations. *Journal of Law and Economics* 22(2): 233–61.

Williamson O E 1981 The modern corporation: origins, evolution, attributes. *Journal of Economic Literature* 19: 1537–68.

Wilson H 1971 *The Labour government 1964–70*. Weidenfeld and Nicolson and Michael Joseph.

Wilson H 1979 *The final term*. Weidenfeld and Nicolson and Michael Joseph.

Winch D, 1972 *Economics and policy*. Fontana.

Worswick D, Trevithick J (eds) 1983 *Keynes and the modern world*. Cambridge U.P.

Worswick G D N 1984 Two great recessions: the 1980s and the 1930s in Britain. *Scottish Journal of Political Economy* 31 Nov.: 209–28.

Wright G A 1984 A firm foundation: a consideration of the nature of firms and markets. Paper presented to the Annual Conference of Polytechnic Teachers of Economics. Bristol Polytechnic, April 1984.

Young A 1928 Increasing returns and economic progress. *Economic Journal*: 527–42.

Young S, Lowe A V 1974 *Intervention in a mixed economy*. Croom Helm.

Zarnowitz V 1985 Recent work on business cycles in historical perspective: a review of theories and evidence. *Journal of Economic Literature* 23.

Ziderman A 1975 The economics of educational policy. In Grant R M, Shaw G K (eds) *Current issues in economic policy*. Philip Allan.

Zis G 1983 Exchange rate fluctuations. *National Westminster Bank Quarterly Review*, August.

Zuckerman Report 1961 *Advisory Council on scientific policy, Committee on scientific manpower*. HMSO Cmnd 1490.

AUTHOR INDEX

SUBJECT INDEX